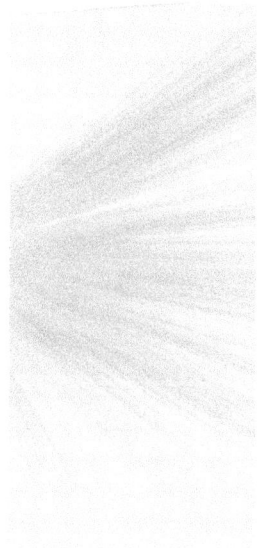

# Equity and Growth
# in a Globalizing World

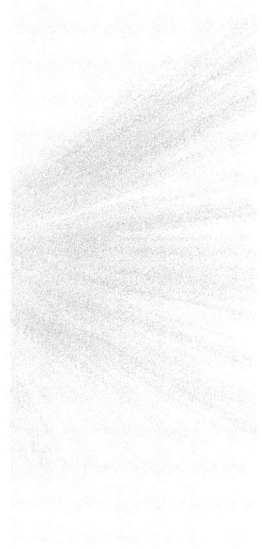

# Equity and Growth in a Globalizing World

*Edited by Ravi Kanbur and Michael Spence*

Contributions by

Ravi Kanbur
Michael Spence
Abhijit Banerjee
Agnès Bénassy-Quéré
Nancy Birdsall
François Bourguignon
Stefan Dercon
Antonio Estache
Francisco H. G. Ferreira
Jérémie Gignoux
Jan Willem Gunning
Gordon Hanson

Ann Harrison
Stephan Klasen
Simon Maxwell
Margaret McMillan
Andrew Morrison
Jean-Philippe Platteau
Lant Pritchett
Dhushyanth Raju
Mark Rosenzweig
Nistha Sinha
Amedeo Spadaro

COMMISSION ON GROWTH AND DEVELOPMENT

© 2010 The International Bank for Reconstruction and Development /
The World Bank
On behalf of the Commission on Growth and Development
1818 H Street NW
Washington DC 20433
Telephone: 202-473-1000
Internet: www.worldbank.org
        www.growthcommission.org
E-mail:  info@worldbank.org
        contactinfo@growthcommission.org

1 2 3 4 13 12 11 10

This volume is a product of the Commission on Growth and Development, which
is sponsored by the following organizations:

Australian Agency for International Development (AusAID)
Dutch Ministry of Foreign Affairs
Swedish International Development Corporation Agency (SIDA)
U.K. Department of International Development (DFID)
The William and Flora Hewlett Foundation
The World Bank Group

The findings, interpretations, and conclusions expressed herein do not necessarily
reflect the views of the sponsoring organizations or the governments they represent.
    The sponsoring organizations do not guarantee the accuracy of the data
included in this work. The boundaries, colors, denominations, and other
information shown on any map in this work do not imply any judgement on the
part of the sponsoring organizations concerning the legal status of any
territory or the endorsement or acceptance of such boundaries.
    All queries on rights and licenses, including subsidiary rights, should be
addressed to the Office of the Publisher, The World Bank, 1818 H Street
NW, Washington, DC 20433, USA; fax: 202-522-2422; e-mail: pubrights@
worldbank.org.

ISBN: 978-0-8213-8180-9
eISBN: 978-0-8213-8181-6
DOI: 10.1596/978-0-8213-8180-9

Library of Congress Cataloging-in-Publication Data has been applied for.

# Contents

## Tables

# Preface

The Commission on Growth and Development was established in April 2006 in response to two insights: people do not talk about growth enough, and when they do, they speak with unearned conviction. Too often, people overlook economic growth when thinking about how to tackle the world's most pressing problems, such as poverty, illiteracy, and unemployment. At the same time, their understanding of the mechanics of growth is less definitive than commonly thought—even though advice is often given to developing countries with great confidence. Consequently, the Commission's mandate is to "take stock of the state of theoretical and empirical knowledge on economic growth with a view to drawing implications for policy for the current and next generation of policy makers."

To help assess the state of knowledge, the Commission invited leading academics and policy makers from around the world to a series of 12 workshops held from 2007 to 2009 in Washington, DC; New York City, NY; New Haven, CT; and Cambridge, MA. It also commissioned a series of thematic papers, reviewing areas such as monetary and fiscal policy, climate change, education, urbanization, health, and inequality—the subject of this volume. In addition, 25 case studies were commissioned to explore the dynamics of growth in specific countries. Each presentation benefited from comments by members of the Commission and other workshop participants from the worlds of policy, theory, and practice.

The workshops turned out to be intense, lively affairs, lasting up to three days. It became clear that experts do not always agree, even on issues that are central to growth. But the Commission had no wish to disguise or gloss over these uncertainties and differences. And it did not want to present a false confidence in its conclusions beyond that justified by the evidence. Researchers do not always know the "model" that would correctly explain the world they observe, and, even if they know the factors that matter, they cannot always measure them convincingly.

While researchers will continue to improve people's understanding of the world, policy makers cannot wait for scholars to satisfy all of their doubts or resolve their differences. Decisions must be made with only partial knowledge of the world. One consequence is that most policy decisions, however well informed, take on the character of experiments, which yield useful information about the way the world works, even if they do not always turn out the way policy makers had hoped. It is good to recognize this fact, if only so that policy makers can be quick to spot failures and learn from mistakes.

In principle, a commission on growth could have confined its attention to income per person, setting aside the question of how income is distributed. But this Commission chose otherwise. It recognized that growth is not synonymous with development. (If it were, the Commission would not have needed the last two words of its title.) To contribute significantly to social progress, growth must lift everyone's sights and improve the living standards of a broad swath of society. The Commission has no truck with the view that growth only enriches the few, leaving poverty undisturbed and social ills untouched. Nor does it subscribe to the simplistic notion that if a country's gross domestic product begins to rise, everything else will take care of itself. In its flagship publication, *The Growth Report: Strategies for Sustained Growth and Inclusive Development*, the Commission faced the question of inequality squarely and urged policy makers to do the same.

Of course, many policy makers need no persuading. They cherish equity as an ethical goal. Indeed, most credible political philosophies are "egalitarian" in some sense, even if they differ vehemently about what equity implies. On the one hand, the philosophies of the left espouse equality of income or wealth, arguing that everyone has an equal claim to the fruits of society. The philosophies of the libertarian right, on the other hand, argue that everyone has an equal claim on the fruits of their own labor and capital.

If policy makers do prize equity in itself, they must pay close attention to the distributional consequences of growth. Is a rising tide of prosperity lifting all boats? Or must some people grow rich first if anyone is to grow rich at all? Are the economic rewards earned by one generation passed on as an unearned inheritance to their offspring?

Even if policy makers do not subscribe to an egalitarian ethic, they have a pragmatic reason to care about the distribution of resources and opportunities. A society that does not provide all of its citizens with a fair chance to flourish is not making the best use of their talents. And a society that entirely neglects growing gaps between rich and poor is also courting trouble. Gross inequalities can undermine the social peace that growth strategies often require.

All of these issues were raised in the workshop on inequality held in September 2007. We were immensely fortunate to benefit from the insights of outstanding researchers and experienced practitioners. We are deeply grateful to the participants, and we hope this volume will give a wider audience an equal opportunity to benefit from their wisdom.

Ravi Kanbur
Michael Spence

# Workshop Participants

**Ahluwalia,** Montek, Commissioner, Deputy Chairman, Planning Commission, India
**Aninat,** Cristobal, Ministry of External Affairs, Chile
**Annez,** Patricia, World Bank
**Banerjee,** Abhijit, Massachusetts Institute of Technology
**Benabou,** Roland, Princeton University
**Bourguignon,** François, World Bank
**Bowles,** Samuel, Santa Fe Institute and University of Siena
**Bruggenkamp,** Ammarens, Embassy of the Netherlands in the United States
**Buckley,** Robert, World Bank
**Dadush,** Uri, World Bank
**Darlington,** Muriel, Growth Commission Secretariat
**Derviş,** Kemal, Administrator, United Nations Development Programme
**Ferreira,** Francisco, World Bank
**Grigonyte,** Dalia, The European Commission
**Hanson,** Gordon, University of California-San Diego
**Harrison,** Ann, University of California-Berkeley
**Joshi,** Manosh, Embassy of India in the United States
**Jousten,** Alain, International Monetary Fund
**Kanbur,** Ravi, Cornell University
**Kharas,** Homi, The Brookings Institution
**Leipziger,** Danny, Growth Commission Vice Chair, World Bank
**Levine,** Ross, Brown University

**Lewis,** Maureen, World Bank
**Lim,** Edwin, China Economic Research and Advisory Program
**Loewald,** Christopher, Ministry of Finance, South Africa
**Lundstrom,** Susanna, World Bank
**MacCallum,** Lisa, The Nike Foundation
**Mahovsky,** Madeleine, The European Commission
**Manevskaya,** Diana, Growth Commission Secretariat
**Manuel,** Trevor, Minister of Finance, South Africa
**Meadows,** Graham, European Research Institute, University of Sussex
**Morrison,** Andrew, World Bank
**Nabli,** Mustapha, World Bank
**Nankani,** Gobind, Global Development Network
**Nowak,** Dorota, Growth Commission Secretariat
**Ozden,** Caglar, World Bank
**Ozer,** Ceren, World Bank
**Perry,** Guillermo, World Bank
**Pritchett,** Lant, Center for Global Development and Harvard University
**Rosenzweig,** Mark, Yale University
**Simler,** Kenneth, World Bank
**Sjoblom,** Mirja, World Bank
**Spence,** Michael, Nobel Laureate and Professor Emeritus, Growth
    Commission Chair, Stanford University
**Srinivasan,** TN, Yale University
**Udry,** Christopher, Yale University
**Venner,** Sir Dwight, Commissioner, Governor, Eastern Caribbean Bank,
    St. Kitts and Nevis
**Zagha,** Roberto, Growth Commission Secretariat
**Zedillo,** Ernesto, Commissioner, Director, Yale Center for Study
    of Globalization

# About the Editors and Contributors

**Abhijit V. Banerjee** is Ford Foundation Professor of Economics in the Department of Economics at the Massachusetts Institute of Technology (MIT), the Director of the Poverty Action Lab, and the past President of the Bureau for Research in Economic Analysis and Development (BREAD). He taught at Princeton and Harvard before joining the MIT faculty in 1996. In 2001, he was the recipient of the Malcolm Adeshesiah Award, and he was awarded the Mahalanobis Memorial Medal in 2000. He is a fellow of the Econometric Society and the American Academy of Arts and Sciences, and has been a Guggenheim Fellow and Alfred P. Sloan Research Fellow. His areas of research are development economics, the economics of financial markets, and the macroeconomics of developing countries.

**Agnès Bénassy-Quéré** is Professor at the University of Paris X-Nanterre. She is currently a Director of CEPII, having been a Scientific Advisor of the Centre until 2003 and Deputy-Director from 2004 to 2006. Agnès Bénassy-Quéré is also a member of the THEMA research unit (Economic Theory, Modelling and Applications–UMR 7536 of the CNRS) and a member of both the Economic Commission of the Nation and the Circle of Economists.

**Nancy Birdsall** is the founding President of the Center for Global Development. Prior to launching the center, Dr. Birdsall served for three years as Senior Associate and Director of the Economic Reform Project at the Carnegie Endowment for International Peace. Her work at Carnegie focused on issues of globalization and inequality, as well as on the reform of the international financial institutions. From 1993 to 1998, Dr. Birdsall was Executive Vice President of the Inter-American Development Bank, the largest of the regional development banks, where she oversaw a $30 billion public and private loan portfolio. Before joining the Inter-American Development Bank, Dr. Birdsall spent 14 years in research, policy, and management positions at the World Bank, most recently as Director of the Policy Research Department. Dr. Birdsall is the author, co-author, or editor of more than a dozen books and monographs. She has also written more than 75 articles for books and scholarly journals published in English and Spanish. Shorter pieces of her writing have appeared in dozens of U.S. and Latin American newspapers and periodicals.

**François Bourguignon** is the Director of the Paris School of Economics. He is former Chief Economist and Senior Vice President, Development Economics of the World Bank (2003–07). Dr. Bourguignon was previously Director of the Development Research Group, a part of the Development Economics Vice Presidency, and Managing Editor of the World Bank Economic Review. He has served as an advisor to many developing countries, the Organisation for Economic Co-operation and Development (OECD), the United Nations, and the European Commission. Since 1985 he has been Professor of Economics at the Ecole des Hautes Etudes en Sciences Sociales in Paris, where he founded and directed the DELTA research unit in theoretical and applied economics. He has held academic positions with the University of Chile, Santiago, and the University of Toronto. He is also a Fellow of the Econometric Society. Dr. Bourguignon has authored and edited several books as well as numerous articles in leading international journals in economics.

**Stefan Dercon** is Professor of Development Economics at the University of Oxford and a Professorial Fellow of Wolfson College. Previously he taught in Belgium and at the University of Addis Ababa. His interest is in applying microeconomics and statistics to problems of development. He has worked on risk and poverty, agriculture and rural institutions, political economy, childhood poverty, social and geographic mobility, micro-insurance, and measurement issues related to poverty and vulnerability. Much of this work involves the collection and analysis of longitudinal data sets, and he is closely involved in seven ongoing longitudinal surveys focusing on rural households in Ethiopia (ERHS), Tanzania (KHDS), and India (new ICRISAT VLS), and on children in Ethiopia, India, Peru, and Vietnam (Young Lives).

**Antonio Estache** is Professor of Economics at the Université Libre de Bruxelles where he holds the Bernard Van Ommeslaghe Chair and is a member of the European Center for Advanced Research of Economics (ECARES). Prior to that, he was Chief Economist for the Sustainable Development Network of the World Bank where he spent 25 years (1982–2007) working across regions on various dimensions of public sector reform. He has published widely on the regulation of network industries (electricity, telecommunications, transport, and water and sanitation), the assessment of the performance of the public sector and the growth, and distributional effects of environmental, fiscal, and sectoral policies in developing countries.

**Francisco H. G. Ferreira** is a Lead Economist with the Development Research Group at the World Bank. He has published widely on both the theory and empirics of poverty and inequality in developing countries, and he was a Co-Director of the team that wrote the World Bank's *World Development Report 2006: Equity and Development.* Outside the World Bank, he taught for three years at the Economics Department of the Catholic University of Rio de Janeiro, and has been closely associated with the Latin American and Caribbean Economics Association and its journal, *Economia.* He has sat on advisory boards for public policy institutes in Brazil and Mexico and has advised a number of Latin American governments on social policy issues. He is presently a Co-Editor of the *Journal of Economic Inequality.*

**Jérémie Gignoux** is an Assistant Professor at the Paris School of Economics, France. He holds a PhD in economics from Paris Institute of Political Studies (Sciences Po) and has been a consultant for the Development Research Group of the World Bank. His research interests include the analysis of inequality and intergenerational mobility, and the analysis and evaluation of human capital policies in developing countries.

**Jan Willem Gunning** is Professor of Development Economics at VU University Amsterdam. He is also a Co-Founder and Co-Director of the Amsterdam Institute for International Development and Member of the Royal Netherlands Academy of Arts and Sciences (KNAW). Professor Gunning started his career as a staff member of the World Bank. He has been Professor of Economics at Oxford where he was the Director of the Centre for the Study of African Economies. He is Co-Founder and Past President of the European Development Research Network (EUDN). For many years he was active as a resource person in the African Economic Research Consortium (AERC). In the Netherlands, he has served on the National Advisory Council for Development Cooperation. He has been Managing Editor of the *Journal of African Economies* and is on the editorial board of the *World Bank Economic Review.* In 2007 he received an honorary doctorate from the University of Auvergne (France) for his leading role in economic research on Africa. His current research interests are statistical impact evaluation of sectorwide programs (education, water supply, and sanitation), microeconomic analysis of economic growth under risk, and vulnerability of rural households.

**Gordon H. Hanson** is the Director of the Center on Pacific Economies and Professor of Economics at the University of California, San Diego (UCSD), where he holds faculty positions in the Graduate School of International Relations and Pacific Studies and the Department of Economics. Professor Hanson is also a Research Associate at the National Bureau of Economic Research and Co-Editor of the *Journal of Development Economics.* Prior to joining UCSD in 2001, he was on the economics faculty at the University of Michigan (1998–2001) and at the University of Texas (1992–98).

Professor Hanson has published extensively in the top academic journals of the economics discipline. His current research examines the international migration of high-skilled labor, the causes of Mexican migration to the United States, the consequences of immigration on labor-market outcomes for African-Americans, the relationship between business cycles and global outsourcing, and international trade in motion pictures. In recent work, he has studied the impact of globalization on wages, the origins of political opposition to immigration, and the implications of China's growth for the export performance of Mexico and other developing countries. His most recent book is *Why Does Immigration Divide America? Public Finance and Political Opposition to Open Borders* (Institute for International Economics 2005).

**Ann Harrison** is Director of Development Policy at the World Bank. Her career experience includes the position of Professor of Agricultural and Resource Economics at the University of California, Berkeley. Her research is in the areas of international trade, foreign investment, and economic development. She has analyzed the impact of globalization on domestic labor markets, the linkages between productivity and trade reform, and the impact of foreign investment on host countries. She recently completed a book, *Globalization and Poverty*, for the National Bureau of Economic Research. Her publications have appeared in top economic journals, including the *American Economic Review*, *Journal of Labor Economics*, *Journal of Development Economics*, *Journal of International Economics*, and *Review of Economics and Statistics*, and among others.

**Ravi Kanbur** is T. H. Lee Professor of World Affairs, International Professor of Applied Economics and Management, and Professor of Economics at Cornell University. He holds an appointment tenured both in the Department of Applied Economics and Management in the College of Agriculture and Life Sciences, and in the Department of Economics in the College of Arts and Sciences. He has taught at the Universities of Oxford, Cambridge, Essex, Warwick, Princeton, and Columbia. Professor Kanbur has served on the staff of the World Bank, as Economic Adviser, Senior Economic Adviser, Resident Representative in Ghana, Chief Economist of the Africa Region of the World Bank, and Principal Adviser to the Chief Economist of the World Bank. He has also served as Director of the World Bank's *World Development Report*. Professor Kanbur's main areas of interest are public economics and development economics. His work spans conceptual, empirical, and policy analysis. He is particularly interested in bridging the worlds of rigorous analysis and practical policy making. His vita lists more than 150 publications covering topics such as risk taking, inequality, poverty, structural adjustment, debt, agriculture, and political economy. He has published in the leading economics journals such as the *American Economic Review*, *Journal of Political Economy*, *Review of Economic Studies*, *Journal of Economic Theory*, and *Economic Journal*.

**Stephan Klasen** is Professor of Development Economics and Empirical Economic Research at the University of Göttingen, where he also heads the Ibero-American Institute. Previously he was Professor of Economics at the University of Munich as well as a Fellow at King's College in Cambridge and an Economist at the World Bank in South Africa. His research interests are in population, labor, welfare, and development economics. His current research interests include an assessment of the relation between labor market events and demographic decisions at the household level, an analysis of the determinants of undernutrition and child mortality in developing countries, the linkages between inequality, growth, and well-being, and the causes and consequences of gender inequality in developing countries.

**Simon Maxwell** until recently was a Director of the Overseas Development Institute, the position he held since 1997. He is an Economist who worked overseas for 10 years—in Kenya and India for the United Nations Development Programme (UNDP), and in Bolivia for UKODA (now Department for International Development, U.K.)—and then for 16 years at the Institute of Development Studies at the University of Sussex, latterly as Programme Manager for Poverty, Food Security and the Environment. He has written widely on poverty, food security, agricultural development, and aid. His current research interests include development policy, aid, poverty, food security, linking relief and development, global governance, and bridging research and policy.

**Margaret McMillan** is an Associate Professor of Economics at Tufts University. She has published widely in the areas of international trade and investment focusing primarily on developing countries. Understanding the distributional consequences of international economic integration is the key focus of her work. She is a Faculty Research Associate of the National Bureau of Economic Research and a recipient of research grants from the National Science Foundation and the Center for AIDS Research. In 2005, she was named the William and Flora Hewlett Foundation Fellow at the Radcliffe Institute for Advanced Study. Professor McMillan's research has been featured in the *New York Times* and the *NBER Digest* and has been published in leading economics journals such as the *Review of Economics and Statistics*, the *Journal of Economic Growth*, the *American Journal of Agricultural Economics*, the *Journal of Development Economics*, and the *Journal of International Economics*. Professor McMillan has worked in several African countries including Ethiopia, Gabon, Kenya, Mali, Tanzania, Uganda, and South Africa. Before coming to academia, she worked for a variety of organizations including the Peace Corps, Lehman Brothers, U.S. Agency for International Development (USAID), UNDP, and the World Bank.

**Andrew Morrison** is Chief, Gender and Diversity Unit, at the Inter-American Development Bank. Prior to that he was Lead Economist in the Gender and Development Group of the Poverty Reduction and Economic Management Network at the World Bank. His current analytical work focuses on labor force participation of women, migration, violence against women, and crime and violence prevention. He has written journal articles on the issues of labor markets, migration, and urbanization, with research support from the National Science Foundation, the Tinker Foundation, and the Fulbright Scholarship program.

**Jean-Philippe Platteau** is Professor of Economics at the University of Namur (Belgium). Most of his research has been related to the understanding of the role of institutions in economic development, and the processes of institutional change, especially under the joint impact of population growth and market penetration. He is an active member of the network on "The Moral and Social Dimensions of Microeconomic Behavior in Low-Income Communities" supported by the Pew Trust Fund. Also, he is a member of the executive committee of the European Development Network (EUDN) that works as a European association of development economists and member of the advisory committee of the World Bank's network for agrarian reform; and of the International Society for the New Institutional Economics (ISNIE). Besides being Associate Editor of several development journals (*Journal of Development Studies*, *World Development* [until 2000], *Development and Change*, and *Oxford Development Studies*), he is active as Referee for a number of journals, including the *American Economic Review*, *Journal of Political Economy*, and *Economic Journal*. Professor Platteau is the recipient of several awards including the Dudley Seers Prize for the best paper of the year in the *Journal of Development Studies* (1996).

**Lant Pritchett** is Professor of the Practice of Economic Development at the Kennedy School of Government at Harvard University. In addition he works as a consultant to Google.org, is a Nonresident Fellow of the Center for Global Development, and is a Senior Fellow of BREAD. He is also Co-Editor of the *Journal of Development Economics*. After graduating from MIT in 1988, Professor Pritchett joined the World Bank, where he held a number of positions in the Bank's research complex between 1988 and 1998. From 1998 to 2000 he worked in Indonesia. From 2000 to 2004 Professor Pritchett was on leave from the World Bank as a Lecturer in Public Policy at the Kennedy School of Government at Harvard University. In 2004 he returned to the World Bank and moved to India where he worked until May 2007. He has been part of the team producing many World Bank reports, including. *World Development Report 1994: Infrastructure for Development; Assessing Aid: What Works, What Doesn't and Why* (1998); *Better Health Systems for India's Poor: Findings, Analysis, and Options* (2003); *World Development Report 2004: Making Services Work for the Poor; and Economic Growth in the 1990s: Learning from a Decade of Reforms* (2005). In addition he has authored (alone or with one of his 22 co-authors) over 50 papers published in refereed journals, as chapters in books, or as articles. In addition to economics journals his work has appeared in specialized journals in demography, education, and health. In 2006 he published his first solo authored book, *Let Their People Come.*

**Dhushyanth Raju** is an Economist at the World Bank. He is currently working on the economics of education in the Education Group, South Asia Region. He has a PhD in economics from Cornell University.

**Mark R. Rosenzweig** is the Frank Altschul Professor of International Economics and Director of the Economic Growth Center at Yale University. He is a development economist who studies the causes and consequences of economic development as well as international migration. He is one of the principal investigators of the New Immigrant Survey, the first national longitudinal survey of immigrants in the United States. Professor Rosenzweig serves as Editor of the *Journal of Development Economics* and was a Director of Research for the U.S. Select Commission on Immigration and Refugee Policy in 1980. He is a Fellow of the Econometric Society and a Fellow of the Society of Labor Economists.

**Nistha Sinha** is an Economist at the World Bank. She was a core team member of *World Development Report 2007: Development and the Next Generation* and of a research report analyzing gender issues in schooling, health, labor force, and community participation in Pakistan. Prior to joining the World Bank, she worked as a Postdoctoral Research Fellow at the Economic Growth Center, Yale University (2001–03). Her research focuses on the role of household behavior and delivery of services in the determination of human development outcomes, and the implications for public policy.

**Amedeo Spadaro** is Professor at the Paris School of Economics and Director of Microsimula. He is also Professor of Public Economics at University of Balearic Islands (Spain). His research activity is mainly concentrated on the theoretical and empirical analysis of the reform of redistribution systems. From a theoretical point of view the work is based on the normative analysis of the taxation and redistribution. From the applied side the main subject of research has been the construction of microsimulation models with behavior reactions and the treatment of the microdata about income and sociodemographic characteristics of European Households. The results of his research have been published in several papers and books. He participates (and also coordinates) in several research projects about tax reforms and their impact on household welfare.

**Michael Spence** is Senior Fellow, the Hoover Institution, and Philip H. Knight Professor Emeritus of Management, Graduate School of Business, Stanford University. He was awarded the Nobel Memorial Prize in Economic Sciences in 2001. Mr. Spence was Philip H. Knight Professor and Dean of the Stanford Business School from 1990 to 1999. Since 1999, he has been a Partner at Oak Hill Capital Partners. From 1975 to 1990, he served as Professor of Economics and Business Administration at Harvard University. Mr. Spence was awarded the John Kenneth Galbraith Prize for excellence in teaching in 1978 and the John Bates Clark Medal in 1981 for a "significant contribution to economic thought and knowledge." He was appointed Chairman of the Economics Department at Harvard in 1983 and served as the Dean of the Faculty of Arts and Sciences from 1984 to 1990. At various times, he has served as a member of the editorial boards of the *American Economics Review*, *Bell Journal of Economics*, *Journal of Economic Theory*, and *Public Policy*. Professor Spence is the Chair of the Commission on Growth and Development.

# Acknowledgments

The editors are most grateful for the strong support provided by the sponsors of the Commission on Growth and Development: the governments of Australia, the Netherlands, Sweden, and the United Kingdom; the William and Flora Hewlett Foundation; and the World Bank. Danny Leipziger, former Vice President of the Poverty Reduction and Economic Management Network of the World Bank, was generous in providing resources for this effort. We are much obliged to the participants in the workshops on equity and growth sponsored by the Commission and held at Yale's Center for the Study of Globalization, especially the chapter authors, for their numerous and diverse insights and the time they dedicated to engaging in discussions of the issues. Roberto Zagha, Secretary of the Commission, was a constant source of good ideas, encouragement, and stimulation. Roberto brings out the best in others while keeping a sharp focus on the driving issues at hand. The level of discussion and the quality of the papers that follow reflect his enthusiasm and wisdom.

A team of colleagues in the Growth Commission Secretariat—Muriel Darlington, Diana Manevskaya, and Dorota Nowak—were dedicated to making every aspect of the Commission's work successful. They gave us what felt like undivided attention in organizing the workshops and producing this book—one of many of the Commission's activities with pressing deadlines and low tolerance for error. The whole process was only possible due to their marvelous organization and steady hard work. Cindy Fisher was pragmatic, accommodating, and rigorous in preparing the manuscript for publication. Stephen McGroarty oversaw the publication process with great skill. We thank Simon Cox of the *Economist* for his excellent work on the preface.

Ravi Kanbur
Michael Spence

# Abbreviations

| | |
|---|---|
| AERC | African Economic Research Consortium |
| BREAD | Bureau for Research in Economic Analysis and Development |
| CGE | computable general equilibrium (model) |
| CPIA | Country Policy and Institutional Assessment |
| DHS | Demographic and Health Surveys |
| GDP | gross domestic product |
| GNI | gross national income |
| HBS | Household Budget Survey (Turkey) |
| HIPC | heavily indebted poor country |
| HYV | high-yielding variety |
| ICOR | incremental capital output ratio |
| ICRISAT | International Crop Research Institute for the Semi-Arid Tropics |
| LSMS | Living Standards Measurement Study |
| MDG | Millennium Development Goal |
| MICS | Multiple Indicator Cluster Survey |
| MPK | marginal product of capital |
| NAFTA | North American Free Trade Agreement |
| NBER | National Bureau of Economic Research |
| NIS | New Immigrant Survey |
| NISP | New Immigrant Survey Pilot |
| ODA | official development assistance |
| OECD | Organisation for Economic Co-operation and Development |
| OWW | Occupational Wages Around the World |

| | |
|---|---|
| PISA | Program for International Student Assessment |
| PPP | purchasing power parity |
| PRSP | Poverty Reduction Strategy Paper |
| ROSCAs | rotating savings and credit associations |
| TDHS | Turkish Demographic and Health Survey |
| UNICEF | United Nations Children's Fund |
| USAID | U.S. Agency for International Development |
| WDI | *World Development Indicators* |
| WTO | World Trade Organization |
| $ | U.S. dollars unless otherwise indicated |

# CHAPTER 1

# Equity within and between Nations

*Ravi Kanbur and Michael Spence*

Income inequality between persons in the world as a whole can be conceptualized as composed of two elements: inequality *within* nations or countries and inequality *between* nations or countries, defined as inequality between the average incomes of these different nations. Some inequality measures, such as the variance of log-income or the generalized entropy family of inequality measures, can be formally broken down into these two components so that they add up to total inequality. In a purely accounting sense, then, inequality within nations and inequality between nations both contribute to global inequality and are thus appropriate policy targets. Even when such a precise formal accounting decomposition cannot be accomplished for income, or even when the discourse on inequality transcends income and touches on broader dimensions such as health and education, the notion of equity between and within nations serves well as a framework for underlying concerns and for organizing discussion and debate.

Inequality within a nation is ordinarily thought to be within the purview of the policymakers and the social and political processes of that nation. In a globalizing world, however, it cannot be insulated from global forces and trends and from policies adopted by other countries or the international community at large. Sometimes, it cannot even be insulated from the social and political processes in other countries, especially neighboring countries. Leaving aside these global influences, whose effects are much discussed, considerable debate has surrounded equity and inequity within a country, its impact on growth and on the fabric of society, and what policies can best be deployed to reduce inequity if that is an ethical goal, or to manage its consequences for growth and development even if equity per se is not an ethical concern. For example, among the fundamental issues to be addressed are the conceptual, empirical, and policy differences between reducing inequality of ex post outcomes and inequality of ex ante opportunities.

As difficult as the questions of equity within nations tend to be, inequality between nations is even more difficult. The difficulties are in part philosophical, arising from a long-standing debate on what exactly constitutes a moral community of concern. Does this moral community move outward from the family in concentric circles of diminishing concern as it reaches the extended family, the immediate neighborhood, the region, the nation, and the world? Or do humanity's deep moral imperatives lead to a flatter world in the sense of a moral community, so that the only morally defensible objective is to reduce inequity between citizens of the world, no matter which nations they happen to inhabit? At the same time, the nature of policy instruments available at the global level is less certain and less clear both in the technical sense of the operation of these global instruments and in the political sense that these instruments exist only as a result of agreements between sovereign nation-states. One of the most difficult global issues, and one on which the nation-state holds greatest sway, is the free migration of labor across national borders.

This volume brings together a significant new collection of papers by leading economists, who address a range of challenging questions on equity within and between nations in the context of a globalizing world. Most of the papers were presented at workshops organized by the Commission on Growth and Development (henceforth the Growth Commission) in the run-up to the publication of *The Growth Report: Strategies for Sustained Growth and Inclusive Development* (Commission on Growth and Development 2008).[1] In its report, the commission emphasizes the importance of equity within nations:

> The Commission strongly believes that growth strategies cannot succeed without a commitment to equality of opportunity, giving everyone a fair chance to enjoy the fruits of growth. But equal opportunities are no guarantee of equal outcomes. Indeed, in the early stages of growth, there is a natural tendency for income gaps to widen. Governments should seek to contain this inequality, the Commission believes, at the bottom and top ends of the income spectrum. Otherwise, the economy's progress may be jeopardized by divisive politics, protest and even violent ethnic conflict. Again, if the ethical case does not persuade, the pragmatic one should. (p. 7)

---

1 The Commission on Growth and Development (2008) was chaired by Michael Spence, http://www.growthcommission.org/index.php.

The report also calls for equity between nations, highlighting the responsibilities of advanced countries, including on trade: "Developing countries cannot grow without the support of the advanced economies. In particular, they need access to the open global trading system. They may also need some latitude to promote their exports, until their economies have matured and their competitive position has improved."

In this introduction and overview, we, the volume editors, highlight what we see as the key issues on equity that emerge for analysts and policymakers from the papers that make up this volume and from the literature more generally. The next section takes up the perspective of equity within nations, and the section that follows looks at equity in the global context. The concluding section pulls together, based on the previous two sections, a policy-focused discussion of what can and should be done to address equity within and between nations.

## Poverty and Inequality within Countries

How have incomes and other dimensions of well-being in developing countries evolved over the last two decades? In chapter 2, François Bourguignon et al. fully answer this question, focusing on the dimensions captured in the Millennium Development Goals (MDGs). The specific indicators proposed for tracking the MDGs include income poverty, malnutrition, school enrollment rates for boys and girls, and infant and maternal mortality rates. Despite the data difficulties (and they are considerable), the authors summarize the analysis of the World Bank and the United Nations as follows:

1. *Global progress is surprisingly good*, especially for the poverty and the gender parity goals, but less so for the child mortality and maternal mortality goals. As is widely acknowledged, however, the progress on global poverty is very much driven by overachievers in East and South Asia, including Bangladesh, China, India, Indonesia, and Vietnam.
2. *There are clear regional patterns in MDG progress* that depend on initial conditions and recent growth performances. If Asian countries are overachievers on the income poverty goal, they perform relatively worse in health and, for India, in education and gender equity. Conversely, Latin America and the Middle East are relative underachievers on the poverty goal, but relative overachievers in health, education, and gender equity. Finally, the Sub-Saharan African countries lag far behind other regions.
3. *Most countries in all regions are off track on most MDGs* (or data are missing to assess progress), even some of those countries that have experienced very good growth performance.
4. *MDG achievements are much lower in "fragile" states.* One of the reasons why Sub-Saharan Africa lags behind on the MDGs is the relatively

large proportion of so-called fragile states in that region. The definition of fragile states used here is that established by the World Bank.[2]

5. In most regions, including those successful in meeting the poverty goal, *progress on reducing childhood undernutrition is extremely slow.*

6. The *poorest regions*, South Asia and Sub-Saharan Africa, *are* the two still seriously *off track for primary school completion rates and for child mortality.*

7. *Progress has been good on gender equity in primary and secondary school enrollments in all regions.* Yet Sub-Saharan Africa and other fragile states still lag seriously behind. Most countries in Sub-Saharan Africa are unlikely to meet this goal.

As Bourguignon et al. note, the overall pattern thus seems to be one of a glass that is half-full and half-empty. But further analysis of the data reveals two important findings relevant to policy. First, even within regions there is considerable country heterogeneity in country performance on the MDGs. Some of these differences stem from structural factors such as geographic location or whether a country is a "fragile" state. But even allowing for these factors, there is significant variation. This variation surely emphasizes another theme of *The Growth Report*: country specificity and context matter, and a uniform policy prescription across countries is inappropriate.

Second, although there is a strong correlation between growth in income per capita and changes in income measures of poverty, for nonincome MDGs Bourguignon et al. conclude:

> The correlation between growth in GDP per capita and improvements in nonincome MDGs is practically zero, . . . [thereby confirming] the lack of a relationship between those indicators and poverty reduction. Because it would be hard to believe that information on nonincome MDGs is so badly affected by measurement error that it is pure noise, this lack of a relationship reflects some relative independence among policy instruments governing progress in the various MDGs. Furthermore, it highlights substantive differences in country policies and circumstances that may affect the relationship between these policies. This interesting finding suggests that economic growth is not sufficient per se to generate progress in nonincome MDGs. Sectoral policies and other factors or circumstances presumably matter as much as growth.

Thus, as *The Growth Report* acknowledges and emphasizes, growth is not an end in itself; it is a necessary but not sufficient condition for development in the broader sense.

Even for income poverty, which has a strong correlation with economic growth, there are still significant variations around the average relationship. Specifically, different countries seem to translate economic growth into reduced income poverty at different rates—that is, the "growth elasticity

---

2   The countries referred to as "fragile" are low-income countries that score below a certain cutoff in the World Bank's Country Policy and Institutional Assessment (CPIA) ratings. These ratings reflect assessments made by Bank staff members in a range of policy and institutional areas, but in practice, fragility is most often linked to present or past conflicts in the national territory or in neighboring states.

of poverty reduction" varies considerably. In countries such as Cambodia, China, Ghana, Honduras, and Uganda, this effectiveness appears to be quite low.

In chapter 3, Ravi Kanbur reviews the growing theoretical and empirical literature, which locates this ineffectiveness in the high and rising inequality that dissipates the poverty reduction benefits of economic growth. In his chapter, Kanbur highlights the disconnect between falling income poverty indices in fast-growth economies, on the one hand, and the growing distributional concerns among the civil societies and polities of these very same countries, on the other. What explains this disconnect? Kanbur argues that official poverty statistics by their very nature tend to understate true poverty and overstate reductions in poverty. One important reason is that such statistics ignore intrahousehold inequality, because official surveys collect data on consumption only at the household level. Thus by ignoring a key dimension of inequity in society—gender inequity within the household— official statistics bias the national representation of the level and trends in poverty. They paint a rosier picture than warranted, thereby misleading the policy debate.

Kanbur also argues that, quite independently of the dissipating effects of high and rising inequality on the growth-poverty reduction relationship, higher inequality in and of itself creates tensions in society that are reflected in the concerns of the polity. This is particularly true when the inequity is across salient sociopolitical groupings such as regions, religions, or ethnicities. The reason why such inequities and the tensions they cause can hold back investment and growth is fairly clear.

However, in chapter 4, Abhijit Banerjee presents an analysis that shows a causal link between inequity pure and simple, even when it does not have ethnic or other group dimensions, and investment efficiency and growth. Banerjee develops a canonical model in which there is no correlation between entrepreneurial talent and wealth, but, because of fixed costs of investment and imperfect credit markets, those with more wealth are better able to invest in their own projects. As a result, "some less talented rich people are able to bid the capital away from some poorer but more gifted entrepreneurs (or, equivalently, the rich father of a mediocre student can bid away a seat in a good college from the poor father of the next would-be genius)." And the problem is not just that the poor are too poor to finance the fixed costs of investment; it is also that the rich can bid away capital because of their better ability to offer collateral. In this sense, too much capital is in the hands of the rich. Banerjee reviews the empirical evidence on credit constraints, which supports the assumptions in his model, and concludes that "there is reason to try to redistribute investible resources, not only toward the poor, but also toward specific groups of the nonpoor, including many established but smaller entrepreneurs."

Further arguments for and evidence of the importance of equity in the promotion of efficiency and economic growth are presented in chapter 5 by Andrew Morrison, Dhushyanth Raju, and Nistha Sinha. They begin by recognizing that the evidence that economic growth, on average and over a long period of time, is associated with greater gender equity is quite strong. This recognition is all the more an argument for promoting economic growth, as *The Growth Report* points out. However, the results of Bourguignon et al. in chapter 2 indicate that there is significant variation around such relationships, and that there is plenty of room for purposive interventions to promote gender equity in order to ensure that the fruits of growth are indeed being shared equitably. Moreover, such direct promotion of gender equity can by itself act as a spur to efficiency and economic growth, which is the burden of the argument in chapter 5. Morrison, Raju, and Sinha conduct a thorough review of the literature and identify not only key findings but also areas for further research in which knowledge is lacking. By and large, they find that gender equity is supportive of efficiency and growth, but they highlight the following areas in which more research is needed: (1) documenting gender disparities; (2) collecting more rigorous evidence on the gender-differentiated effects of increased access by the poor to economic resources and opportunities; and (3) collecting rigorous evidence on the impact of improving gender equity on economic growth.

*The Growth Report* recognizes the distinction between equality and equality of opportunity, a subject much debated in the literature. According to the report, equality refers to outcomes or results, whereas equality of opportunity refers to starting points:

> People care about both kinds of equality. But they understand that markets do not produce equal outcomes. They will tolerate this inequality, provided governments take steps to contain it. . . . Inequality of opportunity, on the other hand, does not involve trade-offs and can be toxic. This is especially so if the opportunities are systematically denied to a group due to its ethnicity, religion, caste or gender. . . . How can governments safeguard equality of opportunity and contain inequality of outcomes? The latter goal is served by redistribution, over and above the informal sharing arrangements that often prevail in extended families and tight-knit communities. Equality of opportunity is best served by providing universal access to public services like health and education, and by meritocratic systems in government and the private sector. (p. 62)

A somewhat different perspective is presented by Kanbur in chapter 3. In reacting to a literature that tries to specify and measure equality of opportunity, he argues that it may be difficult in practice to distinguish between equality of opportunity and equality of outcomes, especially if equality of outcomes appears to differ from equality of opportunity because of individual "effort" or "tastes." For example, the effort or tastes of parents translate into the starting points ("circumstances") of their children. Equalizing starting points for children may then involve, at least to some extent, equalizing outcomes between their parents. Thus the clean distinction breaks down in concept as well as in practice. Nevertheless, it remains true that differences in achievements across broad groups differentiated by gender, ethnicity, caste, and religion have moral significance beyond the fact that they contribute to inequality between persons. If one believes there is no inherent difference in talent across these groups, then differences in things such as wealth, income, and education as a result of belonging to these groups are inefficient and ethically objectionable.

In chapter 6, Francisco H. G. Ferreira and Jérémie Gignoux present a detailed empirical analysis of inequality of opportunity by applying the concept and measurement to Turkey. Using data from the Demographic and Health Survey (DHS), the authors examine variation in the quantity and quality of education. They show that enrollment rates (correcting for age) differ on average across gender, regions, and family backgrounds. Variation in test scores is also affected by these factors and other indicators of a child's "circumstances" such as parents' education and father's occupation. An interesting difference, however, is that, although gender determines differences in enrollment and retention (lower for girls), it is not an important factor in explaining test scores. As Ferreira and Gignoux conclude, "The policy lesson for those concerned with girls' education in Turkey seems to be: get—and keep—them in school. Once there, they seem to do well enough." The analysis by Ferreira and Gignoux illustrates how careful empirical work on microdata not only can shed light on "big picture" conceptual issues such as equality of opportunity, but also can provide pointers to very specific policy interventions to achieve equity in key dimensions.

Part of the story of the literature on equity within nations is the level of aggregation at which the discourse proceeds, or should proceed. Thus, in chapter 2 Bourguignon et al., after giving a detailed cross-country account of how well-being has evolved, emphasize that variations within countries are also important. Chapters 3, 4, 5, and 6 focus on the lowest part of the income distribution (poverty) and on the achievements of broad groupings within countries such as those based on gender and ethnicity. However, a group of particular interest in all developing countries, but particularly in fast-growing ones, is the middle class. This grouping is important because of its central role (literally and figuratively) in generating the income distribution and in determining the tax and transfer policies that affect the well-being of the poor. Thus, for example, in chapter 3 Kanbur argues for transfer policies that cushion the poor against shocks and vulnerabilities. But such policies cannot be introduced without the support of middle-income groups—the imperative of fine targeting for efficiency of the transfer has to be traded against some leakages to middle-income groups to build support for the programs in the first place.

In chapter 7, Nancy Birdsall is motivated by the potential political power (PPP, as she calls it) of the middle class. She begins by answering some empirical questions: How should the middle class be defined? How big is it? What are its characteristics? She defines this middle class as those people with consumption/income of more than $10 a day in 2005 and at or below the 95th percentile of the distribution of their country. She discusses and defends this mixture of absolute and relative criteria in her definition, as opposed to the alternatives in the literature, such as just the middle three quintiles. About the $10 line, she says: "I propose an absolute minimum on the grounds that in the relatively open economies of most developing countries today, with economic security to some extent vulnerable to external as well as internal economic and political shocks (including weather, financial crises, and so on—consider the food and fuel price spikes in 2008), and some consumption standards set at the global level (e.g., a car is not a Lexus everywhere), some absolute minimum makes sense." About the 95th percentile, she says: "The relative maximum, which obviously varies across countries, can be thought of as excluding that portion of a country's population whose income is most likely to be from inherited wealth, or based on prior or current economic rents associated with monopoly or other privileges, and thus is less associated with productive and primarily labor activity than for the nonrich."

Clearly, one can debate the specifics of Birdsall's definition, and she herself recognizes criticisms and addresses them. What is interesting and important, however, is that such a definition provides an empirical basis on which to delve deeper into a specific part of the income distribution. Birdsall then goes on to provide an account of the size and composition of the middle class across countries. In light of this exploration, she concludes that "the real trade-off in policy design is far better thought of as a trade-off between the rich and the rest rather than, as has been the mindset in the international community for several decades, the absolute poor and the rest." Such a conclusion certainly influences the perspective and the framework from which the issue of equity within nations is approached.

## Equity in the Global Context

Chapter 8, by Ann Harrison and Margaret McMillan, marks a transition in this volume from looking at a nation or a country to looking beyond that country at the world at large. The fact that opportunities for international trade and especially knowledge transfer are a central factor in explaining the growth performance of developing countries is the subject of relatively little debate. Sustained high growth in isolation is very unlikely, and there are no counterexamples. But there is considerable debate on what policies best take advantage of these opportunities to promote growth. A prime example of these policies is industrial policies for export promotion and structural diversification of the economy. The debates within the Growth Commission, discussed in *The Growth Report*, are indicative of the different views and continuing debate in this area: "Some skeptics might concede that markets do not always work, but they argue that industrial policies don't either. . . . The risk of failure or subversion is too great. . . . But there is also risk to doing nothing. . . . If an economy is failing to diversify its exports and failing to generate productive jobs in new industries, governments do look for ways to jump-start the process, and they should" (p. 49). Although the debate on the exact nature of outward orientation and its impact on growth will no doubt go on, Harrison and McMillan focus on the impact of this outward orientation on poverty. Rather like chapter 5 on gender, this chapter summarizes its findings, but also lays out an agenda for further research.

Does globalization reduce poverty? Harrison and McMillan sum up their findings as follows. First, "the poor in countries with an abundance of unskilled labor do not always gain from trade reform." This finding may seem surprising in view of the basic teaching of trade theory, especially around the Stolper-Samuelson theorem, but it appears that the conditions of this theorem are not met in practice (it is not the case that all countries produce all goods, that labor is immobile, and so on). Second, "the poor are more likely to share in the gains from globalization when complementary policies are in place." Third, "export growth and incoming foreign investment can reduce poverty. In the countries studied, poverty has fallen in regions where exports or foreign investment is growing." Fourth, "financial crises are costly to the poor." This is a uniform finding in the literature, and, although the evidence base of Harrison and McMillan's chapter predates the current crisis, this finding has relevance for policy responses to the current downturn as well. Fifth, "globalization produces both winners and losers among the poor." The central point is that the poor are heterogeneous in their characteristics and in their engagement with the economy. Thus policies such as broad tariff reduction are bound to have differential impacts on the poor. Even when overall poverty declines, it is possible that a significant number of the poor are impoverished as a result, at least in the short term. Whether this happens or not is, of course, an empirical question, but in chapter 3, Kanbur argues that this could be one of the reasons behind the disconnect between encouraging official poverty figures and ground-level discontent, as expressed by those poor who have been made poorer, even though the majority of the poor have benefited. Harrison and McMillan's final conclusion is that "different measures of globalization are associated with different poverty outcomes. *How* globalization is measured determines *whether* globalization is good for the poor." Their chapter focuses on openness to trade and capital flows, and, indeed, the world economy has undergone considerable globalization over the last few decades. But the one measure in which globalization is not very pronounced is labor flows.

The final three chapters in this volume concentrate on the question of international migration and its impact, or the impact of the lack of international migration, on equity within and between nations. The central empirical questions posed in these chapters are the extent to which labor of the same type earns different returns in different countries, how much migration is thereby stimulated, and the impact of this migration, in turn, on these wage differentials. The implicit or explicit moral challenge in these chapters is the national restrictions on migration in the face of large and persistent wage differentials that exacerbate inequity between nations.

Chapter 9 by Mark Rosenzweig provides an analysis of the nature of global wage differentials using three newly available data sets: the New Immigrant Survey Pilot, Occupational Wages Around the World, and the

New Immigrant Survey. A major finding is that "the data reject the model underlying the Mincer wage specification, which assumes perfect capital and labor markets and no barriers to schooling acquisition (and no permanent differences in lifetime earnings), suggesting that a framework incorporating the determinants of the supply and pricing of skills is better suited to accounting for wage inequality." Focusing then just on the supply and pricing of skills, Rosenzweig finds that pricing of skills is the major influence on wages, and he then draws the following sharp conclusion: "That most of global inequality in incomes is due to intercountry differences in the prices of skills suggests that greater equalization of schooling levels arising from domestic schooling policies will have only marginal effects on global inequality, that domestic development policies in poor countries should focus on the underlying reasons skill are less valued, and that labor is poorly distributed across countries based on global efficiency criteria, given the structure of skill prices." Perhaps it is not surprising that Rosenzweig also finds that the skill price differential is a determinant of migration flows to the United States.

In contrast to Rosenzweig's analysis of specific recently available data, Gordon H. Hanson provides in chapter 10 an overview of the general literature on international migration and development, and thus offers a broader scope in the questions asked and studies consulted. He provides the following summary of the key findings of this literature:

1. Bilateral migration flows are negatively affected by migration costs, as captured by the geographic or linguistic distance between countries, the absence of migration networks, or the stringency of border enforcement against illegal entry. . . .
2. Emigration rates are highest for those in the middle-income group of developing countries and for developing countries with higher population densities. . . .
3. In most developing countries, the more educated are the most likely to emigrate. . . .
4. Emigrants sort themselves across destinations according to income-earning possibilities, and the countries that have the highest incomes for skilled labor attract the most educated mix of immigrants. . . .
5. Empirically, the impact of opportunities for skilled emigration on the stock of human capital in a country is unknown. . . .
6. There is some evidence that emigration puts upward pressure on wages in sending countries. . . .
7. Migrant remittances tend to positively correlate with household consumption and investments in education and entrepreneurial activities in sending countries.

Whether one favors the specific study by Rosenzweig or general survey by Hanson, it is difficult to escape the conclusion that freer movement of labor would enhance global efficiency. It certainly would improve equity between nations, and, although its impact on equity within nations is ambiguous, there are positive forces in this direction as well (e.g., in the finding that emigration leads to upward pressures on wages). It is this huge anomaly in the globalization discourse that motivates, and enrages, Lant Pritchett, the author of the final chapter in this volume.

For Pritchett, globalization as currently envisaged is a sham without freer movement of labor. On this score, there has been, if anything, a retreat since the number of sovereign nations increased over the last few decades. Most important for labor movement, these sovereigns present a "cliff at the border." Pritchett presents considerable evidence of such cliffs and argues that the world is not all flat—far from it. He labels the world as it is now the Proliferation of Sovereigns combined with Everything but Labor Liberalization (POSEBLL). According to Pritchett, "POSEBLL has led, as expected, to equalization of the prices of goods and equalization of the prices of capital. But, perhaps unexpectedly, it has also led to very uneven progress in the newly proliferated sovereigns, and this, combined with binding quantitative restrictions on the movement of labor, has also led to massive gaps in the wages of equivalent labor around the world and sustained divergence in the per capita incomes across nation-states."

Pritchett's main thrust goes beyond the empirical establishment of these distortions to an examination of their implications for equity. In doing so, he takes on what he calls the "nation-state-ization" of equity: "The question is, how does the massive differential treatment of people who are alike in every respect except for their affiliation with a particular nation-state, an essentially arbitrary condition of birth, square with any theory of justice?" His discussion relates very much to our earlier discussion of equality of opportunity. If gender differences and ethnic differences cannot be the basis morally for unequal outcomes for people alike in talent, why should nation of birth have moral salience in evaluating equality of treatment? According to Pritchett, "'Because you are a girl' is no longer considered a socially appropriate rationale for differential treatment. By contrast, people who are exactly identical in every conceivable and observable respect can be treated in ways that cause their well-being to differ by orders of magnitude—for example, one is denied access to a more productive job—with no apparent violation of justice if those otherwise identical individuals happen to be citizens of different countries." Pritchett's discourse critiques many scholars, including John Rawls, the supposed guide to egalitarian instincts, for circumscribing his moral community to that of the nation-state and thereby avoiding the problem altogether.

Although Pritchett's critique is powerful and appeals to moral intuition at one level, a truly global social welfare function in which citizenship does not matter would have its own jarring consequences. In their discussion of the Millennium Development Goals in chapter 2, Bourguignon et al. show that, globally, there has been good progress on income poverty, so much so, in fact, that (before the current global financial crisis) the world was well on its way to meeting the MDG of halving the incidence of poverty between 1990 and 2015. However, as also pointed out and highlighted by Bourguignon et al., this performance is almost entirely explained by China, India, and other large Asian countries because they have had sharp declines in poverty, and because they account for the bulk of the population of developing countries. Sub-Saharan Africa, by contrast, has seen an increase in poverty. If analysts adopted a truly global perspective à la Pritchett, they would presumably be indifferent to whether an Indian or an African was lifted from poverty. But would this also allow them to "cancel out" the increase in African poverty with an equivalent decrease in Asian poverty? The issue presents itself equally within a nation-state as well, and we have already alluded to it. As highlighted in Kanbur's chapter 3, quite often a decline in national poverty has been accompanied by a rise in the poverty of a significant number of people, frequently in groups identified regionally. The impoverishment of an ethnic group, perhaps by the very same policies that have bettered poverty nationally, raises questions beyond the pragmatic ones of likely consequences for social peace. It jars morally as well. The nation-state as a moral community does not seem to be an adequate response. In the same way, the world as a moral community that dominates other groupings may not be an adequate response to many distributional dilemmas. A balance would have to be struck in the ethical conceptualizations of equity within and between nations, just as a balance would have to be struck between national and global policy instruments in addressing inequity in its many dimensions.

## Policy Conclusions

We have not been able to cover the full range of issues that arise in a discussion of equity in a globalizing world. Instead, we have focused on topics covered by the chapters in this volume, thereby omitting many important questions such as the role of development assistance as a response to inequity between nations and as an instrument for reducing poverty and inequality within nations. We also have not discussed the role of global public goods (and global public bads) in equity within and between nations.

Nevertheless, the analysis and evidence presented here provide a useful framework for setting policy priorities. In any country, and especially in developing countries, as well as in the international arena, priorities have to be set, and simply doing everything that sounds meritorious, even if one is sure about the desired direction, is not feasible. Resources—physical, financial, human, and political—are not infinite.

The contributors to this volume make it clear that, if one begins with what people care about, the list is not confined to income or material well-being in the narrow sense. It includes health, education, productive employment opportunity, freedom of expression, a voice in governance and shaping the collective destiny, respect, and more. In each of these fundamental aspects of life, there are citizens who are disadvantaged. And the outcomes in the various dimensions are not perfectly or even very highly correlated within and across countries and regions. It is a multidimensional policy challenge, domestically and internationally.

The contributors to this volume also make it clear that ex ante (opportunity) and ex post (outcomes) equity issues deserve high priority in policymaking for a number of reasons. One reason is moral. People make choices that lead to differing levels of income. But people do not choose to be very poor or to have limited access to basic services. They end up in disadvantaged positions because of constraints of a variety of kinds, including intertemporal ones.

A second reason has to do with preferences. People generally care about equity for both moral and pragmatic reasons. Those reasons are translated into political and social choices and implemented by policy. The political challenge is to avoid the zero-sum game version of this exercise in which one person's gain is another loss. Thus it is important to create and choose policies that deal with equity but also promote (or do not impede) growth and expanding opportunity of an inclusive kind. The challenge must be thought of as an intertemporal one and not simply as a static redistributional one. It would be wrong to pretend that this is an easy challenge or that, in view of the current state of our knowledge, the road map is well understood and agreed on.

The third and related reason concerns the sustainability of the growth and development process. Persistent inequality in its various dimensions leads to political and social instability or very harsh repression. In either case, the chances of growth and intergenerational improvement and poverty reduction decline precipitously.

The case is very strong that the potential for productive economic activity, growth, and employment among poor populations is considerable. However, this potential is untapped because of structural barriers that prevent access to a variety of services that would serve as crucial inputs. Policies directed at removing these barriers and, more generally, at ensuring access to a broad array of basic services—among them, security, financial, and educational—are likely to have a first-order positive impact on growth and intertemporal poverty reduction.

The middle class is important. In a country that is growing and developing, the middle class becomes larger. Moreover, it is increasingly politically important. And many of its members or their parents used to be poor. What does this mean? As Birdsall and others argue, it means that paying attention to equity in growth and development policy terms cannot mean an exclusive focus on the poor. Doing so produces a growing gap between the policy priorities and focus, on the one hand, and the status and aspirations of the majority of the people, on the other. So once again a political and policy balancing act must combine a special concern for the poor and disadvantaged with a focus on policies that broadly improve the circumstances of a majority of citizens.

As highlighted in this volume, some forms of inequality, deprivation, or deficit have particularly long-lived effects. Nutrition; access to basic, quality education; and chronic and debilitating diseases would be among them. Policies that address these issues should be a continuing priority. Because they deal with equity issues, they could have enormously high social and economic returns.

The international dimensions of equity are morally and conceptually complex. The absence of labor mobility clearly has a profound effect on outcomes in terms of efficiency and distribution, although the growing volume of trade in services involving transactions and the processing of information would modify the impact of this constraint.

The contributors to this volume make it clear that the international differences in incomes are not attributable to simple differences in skills; they have more to do with the complementary assets that are in place.[3] Neither tangible nor intangible assets are produced overnight. The full transition from relatively poor to advanced country income levels, even at sustained high growth rates, takes more than half a century, and at lower growth rates it takes much longer than that. Thus these differentials, which are not a function of narrowly defined human capital differences, will be persistent.

Within countries, labor mobility in the relevant economic sense is often not perfect. Present are linguistic issues, constraints on mobility created by infrastructure, and institutions and legal structures that protect subsets of the labor force from competition with other segments. Removal of these barriers is not easy, and it generally will not benefit everyone. The distributional issues come to the forefront in the political process.

The same considerations appear in the international arena. International policies that increase labor mobility have high payoffs in efficiency and equity. But they also have distributional consequences, as does expansion of the tradable sector. Not everyone gains, at least in the short run. International policies on labor mobility therefore meet resistance, and for immigration and emigration the resistance can be very substantial.

A full-scale attempt to change the landscape for labor mobility and immigration is not likely to succeed. One way to reduce the distributional resistance to labor mobility internationally is to focus on opening channels from surplus labor environments to labor shortage markets. The contributors to this volume suggest that this process works in practice—a kind of sorting process in which immigration constraints are relaxed in response to a perceived need. But the process is far from perfect. The potential for exploitation and abuse invites the setting of international standards and the proper supervision of transnational labor flows.

Research conducted over the last 15 years has dramatically increased the understanding of inequality, its quantitative dimensions, and its causes. Major progress has been made in thinking about policies that deal effectively with equity. The contributors to this volume bring together much of that thinking and progress in a highly accessible form. Our hope is that their contributions will provide a useful framework

---

3   There is ample evidence for this conclusion. Well-trained professionals in many fields who move from a developing country to an advanced country find that their incomes rise, reflecting a jump in productivity associated with the change in productivity-enhancing complementary assets.

for political and policy leaders as they wrestle with these important and challenging issues.

## Reference

Commission on Growth and Development. 2008. *The Growth Report: Strategies for Sustained Growth and Inclusive Development.* Washington, DC: World Bank. http://www.growthcommission.org/index.php?option=com_content &task=view&id=96&Itemid=169.

# CHAPTER 2
# The Millennium Development Goals: An Assessment

*François Bourguignon, Agnès Bénassy-Quéré, Stefan Dercon, Antonio Estache, Jan Willem Gunning, Ravi Kanbur, Stephan Klasen, Simon Maxwell, Jean-Philippe Platteau, and Amedeo Spadaro*

The Millennium Development Goals (MDGs) express the international community's strong commitment to universal development and poverty eradication. It made this commitment in September 2000 in the United Nations (UN) Millennium Declaration. The goals include halving world poverty and hunger by 2015, as well as reaching universal primary education, reducing under-5 and maternal mortality by two-thirds, and halving the number of people without access to safe drinking water (see box 2.1). The declaration also calls for a new partnership between the developed and developing countries, determined "to create an environment, at the national and global levels alike, which is conducive to development and the

This chapter is extracted from a longer and more comprehensive paper by Bourguignon et al. (2008) entitled "Millennium Development Goals at Midpoint: Where Do We Stand and Where Do We Need to Go?" written for the Directorate General for Development of the European Commission as a background paper for the 2009 *European Report on Development*. The paper was funded by the UK Department for International Development.

Box 2.1 Millennium Development Goals

The following list of Millennium Development Goals is accompanied by the targets developed in 2002 and used until 2007 to measure progress toward the goals.

**Goal 1: Eradicate extreme poverty and hunger.**
Target 1.A: Halve, between 1990 and 2015, the proportion of people whose income is less than one dollar a day.
Target 1.B: Achieve full and productive employment and decent work for all, including women and young people.*
Target 1.C: Halve, between 1990 and 2015, the proportion of people who suffer from hunger.

**Goal 2: Achieve universal primary education.**
Target 2.A: Ensure that, by 2015, children everywhere, boys and girls alike, will be able to complete a full course of primary schooling.

**Goal 3: Promote gender equality and empower women.**
Target 3.A: Eliminate gender disparity in primary and secondary education, preferably by 2005, and in all levels of education no later than 2015.

**Goal 4: Reduce child mortality.**
Target 4.A: Reduce by two-thirds, between 1990 and 2015, the under-five mortality rate.

**Goal 5: Improve maternal health.**
Target 5.A: Reduce by three-quarters, between 1990 and 2015, the maternal mortality ratio.
Target 5.B: Achieve, by 2015, universal access to reproductive health.*

**Goal 6: Combat HIV/AIDS, malaria, and other diseases.**
Target 6.A: Have halted by 2015 and begun to reverse the spread of HIV/AIDS.
Target 6.B: Achieve, by 2010, universal access to treatment for HIV/AIDS for all those who need it.
Target 6.C: Have halted by 2015 and begun to reverse the incidence of malaria and other major diseases.

**Goal 7: Ensure environmental sustainability.**
Target 7.A: Integrate the principles of sustainable development into country policies and programs and reverse the loss of environmental resources.
Target 7.B: Reduce biodiversity loss, achieving, by 2010, a significant reduction in the rate of loss.*
Target 7.C: Halve, by 2015, the proportion of people without sustainable access to safe drinking water and basic sanitation.

**Goal 8: Develop a global partnership for development.**
Target 8.A: Develop further an open, rule-based, predictable, nondiscriminatory trading and financial system. Includes a commitment to good governance, development, and poverty reduction—both nationally and internationally.
Target 8.B: Address the special needs of the least-developed countries. Includes: tariff- and quota-free access for the least-developed countries' exports; enhanced program of debt relief for heavily indebted poor countries (HIPC) and cancellation of official bilateral debt; and more generous ODA for countries committed to poverty reduction.
Target 8.C: Address the special needs of landlocked developing countries and small island developing states (through the Programme of Action for the Sustainable Development of Small Island Developing States and the outcome of the twenty-second special session of the General Assembly).

Target 8.D: Deal comprehensively with the debt problems of developing countries through national and international measures in order to make debt sustainable in the long term.

*Source:* The Millennium Development Goals and targets are taken from the Millennium Declaration, signed by 189 countries, including 147 heads of state and government, in September 2000 (http://www.un.org/millennium/declaration/ares552e.htm) and from further agreement by member states at the 2005 World Summit (resolution adopted by the General Assembly, A/RES/60/1, http://www.un.org/Docs/journal/asp/ws.asp?m=A/RES/60/1).
* Targets added at the 2005 UN World Summit.

elimination of poverty." Developed countries are to improve market access, channel financial resources, and provide development assistance to the developing world, as well as reduce its debt burden. The developing world, for its part, is to improve governance and conduct effective development policies.

A year and a half later, in March 2002, the International Conference on "Financing for Development," held in Monterrey, Mexico, reiterated the need for such a partnership. With respect to official development assistance (ODA) in particular, it established a compact between developed and developing countries by which developed countries would increase the volume of aid and its quality through better coordination, while developing countries would strive to use aid more effectively through improved governance and development management. At the same time, the arrangement called for development strategies to be fully owned by developing countries. In both the Millennium and the Monterrey declarations, the focus was on low-income countries, with particular emphasis on those in Sub-Saharan Africa.

This chapter is a contribution to the current debate on the MDG program of action. It begins with an empirical assessment of progress on the MDGs. We show that achievements are mixed, with great heterogeneity across countries, within countries, and across MDGs. We then discuss the conceptual foundations of the MDG process and the components of an "MDG Plus" strategy in light of experience and the conceptual foundations of the MDGs. The chapter ends with our conclusions.

## Where Does the International Community Stand on the MDGs?

Before reviewing the stylized facts on MDG achievements so far, we must say a word about data. Compiling a clear picture of progress toward meeting the MDGs is not an easy task. The vast majority of developing countries do not produce reliable regular figures on, for example, life expectancy, infant and child mortality, water access, or poverty. Many among the poorest and most vulnerable countries do not report any data on most MDGs. And, where available, data are often plagued with comparability problems, and MDG indicators often come with considerable time lags.

Most of the information from low-income countries is generated in donor-funded data-gathering exercises, such as the Living Standards Measurement Study (LSMS, World Bank), Demographic and Health Survey (DHS, U.S. Agency for International Development), and Multiple Indicator Cluster Survey (MICS, UNICEF). Only a limited number of countries in Latin America, together with China, India, Indonesia, South Africa, and Thailand, are equipped with national statistical agencies that produce high-quality national survey programs and provide the information needed to rigorously monitor the MDGs. Extending such high-quality national data gathering to more countries should be a central focus of the second half of the MDG time frame and beyond. Reliable data and indicators are essential, not only to enable the international development community to follow progress on the MDGs, but also to allow individual countries to effectively manage their development strategies.

In addition to the problem of data availability, technical issues are associated with defining several of the indicators currently used in monitoring the MDGs. For example, international poverty data were recently revised, based on the results of the International Comparison of Prices project. This revision has led to drastic changes in the level of poverty for several countries, some of which are difficult to interpret. Moreover, hunger indicators are severely deficient, and maternal mortality indicators are most often model-generated and thus lack a measured baseline as well as reliable measures of progress.[1]

### Stylized Facts on Overall MDG Progress

The 2008 *Global Monitoring Report* (World Bank 2008) and the *Millennium Development Goals Report 2007* (United Nations 2007) provide the following stylized facts on MDG progress:

1. *Global progress is surprisingly good*, especially for the poverty and the gender parity goals, but less so for the child mortality and maternal mortality goals. As is widely acknowledged, however, the progress on global poverty is very much driven by overachievers in East and South Asia, including Bangladesh, China, India, Indonesia, and Vietnam.
2. *There are clear regional patterns in MDG progress* that depend on initial conditions and recent growth performances. If Asian countries are overachievers on the income poverty goal, they perform relatively worse in health and, for India, in education and gender equity. Conversely, Latin America and the Middle East are relative underachievers on the poverty goal, but relative overachievers in health, education, and gender equity. Finally, the Sub-Saharan African countries lag far behind other regions.

---

1 These issues are considered in greater detail in Bourguignon et al. (2008).

3. *Most countries in all regions are off track on most MDGs* (or data to assess progress are missing), even some of those countries that have experienced very good growth performance.[2]

4. *MDG achievements are much lower in "fragile" states.* One of the reasons why Sub-Saharan Africa lags behind on the MDGs is the relatively large proportion of fragile states in that region. The definition of fragile states used here is that established by the World Bank.

5. In most regions, including those successful in meeting the poverty goal, *progress on reducing childhood undernutrition is extremely slow.*

6. The *poorest regions*, South Asia and Sub-Saharan Africa, *are* the two still seriously *off track for primary school completion rates and for child mortality.*

7. *Progress has been good on gender equity in primary and secondary school enrollments in all regions.* Yet Sub-Saharan Africa and other fragile states still lag seriously behind. Most countries in Sub-Saharan Africa are unlikely to meet this goal.

Overall, the picture is that of a glass half-full and half-empty. Global progress on income poverty has been outstanding thanks to the high performance of mostly the Asian countries. Thus the global income poverty target should be reached. Other regions of the world have performed poorly, especially Sub-Saharan Africa. However, the picture probably would be brighter in that region because of somewhat better growth performances if indicators for the most recent years were available. Of the other MDGs, gender parity in primary and secondary schools is the only goal on which developing countries seem to be on track overall. The world is off track on the others, and the gap is the largest in the poorest regions in South Asia and Sub-Saharan Africa.

### Country Heterogeneity in MDG Performance

Within regions and fragile versus nonfragile states, country heterogeneity remains considerable. For example, poverty in Sub-Saharan Africa ranged from an annual rate of 4.6 percent in Ghana between 1999 and 2006 (a decline) to 3.8 percent in Uganda between 2000 and 2003 (an increase), despite the two countries having comparable growth rates of gross domestic product (GDP) per capita of about 2.5 percent a year. Similarly, in the 10 countries in which poverty declined most, mortality declined at an annual rate greater than or equal to 2 percent, but increased at a rate of over 1 percent per year in the six worst-performing countries.[3] Measurement problems may be contributing to the variance of these results, but there certainly is a great deal of specificity in the patterns of progress, or

---

2   This fact may appear to be in conflict with the first one, but that is not so. As noted in number 1, the good global performance is driven by the good performance of a number of countries that account for the bulk of the developing world's population. The performance of the many countries in Sub-Saharan Africa accounts for number 3.

3   These terrible performances are mostly explained by HIV/AIDS. However, the worst-performing countries among countries less affected by this pandemic still do rather badly.

Figure 2.1 Change in Poverty (MDG1) between 1990 and 2006, Fragile States (CPIA Definition)
(poverty headcount ratio at $1 a day [PPP], percentage of population)

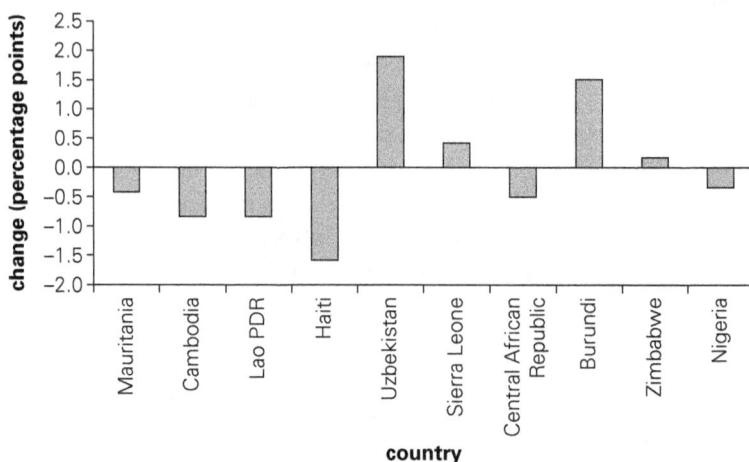

Source: Author's calculation(s) based on World Development Indicators.
Note: CPIA = Country Policy and Institutional Assessment, World Bank.

lack thereof, toward meeting the MDGs. In primary education, the nine best Sub-Saharan African performers increased their enrollment rates at an annual rate of over 5 percent, whereas the five worst performers saw a decline in primary school enrollment.

It is unlikely that such a variable MDG performance in Sub-Saharan Africa stems entirely from the measurement problems noted earlier. Besides, MDG performances in other regions also exhibit substantial variability. The issue then arises of whether these disparities can be explained by some specific factor within the region.

The distinction between fragile and nonfragile states comes to mind. However, if there is a clear difference between the two groups of countries in terms of the *levels* of the various indicators, the distinction between them explains very little of the variability in terms of the *rates of change* of MDG indicators. This is true whether one uses either the World Bank's definition of fragile states or that of other agencies. In other words, the variability of performances remains extremely high within both fragile and nonfragile state groups.

This finding is illustrated in figure 2.1, which shows changes in the poverty headcount between 1990 and the latest available year after 2000 for fragile states (according to the World Bank definition) and in figure 2.2, which shows the same information for nonfragile states. Countries such as Cambodia, Nigeria, or Ethiopia saw very rapid poverty reduction, whereas in Niger and Zimbabwe, poverty increased dramatically over the period.[4] The number of states with high levels of poverty reduction exceeds the number with large increases in poverty, indicating that at the global

---

4   A forthcoming *European Development Report* will focus on development challenges in fragile states.

Figure 2.2 Improvements in MDGs between 1990 and 2006, Nonfragile States (CPIA Definition) (poverty headcount ratio at $1 a day [PPP], percentage of population)

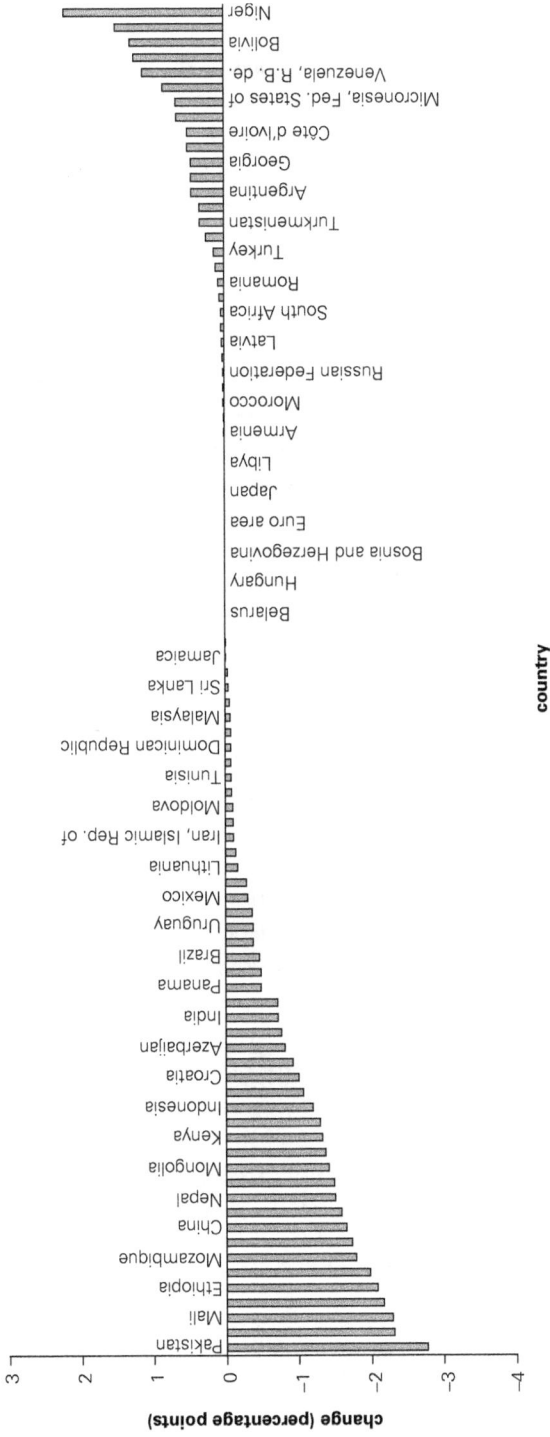

Source: Author's calculation(s) based on World Development Indicators.
Note: CPIA = Country Policy and Institutional Assessment, World Bank.

level, on average, poverty reduction is more rapid for nonfragile states than for fragile states. Nevertheless, disparities across countries are comparable and sizable. The same is true for primary completion rates. Both fragile and nonfragile countries were able to make progress, but progress differs greatly across countries. The same applies to the under-5 mortality MDG.

Intraregional country heterogeneity might be explained by other country-specific characteristics. In its recent analysis of growth, the African Economic Research Consortium (AERC) found it convenient to distinguish between landlocked, coastal, and resource-rich states in Sub-Saharan Africa, a classification that would presumably also apply to other regions.[5] As for the fragile/nonfragile distinction, however, if there are noticeable patterns across those three groups in the *levels* of the MDG indicators, no clear patterns emerge in MDG *progress*.[6] It appears that the resource-rich countries have to date not benefited from the poverty reduction taking place elsewhere in Africa. However, since 1995 the trend in poverty reduction for the minority of countries where data are available is similar across the three groups. The same is true for the under-5 mortality rate.

It follows that country heterogeneity in relation to MDG performance must be explained by a complex combination of specific country characteristics and initial conditions rather than a few geographic and institutional features. This is particularly true for Sub-Saharan Africa and to a lesser extent for other regions.

**Heterogeneity across MDGs**

Regarding progress in any given MDG, there is heterogeneity across countries in the same region and within a given category. Moreover, progress is also heterogeneous across MDGs in a given country. Figure 2.3 is composed of simple scatter graphs that plot progress for pairs of MDGs. The results demonstrate that there is often little correlation between the MDGs—as if they were influenced by wholly independent factors and policies.

Figure 2.3 shows correlations between poverty reduction and other MDGs, as well as between the different nonpoverty MDGs. Hardly any correlation is evident between poverty reduction and changes in under-5 mortality. The same applies to poverty reduction and changes in primary school completion rates. Somewhat surprising, however, is the strong correlation between poverty reduction and changes in underweight (see Klasen 2008b), although there is virtually no correlation between poverty reduction and undernourishment. The correlation is close to zero between different

---

5   The Explaining African Economic Growth Performance Project was conceived in 1997 as a collaborative effort among Harvard University, Oxford University, and the African Economic Research Consortium. The project is designed to produce the first major comprehensive assessment by African research economists of the continent's growth experience in the post-independence period. See http://www.aercafrica.org/programmes/research_collab_growth.asp. See also Ndulu et al. (2007).

6   The distinction between levels of indicators and progress is important. Interestingly, a cluster analysis of a large number of developing-country characteristics carried out for the Chronic Poverty Research Centre (2008) leads to a classification of developing countries based on those two variables.

Figure 2.3 Heterogeneity across MDGs

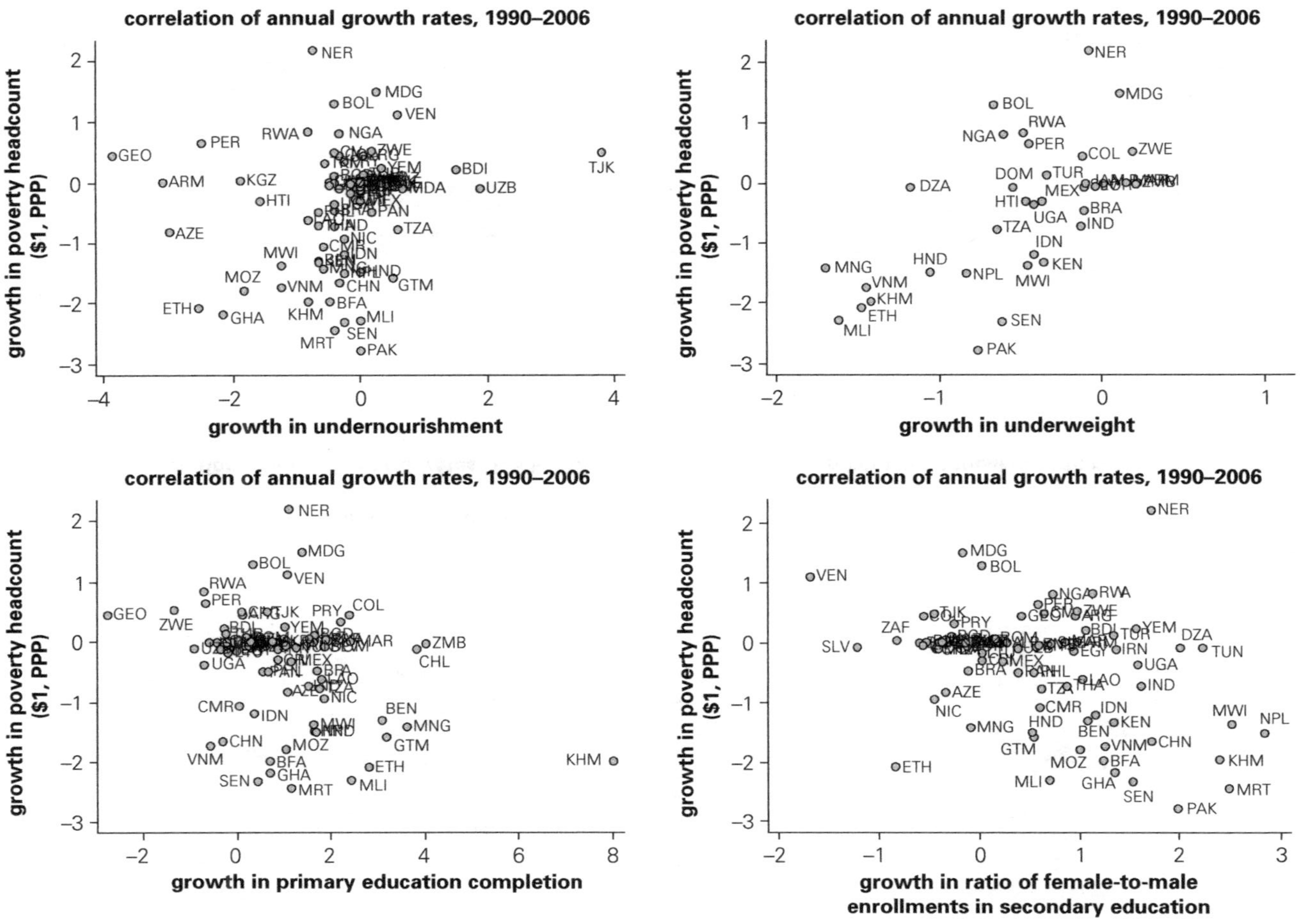
correlation of annual growth rates, 1990–2006
growth in poverty headcount ($1, PPP)
growth in undernourishment
correlation of annual growth rates, 1990–2006
growth in poverty headcount ($1, PPP)
growth in underweight
correlation of annual growth rates, 1990–2006
growth in poverty headcount ($1, PPP)
growth in primary education completion
correlation of annual growth rates, 1990–2006
growth in poverty headcount ($1, PPP)
growth in ratio of female-to-male enrollments in secondary education

Figure 2.3 (continued)

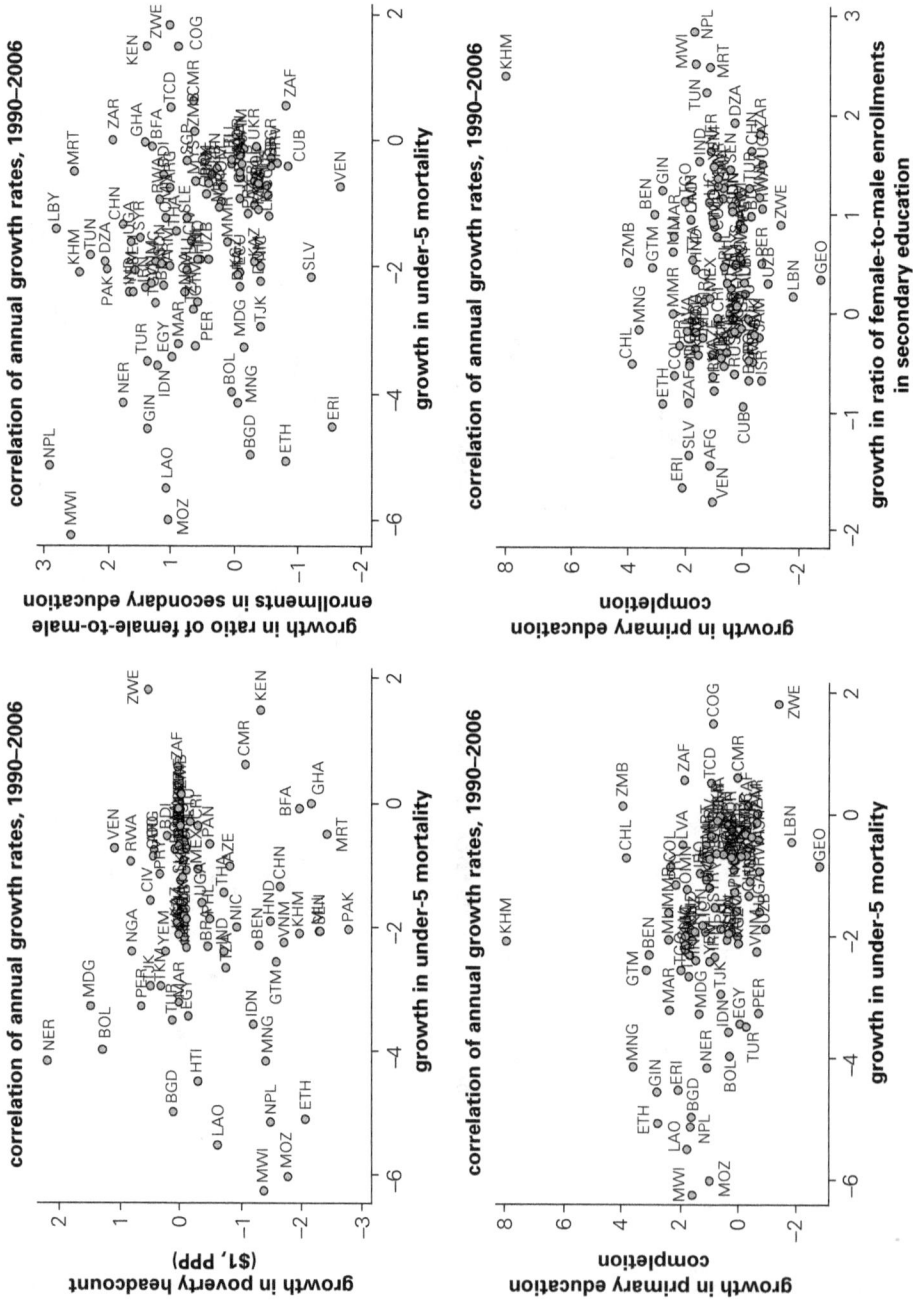

Source: Survey means from POVCAL.

nonincome MDGs, as illustrated in figure 2.3 for primary education and under-5 mortality. These low correlations, as well as the puzzling difference between the correlation of underweight and undernourishment indicators with poverty reduction, could be driven in part by measurement errors and comparability issues. Nevertheless, it is hard to believe that the available data reflect only pure noise.

If the MDGs are weakly correlated among themselves, would they be more strongly correlated with some general economic indicator? In particular, it is to be expected that poverty reduction, and possibly progress on other MDGs, is positively tied to economic growth, because growth should progressively relax the budget constraint of public and private economic agents and ease the pursuit of various MDGs. As shown in figure 2.4, poverty reduction is closely correlated with growth in household per capita income.[7] The importance of economic growth at the national level emphasizes the importance of growth at the global level and the feedback effects of global growth on developing country prospects. Bourguignon et al. (2008) present a detailed assessment of these linkages and consider the impact of the 2008–2009 global crisis on poverty—the direct impact through lost output and remittances and the indirect impact through a possible rise in protectionism and thus further negative consequences for growth in developing countries.

On average, 1 percent growth in mean income generates a 1 percent drop in the poverty headcount. However, this effect appears lower in quite a few countries, including Cambodia, China, Ghana, Honduras, and Uganda. The relatively low effect of growth on poverty reduction in the mean income of the population is related to the rising income inequality since the 1990s. As Jäntti and Sandström (2005) show using the WIDER World Income Inequality Database, in a majority of developing countries inequality began rising significantly in the mid-1980s after a period of decline. As shown by Bourguignon (2003), such an increase in inequality both slows the pace of future growth and reduces its impact on poverty reduction. Conversely, the recent decline in inequality in some highly unequal Latin American countries (including Brazil and Chile) was related to a more stable macroeconomic environment, coupled with sizable pro-poor social protection programs that have accelerated poverty reduction there.

In figure 2.4, growth is defined by the rate of annual increase in the mean household per capita income as observed in surveys used to calculate poverty indices. The correlation between growth and poverty reduction would still be visible and statistically significant, although less severe, had the growth in GDP per capita been used because of differences between the definition of household income in national accounts and in household surveys and because the distribution of national income across various uses changes over time. For example, a higher share may be devoted to

---

7   In this relative assessment, we excluded all observations in which the initial poverty headcount was below 5 percent, because percentage changes in such small figures can be very large and rather erratic. See Klasen and Misselhorn (2007) for a discussion.

Figure 2.4 Correlation of Annual Growth Rates, 1990–2006

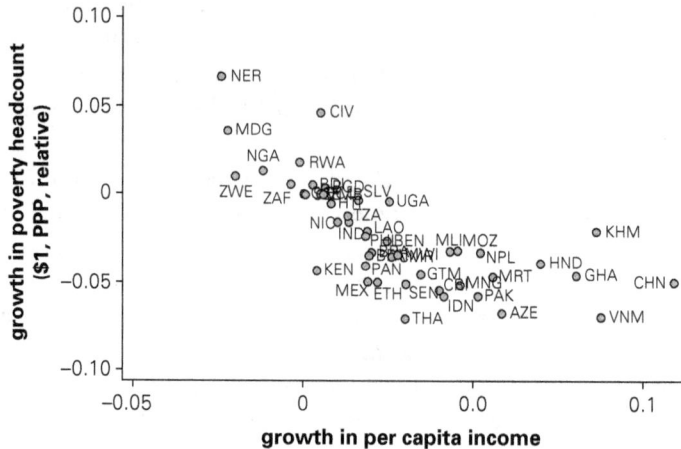

Figure 2.4 Correlation of Annual Growth Rates, 1990–2006

*Source:* Survey means from POVCAL.

investment or to public spending. If so, household income will grow more slowly than national income.

The correlation between growth in GDP per capita and improvements in nonincome MDGs is practically zero, as illustrated in figure 2.5 for Sub-Saharan countries. This figure confirms the lack of a relationship between those indicators and poverty reduction. Because it would be hard to believe that information on nonincome MDGs is so badly affected by measurement error that it is pure noise, this lack of a relationship reflects some relative independence among policy instruments governing progress in the various MDGs. Furthermore, it highlights substantive differences in country policies and circumstances that may affect the relationship between these policies. This interesting finding suggests that economic growth is not sufficient per se to generate progress in nonincome MDGs. Sectoral policies and other factors or circumstances presumably matter as much as growth. It should be noted, however, that most of the scatter plots in figures 2.3 and 2.4 refer to a 15-year period during which the MDGs have been explicitly relevant for only a few years.

A point seldom emphasized by those analyzing nonincome MDG performance is the distribution of progress within the population. Because MDGs are presented as independent goals, they tend to be evaluated independently. It presumably makes a difference whether progress on access to water (MDG7) or health care (MDG3 and MDG4) takes place exclusively in urban areas, and therefore in the top half of the distribution of income, rather than in rural areas, which is presumably home to the poorest segment of the population. Unfortunately, the data needed to look at this distribution of progress are all too rarely presented. In principle, collecting such data should not be an insurmountable hurdle. Indeed, an analyst can use the same household surveys used to study changes in the distribution of income to examine changes in the distribution of progress in

Figure 2.5 Correlation between Growth and Change in Primary School Completion Rate, Sub-Saharan Africa Countries, 1996–2006

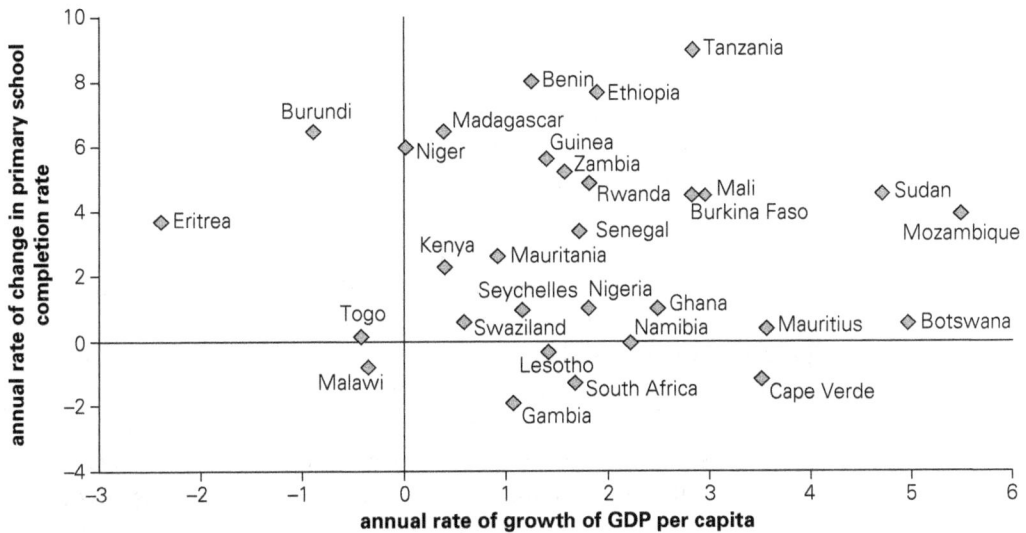

*Source:* Author's calculation(s) based on World Development Indicators.

nonincome MDGs. For example, as shown in Klasen (2008a) and Grosse, Harttgen, and Klasen (2008a, 2008b), one can draw nonincome MDG progress incidence curves that plot the distribution of progress in enrollment rates, vaccination rates, access to water, under-5 mortality, and so forth against the relative level of income. Work of this type could reveal possible biases in the progress in nonincome MDGs and help monitor the MDGs more closely.

This short review of evidence on the MDGs at the midpoint of the 2015 horizon has revealed that most developing countries have been lagging behind on the income poverty front. In middle-income countries and in those countries with fast growth, filling these gaps may be essentially a question of implementing adequate MDG-oriented policies, because growth should provide the budgetary resources needed to implement such policies. In other countries, accelerating broad-based growth and generating budget resources may be as important as policies targeted directly at the MDGs. From that point of view, the focus of the international development community on Sub-Saharan Africa and the problems arising from its low growth performance, as stated, for example, in the Millennium Declaration, is fully justified.

However, heterogeneity in MDG achievements extends well beyond regions. Differences between fragile and nonfragile states are important, even though they are less important in MDG progress than in MDG levels. It turns out that a considerable part of the observed differentials in MDG achievements cannot be explained by any simple categorization of countries. This finding suggests that particular country circumstances and initial conditions play a big role in explaining MDG achievements so far.

Any program aimed at accelerating progress toward the MDGs must take this country specificity into account.

## "MDG Plus": The Road Ahead

The difficulty with getting the MDGs on track, even in countries with excellent economic growth, raises the question of whether this set of goals is an appropriate summary of the general objective of development. Related to this question, the great heterogeneity in performance—within countries, between countries, and across MDGs—raises other questions about the determinants of economic performance and about what the goals of development should be. Two lines of thought seem to be developing on this issue. The first tends to add monitoring indicators, thereby allowing both domestic policymakers and donors to see more clearly why progress is slow or fast on particular goals. In some sense, this line of thought reinforces the initial UN plan that combined the eight development goals with 18 "quantifiable targets" based on some 60 indicators (see box 2.1). According to this view, those targets are useful, but they miss some important aspects of the process to achieve the MDGs. The second school of thought favors simplifying the existing MDGs, possibly replacing some of them with other important dimensions of development in order to satisfy the need for more coherent development strategies that fully take into account country specificity. Thus there is an "MDG Plus" view in favor of enlarging the scope and number of MDGs, and a more compact view in favor of making the MDGs simpler and more consistent with fully articulated development strategies.

Midway to the 2015 deadline this debate is still relevant, and its answers may help countries pursue the MDGs more efficiently. This section outlines some of the lessons learned from the experience accumulated in recent years and reviews the main arguments on both sides of the debate in the light of some general conceptual remarks on the foundations of the MDGs.

### Conceptual Foundations of the MDG Process

When discussing the achievements and the future of the MDGs, two fundamental questions must be addressed: First, in what precise sense are the MDGs the goals of the development process? Second, how does goal setting aid the development process? Each of these questions leads, in turn, to some subquestions that both unpack the possible rationale behind the MDGs and their process and highlight the strengths and weaknesses of them.

#### MDGs as Goals of Development

If they are to have any impact, the MDGs must surely represent some sort of international consensus on the goals of the development process. They fare best when viewed as a minimal set of objectives to which all or most in the international community would subscribe. However, some of them— gender (MDG3), environment (MDG7), and international cooperation

(MDG 8)—raise questions that apply not only to the other MDGs but also to the MDG process as a whole:

1. Do the MDGs command universal agreement, and, if not, are there excluded elements that might garner a level of agreement comparable to that of some of the MDGs?
2. If the MDGs are indeed the final goals of development, how do analysts weigh them in relation to each other?
3. Are the MDGs really the final "goals" of development? Are they outcomes, outputs, or inputs?

*Excluded elements of MDGs.* Each MDG is broad enough to allow many subgoals, satisfying many constituencies, to be brought together. Nevertheless, some categories of subgoals are excluded, the most prominent of which are voice and accountability as independent goals of development. The issue of voice and accountability as an instrument to achieve other objectives such as poverty reduction has been much discussed in the literature. However, from both a conceptual and a normative point of view the questions should be: What consensus would be commanded by these governance principles as an objective of development? How would analysts measure this consensus? Would this consensus be lesser or greater than, for example, the consensus on gender equality?

*Trade-offs between MDGs.* In a world of limited resources, it is likely that often progress on one MDG will have to be at the expense or postponement of another. Suppose country A rushes ahead on MDGx but falls behind on MDGy, whereas for country B the reverse is true. How is the MDG performance of the two countries to be assessed? Whose trade-off weights are to be used—country A's, country B's, or a universal trade-off determined internationally? This question would be particularly relevant if aid allocation were tied to the MDGs, which would be the case if aid were more results-based.

*MDGs: Outcomes or inputs?* Spending on teachers is an input; the number of teachers hired is an output from that input; and the outcome (of this and other inputs) could be the number of children taught in primary school. However, is the number of children taught really the final outcome of concern? The quantitative measure of the number of children attending school ignores the quality of this education. A more satisfactory measure of outcome would be quality-adjusted years of schooling given to children, where quality is measured, for example, through test scores. With limited resources, there may be a trade-off between quantity and quality in education, especially as universal enrollment is approached. Scarce resources could be used to expand access at a given level of quality, or even at a lower level, or to improve quality for those who already have access to education. Again, this issue raises the question of assessment. How can anyone compare two countries, one of which emphasizes quality, while the other emphasizes quantity? Such trade-offs are present in each of the MDG categories, especially those dealing with education and health. Even within poverty and hunger, there can be a trade-off between alleviation for those close to the poverty or hunger threshold and those far below it. As currently specified, MDG1 tends to draw attention and resources toward those persons just below the poverty threshold, because the incidence of poverty can be most easily reduced by lifting these people out of poverty.

### Goal Setting as an Aid to Development

Lack of clarity on the MDGs as goals can hamper their use in the development process. However, suppose more and more clarity is achieved in the future. To what extent can goal-setting exercises of this type help development itself? Three arguments can be made in this regard:

1. Goal setting at the national level focuses debate, decision, and action.
2. Goal setting helps to quantify resources needed from the outside and helps to mobilize world opinion for development assistance.
3. Goal setting and performance assessment help to target aid resources to countries where they would be used most effectively.

All countries set themselves developmental goals, which can be broad or narrow, implicit or explicit. In countries in which governments are elected, the goals are implicitly, sometimes explicitly, set in the election manifestos. Sometimes there is an explicit process, perhaps constitutionally mandated, through long- and short-term planning. India's five-year plans are an example of mixing shorter-term political imperatives and longer-term perspective planning exercises. In many African countries, the Poverty Reduction Strategy Paper (PRSP) process plays the role of goal setting as well as strategy making.

Goal setting is thus very much part of national processes. What role, then, can the MDGs play? One possibility is that they can act as "international standards." If countries are generally adopting the goal of halving poverty by 2015, it is difficult to imagine domestic policymakers being any less ambitious. In this sense, the MDGs may help in raising the sights of policymakers and populations. Certainly, the rhetoric of domestic goal setting has adopted some of the MDG language.

However, as repeatedly emphasized earlier, it must not be forgotten that the domestic debate and its outcomes should be given priority. If the outcome of the domestic debate is to agree to be more ambitious on some goals but less ambitious on others, that outcome must be accepted. Some confusion may be caused by the outcomes/input distinction. For example, if a country's policymakers feel that building roads is a key input to achieving many objectives, including education and health, they may spend more on infrastructure and less on education and health. Nevertheless, these input indicators should not necessarily be used as a gauge of their progress toward outcomes.

*Goal setting and resource mobilization at the national and international levels.* National-level goal setting on outcomes can be a useful first step in quantifying resources needed. A crucial requirement, however, is a credible model, in terms of both the economy and government intervention, through which the resources needed, especially aid, to achieve a particular outcome can be established. Such exercises are now routine in finance ministries and ministries of planning in developing countries and in aid agencies of donor countries. They also can be carried out for several of the MDGs. For example, the cost of achieving universal enrollment can be calculated, and has been calculated, country by country by the UN's MDG project. Nevertheless, these calculations are only as good as the assumptions and data on which they are based (such as teacher-to-pupil ratios, teacher absentee rates, trajectory of teachers' salaries, cost of fees exemption).[8] In view of these assumptions, for any particular goal, such as primary school enrollment, the cost of achieving alternative targets can be simulated and the aid requirements estimated.

Analysts need not rely on the MDG process to conduct the kind of analysis just described. Indeed, before the MDG process many countries were already undertaking such analyses. However, not only has the MDG process made this type of calculation much more common, but also discussions about them, at least among development professionals, have become more routine. Such analyses also have the potential, if all donors focus on achieving specified MDG targets, to put donor assessments of resource needs on a common footing. In addition, the MDGs can be used to estimate both resource needs and, more important, to assess performance and thus to inform aid allocation and reallocation.

Perhaps more important than quantifying resource requirements is the willingness of the international community to devote more resources and policy attention to development issues in general, and in particular to poverty reduction. As discussed earlier, the MDGs have been quite successful in this respect. However, efforts to turn them into precise national targets or quantified resources have, for good reasons, not been as successful. In this sense, in the future the overarching goal of the MDGs should be to keep development issues high on the international agenda and promote lobbying for more policy coherence, greater aid flows, and better delivery.

*MDGs and performance assessment.* If the MDGs capture, however imperfectly, an international consensus on the objectives of development, then they can be used to assess *performance* as well as need. The alternative performance assessment method would be to rely on the inputs employed to achieve a specific result on a particular MDG. However, the complexity and the context-specific nature of the process that transforms inputs into outcomes may be such that it is easier to assess development efforts and performances than to rely on the MDG itself.

---

8  Such exercises are much more complex when the interaction between the various MDGs is taken into account. Investing in education rather than in infrastructure, for example, clearly has a cost in foregone growth and poverty reduction. At the same time, faster accumulation of human capital may accelerate growth at a later stage in the development process. These interactions are at the core of the MDG modeling tool MAMS (see Bourguignon, Diaw-Bonilla, and Löfgren 2008).

For example, MDG4 calls for reducing under-5 mortality by two-thirds. Very few would disagree with this goal as an objective of development. The question, however, is how to achieve it. Typically, debates revolve around direct and indirect routes. Some development experts suggest that policies and interventions that maximize economic growth will achieve the objective and would also have a beneficial impact on MDG1. However, some also argue that other indirect routes (e.g., improving women's education and empowerment) have a significant effect on child mortality. Direct interventions (e.g., vaccinating against diseases that kill small children) are also suggested, and sometimes championed, as the principal intervention for achieving particular objectives. There is, then, little consensus on how exactly to proceed and on the combination of approaches to use. Thus assessing performance through the input side—whether the policies and interventions are conducive to poverty-reducing growth, whether they are good for women's empowerment and thus good for infant mortality, or whether the direct interventions such as vaccinations are effective for the task at hand—is bound to be a contentious issue. Suppose the local government heavily favors one of the three routes because it interprets the evidence differently from outsiders. Should it then be marked down in the performance assessment by outsiders and perhaps given less aid as a result?

One issue is the use of levels rather than rates of change of MDGs as a measure of performance. For example, the *rate of improvement* in child mortality might be used as a measure of performance, but that measure raises its own questions. If improvement in child mortality is to be used as a performance indicator, how are analysts to benchmark it? Relative to a country's past performance? Relative to the performance of countries that have similar levels of child mortality? Or relative to an exogenously given target, such as reducing child mortality by two-thirds? These open questions require further research, but they are important in considering the future of the MDGs. After all, the fact that some countries that perform well in economic growth do not perform well on goals such as infant or maternal mortality may simply mean that these goals were not set in a realistic or developmentally consistent manner.[9]

### The Case for Broadening MDGs to Obtain Better Development Monitoring

Another possible way out of the dilemma just described is to combine both inputs (MDGs) and outcomes (the means to reach the MDGs) in monitoring pursuit of the goals. Practically, this approach implies upgrading the MDGs by adding a set of input-based monitoring indicators to the standard indicators that are usually part of MDG assessments. Of course, such a change requires some consensual understanding of some of the minimum

---

9  On the implications of formulating MDG4 and MDG5 in proportional terms (two-thirds), see Easterly (2007).

requirements that must be met to reach a specific MDG, something that does not apply to the example of child mortality just given.

In view of the various determinants of the progress toward an MDG such as access to water or possibly schooling, the monitoring gaps currently not covered by the MDGs seem to be as follows:

- Should the financial, human, and institutional absorptive capacities be monitored just as systematically as the MDGs are?
- Should the interpersonal, interregional, and intertemporal equity of the MDG implementation strategies be monitored?
- Should the voice revelation mechanisms be monitored?
- Should outcomes or inputs be monitored?

The first question clearly is more general than any particular MDG (except probably MDG1) because it deals essentially with the macroeconomic circumstances surrounding the MDGs and the macroeconomic constraints in absorbing the aid that might be needed to fund their achievement. Although macroeconomic coherence is central to the success of any MDG strategy, it may seem too far removed from the MDGs themselves to be taken as part of MDG monitoring indicators. Moreover, there are simply too many degrees of freedom in the relationship between macropolicy and MDGs for the macropolicy to be monitored in any sensible and simple way that is meaningfully comparable to the MDGs.

Equity has often been mentioned as one of the missing MDGs. In fact, in some countries inequality has increased so much that it considerably weakened the poverty reduction impact of growth. The World Bank's 2006 *World Development Report* documented in enormous detail the need for equity to increase the efficiency of developing economies, in particular in some MDG-linked areas such as education and health care. Both general development and MDG strategies should pay attention to this important point, provided that equity is interpreted as equality of opportunities rather than just incomes. However, caution is required. It is possible that a progressive development path, and efficient pursuit of the MDGs, may at an interim stage result in a worsening of the distribution of both income and perhaps opportunities. However, as long as this worsening remains a temporary phenomenon, without longer-term implications, it may not pose a significant threat. Again, this is an issue that requires general monitoring by policymakers, but not necessarily in close relationship with the MDGs.

Voice is another area often mentioned as another possible MDG. Our discussion of participatory governance has shown that this area should be viewed with great care. A greater voice by poor people at the local level may be counterproductive if it leads to capture by the elite. And yet it may be beneficial to the welfare of the poor and the pursuit of the MDGs in different contexts. Here, too, defining indicators that have uniform validity across countries and contexts seems inappropriate at this stage.

Most of the MDGs have been defined as outcomes, not inputs. Yet there is a sense that part of the difficulty in implementing them is that many countries have underestimated the importance of inputs. In cases in which inputs can be identified without too much uncertainty, it should indeed be possible to introduce an indicator to allow the monitoring of progress in a specific MDG. In the water sector, for example, the initial focus was on increasing the access rates to improved water sources. However, because of the budget constraints and the urgency, the debate soon moved to the optimal form of delivering access. Should countries promote large-scale utilities to deliver access, knowing that their investments might be slow to materialize, or should more resources be allocated to installing water pumps that are cheaper and may require replacements more often, but that are easier and quicker to install? Because of the nature of these questions, it is unclear whether we can ascertain a single indicator that describes the situation of a particular country in this sector. Again, context specificity is of great importance.

Overall, then, it appears that, despite the views of some analysts, there is little justification for broadening the scope of the MDGs by adding more goals or more monitoring indicators. Such additions may be possible only in some very precise areas where it is known that a specific input is absolutely necessary for a particular outcome. Immunization against various diseases may well be indispensable for reducing child mortality (immunization against measles is actually one of the MDG targets), but on its own this step may not be sufficient. And yet difficulties in achieving immunization campaigns may themselves be the result of more important and deep-rooted problems that must be addressed. Moving in the direction of accuracy and specificity may be a useful exercise when thinking about *strategies* to implement the MDGs. As for the MDGs themselves, which already provide overall direction and focus on poverty in its multiple dimensions, broadening their scope or adding detail and precision does not seem warranted and would, in any case, require dealing with many of the MDG-related problems detailed at the outset of this chapter.

### Concentrating on the Core of the MDGs

Arguments have also been heard for reducing the importance of the MDGs and focusing more on general development objectives. But this does not mean losing sight of the MDGs. Quite the contrary, it means keeping them as either consequences or inputs in a dynamic process of development. And yet by introducing a set of universal imperfect targets that mix up means and ends and confuse stocks, needs, financial flows, or performances, we might weaken the process of development and also the process of assisting development. For example, the broad use of headcounts for many of the indicators (such as income poverty in MDG1 or school enrollment in MDG2) provides incentives to offer quick gains to those closer to the target.

Alternatively, a case can be made for retaining the overall approach of the MDGs, but with a focus on a smaller set of essential MDGs. To capitalize on the main feature of the MDGs, an international focus on multidimensional poverty reduction, concentrating on fewer indicators (e.g., just income poverty, health, education, and sustainability) might be sufficient. More effort should then be concentrated on ensuring that the selected indicators make sense, can be measured effectively, and are easy to understand, communicate, and interpret.

There is also the question of whether the MDGs, which were set at a global level (and never actually designed to be goals for each country), should explicitly take account of regional and country heterogeneity. To succeed down the road, the MDGs would have to reflect the realistic aspirations of a population for their desired condition at a particular point in the future, and the goals would have to be expressed in the form of a set of ambitious, forward-looking indicators. They would then be relevant to the current generation and their children. In fact, the current MDGs could have been used in this way had they not been applied indiscriminately to incomparable sets of contexts, and had the resulting industry of rhetoric and monitoring not served to significantly undermine their objectives.

In the future, MDGs will have to assume a form that ensures that differing low-income countries are treated differently. At one level are those countries whose overall outlook is one of hope, even if they are currently facing low incomes and considerable deprivation. They tend to experience continued deprivation in many dimensions, and will not necessarily achieve the MDGs. However, with an optimistic outlook of what development can deliver in the decades ahead, using reasonably clear trajectories, these countries will achieve the goals shortly after 2015. Much of Asia is in this category, and a few countries in Africa may graduate to this group soon. A strong case could be made for considering as one group these countries together with the middle-income countries that have still failed to make sufficient progress on particular MDGs, but whose well-defined development trajectories could make those goals achievable.

The other group is of more concern. It is made up of countries with limited signs of hope that are currently often sliding rather than progressing in meeting the MDGs, including, but by no means limited to, many fragile states and often countries with severe and widespread deprivation but relatively high incomes such as Nigeria. A full compendium of MDGs does not make much sense here. A small number of priorities, offering the framework for sustainable development processes, may be preferable. These priorities could focus on the reduction in income poverty, human capital formation in terms of education, health, and nutrition, and basic accountability of the state relative to its population.

For both types of countries, but perhaps more so for the second, the practice of monitoring MDGs has to be changed fundamentally. Too often, the MDGs have been used as pure backward-looking indicators. Clearly, it would be dangerous to stick exclusively to such a view. An analysis of why and how a country is lagging behind on specific MDGs should be given much more importance than has been done to date. Such an analysis implies that the donor community will call into question the supremacy of measuring MDGs over understanding the processes leading to their most effective implementation. Under the guise of requiring evidence-based policymaking, a whole industry of monitoring the MDGs has indeed sprung up, and it risks concealing the need for a more analytical approach to MDG-achieving trajectories. Equally pertinent, reducing the number of indicators and paying more attention to modeling and understanding the overall development process that leads to success or failure in promoting the MDGs seem to be a more promising avenue.

Every country in the world (and every large financial institution) has developed relatively careful mechanisms for assessing growth in its own economy, based on the use of forecast models. But for poverty and the MDGs such mechanisms are almost uniformly lacking. In the context of the MDGs, the business of backward-looking performance monitoring has to be transformed into a forward-looking strategic monitoring business. A forward-looking strategy would harness knowledge of the past and of the heterogeneous processes involved in achieving different MDGs. This strategy would, in turn, allow for the careful development of scenarios outlining if and how the core set of MDGs can be delivered.

## Conclusions

Two main conclusions can be derived from the discussion in this chapter. First, the central message on MDG achievements is one of heterogeneity of outcomes—between countries, within countries, and across MDGs. Some of this observed heterogeneity, and the lack of correlation between different MDG dimensions, simply reflects the quality of the data, and we certainly call for greater investment in better information for monitoring and assessment. Yet another explanation is that the MDGs as currently constituted combine measurement of stocks with measurement of flows, and do not distinguish clearly between inputs and outputs. But even with these qualifications, the lack of correlation remains surprising. The heterogeneity calls for more detailed country-specific analysis of the policy and structural determinants of well-being and poverty. The second main conclusion derived from this chapter is thus that the practice of monitoring MDGs must be changed fundamentally from a backward-looking exercise to one that uses the information to understand why one country is lagging behind and another is succeeding and to understand better the country- and context-specific reasons for success and failure.

## References

Bourguignon, F. 2003. "The Growth Elasticity of Poverty Reduction." In *Inequality and Growth,* ed. T. Eicher and S. Turnovsky. Cambridge, MA: MIT Press.

Bourguignon, F., et al. 2008. "Millennium Development Goals at Midpoint: Where Do We Stand and Where Do We Need to Go?" Paper written for the Directorate General Development of the European Commission as a background paper for the *2009 European Report on Development.*

Bourguignon, F., C. Diaw-Bonilla, and H. Löfgren. 2008. "Aid, Service Delivery and the Millennium Development Goals in an Economy-wide Framework." In *The Impact of Macroeconomic Policies and Income Distribution*, ed. F. Bourguignon, M. Bussolo, and L. Pereira da Silva. London: Palgrave Macmillan; Washington, DC: World Bank.

Chronic Poverty Research Centre. 2008. *Chronic Poverty Report: Escaping Poverty Traps.* Manchester, UK: Chronic Poverty Research Centre.

Easterly, W. 2007. "How the Millennium Development Goals Are Unfair to Africa." Working Paper 14, Brookings Global Economic Development, Washington, DC.

Grosse, M., K. Harttgen, and S. Klasen. 2008a. "Measuring Pro-Poor Growth Using Non-Income Indicators." *World Development* 36 (6):1021–47.

———. 2008b. "Measuring Pro-Poor Progress towards the Non-income MDGs." In *Achieving the Millennium Development Goals,* ed. M. McGillivray. London: Palgrave Macmillan.

Jäntti, M., and S. Sandström. 2005. "Trends in Income Inequality: A Critical Examination of Evidence in WIID2." World Institute for Development Economics Research, Helsinki.

Klasen, S. 2008a. "Economic Growth and Poverty Reduction: Measurement Issues in Income and Non-income Dimensions." *World Development* 36 (3): 420–45.

———. 2008b. "Poverty, Undernutrition, and Child Mortality: Some Inter-regional Puzzles and Their Implications for Research and Policy." *Journal of Economic Inequality* 6 (1): 89–115.

Klasen, S., and M. Misselhorn. 2007. "Determinants of the Growth Semi-Elasticity of Poverty Reduction." University of Göttingen, Göttingen, Germany.

Ndulu, B. J., S. A. O'Connell, R. H. Bates, P. Collier, and C. C. Soludo, eds. 2007. *The Political Economy of Economic Growth in Africa, 1960–2000.* Cambridge, UK: Cambridge University Press.

United Nations. 2007. *The Millennium Development Goals Report 2007.* New York: United Nations.

World Bank. 2008. *Global Monitoring Report.* Washington, DC: World Bank.

# CHAPTER 3

# Globalization, Growth, and Distribution: Framing the Questions

*Ravi Kanbur*

The discourse on globalization, economic liberalization, and growth is contentious partly, perhaps mainly, because of the distributional dimension. The "anti-globalizers," if one is permitted that shorthand with all its problems, point to the negative distributional consequences of the conventional policy package of economic liberalization combined with trade and financial integration into the global economy, even if they accept (which many do not) that these policies are associated with  higher growth rates. Some "globalizers," while standing firm on the close link between the conventional policy package and growth, nevertheless worry about its distributional outcomes. Others, however, argue that the package is good for both growth and distribution, at least in the long run.[1]

I will argue in this chapter that this discourse is characterized by many misunderstandings. These misunderstandings arise because different questions are being asked and answered, different perspectives are being brought to bear on economic processes, and different analytical frameworks are

---

[1]  The literature is by now too vast to enumerate even partially. For publications that target general audiences, see Stiglitz (2003) and Bhagwati (2004). Recent publications that target an academic audience include Nissanke and Thorbecke (2006) and Harrison (2007).

being used to understand and interpret ostensibly the same phenomena. As long as these misunderstandings persist, it is difficult to make progress in the discourse. Implicit pejorative characterizations of one side or the other (as "good-hearted but stupid" or as "clever but a tool of international capital") will continue, even among people who may, again ostensibly, all share a common objective—such as poverty reduction.

My focus here is primarily on developing economies rather than the rich countries (including the transition economies of Eastern Europe, although I allude to their experience). I also focus primarily on economic growth and income distribution, leaving to one side the vast topic of the noneconomic dimensions of well-being. I eventually cover in some detail aspects of how income distribution data are generated and their role in the debates I just described. For now, however, imagine an "ideal" income distribution—a distribution of individuals by real income with all the corrections for price differentials, household composition, and so forth that one is advised to make in the research manuals. Define poverty as a measure on the lower tail of the income distribution, below some cutoff called the "poverty line." Also for now, leave to one side the vast literature on poverty lines and poverty indices. Rather, think simply of the percentage of people below some nationally accepted cutoff.

A few accounting properties of such income distributions will prove useful as an anchor. Speaking loosely, but I believe intuitively, an increase (a decrease) in the mean, holding constant the inequality of the distribution, will reduce (increase) poverty. A decrease (increase) in inequality, holding the mean constant, will decrease (increase) poverty.[2] So, if the mean increases and inequality declines (a stylized representation of the East Asia miracle of the 1960s, 1970s and 1980s), poverty will fall. If the mean decreases and inequality increases (a stylized representation of some transition economies in the 1990s), poverty will rise. I refer to an increase in the mean of the income distribution as growth. If growth is accompanied by an increase in inequality, the effect on poverty is ambiguous and depends on the relative strength of the two forces. Finally, notice that even if inequality does not change, the initial level of inequality will affect the impact of growth on poverty. Intuitively, the more unequal the distribution to which a given growth rate is applied, the lower will be the impact on poverty reduction.[3]

To my mind, the central stylized fact of distributional evolution in developing countries over the last 20 years is that in countries where there has

---

2 These statements can be made more precise. For example, if by decreasing inequality is meant an inward movement of the Lorenz curve (or, equivalently, a second order dominating shift in the income distribution), then all members of the FGT family of poverty indices (Foster, Greer, and Thorbecke 1984) for poverty aversion greater than or equal to one will decline. However, whether the headcount ratio—the proportion of population below the poverty line—declines depends more intimately on the shape of the distribution and the position of the poverty line. For example, if the distribution is symmetric and the poverty line is less than the mean, then a decrease in inequality will reduce poverty (see Haddad and Kanbur 1990).

3 For a formal statement of these relationships, see Ravallion (1997, 2000).

been high growth it has been accompanied by an increase in inequality, but the growth effect has been sufficiently strong that poverty has fallen.[4] It is this constellation of outcomes—high growth, increased inequality, and poverty reduction—that forms the nexus of debate, not only for these countries but also for those countries languishing at low growth rates and low poverty reduction. For the latter, the high-growth countries offer a model—but of what sort?

In country after country where there has been significant growth, policymakers continue to worry about distributional outcomes. The statistics of poverty reduction do not seem to have registered with the population or the polity. The newspapers, and civil society at large, speak of "those left behind." Growing gaps between rich and poor are the basis of much social commentary, and also much social unrest. In China, despite spectacular growth and poverty reduction, policy attention is focusing on the growing protests, not only in the vast hinterland but also in the fast-growing coastal provinces.[5] In India, the last election brought in a government with a commitment to addressing the distributional consequences of the high-growth trajectory.[6] In Ghana, the North-South divide looms larger than ever in the political economy, despite a decade or more of growth that has reduced measured poverty significantly (Aryeetey and McKay 2007). In South Africa, the first postapartheid decade was characterized by low growth and rising inequality and poverty (see Bhorat and Kanbur 2006). Over the last five years, despite a pickup in growth rates, inequality has continued to increase and income poverty reduction has languished, spurring the government to start a discourse on a "second economy" that is disconnected from the "first economy," which is reaping the benefits of growth. In Chile, spectacular growth and poverty reduction over the last quarter-century have not allayed distributional concerns about growing inequality.[7] In Mexico, overall low growth rates have held back poverty reduction, but even when growth rates have been high, their impact on poverty reduction has been diluted significantly by rising inequality.[8]

These country stories could be multiplied many times over. They raise the question: what is going on in those countries where growth has been high enough to reduce poverty, and yet there is popular discontent about

---

4   I highlighted increasing inequality as an emerging phenomenon in a review paper I wrote in the mid-1990s (Kanbur 2000).

5   For evidence of the magnitude of the growing spatial inequality in China, see Kanbur and Zhang (2005).

6   For a recent account of the evolution of income distribution in India, see Deaton and Dreze (2002).

7   Birdsall and Szekely (2003) note: "Between 1992 and 1996, Chilean GDP per capita expanded by more than 30 percent in real terms and moderate poverty (headcount ratio) declined by 20 percent. But income inequality increased (the Gini index increased by 7 percentage points). Had the income distribution remained as in 1992, the proportion of poor would have actually declined much more, by 50 percent."

8   See Birdsall and Szekely (2003), who observe: "Between 1996 and 1998, GDP per capita increased in Mexico by 9.7 percent in real terms, a spectacular gain compared to the previous 16 years. However, poverty hardly declined. . . . The huge increase in mean income was due entirely to the income gains among the richest 30%—particularly the richest 10%—of the population."

distribution that policy makers feel they have to address? A second question is: what can and should be done to address these concerns without jeopardizing growth performance—what, if any, are the trade-offs? Answers to these questions are important for high-growth countries, and for low-growth countries seeking to accelerate their growth rates.

In answering the first question, the possibility arises that the poverty numbers are misleadingly optimistic about well-being at the lower end of the income distribution because they miss or misrepresent key trends that are relevant in terms of ground-level realities. There is also the conceptual issue of whether the evolution of poverty captures the full dimensions of social welfare as perceived by the population and policymakers, especially when inequality is on the rise. In answering the second question, we might first consider the possibility that the rising phase of inequality is temporary and will end soon enough, so that the short-run price will be worth paying from the long-run perspective. If the increase in inequality is nevertheless a problem, the issue arises as to whether and how the increase can and should be curtailed. Finally, even if poverty were the only concern, and even if it were measured accurately by the numbers, the concern might be that rising inequality could threaten the growth trajectory and therefore future poverty reduction.

The following sections frame a series of specific questions on the issues just identified, starting with why rising inequality might be a concern, followed by what might be done about it. Even when answers to these questions are not easily available, I hope that framing the questions in this way serves to illuminate key features of the debate and highlights what further analysis may be needed to arrive at a resolution.

## Is Something Missing from the Poverty Numbers?

Policymakers are used to members of civil society greeting official growth rates with disbelief. The latter often argue that high growth rates are all very well, but that the beneficial impact on the population at large, in particular on the poor, is a different matter altogether. Poverty statistics from nationally representative household survey data should address this concern. Poverty data are now produced at regular intervals for most developing countries by their national statistical agencies or by international agencies. The publication of these numbers is a major event, leading in most countries to a national debate on what the numbers represent and what they imply about the efficacy of government policy. The recent controversy in India over poverty statistics is perhaps an extreme example of such a debate (see Deaton and Kozel 2005).

It would be fair to say that there is considerable skepticism among members of civil society about these poverty numbers. Especially in countries where these statistics are showing declining poverty, they are challenged by many elements of civil society as not representing the reality on the ground, which, they claim, shows a worsening of well-being at the lower end of the income distribution. Such claims are often dismissed by economists, official statisticians, and some in government as the biased views of those with an interest in attacking economic liberalization policies. But sooner or later, those in government do pay attention to these views, because they often represent those of the voters at large, or they spill over into violent protests. This situation explains policymakers' continued worries on the distributional front despite good poverty reduction figures. Analysts, however, might ask whether the poverty figures conventionally published are missing out on key features of ground-level reality—features that might explain the disconnect between the official statistics and the perceptions of the population.[9]

## Population Normalization

Consider an economy in which the incidence of poverty (the fraction of the population below the poverty line) has been falling at a rate of one percentage point per annum—a pretty good rate of decline, especially for an African country. At this rate, depending on the initial level of poverty, an economy would be well on track for achieving the first Millennium Development Goal on reducing the incidence of income poverty. But suppose that population growth in this economy is two percentage points per annum. In this case, although the fraction of the poor population is falling at a rate of one percentage point per annum, the absolute number of the poor is rising at a rate of one percentage point per annum. For a nongovernmental organization (NGO) working with the poor on the ground, the soup kitchens are fuller than ever, there are more street children than ever, there are more distressed farmers than ever—and yet the official statistics seem to proclaim a reduction in poverty. The disconnect is, of course, sharpest in economies with relatively low poverty-incidence reduction and relatively high population growth, such as those in Africa. But the tendency is present in all economies. Even in the fast poverty reduction case of China, where the incidence of poverty and the absolute number of poor have both fallen spectacularly, the rate of decline of the former is higher than the rate of decline of the latter.

The practice of normalizing by total population goes back at least as far as Sen's axiomatic treatment of poverty measurement (Sen 1976). One of those axioms effectively states that replicating every individual in an economy—so that there are twice as many poor but twice as many rich as well—should leave the poverty measure unchanged. This replication leads to the characteristic form of all standard poverty measures: total population size appears in the denominator. Economists and poverty statisticians have clearly bought into this axiom, perhaps somewhat unthinkingly. Those working at the ground level with the poor, however, have not. Policymakers need to be aware of this rejection and look at figures for absolute numbers of the poor to better understand popular perceptions of poverty. The

---

9 Some of the points in this section are developed in Kanbur (2001).

World Bank is now producing both sets of figures for its global poverty data, which is a good start.[10]

### Value of Public Services

Household surveys are excellent at capturing the value of market goods and services bought and sold. Expenditure data generated from respondents are the building blocks of poverty data in countries such as India and Ghana.[11] Over the years, these surveys have become better and better at capturing the value of nonmarket activities such as production for home consumption—for example, through questions that try to ascertain how much it would have cost to purchase home-grown maize at the market. Housing in rural areas is also not traded very much. Even so, descriptive information on the house (such as type of construction, square footage) could, in principle, be used to construct hedonic estimates of the value of housing services, based on information from what little trading there is in the sample. And so on.

Household surveys are not good, however, at capturing the value of public services such as health, education, and transportation. Conceptually, there is no particular difficulty in incorporating these services into the standard money metric measures of well-being. And yet empirically there are severe difficulties in estimating the shadow value of these services for each household. In any event, this estimation is simply not done in official statistics. Household surveys do collect information on the availability, quality, and other measures of health, education, water, sanitation, and other services, but there is no integration of the value of these services into the income/expenditure measure of well-being from which the poverty rates are calculated.

Consider then an economy in which there is a reorientation from a heavily publicly provided services past to a more private sector–oriented future, which is precisely what, as some may argue, is leading to the higher growth rates. The household survey data will capture transactions in the expanded private sphere, but they will not capture the corresponding reduction in public services, which, no matter how inefficiently and ineffectively provided, had at least some value to households. Because the value of public services is not accounted for in standard household survey–based money metric measures of well-being, standard official poverty statistics will overstate the improvement in well-being throughout the distribution, including at the lower tail. Thus the statistics will overstate the reduction in poverty.[12]

This disconnect works in both directions. If for some reason basic public services are expanded, the monetary equivalent of the expansion will not

---

10 For a formal analysis of poverty measurement without Sen's population axiom, see Chakravarty, Kanbur, and Mukherjee (2006).

11 Although expenditure surveys are increasingly coming to Latin America, the primary sources of information are income surveys from the labor market. However, the issue of neglect of public services is still present in these surveys as well.

12 Some of these ground-level realities may be better captured in smaller-scale qualitative assessments based on in-depth unstructured interviews with respondents. See Kanbur and Shaffer (2007).

be captured in household surveys, and the poverty statistics based on them will understate improvement in well-being and thus understate improvement in poverty. This was arguably the case for postapartheid South Africa, as documented in Bhorat and Kanbur (2006). It is a measure of the sharp increases in income inequality in South Africa that they loom so large in the population's perceptions and evaluations of distributional evolution—indeed, so large that even vast improvements in the supply of public services to the previously deprived black population cannot make up for it. In any event, the way in which standard poverty statistics are calculated is likely to be misleading during a period of major changes in the provision of public services.

### Gender and Intrahousehold Inequality

Another defining feature of standard household income/expenditure surveys is that all money metric information is collected at the household level. The usual way of converting this information into individual levels of well-being is to divide by household size and to assign the per capita household income or consumption of the household to each individual in the household. Sometimes in analytical work an adjustment is made for household composition by using adult-equivalent conversions, but it would be fair to say that this is almost never done in official poverty statistics. In any event, even if this correction were made to account for differing consumption needs, the assumption is still that consumption is allocated in proportion to need—in other words, that there is no intrahousehold inequality in real terms.

Some of the most vocal critics of official government narratives of poverty decline tend to be women's groups. One possible explanation for their disconnect is that household survey–based methods do not allow for intrahousehold inequality in consumption, especially between the genders. Of course, there are many nonconsumption-based indicators of gender inequality, such as anthropometric measures for babies, educational and health access for children and adults, differential mortality rates, and so on. Analyses of these various measures strongly indicate that gender inequality is present.[13] But my focus is on the disconnect with the standard income/consumption-based measures of poverty and inequality. How big might intrahousehold inequality in consumption be, and what difference can it make to measured poverty and inequality? This is a difficult question to answer, because, by definition, individual-level consumption data are not available from the standard sources—and if the information were available as a matter of routine, there would be no disconnect problem to start with. In an analysis of a specially designed survey in the Philippines, Haddad and Kanbur (1990) used information on individual calorie intakes within households to calculate food consumption–based measures of poverty and inequality. Because they had individual-level data, they could simulate the

---

13 For an early example of this type of work, see Kynch and Sen (1983).

standard situation in which only household-level data are available and household equality is assumed. The results are striking. Ignoring intra-household inequality understates true inequality and poverty by as much as 30 percent.

Gender inequality is a deep structural phenomenon, amenable only to equally deep structural changes over the long term. How might the fact of gender inequality within households play into the disconnect between official poverty statistics and ground-level reality over the relatively short period of a decade? In particular, how might the disconnect play out in periods of rapid growth? The accounting framework in the introduction to this chapter can provide one answer. There it was pointed out that if one takes two distributions with different degrees of inequality and then applies the same growth rate to each without a change in inequality in either, the poverty reduction will tend to be lower in the distribution with the greater inequality. For intrahousehold inequality, the true income distribution is more unequal than the standard income distributions produced by official statistical agencies. Thus even if there were no increase in inequality in the true distribution, the poverty reduction would be scored as being greater in the official statistics than the true income distribution would show—if only analysts had the data to calculate it. But because they do not have this data, they are left with a disconnect between the (more optimistic) official poverty reduction narrative and the true situation on the ground.

There is a second reason why a disconnect might appear in a rapidly transforming economy, especially one that is opening out to the outside world. Consider an economy that is moving in a direction in which tradable activities are earning relatively higher returns than in the past, and non-tradable activities are earning lower returns than in the past—a standard adjustment that is a feature of global integration, and one that is argued to be the basis of faster growth. Clearly, then, individuals whose incomes come from tradable activities will benefit, and those whose incomes come from nontradable activities will lose. If there is full mobility among the activities, then in the long run those factors used intensively in nontradable activities will lose out relatively. If, structurally, women are more restricted to nontradable activities, then their incomes from this source would decline. Such a decline would not matter if there was full income pooling within the household. If each household was a microcosm of the economy as a whole, and there was perfect income sharing within the household, then the growth in the economy that follows greater global integration should be reflected in household incomes and in the individual consumption of men and women. But a fair amount of evidence points to no income pooling within the household—that is, in the short run at least, the consumption of men and women reflects the income they bring to the household.[14] Thus,

---

14 The literature on this factor is large. By the mid-1990s, the evidence against income pooling was already strong, which led Alderman et al. (1995) to argue that the burden of proof should shift to those who would argue that there was such pooling. Since then, the evidence has continued to mount.

to the extent that women are structurally tied to nontradable activities, the average improvement will not be reflected in their well-being to the same extent and will lead to the disconnect.

The extent and nature of the disconnect through this channel will be context-specific. In many parts of West Africa, for example, men traditionally tend the internationally traded cash crop (e.g., coffee or cocoa) and control the income from it, while women tend the root crops (e.g., cassava or yam) and dispose of the income from them. Furthermore, if childbearing and childrearing could be argued to be quintessentially nontradable activities worldwide—at least in rural areas of poor countries—then the structural nature of gender roles in most countries would suggest a decline in the well-being of women from a general policy shift that increases returns to tradable activities over nontradable activities, if income pooling is not perfect within the household.

Of course, these explanations for a possible disconnect between official poverty figures and the reality of women's well-being cannot be tested directly through household survey data. However, the body of evidence on intrahousehold inequality gives a reasonable indication that policymakers should be aware of this as a reason why the population's response to official poverty statistics is not the same as that of the economists or the statisticians who produce those figures.

## Poor Winners and Poor Losers

The official poverty statistics are snapshots of different points in time. They do not follow the same individuals over time to track their fortunes. If they did, they might find considerable churning into and out of poverty between two points in time. Certainly, specialized panel surveys that do follow households and individuals over time seem to find this to be a systematic phenomenon. This evidence has spawned a growing literature on risk, vulnerability, and poverty. The focus in this literature is that even around a given steady state of average outcomes there are shocks, and these affect the time path of well-being around a given average.[15]

The stylized fact I am focusing on is not a steady state, but rather decreasing poverty with increasing inequality when there are high growth rates. However, the basic lesson from the risk and vulnerability literature—that tracking individual well-being matters—is perhaps relevant in understanding why declining official poverty figures do not elicit as positive a response from the population as they might be expected to. Consider a country in which major structural changes are under way. These changes will, in general, create winners and losers in the short run and long run. If the poor are all winners, or if there are some poor winners and no poor losers, poverty will, of course, decline. But measured poverty may also decline even if a significant number of the losers are poor, because their losses are outweighed

---

15 Here are some recent works in this growing literature: Grootaert, Kanbur, and Oh (1997); Baulch and Hoddinott (2000); Dercon and Krishnan (2000); Jalan and Ravallion (2000); Ligon and Schecter (2003); Dercon (2004); and Agüero, Carter, and May (2007).

by the gains of the other poor. The anguish of increasing poverty among some, perhaps a sizable number, of the poor will not be captured by the national-level decline in poverty. There will be a disconnect between those who focus on these official statistics and those who focus on the poor losers.

The discourse on economic liberalization, globalization, and distribution is often cast as a battle between rich and poor. Those in favor of liberalization argue that the old controls favored the rich and powerful. Those against point to the gains made by the rich during liberalization and the losses incurred by the poor. What is missing from this discourse is recognition that the blunt instruments of economic reform often pit one group of poor against another group of poor. It may be true that, on average, households whose incomes come primarily from the nontradable sector (e.g., government employees) have lower poverty than households in the tradable sector, so that global integration of the standard sort in favor of tradables should reduce poverty. However, there are poor people in the nontradable sector as well. These people will be negatively affected by adjustment, at least in the short run. Even if overall poverty comes down, the poverty of many, not the majority but still a significant number, will increase.[16]

Because national-level poverty data are calculated from snapshot surveys, analysts cannot test this logic directly. The available panel data do show a significant amount of worsening of well-being for significant portions of the population, which provides some weak support for the hypothesis, but analysts have not used these data to identify the effects of liberalization or global integration. However, the increasing inequality observed in the periodic surveys that underpin national poverty data may indicate that this logic might be playing out. Certainly, there is a wide variation in the rates of poverty reduction across regions within a country. In Ghana, for example, during the 1990s national poverty declined, but poverty in the northern part of the country remained stagnant or, for some measures, actually increased. In Mexico in the late 1980s and early 1990s, the declines in poverty at the national level were not reflected in the poor south of the country.[17] In other countries, poverty measures that emphasize the depth of poverty decreased less, indicating a problem in the depths of the income distribution compared with close to the poverty line.[18] Thus, rising inequality could be an indirect, though not conclusive, indicator of a significant number of people who are becoming worse off even during a period of overall poverty reduction.

---

16 The technical specifics of this analysis for decomposable poverty measures were developed in Kanbur (1987a).

17 For a comprehensive compilation of information on the increasing spatial inequality worldwide, see Kanbur and Venables (2005).

18 See, for example, Deaton and Dreze (2002) for India and Aryeetey and McKay (2007) for Ghana.

So far, I have considered reasons why the poverty numbers used to evaluate distributional outcomes might be missing key features of ground-level reality. I have also argued that rising inequality might be an indirect indicator that this type of phenomenon is in play. But suppose that the poverty numbers are not missing anything—that they actually do capture the true snapshot of the evolution of well-being at the lower tail of the distribution. Then why should rising inequality matter if poverty is falling? The question leads to a number of considerations.

### The Welfare Function

The standard Bergson-Samuelson social welfare function, in which the well-being of each individual in the snapshot counts positively but at a diminishing rate at the margin, would justify concern with inequality. All else being equal, it would be better to have a more equal distribution for a given mean. Furthermore, if the social welfare function were particularly inequality-averse, it would emphasize improvement and worsening of well-being in the lower tail of the distribution, which is what poverty measures do. In the extreme, only poverty of the poorest would matter—it would be the centerpiece of evaluation, and overall inequality would fade away as a policy-relevant phenomenon. The gaps between rich and poor would not matter; only the well-being of the poorest would count. If this is the case (assuming the data are not missing anything as discussed previously), the central stylized fact I have been exploring would be a cause for unalloyed celebration, and policymakers should not be concerned at all about rising inequality.

But policymakers are concerned, and that is the motivation for much of the discourse. Why might this be? One argument is that they are indeed concerned about inequality in its own right as a normative assessment, separate from poverty. But they are concerned about both. Despite the technical difficulties of assigning independent roles to both poverty and inequality as a reduced form of a general social welfare function of individual well-being, analysts may just have to accept that this is what policymakers care about and thus analysts must carry both elements in their evaluations—although the lack of a formal foundation makes it difficult to discuss the relative weighting of the two components.[19]

### Groups and Inequality

The standard measures of inequality, like the Gini coefficient or the Theil measures, are individualistic. They calculate the inequality in the distribution

---

19 Fields (2006) refers to such a reduced-form welfare function, with poverty and inequality appearing independently, as BLEND. He says, "You might also try to axiomatize BLEND. I have been singularly unsuccessful in getting anywhere with it; I think this is because it is unclear to me what the primitive concept of BLEND is" (p. 71).

of income by person. These are the measures whose rise is the center of so much discussion and concern. As detailed earlier, for some analysts a change in such inequality is of second-order importance in evaluation compared with a change in poverty in the individualistic social welfare function framework. But consider now a society divided into broadly defined groups such as ethnic, racial, religious, and regional. A given change in overall interpersonal inequality, or even no change at all, can go hand in hand with many different patterns of change in the distribution between these groups.

For certain inequality measures, overall inequality can be decomposed into a between-group component and a within-group component. The between-group component is the inequality that would remain if all incomes in each group were equal to the mean income of that group. The within-group component is the inequality that would remain if all group means were equalized to the national mean. This empirical technique is commonly used to gauge the quantitative contribution of group mean differences to overall inequality. For most actual exercises with between half a dozen and a dozen groups, it turns out that the between-group component is from 10 to 30 percent.[20]

I suggest that an increase in the between-group component of inequality, reflecting growing average differences between salient groupings within a country, is much more significant in a population's perceptions of inequality than an equivalent increase in the overall national measure of inequality.[21] To the extent that policymakers reflect this thinking, their concerns are often about divisions across groups, whose evolution can be more exaggerated than the evolution of national-level inequality. To take an extreme example for illustrative purposes, suppose an increase in the between-group component of inequality is matched exactly by a decrease in the within-group component of inequality, leaving national inequality unchanged. It is easy to see that the stable national level of inequality may not capture the key elements of rising tension in the society, which policy makers will pick up but which will be missed by distributional analysts and national-level inequality indices.

The reasoning behind the importance of group differences can be related to the recent economic literature on identity, which characterizes individual well-being not only in terms of standard consumption inputs but also in terms of an exogenously given feature of individuals defining their belonging to a group (Akerlof and Kranton 2000; Basu 2005). From this, it is a short step to making the average consumption of an individual's group an input into the well-being of that individual. A more direct way is to simply think in terms of forms of income sharing within a group that are not captured very well in the household survey data. Thus, for example, free food at the temple or the mosque, provided by rich Hindus or rich Muslims but largely consumed by poor Hindus or poor Muslims, should, in principle, be

---

20 See references in Kanbur (2006).
21 This argument is developed in Kanbur (2006).

captured in the household survey data. To the extent it is not, analysts are missing the effect of group means on individual well-being.

I am not aware of any direct empirical studies to substantiate the possible explanation just given of why rising inequality might be a concern over and above the simple national inequality measure. However, the growing economics literature provides indirect support for the mechanisms suggested. For example, the theoretical propositions in Dasgupta and Kanbur (2007) formalize group antagonism in a model of contribution to group-specific public goods; Miguel (2004) and Gugerty and Miguel (2005) examine the role of ethnic divisions in the underprovision of public goods in Africa; and Alesina, Baqir, and Easterly (1999) argue that ethnic divisions explain the undersupply of local public goods in the United States.

## Equality of Opportunity

If the argument about groups points toward concern for (certain types of) distributional change greater than that captured by standard national inequality measures, there is another line of argument that in fact this concern should be less. What is important normatively, it is argued, is equality of opportunity—and measured interpersonal inequality does not necessarily capture this equality well. Indeed, measured inequality may overstate the true degree of inequality of opportunity. Perhaps the most famous statement of a disconnect in this direction was by Milton Friedman (1962):

> Another kind of inequality arising through the operation of the market is also required, in a somewhat more subtle sense, to produce equality of treatment, or, to put it differently, to satisfy men's tastes. It can be illustrated most simply by a lottery. Consider a group of individuals who initially have equal endowments and who agree voluntarily to enter a lottery with very unequal prizes. The resultant inequality of income is surely required to permit the individuals in question to make the most of their initial equality. . . . Much of the inequality of income produced by payment in accordance with the product reflects "equalizing" difference or the satisfaction of men's tastes for uncertainty. . . . Redistribution of income after the event is equivalent to denying them the opportunity to enter the lottery.

In the present context, and in the frame of my central stylized fact of growth with rising inequality, the argument might run as follows. Consider a scenario in which, after a long period of being denied the opportunity to enter the lotteries of economic entrepreneurship and risk taking, economic liberalization opens up these opportunities. Some people take up these lotteries; others do not. Those who do will, on average, do better than those who do not. But even among those who do, there will, of course, be winners and losers. The economic opening up will increase the size of the pie and will introduce inequality of outcome where there was none. But there will be no inequality of opportunity.

In the extreme example given by Friedman (1962), there is no inequality that should cause concern. The inequality observed is the result of decisions freely taken by initially equal individuals. In reality, of course, individuals are not initially equal. If this inequality affects their decisions, then the further inequality caused by these decisions is, to some extent, influenced by the initial inequality.[22] But the basic argument remains: part of the increase in inequality can be attributed to decisions taken freely by individuals in accordance with their tastes in response to new opportunities, and this increase in inequality should not cause normative concern.

To get at the level and evolution of inequality of opportunity, analysts would have to allow for the decisions made by the initially unequal people. More generally, analysts can separate out the factors beyond the individual's control and the decisions under the individual's control, such as the effort a person expends on economic activity according to his or her tastes. This line of argument is developed by Roemer (1998). For example, identical distributions of income within each category of individuals with identical exogenous conditions might be described as equality of opportunity—differences are caused by effort or luck, not by initial exogenous circumstances. More narrowly, analysts might require only that the means of the distributions by type be the same for equality of opportunity. As recognized by Bourguignon, Ferreira, and Walton (2007), "These are the definitions of equal opportunities implicit in the [*World Development Report 2006*]."

But Bourguignon, Ferreira, and Walton (2007), who are among the principal authors of the World Bank's *World Development Report 2006*, find that they need to go beyond equality of opportunity to capture their value judgments because, in principle, a policy to equalize opportunity might be consistent with severe deprivation of actual outcomes for some. They handle this by keeping (a Rawlsian maximin version of) opportunity in the objective function, but introducing a constraint that the actual well-being of any individual not be allowed to fall below a critical value:

> We find the above formulation appealing in that it makes "poverty reduction" (understood in this context as enforcing a minimum level of [well-being] for all, regardless of *both* circumstance *and* efforts) a necessary *requirement* for equitable policy, but not its ultimate *objective*. The ultimate objective goes beyond the elimination of absolute deprivation, and is the pursuit of "equal opportunities" in the Rawls-Roemer sense. (Bourguignon, Ferreira, and Walton 2007: 240, emphasis in original)

I am not sure that the separation the authors intend is as clean as they wish it to be, because the constraint comes from government preferences, not from technology. If one were to take the formulation literally, then almost no recent distributional evolution could pass the constraint, because, as argued earlier, significant new poverty has been created under the aggregate umbrella of an overall improvement. If analysts were to get around this by allowing some increase in poverty at the individual level, then they are back to having some combination of poverty and equality. In any event, Bourguignon, Ferreira, and Walton (2007) seem to have brought this chapter full circle. Note the arguments of those who would not be as concerned about rising inequality over the last 20 years, because it is an increase in inequality of outcomes

---

22  See Sen (1980) for an early discussion of what the concern about inequality should be.

brought about by new opportunities that are differentially accessed because of individual preferences—it is not an increase in inequality of opportunity. This is a move away from the focus on outcomes. But Bourguignon, Ferreira, and Walton (2007) are not willing to abandon an outcomes-based approach. So they reintroduce poverty, requiring, I would argue, a weighing of poverty outcomes against the increase in inequality. Albeit in the context of a definition of equality of opportunity, analysts are effectively in the BLEND scenario of Fields (2006) and all of the conceptual problems it raises.

But I want to go further. I want to argue that the idea of equality of opportunity, although persuasive and elegant in the abstract, may not have cutting power in practice because of the difficulty, in my view, of separating out those factors that are under the individual's control and those that are truly exogenous. A child's home circumstances are exogenous to the child, but are a consequence of the choices made by the child's parents. Those choices, in turn, were influenced by the home backgrounds of their parents. Where exactly can the line be drawn? Where is the original position from which to start to define equality of opportunity? Put another way, parents' free choices create the circumstances for their children. Equalizing these circumstances for the children surely goes against the principle of not taking into account inequality in the outcomes of the parents' free choices. By the same token, when I see information about the life chances of babies born into different racial and ethnic caste groups, or information about differing wages for the same educational achievements across racial groups, I find it important because these findings affect the distribution of outcomes.

Finally, it is not at all clear which way moral intuition runs on bad luck from an equal starting point. The equality of opportunity view would say that this should not count in this assessment. But an equally strong intuition, I would argue, is that the one who is down must be helped precisely because he had bad luck despite all his efforts.[23] Thus, I wish to argue that the palpable concern among populations and their policymakers about increasing inequality of outcomes cannot be easily assuaged by equality of opportunity arguments. Opportunity is abstract. It is the translation into actual outcomes that matters.

## What Can and Should Be Done?

The palpable concern among populations and policymakers about the increasing inequality despite poverty reduction because of high growth worries some economists and policy advisers, because they fear this concern will lead to measures that may hold back the rise in inequality but will reduce growth and thus hamper poverty reduction. Two questions then arise: First, might it all blow over with the passage of time, with inequality

---

23 This argument is developed in Kanbur (1987b).

declining after a period, and if so, why not wait? Second, if redistributive measures have to be taken, what are their consequences for growth?

**Will It All Blow Over, and So What If It Does?**

What if increasing inequality is only a phase, and so it eventually will begin to decline? The best-known hypothesis in this regard is that of Kuznets (1955), which posits that as development proceeds and mean income grows, inequality first increases and then decreases. Kuznets himself supported this hypothesis with time series data for England, Germany, and the United States over periods of decades. But since the 1970s, testing of the "Kuznets inverted-U shape" for developing countries has been conducted on cross-country data. The most famous test of the Kuznets hypothesis on cross-country data (Ahluwalia 1976) spawned a large volume of literature, much of which supported the hypothesis. Surveying the early literature, Fields (1980: 122) concluded: "Research studies suggest that the relationship between relative inequality and per capita GNP tends to have an inverted-U shape."

Thus, according to the empirical literature of a quarter-century ago, increasing inequality would be followed by decreasing inequality. Characteristically, the policy conclusions drawn from this finding were diametrically opposed. One group (including some at the World Bank—see Chenery et al. 1974) focused on the initial increasing inequality phase and how to make growth more equitable. A second group focused on the declining phase to argue that increasing inequality was not inevitable but a phase—policymakers should continue to pursue growth and wait it out until the declining inequality set in, because addressing distribution early on might jeopardize the growth itself.

However, careful data and econometric work in the 1980s and 1990s, after the initial burst of research in the 1970s, raised serious questions about the empirical basis of the Kuznets relationship in the cross-country data. Using the same data set as Ahluwalia (1976), work in the 1980s by Anand and Kanbur (1993a, 1993b) argued that an inverted-U shape could not be easily confirmed. Then in the 1990s came a new and more comprehensive data set put together by Deininger and Squire (1998), which, in turn, led to an explosion of attempts to test for the Kuznets hypothesis empirically. Although there are variations in the findings of the many papers in this literature, it would be fair to say that, by and large, the inverted-U shape has not been found in cross-sectional analysis, including by Deininger and Squire (1998) themselves. The difficulties in convincingly finding such a relationship are partly related to the usual problems of cross-country econometric analysis, but, to the extent that the cross section is thought to represent the long-run outcome, a summary of the current literature is that there is no long-run relationship between economic growth and inequality in the data.

Plenty of time series evidence indicates that inequality has increased in countries with high growth rates over the last two decades. If the cross-country empirical finding of a Kuznets curve, or of no curve at all, was assumed to be the long-run outcome, the prescription of holding onto the growth path despite the current increases in inequality could still have some force. But there are two important challenges to such a conclusion, one normative and the other analytical.

The normative challenge is how to balance the losses of today with the gains of tomorrow. Suppose there is indeed an iron law that distributional changes will in the long run reverse themselves, how long is the long run? Kuznets's original data were collected over several decades, which may be too long to wait. This could be a straightforward political economy issue— asking policymakers to stick to policies that are increasing inequality may be tantamount to asking them to sign their own resignation from office. But it is also an issue about the nature of the social welfare function. How are analysts to compare across, say, a half-century the welfare of two populations that are most likely a considerably different set of individuals? Sacrifices on the part of some individuals at the start of the half-century could, in principle, be aggregated with the benefits to them if they were still alive 50 years hence, with an appropriate discount rate. Their sacrifices could perhaps also be aggregated with the gains of their descendants 50 years hence, again applying a suitable discount rate. Aggregating the sacrifices of some today with the benefits to unrelated individuals tomorrow is more problematic, but could nevertheless be forced through the social welfare function.[24]

The key normative question, then, turns on the choice of discount rate and how benefits are aggregated and compared across unrelated individuals. A high discount rate obviously justifies a greater concern about sacrifices today. At the same time, if future generations are going be wealthier than the present generation because of exogenous trends in, say, technology, then sacrificing in the present in return for future gains will appeal less the more egalitarian are the normative sentiments. Many of the disputes in the globalization, growth, and distribution discourse, while seemingly about the efficacy of this or that policy instrument, are really about such trade-offs.

The second challenge, an analytical one, is simply this: treating the evolution of distribution as an iron law does not make sense. Although Kuznets (1955) did indeed have a specific model in mind that generated an inverted-U shape,[25] he recognized that much of the force behind distributional change—for example, the decline in inequality in the first half of the 20th century—was to do with politics and then policy. Specific and purposive redistributional policy had played the central role in declining inequality. This view is summarized well by Piketty (2006) in his recent overview, when he said that "there exists a myriad of country-specific institutions (from educational and labor market institutions to corporate governance and social norms) that play a key role to shape the interplay

---

24 The problem becomes particularly acute when there are deaths because of increasing poverty, and these deaths serve to reduce measured poverty by taking the poor out of the count. See Kanbur and Mukherjee (2007).

25 See Anand and Kanbur (1993b) for a formalization of the "Kuznets Process."

between development and inequality. Rising dispersion of income is not the mechanical and largely unavoidable consequence of technical change. Nor is the trend going to reverse in a spontaneous fashion. Inequality dynamics depend primarily on the policies and institutions adopted by governments and societies as a whole."

### Are Growth-Enhancing Policies Bad for Equality?

So now we come to the central policy questions: Will measures to stem the rise in inequality that has accompanied high rates of economic growth invariably be detrimental to that growth? Will rising inequality by itself act as an impediment to economic growth? What, if any, are the policies and interventions that help growth without harming equality, and help equality without harming growth? For practical policymaking, all of these questions should be asked over a relevant policy horizon of at most a generation, but more likely over a decade or perhaps even less. Beyond this horizon, the predictive value of analysis based on previous history can be questioned, and the interest of current policymakers may wane.

The following representation of the questions might be helpful. Think of an instrument panel on which there are a number of buttons, each representing a particular type of policy or intervention such as monetary policy, exchange rate policy, trade policy, tax policy, government expenditures of different types, or laws and regulations. The instrument panel works in conjunction with a box representing the economy to produce various outcomes—in particular, the distribution of well-being to individuals in society. The model of the economy in the box has features that describe structural aspects of the economy and society, including social norms that govern behavior, factor endowments, and infrastructure. Some of these features can be changed over the relevant time horizon; others change so slowly that they can be taken as given for this discussion. Once this panel and box are set up, we can ask, instrument by instrument, whether its application will lead to a trade-off between growth and equity over the relevant time horizon. Then we can ask whether packages of instruments would allow one to avoid the trade-off.

The classic policy instrument debated and discussed has been global integration in trade, and I will focus on this instrument for concreteness and illustration. The literature on the impact of such "openness" on growth and on distribution is now substantial. A key technical question has been how to measure openness, because trade flow–based measures suffer from being endogenous. Using genuine policy variables such as tariffs weakens the results considerably. On trade liberalization, the recent study by Harrison (2006: 38–40) concludes:

> The evidence suggests that there is no significant relationship between globalization (measured using average import tariffs) and poverty. Poverty is measured as the percentage of households in a country living on less than a $1 a day, measured in 1993 PPP dollars. . . . One strong possibility, which is clearly revealed in the country case studies that make use of micro data using households or firms, is that there is too much heterogeneity in the effects of trade reforms on the

poor. . . . The lack of any robust positive association between trade and poverty reduction could indicate that the growth gains from trade have failed to trickle down to the poor because they simply do not participate in the benefits. This interpretation of results is consistent with the fact that a number of studies find that globalization is associated with increasing inequality.

Goldberg and Pavcnik (2004) find that trade liberalization has a negative effect on unskilled workers in the short and medium run because "the most heavily protected sectors in many developing countries tend to be sectors that employ a high proportion of unskilled workers earning low wages" (p. 40). The topic of openness and distribution is controversial, and results counter to these have been propounded. Perhaps the best known of recent results are those by Dollar and Kraay (2001), who argue that because openness leads to growth and because growth does not lead to much distributional change, openness benefits the poor.[26]

Where do I come down on the question of trade, growth, and distribution? Although there are technical problems with measuring openness using trade flows, it seems clear to me that strong growth benefits can be had from integration into the global economy, but that these benefits come at a short-run cost of worsening distribution—either in the sense that inequality increases or in the sense that a significant number of people are made worse off even if an equivalent or greater number are made better off, or both. I find myself not too far from the middle ground proposed in the review by Winters (2000: 53):

> Open economies fare better in aggregate than do closed ones, and there is no evidence that, overall, they experience worse poverty than closed ones. . . . On the other hand, it is absurd to pretend that liberalization never pushes anyone into poverty, nor even that liberalization cannot increase the extent or depth of poverty in some circumstances. Thus in contemplating and managing a liberalization care is required to minimize adverse poverty impacts (care that has not always been taken in the past), and, wherever possible, to tailoring the program to play a positive role in poverty alleviation.

Thus, Winters (2000) and Harrison (2006) seem to be advocating a *package* of policy measures to make the most of the benefits of trade liberalization, while addressing the negative distributional consequences. What might these measures be? A key choice is between what Winters (2000) calls specific compensatory policies and general compensatory policies. The difficulty with specific compensatory policies is that they are difficult and costly to design and tailor to each circumstance—by trade reform and by subsector, for example. General compensatory policies avoid this problem. According to Winters (2000: 44),

> These policies—often referred to as safety nets—are designed to alleviate poverty from any source directly. They replace the problem of identifying the shock with one of identifying the poor. Ideally, countries should already have such programmes in place. Indeed, a major part of their effect arises from their mere

---

26 A critique of the Dollar-Kraay paper has been provided, in turn, by Rodrik (2000). For an earlier analysis of openness and distribution, see Bourguignon and Morrison (1990).

existence rather than their use: they facilitate adjustment by assuring the poor that there is a minimum (albeit barely acceptable) below which they will not be allowed to fall. If trade-adjusting countries do already have these schemes, they have the advantages over tailor-made schemes of automaticity, immediacy and a degree of 'road-testing', and they also avoid the problems of targeted trade adjustment assistance. Sensibly constructed, they need not entail huge expenditure; there is rather little chance of moral hazard problems if the thresholds are set low enough; and, since relieving poverty is more or less universally recognised as a responsibility of the state, there is little argument about the legitimacy of such interventions.

Examples of such general compensatory schemes include various public works schemes such as the famous Employment Guarantee Scheme of Maharashtra in India (Ravallion 1991). This scheme has now been strengthened and introduced as a national-level scheme by the government elected in 2004 on a platform of addressing the distributional consequences of the India's high-growth trajectory (Basu, Chau, and Kanbur 2007). Although some analysts may disagree with this classification, the recent crop of conditional cash transfer schemes such as Oportunidades-Progresa in Mexico (Levy 2006) can also be put into the general compensatory schemes category. However, by means of their conditionalities such schemes attempt to achieve other objectives as well, such as keeping children in school or increasing prenatal visits to health centers.

Such general compensatory programs or safety nets do raise a large number of questions. Issues arise of targeting, implementation, and monitoring (e.g., see Besley and Kanbur 1988; Ravallion 1991; Coady, Grosh, and Hoddinott 2004). However, the evaluation of these schemes has always been on their own terms—whether they target the poor, whether they make efficient use of resources, and so forth. What the argument just made suggests is that such schemes have a value over and above the direct value of poverty alleviation from a given starting point. Also important, they help to mitigate the negative distributional consequences of broad-based economic reform, which, alongside the average growth benefits, do tend to create winners and losers because of the great heterogeneity of the population, especially the poor. Apart from this direct impact on the social welfare function, such schemes can also ease the political economy of economic reform and liberalization (in general, not just trade liberalization) by reducing the incentives of the losers to band together and resist the reforms (Kanbur 2005).[27]

### Are Equality-Enhancing Policies Good for Growth?

Now we come to the debate on the causal link between equity and growth. In the earlier discussion, we started off from the empirical observation that in the last decade or two greater openness to trade has led to more growth,

---

27 Rodrik (1999) has put forward the argument that because efficient adjustment to shocks almost invariably involves distributional consequences, those societies that resolve these distributional issues, or at least minimize them, will be better placed to make efficient adjustments and thus to grow faster.

but also to more inequality. If inequality is a concern, policymakers may be moved to address it. Clearly, addressing inequality by reversing open trade sacrifices growth—thus the compensation argument. If the compensation could be given in a way that it does not jeopardize growth, at least not too much, then the policy package of openness plus compensation could be recommended. Some economists worry that compensation schemes may lead to excessive fiscal exposure and corruption, and may have adverse incentive effects on effort, thereby lowering growth rates. But without compensation schemes, the only advice one can offer policy makers is to wait out the rising inequality and the increase in poverty for which it might be an indicator. This advice is not very helpful, however, and, in any event, the backlash from the population may force a closing down of trade. This is one way in which equality-enhancing policies, such as general compensation mechanisms or safety nets, could help the growth process itself.

The other theoretical arguments on why equality per se could enhance growth counter the classical argument that because of the shape of the savings function, the saving rate is higher with a more unequal distribution of income.[28] Indeed, there is no shortage of theoretical models to counter the classical argument. They all rely on some form of market failure, which interacts with an unequal distribution of income to produce a brake on growth. Thus, for example, if a threshold level of investment is required for human capital investment and if credit market failures mean that the amount that can be invested is determined by one's own wealth, then those with low wealth will not invest in their own human capital. If human capital investment by the wealthy is diminishing at the margin, a redistribution of wealth will increase overall investment in human capital and, where this mechanism is tacked on to an endogenous growth model, the steady-state growth rate as well. There are many other types of mechanisms, including political economy ones such as that in Alesina and Rodrik (1994) in which in a voting model more inequality induces more inefficient policies (specifically, a higher level of a distortionary tax) to be chosen.[29]

The real difficulties lie not so much in developing models that demonstrate a causal connection between equality and growth, but in actually showing this causal connection empirically. Certainly, this has not proved easy in the cross-sectional data, as might be expected from the Kuznets curve literature. A recent review by Birdsall and Szekely (2003: 6) concludes as follows:

> Empirical evidence from cross-country studies supports the general proposition for the case of developing countries that those with high levels of income inequality have experienced lower levels of growth. Best known but problematic are the early studies of Persson and Tabellini (1994) and Alesina and Rodrik (1994). These relied on cross-sectional estimates without controlling for fixed effects. . . . More recent studies including developed as well as

28 The classical savings assumption that capitalists save their incomes but workers do not drives growth in the famous Lewis (1954) model. Surplus labor holds wages down, whereas investment creates ever more profits to be invested.

29 For reviews, see Aghion et al. (1999) and Kanbur and Lustig (2000).

developing countries and controlling for fixed effects tend to come to the opposite conclusion (Forbes, 2000). But Barro (2000) shows that . . . [i]n developing but not developed countries, inequality does seem to reduce growth.

As much as I am convinced by the theoretical models, I am not sure I would endorse Birdsall and Szekely's opening sentence so far as the "cross-country studies" on income inequality are concerned. All the well-known problems of drawing inferences from cross-country regressions will continue to bedevil these analyses. In an added twist, Banerjee and Duflo (2003) argue that in their analysis of the cross-country data "changes in inequality (in any direction) are associated with reduced growth in the next period."

But perhaps the most striking argument against any systematic relationship between inequality and growth at the national level is the very same stylized fact that motivates this chapter. A significant number of countries now have experience with increasing inequality over the last decade or two, but this increase does not seem to have negatively influenced their growth performance. Of course, the counterfactual is important—had they not had the increase in inequality, perhaps their growth would have been higher. Establishing such counterfactuals is difficult, but for 20 years now China has had ever-increasing inequality with spectacular growth rates, and the same is true for a decade or more for Bangladesh, Ghana, India, and Vietnam. Thus any simple relationship between overall inequality and growth may be difficult to establish. Furthermore, Voitchovsky (2004) argues that the effects are different at either end of the distribution, with inequality at the top end positively associated with growth and inequality at the bottom end negatively associated with growth.

The evidence is perhaps somewhat stronger when we move from inequality defined as income inequality to inequality defined in broader terms: inequality in physical and human capital or gender inequality. Birdsall and Londoño (1997) argue that this link between inequality and growth applies to Latin America for land and education, and Klasen makes the same argument for gender inequality. Klasen (1999: 1) concludes: "Point estimates suggest that between 0.4–0.9% of the differences in growth rates between East Asia and Sub-Saharan Africa, South Asia, and the Middle East can be accounted for by the larger gender gaps in education prevailing in the latter regions."

Again in a broader sense, it has been argued that group inequalities hold back growth. The empirical evidence for ethnic and other forms of fractionalization and growth has been presented in the literature, including by Easterly and Levine (1997) and Collier (2001), but questioned by Arcand et al. (2000) and Temple (1998). Temple asks and answers his questions as follows: "Should the origins of slow growth be traced to Africa's social arrangements, high inequality, and ethnic diversity? Based on cross-country empirical work, this paper argues that the best answers are yes, no, and maybe."

Overall, then, the macroeconomic evidence for a causal connection between equity and growth is not particularly strong. Almost a decade ago, Kanbur and Lustig (2000) concluded their review by saying that "the jury is still out." The best-known recent overview appeared in the World Bank's *World Development Report 2006*:

> Most studies that look at the cross-sectional relationship between inequality and subsequent growth over a relatively long period in cross-country data, and especially those that use measures of asset inequality, find a negative relationship, often significant. By contrast, most studies that look at the relationship between changes in inequality and growth, including several studies that do analysis at the sub-national level within the same country, find a positive effect. . . . Most important among the many reasons for both cross-sectional and the time series evidence to be misleading are the following: the possibility of a non-linear relationship between inequality and growth, problems with comparability of cross-country data, and the difficulty of identifying the direction of causality when both variables are likely to influence one another. . . . Despite great attention devoted to the question of a systematic relationship between overall inequality and growth at the country level, the body of evidence remains unconvincing. But there is clearly a strong presumption that reducing a specific inequality would promote better investment. (World Bank 2005: 103)

What is left at the end? Managing the distributional consequences of economic reform, as discussed in the previous section, is a strong imperative on ethical and political economy grounds. Proactively addressing inequality is an ethical imperative if inequality is a factor in the social welfare function over and above poverty, and even if only poverty matters, because the same growth rate applied to a more equal distribution will lead to greater poverty reduction. However, the argument about inequity being a drag on growth cannot be made in general with confidence. The theoretical and empirical arguments are stronger for specific forms of inequality—inequality of assets such as human capital and inequality between salient socioeconomic groups such as those defined by gender or ethnicity.

## Conclusion: Where to Focus Future Analysis to Best Help Policymakers

This chapter provides an overview of globalization, growth, and distribution, motivated by the stylized fact that most countries that have experienced high growth have also experienced rising inequality, but the growth has been fast enough to reduce poverty in the official statistics. And yet despite the reduction in poverty, strong distributional concerns persist in the populations at large and among policymakers. Some economists and policy analysts dismiss these concerns as irrelevant or overstated. But these concerns frame the discourse on globalization, and in this chapter I, in turn, frame a series of questions motivated by the stylized fact and the concerns it raises. First, I ask why rising inequality should be a concern if poverty is falling. One possible answer is that the official poverty statistics are missing key features of ground-level reality, which are captured, albeit indirectly and imperfectly, in the rising inequality. Another answer is that rising inequality is a matter of normative concern over and above falling poverty.

Second, I ask: if the concern is accepted, what can and should be done? I argue that waiting for the rise in inequality to blow over is not an option ethically or in terms of political economy. Economic reform and global integration create winners and losers, and addressing the losers' concerns is an ethical and political economy imperative. Generalized compensation mechanisms embodied in safety nets, suitably designed, seem the best option for addressing these concerns. Finally, although the evidence is weak on a causal link between overall income inequality and growth, there is some evidence that addressing specific forms of inequality—in assets, between genders, and between ethnicities and other salient groups—can lay the foundation for higher growth.

Based on all these considerations, where might further analysis most fruitfully focus to help policymakers address the concerns raised by rising inequality in a high-growth environment? It is fairly clear that the marginal social value of yet another cross-country regression between inequality and growth is by now pretty low. Instead, I suggest three areas of focus: (1) improving official statistics to reduce the disconnect between those statistics and the ground-level realities of distributional evolution; (2) analyzing and exploring a range of compensation mechanisms for addressing the distributional consequences of economic reform, technical change, and global integration; and (3) addressing the specific structural inequalities that constrain growth and development.

I have presented several possible explanations for the disconnect between official poverty statistics and perceived ground-level realities. The evidence for these channels of disconnect is mostly indirect, or even anecdotal, because by their very nature the official statistics cannot be further organized to reduce the disconnect. For example, it is difficult to see how within the current framework the standard large national-level household income and expenditure surveys could be easily modified to explore individual-level consumption. In principle, it could be done, but it would be prohibitively expensive. However, smaller-scale specialized surveys could be launched, such as the one analyzed in Haddad and Kanbur (1990). The results of such a survey could be used to provide policymakers with at least an estimate of the impact on official statistics of ignoring intrahousehold inequality in consumption. The same is true for public services. Specialized surveys and analyses that attempt to bring the consumption of publicly provided services into the same framework as money metric measures of well-being could give policymakers an adjustment to the official statistics on poverty, taking into account the evolution of these nonmarket sources of consumption. Panel data could aid in tracking the patterns of winners and losers as the distribution evolves, thereby helping policymakers and analysts to resolve whether the aggregate poverty reduction (if that is the trend) shown in official statistics hides a significant number of poor people (and even some just above the poverty line) who are being made worse off. Over the last two decades, panel data have become much more prevalent in developing countries, but their institutionalization as a standard part of the monitoring mechanisms of government is some way off.[30] Finally (and this does not necessarily require new data), analysts and policymakers should pay much greater attention to the evolution of mean differences between salient socioeconomic groups as opposed to a measure of overall income inequality at the national level.

If the concerns about the poor losers from economic reform, technical change, and global integration are strong enough to warrant addressing— and I would argue that they are—then compensation mechanisms should be considered. I have argued that this perspective calls for looking at generalized compensation schemes of different types (public works schemes, food subsidies, conditional cash transfers, and the like) in a new light—not just as redistributive mechanisms in their own right, but also as mechanisms that address the well-being of losers from policy changes at the macro level. There is already a large literature on the evaluation and design of these types of interventions as income transfer mechanisms—the efficacy of their targeting, their administrative and fiscal costs, and their incentive effects. However, policymakers might benefit from an analysis of the operation of these mechanisms in the context of broad economic policy changes such as greater global integration—analysis that asks how successful these mechanisms are in compensating the losers from such reforms. Such an analysis will require, among other things, collecting more detailed information about participants in these schemes and examining these schemes in detail over time. Finally, policymakers would be helped by an assessment not just of each scheme separately, but also of the schemes as a whole to determine whether they are working to compensate the losers from efficient policy changes, thereby addressing political economy as well as ethical concerns.

Finally, although in my view the inequality-growth cross-country regressions literature has hit a plateau, investigation of the return to specific interventions to reduce inequality in assets and across groups will continue to have a high payoff. Such an approach will take analysts, whether the issue is land inequality, gender inequality, caste inequality, or ethnic inequality, into a deeply structural and often cultural domain, where economic analysis and economic interventions can play only a partial role, and the analysis and the prescriptions will have to be highly context-specific. But if reducing such inequalities can increase the poverty-reducing impact of a given growth rate, and perhaps even increase that growth rate, then it is a strategy worth pursuing.

Thus, the nexus of high growth with falling poverty but rising inequality not only frames the questions for current debate, but also frames the future research and policy analysis agenda.

---

30 For all of these, economists' standard fixed-response survey methods can be complemented by the qualitative methods of other disciplines. Indeed, some of the disconnect has been highlighted by methods such as "participatory poverty appraisal." See, for example, Kanbur and Shaffer (2007).

# References

Aghion, Philippe, Eve Caroli, and Cecilia Garcia-Penalosa. 1999. "Inequality and Economic Growth: The Perspective of the New Growth Theories." *Journal of Economic Literature* 37 (December): 161–66.

Agüero, J., M. R. Carter, and J. May. 2007. "Poverty and Inequality in the First Decade of South Africa's Democracy: What Can Be Learnt from Panel Data?" *Journal of African Economies* 16 (5): 782–812.

Ahluwalia, Montek. 1976. "Inequality, Poverty and Development." *Journal of Development Economics* 3: 307–42.

Akerlof, G., and Kranton, R. 2000. "Economics and Identity." *Quarterly Journal of Economics* 115: 715–53.

Alderman, Harold, Pierre-Andre Chiappori, Lawrence Haddad, John Hoddinott, and Ravi Kanbur. 1995. "Unitary versus Collective Models of the Household: Is It Time to Shift the Burden of Proof?" *World Bank Research Observer* 10 (February): 1–19.

Alesina, Alberto, and Dani Rodrik. 1994. "Distributive Politics and Economic Growth." *Quarterly Journal of Economics* 109: 465–89.

Alesina, Alberto, Reza Baqir, and William Easterly. 1999. "Public Goods and Ethnic Divisions." *Quarterly Journal of Economics* 114 (4): 1243–84.

Anand, Sudhir, and Ravi Kanbur. 1993a. "Inequality and Development: A Critique." *Journal of Development Economics* 41: 19–43.

———. 1993b. "The Kuznets Process and the Inequality-Development Relationship." *Journal of Development Economics* 40: 25–52.

Arcand, Jean-Louis, et al. 2000. "How to Make a Tragedy: On the Alleged Effect of Ethnicity on Growth." *Journal of International Trade and Development* 12 (October): 925–38.

Aryeetey, Ernest, and Andrew McKay. 2007. "Growth with Poverty Reduction, But Increased Spatial Inequality: Ghana over the 1990s." In *Determinants of Pro Poor Growth: Analytical Issues and Findings from Country Cases,* ed. M. Grimm, S. Klasen, and A. McKay, chap. 3. London: Palgrave Macmillan.

Banerjee, Abhijit, and Esther Duflo. 2003. "Inequality and Growth: What Can the Data Say?" *Journal of Economic Growth* 8: 267–99.

Barro, Robert. 2000. "Inequality and Growth in a Panel of Countries." *Journal of Economic Growth* 5: 1.

Basu, Arnab, Nancy Chau, and Ravi Kanbur. 2007. "The National Rural Employment Guarantee Act of India, 2005." In *The Oxford Companion to Economics in India,* ed. K. Basu. New Delhi: Oxford University Press.

Basu, Kaushik. 2005. "Racial Conflict and Malignancy of Identity." *Journal of Economic Inequality* 3 (3): 221–41.

Baulch, R., and J. Hoddinott. 2000. "Economic Mobility and Poverty Dynamics in Developing Countries." *Journal of Development Studies* 36 (6): 1–24.

Besley, Timothy, and Ravi Kanbur. 1988. "Food Subsidies and Poverty Alleviation." *Economic Journal* 98: 701–19.

Bhagwati, Jagdish. 2004. *In Defense of Globalization.* London: Oxford University Press.

Bhorat, Haroon, and Ravi Kanbur, eds. 2006. *Poverty and Policy in Post-Apartheid South Africa*. Pretoria: HSRC Press.

Birdsall, Nancy, and Juan Luis Londoño. 1997. "Asset Inequality Does Matter: Lessons from Latin America." *American Economic Review* 87: 2.

Birdsall, Nancy, and Miguel Szekely. 2003. "Bootstraps, Not Band-aids: Poverty, Equity and Social Policy." Working Paper No. 24, Center for Global Development, Washington, DC. http://www.cgdev.org/content/publications/detail/2766.

Bourguignon, François, and Christian Morrison. 1990. "Income Distribution, Development and Foreign Trade: A Cross-Sectional Analysis." *European Economic Review* 34: 1113—32.

Bourguignon, François, Francisco Ferreira, and Michael Walton. 2007. "Equity, Efficiency and Inequality Traps." *Journal of Economic Inequality* 5 (August): 235–56.

Chakravarty, Satya, Ravi Kanbur, and Diganta Mukherjee. 2006. "Population Growth and Poverty Measurement." *Social Choice and Welfare* 26: 471–83.

Chenery, Hollis B., et al. 1974. *Redistribution with Growth*. London: Oxford University Press.

Coady, David, Margaret Grosh, and John Hoddinott. 2004. "Targeting of Transfers in Developing Countries: Review of Lessons and Experience." International Food Policy Research Institute and World Bank, Washington, DC. http://www.ifpri.org/pubs/cp/targettoc.pdf.

Collier, Paul. 2001. "Implications of Ethnic Diversity." *Economic Policy* 32 (April): 127–55.

Dasgupta, Indraneel, and Ravi Kanbur. 2007. "Community and Class Antagonism." *Journal of Public Economics* 91: 1816–42.

Deaton, Angus, and Jean Dreze. 2002. "Poverty and Inequality in India: A Reexamination." *Economic and Political Weekly*, September 7, 3729–48.

Deaton, Angus, and Vaerie Kozel, eds. 2005. *The Great Indian Poverty Debate*. New Delhi: Macmillan.

Deininger, K., and L. Squire. 1998. "New Ways of Looking at Old Issues: Inequality and Growth." *Journal of Development Economics* 57 (2): 259–88.

Dercon, Stefan. 2004. *Insurance against Poverty*. London: Oxford University Press.

Dercon, S., and P. Krishnan. 2000. "Vulnerability, Seasonality and Poverty in Ethiopia." *Journal of Development Studies* 36 (6): 25–53.

Dollar, David, and Art Kraay. 2001. "Trade, Growth and Poverty." Working Paper 2615, World Bank, Washington, DC. http://econ.worldbank.org/files/24896_wps2615.pdf.

Easterly, William, and Ross Levine. 1997. "Africa's Growth Tragedy: Policies and Ethnic Divisions." *Quarterly Journal of Economics* 112 (November): 1203–50.

Fields, Gary. 1980. *Poverty, Inequality and Development*. Cambridge, UK: Cambridge University Press.

———. 2006. "Should Poverty and Inequality Measures Be Combined?" In *Poverty, Inequality and Development: Essays in Honor of Erik Thorbecke*, ed. Alain de Janvry and Ravi Kanbur. New York: Springer.

Forbes, Kristin. 2000. "A Reassessment of the Relationship between Inequality and Growth." *American Economic Review* 90 (4): 869–87.

Foster, James, Joel Greer, and Erik Thorbecke. 1984. "A Class of Decomposable Poverty Measures." *Econometrica* 52 (May): 761–66.

Friedman, Milton. 1962. *Capitalism and Freedom.* Chicago: University of Chicago Press.

Goldberg, Pinelopi, and Nina Pavcnik. 2004. "Trade, Inequality and Poverty: What Do We Know? Evidence from Recent Trade Liberalization Episodes in Developing Countries." NBER Working Paper 10593, National Bureau of Economic Research, Cambridge, MA.

Grootaert, Christiaan, Ravi Kanbur, and G-T Oh. 1997. "The Dynamics of Welfare Gains and Losses: An African Case Study." *Journal of Development Studies* 33 (5): 635–57.

Gugerty, Mary Kay, and Edward Miguel. 2005. "Ethnic Divisions, Social Sanctions, and Public Goods in Kenya." *Journal of Public Economics* 89 (11–12): 2325–68.

Haddad, Lawrence, and Ravi Kanbur. 1990. "How Serious Is the Neglect of Intrahousehold Inequality?" *Economic Journal* 100 (September): 866–81.

Harrison, Ann. 2006. "Globalization and Poverty." NBER Working Paper 12347, National Bureau of Economic Research, Cambridge, MA.

———, ed. 2007. *Globalization and Poverty.* Chicago: University of Chicago Press.

Jalan, J., and M. Ravallion. 2000. "Is Transient Poverty Different? Evidence from Rural China." *Journal of Development Studies* 36 (6).

Kanbur, Ravi. 1987a. "Measurement and Alleviation of Poverty: With an Application to the Effects of Macroeconomic Adjustment." *IMF Staff Papers* 30: 60–85.

———. 1987b. "The Standard of Living: Uncertainty, Inequality and Opportunity." In *The Standard of Living,* ed. Geoffrey Hawthorn. Cambridge, UK: Cambridge University Press.

———. 2000. "Income Distribution and Development." In *Handbook of Income Distribution,* vol. 1. ed. A. B. Atkinson and F. Bourguignon. Amsterdam: Elsevier.

———. 2001. "Economic Policy, Distribution and Poverty: The Nature of Disagreements." *World Development* 29 (6): 1083–94.

———. 2005. "Pareto's Revenge." *Journal of Social and Economic Development* 7 (1): 1–11.

———. 2006. "The Policy Significance of Inequality Decompositions." *Journal of Economic Inequality* 4 (December): 367–74.

Kanbur, Ravi, and Nora Lustig. 2000. "Why Is Inequality Back on the Agenda? In *Annual World Bank Conference on Development Economics 1999,* ed. Boris Pleskovic and Joseph E. Stiglitz, 285–313. Washington, DC: World Bank.

Kanbur, Ravi, and Diganta Mukherjee. 2007. "Premature Mortality and Poverty Measurement." *Bulletin of Economic Research* 59 (4): 339–59.

Kanbur, Ravi, and Paul Shaffer, eds. 2007. *Experiences of Combining Qualitative and Quantitative Approaches in Poverty Analysis.* Special issue of *World Development* 35 (February).

Kanbur, Ravi, and Tony Venables. 2005. "Spatial Inequality and Development: Overview of UNU-WIDER Project." http://www.arts.cornell.edu/poverty/kanbur/WIDERProjectOverview.pdf.

Kanbur, Ravi, and Xiaobo Zhang. 2005. "Fifty Years of Regional Inequality in China: A Journey through Revolution, Reform and Openness." *Review of Development Economics* 9 (1): 87–106.

Klasen, Stephan. 1999. "Does Gender Inequality Reduce Economic Growth? Evidence from Cross-Country Regressions." http://siteresources.worldbank.org/INTGENDER/Resources/wp7.pdf.

Kuznets, Simon. 1955. "Economic Growth and Income Inequality." *American Economic Review* 45: 1–28.

Kynch, J., and A. K. Sen. 1983. "Indian Women: Well-being and Survival." *Cambridge Journal of Economics* 7 (3/4): 363–80.

Levy, Santiago. 2006. *Progress against Poverty: Sustaining Mexico's Progresa-Oportunidades Program*. Washington, DC: Brookings Institution Press.

Lewis, W. Arthur. 1954. "Economic Development with Unlimited Supplies of Labor." *Manchester School* 22: 139–81.

Ligon, E., and L. Schechter. 2003. "Measuring Vulnerability." *Economic Journal* 113 (486): 15–102.

Miguel, Edward. 2004. "Tribe or Nation? Nation-Building and Public Goods in Kenya versus Tanzania." *World Politics* 56 (3): 327–62.

Nissanke, Machiko, and Erik Thorbecke. 2006. *The Impact of Globalization on the World's Poor*. London: Palgrave Macmillan.

Persson, Torsten, and Guido Tabellini. 1994. "Is Inequality Harmful for Growth? Theory and Evidence." *American Economic Review* 84 (3): 600–621.

Piketty, Thomas. 2006. "The Kuznets Curve, Yesterday and Tomorrow." In *Understanding Poverty*, ed. Abhijit Banerjee, Roland Benabou, and Dilip Mookherjee. New York: Oxford University Press.

Ravallion, Martin. 1991. "Reaching the Rural Poor through Public Employment: Arguments, Experience, and Lessons from South Asia." *World Bank Research Observer* 6: 153–75.

———. 1997. "Can High-Inequality Developing Countries Escape Absolute Poverty?" *Economics Letters* 56: 51–57.

———. 2000. "On Decomposing Changes in Poverty into Growth and Redistribution Components." *Journal of Quantitative Economics* 16 (1): 105–18.

Rodrik, Dani. 1999. "Where Did All the Growth Go? External Shocks, Social Conflict and Growth Collapses." *Journal of Economic Growth* (December).

———. 2000. "Comment on 'Trade, Growth and Poverty,' by D. Dollar and A. Kraay." http://ksghome.harvard.edu/~drodrik/Rodrik%20on%20Dollar-Kraay.PDF.

Roemer, John E. 1998. *Equality of Opportunity*. Cambridge, MA: Harvard University Press.

Sen, Amartya. 1976. "Poverty: An Ordinal Approach to Measurement." *Econometrica* 44: 219–31.

————. 1980. "Equality of What?" In *Tanner Lectures on Human Values*, ed. S. McMurri Cambridge, UK: Cambridge University Press.

Stiglitz. Joseph E. 2003. *Globalization and Its Discontents*. New York: Norton.

Temple, Jonathan. 1998. "Initial Conditions, Social Capital, and Growth in Africa." *Journal of African Economies* 7 (3): 309–47.

Voitchovsky, Sara. 2004. "The Effect of Inequality on Growth: A Review of the Recent Empirical Literature." Oxford University. Processed.

Winters, L. Alan. 2000. "Trade Liberalization and Poverty." http://www.sussex.ac.uk/Units/PRU/wps/wp7.pdf.

World Bank. 2005. *World Development Report 2006: Equity and Development*. Washington, DC: World Bank; New York: Oxford University Press.

# CHAPTER 4

# Investment Efficiency and the Distribution of Wealth

*Abhijit V. Banerjee*

One of the potentially most attractive features of a market economy is that it puts investment decisions in the hands of those who have the talent and the drive to do that job well. Unfortunately, none of this is quite automatic; it all turns on assets markets doing their job well.

To appreciate the issue, consider an economy in which wealth has some distribution $G(w)$, with mean wealth $W$. This economy has only one good and one production technology. This technology requires a minimum investment of $K$, but then yields an output of $aK$ some time later, where $a$ is the talent level of the entrepreneur making the investment. Assume that $a$ is distributed, once again uniformly, between $\underline{a}$ and $\bar{a}$ and that talent is distributed independently of wealth.

I will speak about this investment as if the outputs were widgets, but there is nothing in this formulation that prevents them from being educated or healthy children. In other words, the basic logic applies as much to investment in human capital as to any other kind.

How do those whose wealth is below $K$ get to invest? The obvious answer is that they borrow. Suppose the interest rate is $r$. Then every entrepreneur

The author is grateful to Roberto Zagha for his encouragement.

who has a return of $a \geq 1 + r$ would be happy to borrow to invest. So assuming that there is not enough capital to make it worthwhile for everyone to invest—that is, the average wealth in the economy, $W$, is less than $K$, the minimum required investment—the interest rate will have to clear the capital market. Only those whose $a$ is high enough will invest, and the rest will lend them their wealth. In particular, the marginal investor will be such that

$$\frac{\bar{a} - a^m}{\bar{a} - \underline{a}} K = W, \tag{4.1}$$

or

$$a^m = \bar{a} - (\bar{a} - \underline{a})\frac{W}{K}, \tag{4.2}$$

and the market clearing interest rate will be $1 + a^m$.

To illustrate the workings of this model, I will set the value of W/K at 0.1. Is this a reasonable assumption? Davies et al. (2006) estimate the per capita wealth to be $1,100 in India ($144,000 in the United States), which means that average household wealth is about $5,500 (average family size is five). Of this, about 30 percent is real estate (Davies et al. 2006). The rest, about $4,000, is available for investment. I am therefore setting the minimum efficient scale in India at $40,000, which is equivalent to about $250,000 in U.S. prices. In the United States, $250,000 is the price of a very small business. Therefore, *prima facie*, there seems no reason to rule out a W/K ratio of 0.1 or even less.

If W/K were 1/10, for example, it would imply that the market clearing interest rate would have to go up to the point at which only the top 10 percent of the most talented people would invest. The average productivity of those who invest will be

$$A_{av} = \frac{\bar{a} + a^m}{2}$$
$$= \bar{a} - \frac{1}{20}(\bar{a} - \underline{a}). \tag{4.3}$$

The problem with this happy narrative is that it requires some people to borrow a very large multiple of their wealth (think of the person who has almost no wealth but invests an amount $K$). Suppose as an alternative that people can borrow only multiple $\lambda(r)$ of their wealth, where $r$ is the going interest rate. Most models of credit markets suggest that $\lambda$ should go down when $r$ goes up. This ought to make sense—lenders try to limit their lending to individuals because they are worried about not getting repaid, and they must worry more when the interest rate is higher and therefore more must be repaid.

The presence of credit constraints immediately means that not everyone has the option of investing: in order to reach $K$, one's wealth has to be at least

$K = (1 + \lambda(r))$. What is a plausible value for $\lambda(r)$ that applies to an average Indian firm? Unfortunately, not very much is known about this. The one exception is Timberg and Aiyar's 1984 study of nonbank lenders in India. They report that some of the Shikarpuri and Rastogi lenders set an explicit credit limit that was proportional to the borrower's net worth. Several lenders said they would lend no more than 25 percent of the borrower's net worth, though another said he would lend up to 33 percent—in other words, $\lambda = 1/3$ or less. I will assume that $\lambda$ is no more than 1. A $\lambda$ of 1 corresponds, for example, to the case in which an entrepreneur invests all of his assets in a factory and then is able to mortgage the full value of the factory to raise working capital. In this case, the minimum wealth for someone to start a business will be $K/2$, which, based on the assumptions above, is about $20,000.

How many people in India have $20,000 in wealth? Davies et al. (2006) report that the top 10 percent of Indians possess 53 percent of the wealth and the top 5 percent possess 38 percent. Thus, the average wealth of those between the 90th and 95th percentiles in the wealth distribution is three times the average overall wealth (assumed to be about $6,000[1]), or $18,000. Only those in the top 10 percent of the population can therefore start a business.

Because only the top 10 percent can start a business, as compared with the entire population when there are no credit constraints, the fraction of that segment that starts a business must be 10 times as large. This situation means dipping much deeper into the talent distribution. To see how much difference this makes, observe that the lowest $a$ person who starts a business in this case, $a^c$, must be given by

$$\frac{\bar{a} - a^c}{\bar{a} - \underline{a}} = 10 \frac{\bar{a} - a^m}{\bar{a} - \underline{a}}, \tag{4.4}$$

from which it follows that the average productivity of those who invest in this case will be

$$A_{av} = \bar{a} - \frac{1}{2}(\bar{a} - \underline{a}), \tag{4.5}$$

compared with

$$\bar{a} - \frac{1}{20}(\bar{a} - \underline{a}) \tag{4.6}$$

absent credit constraints.

If $\bar{a} = 2$ and $\underline{a} = 1$, the average productivity would go down from 1.95 to 1.5. As is well known, in this linear production model the growth rate of this economy is simply proportional to the average net productivity, $A_{av} - 1$.

---

1 Note that I am allowing people to borrow against their total wealth and not just their non-housing wealth.

Given the numbers I have assumed, this would imply that the growth rate is effectively halved in the presence of credit constraints.

## Why the Distribution of Wealth Matters

Suppose that the example in the previous section was altered so that everyone had equal wealth. Then, the imperfect credit markets notwithstanding, if the capital markets clear, the outcome would be as if the capital market were working perfectly. The reason is that if people are using the capital, they must include the most productive people (because they are willing to outbid everyone else to get the capital), who are the same people who would have done the investing absent credit constraints.[2] In other words, the credit constraints are hurting in that example because some less talented rich people are able to bid the capital away from some poorer but more gifted entrepreneurs (or, equivalently, the rich father of a mediocre student can bid away a seat in a good college from the poor father of the next would-be genius). This is what Caballero and Hammour (1998) call scrambling—the order of who gets to invest is all scrambled up.

Scrambling could actually be the best thing that could happen under these circumstances. I have been assuming all along that the capital market actually clears—that is, the interest rate falls enough to make $\lambda(r)$ large enough that borrowers are able to absorb the entire amount of available capital. But what if this implies that the interest rate paid to lenders has to be negative? Clearly if, for example, lenders prefer to stuff the money into their mattresses rather than lend it out at negative rates, the interest rate may not fall all the way to clear the market. Then things could be even worse: some of the capital might end up "invested" in the "mattress" technology, which presumably earns no return, even if all the potential investors are highly productive.

The central point is that lenders do not care what the borrower does with the money. What matters to them is that they get their money back with enough interest. If not, they would prefer not to lend or to lend to those potentially less productive people who are preferred borrowers. The distribution of wealth matters—and potentially can matter a lot, as described earlier—because being a preferred borrower might have a lot to do with the ownership of wealth.

## What Is Known about the Ability to Borrow?

A well-functioning credit market, as every student of basic economics knows, is one in which there is a single interest rate and everyone can borrow or lend as much as they want at that rate.

---

2  Actually in this case there are many equilibria, including the one I described earlier, but almost any perturbation of the model that allows the credit supply to respond even a little bit to productivity would pick out the one I chose.

How close are real markets to this idealized market? Chambhar is a market town in Sindh, on the east bank of the Indus River in Pakistan. In 1980–81, farmers from the area around Chambhar obtained most of their credit from about 60 professional moneylenders. Based on detailed data from 14 of these lenders and 60 of their clients (see Aleem 1990), these lenders charged borrowers an average interest rate of 78.5 percent. By contrast, if these farmers wanted to lend their money, the banking system would pay them only about 10 percent. However, it is possible that the farmers may not have been depositing their money in the banks. An alternative measure of the deposit rate relevant for these farmers is the opportunity cost of capital to these money lenders, which is 32.5 percent. In either case, it suggests a gap of at least 45 percentage points between the borrowing and lending rates. The borrowing rate also varied enormously across borrowers: the standard deviation of the interest rate was 38.14 percent, compared with an average lending rate of 78.5 percent. In other words, an interest rate of 2 percent and an interest rate of 150 percent are both within two standard deviations of the mean. One possibility is that these differences reflect differences in the default rate—that is, perhaps the expected repayment is the same for everybody because those who pay higher rates are more likely to default. Also, the expected repayment could be equal to the actual interest rate paid to the depositors if the default rate is high enough. However, default is actually very rare. The study gives default rates for each individual lender. The median default rate is between 1.5 and 2 percent, and the maximum is 10 percent.

The same pattern—high and variable borrowing rates, much lower deposit rates, and low default rates—also shows up in the *Reports on Informal Credit Markets in India: Summary* (Dasgupta 1989), which reports results from case studies commissioned by the Asian Development Bank and carried out under the aegis of the National Institute of Public Finance and Policy. For the urban sector, the data are based on various surveys of specific classes of informal lenders. For the broad class of nonbank financial intermediaries called finance corporations, it is reported that the maximum deposit rate for loans of less than a year is 12 percent, and the minimum lending rate is 48 percent. These corporations offer advances for a year or less at rates that vary from 48 percent a year to the utterly astronomical rate of 5 percent a day. The rates on loans of more than a year vary between 24 percent and 48 percent. Default, once again, is only a small part of the story. Default costs account for only 4 percent of total interest costs. The same report also relates that for hire-purchase companies in Delhi the deposit rate is 14 percent and the lending rate is at least 28 percent, and could be as high as 41 percent. Default costs are 3 percent of total interest costs.

Table 4.1 reports borrowing rates from the rural version of the same report. They are based on surveys of six villages in Kerala and Tamil Nadu carried out by the Centre for Development Studies in Trivandrum. Interest rates are high, but they are also variable, and the rich (those with Rs 100,000 or more in assets) receive most of the credit (nearly 60 percent) and pay a

Table 4.1 Asset Groups and Loans, Six Villages in Kerala and Tamil Nadu

| Asset group (Rs) | Average loan size (Rs) | Average interest rate (% per annum) | Cumulative proportion of credit |
|---|---|---|---|
| 0–5,000 | 799.84 | 50 | 10.23 |
| 5,000–10,000 | 116.67 | 120 | 10.79 |
| 10,000–15,000 | 633.37 | 35 | 12.31 |
| 15,000–20,000 | 285.91 | 71 | 13.91 |
| 20,000–30,000 | 668.00 | 104 | 21.93 |
| 30,000–50,000 | 652.50 | 58 | 27.15 |
| 50,000–100,000 | 1,267.83 | 48 | 41.34 |
| 100,000 and above | 4,075.00 | 33 | 100.00 |

*Source:* Dasgupta 1989.

relatively low rate (33 percent), while those with assets between Rs 20,000 and Rs 30,000 pay rates of 104 percent and receive only 8 percent of the credit. Not reported in the table, the average interest rate charged by professional moneylenders (who provide 45.61 percent of the credit) in these surveys is about 52 percent. Although the average deposit rate is not reported, the maximum from all the case studies is 24 percent, and the maximum in four out of the eight case studies is no more than 14 percent. Within the category of professional moneylenders, about half of the loans are made at rates of 60 percent or more, but another 40 percent or so are made at rates below 36 percent. Default rates are higher than in the urban sector, but still cannot explain more than 23 percent of the interest costs (see also Swaminathan 1991).

The same Asian Development Bank project that reported interest rates in India also surveyed borrowers in Thailand. Ghate (1992), who reports on that survey, finds interest rates of 2–3 percent a month in the more developed south, but much higher rates—5–7 percent a month (i.e., between 80 and 125 percent a year)—in the north and northwest. Note also that 5 percent a month and 7 percent a month are hardly the same rate.

None of these facts is necessarily surprising. Contract enforcement in developing countries is often difficult, and, in particular, courts are reluctant to punish recalcitrant borrowers (see Djankov et al. 2003). As a result, lenders often expend significant resources on ensuring that their loans are repaid. It is plausible that these resources drive a wedge between the borrowing rate and the lending rate. Indeed, a paper by Aleem (1990) actually calculates the amount of resources spent by lenders on monitoring borrowers and shows that they are enough to explain the nearly 50 percentage point gap between the lending and borrowing rates in his data. Moreover, it is easy to imagine that borrowers who are easier to monitor will enjoy better rates, which would explain why lending rates vary so much.

Taken together, these observations make clear that there are favored borrowers. The fact that borrowing rates and lending rates are so different, for example, means that people have very different returns from investing in their own firms and lending to others: the most preferred borrower typically is one's own self. Richer people thus have a strong reason to invest more. The same argument also implies that those with strong social connections with wealthy people will be in a better position to invest than others, because lenders (those who have wealth to lend) presumably have more leverage over such connected borrowers. More generally, the fact that interest rates vary so much means that some people will invest even when their returns are relatively low, whereas others with higher returns will not invest. Because richer people typically have both lower interest rates and more lax borrowing constraints, there is, in particular, a tendency toward overinvestment by the rich and underinvestment by the poor, although this observation will have to be qualified in light of the comments I make in the penultimate section of this chapter.

## Mitigating Factors

The world described in the opening example in this chapter is, of course, very stylized in many different ways. I have assumed, for one thing, that those who cannot invest at least $K$ get nothing from their investment. This is obviously an exaggeration: the world, and especially the developing world, is full of very small businesses. The presence of these small businesses means that an alternative now dominates lending to the most inept entrepreneurs. However, in view of how small these firms tend to be, it is not clear how much this alternative helps. Moreover, there is some disagreement about how productive these businesses are, and therefore about their capacity to absorb capital.

Similarly, the assumption that there is no point in investing more than $K$ means that many rich people cannot invest as much as they could. If the rich can invest more without facing significant diminishing returns, then a lot more capital would find productive uses.

I also have assumed that richer people are not more likely to be more talented than poorer people. One does not need to believe in the innate superiority of the rich to find this implausible; after all, the fact that more able people tend to make more money must, over the medium run, make them richer than the average person. Caselli and Gennaoli (2005), who calibrate a model to assess the importance of this mechanism, conclude that in the long run it does serve to limit the effects of credit constraints. However, even then productivity remains 20 percent below what it would be, absent credit constraints. In more recent work, Buera, Kaboski, and Shin (2008) conclude that the steady output distortion could be much larger (50 percent) if there are fixed costs.

Finally, credit constraints are an inducement to save. By saving more, people not only receive the additional resources from their own saving but also are in a position to borrow more. In other words, they have the incentive to save their way out of whatever inefficient situation they might be in. However, after reviewing data from household surveys from 13 poor to middle-income countries, Banerjee and Duflo (2007) conclude that the poor do not save as much as they are able. The average poor family spends very substantial fractions of its total expenditures (more than 15 percent in many countries) on a combination of alcohol, cigarettes, sugar,[3] and entertainment, all of which it could, in principle, save without compromising its nutrition or any of its other investments. One reason why such a family may be reluctant to save is the logic of credit constraints: saving only works if one is close enough to the point at which the extra resources start to pay off. In the world of my opening example, if a person is so far from $K$ that he cannot expect to get anywhere close to it in his lifetime even if he saves everything he earns, he will not want to take it on (see Buera 2008 for a formalization of this idea). Banerjee and Mullainathan (2008) suggest that the view of savings implicit in this claim may be somewhat naive, at least where the poor are concerned. We argue that for the poor, many things that everyone else takes for granted—an extra cup of tea, a glass or two of wine, a surprise present for a child—is a temptation they are meant to resist. For this reason, for them saving is a particular challenge.

## Reinforcing Factors

So far I have been assuming that the only constraint on investment is lack of access to credit, which creates the impression that everyone wants nothing more than an opportunity to invest. This is neither *a priori* obvious nor clear in the data. For various reasons people might be reluctant to invest even if they had the capital. The reasons are described in the following sections.

### Lack of Insurance

Starting a business typically involves bearing some risk. Insurance markets, of which the stock market is an important example, exist in part to allow business owners to reduce the amount of risk they have to bear by selling a part of their revenue streams to others. Such markets also allow owners to get rid of any other risks—such as a health expenditure risk—that might discourage them from taking on the additional risk implied by starting a new business.[4] Exposure to risk might be a particular problem for the poor, because for them failure can mean starvation or worse. Yet formal insurance markets typically do not reach out to the poor,[5] primarily because substantial transaction costs are involved, especially compared with what the poor can pay. And only the biggest companies are able to sell their assets

---

3  It is true that sugar is a source of calories, which the poor need, but there are many much cheaper (and healthier) ways to get those calories.

4  For a wide class of standard preferences, including both constant relative and absolute risk aversion, an increase in background risk causes investors to take less risk.

5  See, for example, the evidence presented in Banerjee and Duflo (2006).

on the stock market, largely because of the (rather elaborate) regulatory requirements for being a traded company.

The poor therefore rely heavily on informal insurance, which is another name for a tacit or explicit agreement to help each other out in times of need. The question is, how effective are these arrangements? The ideal insurance market is one in which people bear no avoidable risks. In a setting in which a single village constitutes a separate insurance market closed to the rest of the world (so that only people in the village can insure other people in the village in some kind of mutual insurance arrangement), this comes down to the requirement that individual consumption should respond only to aggregate (village-level) income fluctuations and not to fluctuations in the income of specific individuals. Or to put it in less abstract terms, income fluctuations should not translate into fluctuations in one's own consumption as long as aggregate consumption is unchanged. Because what an individual does has very little impact on aggregate uncertainty, when insurance markets work well, risk considerations should not have a significant impact on the choices made by people, whatever their wealth.

Although a perfect insurance market is more complex than a perfect credit market and thus harder to detect, some attempts have been made to test the prediction about the irrelevance of fluctuations in personal income. The Côte d'Ivoire Living Standards Measurement Surveys provide panel data on the income and consumption of up to 800 households. Each household is tracked for two consecutive years (1985–86 or 1986–87). The relation between changes is reported in table 4.2 separately for the three main regions and separately for 1985–86 and 1986–87. The first row of the first panel for each year reports the basic correlation between income and consumption: a fall in income always hurts consumption, though the coefficient varies between a low of 0.09 (a $1 reduction in income means that consumption goes down by 9 percent) to a high of 0.46. In other words, insurance is far from perfect. However, this potentially quite strong positive correlation may be a result of comparing across villages. If those who gained income all lived in one village and those who lost lived in the other, and there were no informal insurance links that cut across villages, then the fact that some people gained in another village would have no consequence for those whose income went down—everyone who could have helped them also lost income, and thus they are unable to get much help and end up with lower consumption. If this were true, the positive correlation between income shocks and consumption shocks should vanish (or at least shrink) when one compares only people within the same village. I find no evidence for this—as the next pair of columns shows, the coefficients remain almost exactly the same when comparing within the village.[6]

Not all the evidence is quite so pessimistic. Townsend (1994) uses detailed household-level data from four villages intensively studied by the International Crop Research Institute in the Semi-Arid Tropics (ICRISAT) in India to see whether perfect insurance within the village is consistent

---

6   See Deaton (1997) for more details.

Table 4.2 OLS and IV Estimates of the Effects of Income on Consumption, Three Regions of Côte d'Ivoire

| | West forest | | East forest | | Savannah | | All rural | |
|---|---|---|---|---|---|---|---|---|
| | OLS 1985–86 | | | | | | | |
| No dummies | 0.290 | (6.2) | 0.153 | (3.2) | 0.368 | (5.8) | 0.259 | (8.8) |
| Village dummies | 0.265 | (5.7) | 0.155 | (3.5) | 0.373 | (5.7) | 0.223 | (7.7) |
| Own income | 0.265 | (5.3) | 0.155 | (3.2) | 0.373 | (5.6) | 0.223 | (7.1) |
| Village income | 0.199 | (1.4) | −0.031 | (0.2) | −0.050 | (0.2) | 0.252 | (3.0) |
| | IVE 1985–86 | | | | | | | |
| No dummies | 0.192 | (3.9) | −0.003 | (0.1) | 0.271 | (4.0) | 0.126 | (4.0) |
| Village dummies | 0.171 | (3.5) | 0.029 | (0.6) | 0.270 | (3.8) | 0.107 | (3.4) |
| Own income | 0.171 | (3.2) | 0.029 | (0.5) | 0.270 | (3.7) | 0.107 | (3.1) |
| Village income | 0.161 | (1.1) | −0.417 | (2.0) | 0.020 | (0.1) | 0.144 | (1.6) |
| | OLS 1986–87 | | | | | | | |
| No dummies | 0.458 | (8.8) | 0.162 | (5.3) | 0.168 | (4.0) | 0.239 | (10.4) |
| Village dummies | 0.424 | (8.1) | 0.173 | (5.6) | 0.164 | (3.8) | 0.235 | (10.1) |
| Own income | 0.424 | (7.9) | 0.173 | (5.3) | 0.164 | (3.8) | 0.235 | (9.7) |
| Village income | 0.350 | (2.0) | −0.094 | (1.0) | 0.061 | (0.4) | 0.039 | (0 5) |
| | IVE 1986–87 | | | | | | | |
| No dummies | 0.418 | (7.8) | 0.090 | (2.8) | 0.088 | (2.0) | 0.177 | (7.4) |
| Village dummies | 0.388 | (7.3) | 0.105 | (3.2) | 0.087 | (1.9) | 0.177 | (7.3) |
| Own income | 0.388 | (7.1) | 0.105 | (3.1) | 0.087 | (1.9) | 0.177 | (7.0) |
| Village income | 0.353 | (2.0) | −0.127 | (1.3) | 0.015 | (0.1) | −0.002 | (0.0) |

*Source:* Deaton 1997.

*Note:* Absolute values of *t*-values are shown in brackets. The first row of each panel shows the coefficient on income change of a regression of consumption changes on income changes. The second row reports the same result when village dummies are included in the regression. The third and fourth rows show the estimates from a regression of consumption changes on individual household and village average changes in income. The IV regressions use the change in the value of cash income, individual and village average, as instruments for total income, including imputations; the *t*-values on these instruments in the first-stage regressions are large, typically larger than 30. Because village dummies "sweep out" the village means, the coefficients—but not the standard errors—are identical in the second and third rows of each panel.

with the evidence. He finds that although the data do reject the exact prediction, they do not miss by very much. His evidence thus suggests that villagers do insure each other to a considerable extent. Movements in individual consumption in his data seem largely uncorrelated with movements in income.

However, later work by Townsend based on data he collected in Thailand turned out to be less encouraging (see Townsend 1995). Some villages seemed to be much more effective than others in providing insurance

Investment Efficiency and the Distribution of Wealth

to their residents. Townsend describes in detail how insurance arrangements differ across villages. One village will have a web of well-functioning, risk-sharing institutions, whereas the situations in other villages are different. In one village the institutions exist but are dysfunctional; in another village they are nonexistent; and in a third village, close to the road, there seems to be no risk-sharing whatsoever, even within families.[7]

As it is for credit, it is possible that the failure of insurance has something to do with informational asymmetries. It is not easy to insure someone against a shock that he alone observes, because he has every incentive to always claim that things have gone badly. However, as Duflo and Udry (2004) demonstrate, spouses in Côte d'Ivoire do not seem to be willing to insure each other fully against the rainfall shocks that affect them differentially. Because rainfall is observable, the problem has to be elsewhere. One possibility is that the problem is limited commitment. People may be happy to claim what was promised to them when it is their turn to be paid and then default when it comes time for them to pay. This situation may arise easily in a setting in which the social relations between the set of people who are insuring each other are not particularly close. Perhaps that is why Townsend finds no insurance in the village closest to the road.

## The Limitations of the Land Market

The land market is crucial for investing for the simple reason that starting a business requires real estate. Land is especially an issue for the poor, because agriculture is one of the industries on which the poor tend to concentrate. Moreover, land is often the one asset they own.

The ideal land market is one in which people can buy or lease as much land as they want for as long as they want at a price that depends only on the quality of the land (and the length of the lease). Moreover, the lease should be at a fixed rent, so that the lessor is the residual claimant to the products of the land. The fact that land can be freely bought and sold ensures that no particular advantage or disadvantage accrues to owning land in relation to any other asset of comparable value. The fact that the lessor is the residual claimant means that the land is put to optimal use.

In practice, both conditions fail systematically. Many developing (and some developed countries) countries have regulations about who can buy land and how much or how little. Binswanger, Deininger, and Feder (1995) argue that almost every developing country has passed through a phase in which its regulations on land ownership were intended to concentrate land ownership. By contrast, Besley and Burgess (2000) provide a list of regulations from different states in India, each an attempt to limit the concentration of ownership of land. It is also often unclear who has the right to sell a particular plot of land, because frequently no single person or family has a clear, undisputed legal title to the land. This situation, in turn, reflects the

---

7  Fafchamps and Lund (2003) find that in the Philippines, households are much better insured against some shocks than against others. In particular, they seem to be poorly insured against health risk, a finding corroborated by Gertler and Gruber (2002) in Indonesia.

importance of encroachments and land grabs in the evolution of land rights, as well as the importance of custom in governing land relations, especially in Africa. The recent popularity of land titling as a social intervention is a direct consequence of the growing recognition of this fact.

Where lease contracts exist, they are not always of the fixed-rent type, at least when the land is used for cultivation. Many countries, including the United States, have a long tradition of an alternative contractual form, sharecropping. Under sharecropping, the farmer receives only a fraction of the products of the land, but he does not have to pay a fixed rent. As Alfred Marshall pointed out more than a hundred years ago, this arrangement weakens incentives and reduces the productivity of the land, but the near universality of sharecropping suggests that it is a response to a real need. There is some disagreement among economists about the exact nature of that need,[8] but it is plausible that it is related to the fact that farmers are often poor, and making them pay the full rent when their crop does poorly is probably not desirable.

Finally, leaseholds in developing countries tend to be relatively short-lived—the norm is either a year or a season. Longer leases are not unknown but are rare, perhaps reflecting the fact that custom rather than law secures most of these leases. Perhaps it is too much to rely on custom to enforce leases of arbitrary length.

### Peculiarities of the Family

One thing that makes human capital different is that a lot of the decisions are made by parents (or other family members) on behalf of their children. In other words, those who are making these decisions are often different from those who embody the human capital. Gary Becker's classic formulation of the problem of investment in human capital avoids this problem by assuming that the family can borrow against the child's future income, thereby turning the problem into a conventional investment decision. The amount invested in that scenario will not depend on families' wherewithal.

In the more plausible circumstance in which parents cannot borrow against their children's future income, they might still hope that when the child grows up and reaps the benefits of their investment, he might pay them back by taking care of them in their old age, but they know that he has no legal obligation to do so. If he does, it is either because he feels for his parents or because society expects him to do so. But then it is not clear that he would feel comfortable in entirely abandoning his parents if they failed to educate him. This is not to say that parents do not benefit by making their children richer, or even that they do not vicariously enjoy their children's success, but to suggest that investment in human capital may be driven as much by parents' sense of what is the right thing to do as by any calculation of costs and benefits.

Once one accepts this premise, it becomes clear that children's human capital is not very different from any other consumption good, and

---

8   See Banerjee (2000) for a discussion of the alternative views.

therefore richer families will tend to invest more in their children's health and education. Also, as a consumption decision, a human capital decision may be more a product of culture and tradition than a cold calculation of benefits. This is not to say that the benefits are irrelevant, but that the responsiveness to them may not be as large as one might have expected.

## The Evidence on Underinvestment

The argument so far has been that there are many reasons why those who do not have enough wealth of their own might underinvest. Is this actually a real issue in the world?

### Evidence from Industry and Trade

Direct estimates of the marginal product of capital suggest that there are in fact a lot of unexploited investment opportunities. Figure 4.1 plots a non-parametric relationship between firm earnings and firm capital in Mexico (McKenzie and Woodruff 2006, table 1). Even ignoring the astronomical returns at the very low values of firm capital, this figure suggests huge returns to capital for these small firms. For firms with less than $200 invested, the rate of return reaches 15 percent a month, well above the informal interest rates available in pawn shops or through microcredit programs (on the order of 3 percent a month). Estimated rates of return decline with investment, but remain high (7–10 percent a month for firms with investment of between $200 and $500 and 5 percent for firms with investment of between $500 and $1,000). These firms are therefore all too small, given that the real interest rates on savings in Mexico are substantially less than 10 percent a month.

Trade credit is an important form of credit everywhere and perhaps especially where the formal institutions of the credit market are underdeveloped.

Figure 4.1 Parametric Returns to $0–$1,000 in Capital, Mexico

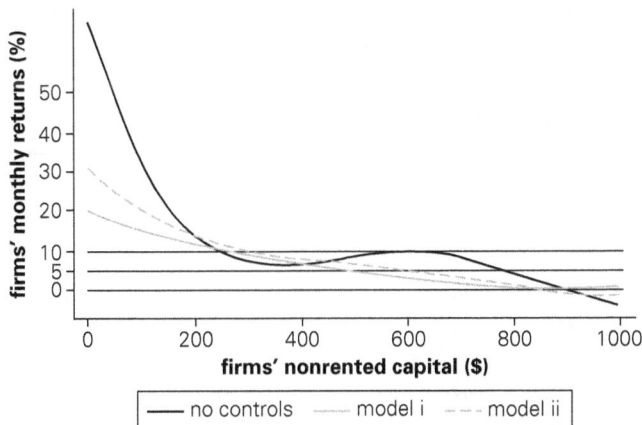

*Source:* McKenzie and Woodruff 2006.

Fisman (2001) looks at the relation between access to trade credit and capacity utilization in a sample of 545 firms in Côte d'Ivoire, Kenya, Tanzania, Zambia, and Zimbabwe and finds that firms that receive trade credit from its three main suppliers (on average about one out of the three suppliers provides trade credit) have 10 percent better capacity utilization than firms that have no trade credit. Moreover, the relation is much stronger in industries in which it is important to carry large inventories.

However, such studies present serious methodological issues. The basic problem is that investment levels are likely to be correlated with omitted variables. For example, in a world without credit constraints investment will be positively correlated with the expected returns to investment, generating a positive "ability bias" (Olley and Pakes 1996). McKenzie and Woodruff (2006) attempt to control for managerial ability by including the firm owner's wage in previous employment, but this goes only part of the way if individuals choose to enter self-employment precisely because their expected productivity in self-employment is much larger than their productivity in an employed job. Conversely, there could be a negative ability bias if capital is allocated to firms to prevent their failure.

Banerjee and Duflo (2003a) take advantage of a change in the definition of the "priority sector" in India to circumvent these difficulties (Banerjee and Duflo 2003a). All banks in India are required to lend at least 40 percent of their net credit to the priority sector, which includes small-scale industry, at an interest rate of no more than 4 percent above banks' prime lending rate. In January 1998, the limit on total investment in plants and machinery that a firm had to meet to qualify for inclusion in the small-scale industry category was raised from Rs 6.5 million to Rs 30 million. We first show that after the reforms newly eligible firms (those with investment between Rs 6.5 million and Rs 30 million) received on average larger increments in their working capital limit than smaller firms. We then show that the sales and profits increased faster for these firms during the same period. Putting these two facts together, we use the variation in the eligibility rule over time to construct instrumental variable estimates of the impact of working capital on sales and profits. After computing a nonsubsidized cost of capital, we estimate that the returns to capital in these firms must be at least 94 percent.

A very different kind of evidence of underinvestment is that many people pay the very high interest rates reported in the previous subsection. Because this money typically goes into financing trade and industry, my presumption is that the people borrowing at these rates of often 50 percent or more must have a marginal product of capital that is even higher. And yet the average marginal product in developing countries seems nowhere close to 50 percent. One way to arrive at the average of the marginal products is to look at the incremental capital output ratio (ICOR) for the country as a whole. The ICOR measures the increase in output predicted by a one-unit increase in capital stock. It is calculated by extrapolating from the past experience of the country and assumes that the next unit of capital will be used as efficiently (or inefficiently) as the last one. The inverse of the

ICOR therefore gives an upper bound for the average marginal product of the economy—it is an upper bound because calculation of the ICOR does not control for the effect of the increases in the other factors of production, which also contributes to the increase in output.[9] The International Monetary Fund (IMF) estimates, that for the late 1990s, the ICOR was over 4.5 for India and 3.7 for Uganda. The implied upper bound on the average marginal product was 22 percent for India and 27 percent for Uganda.

The fact that many firms in India have a marginal product of 50 percent or more while the average marginal product is only 22 percent or so is strong *prima facie* evidence of the misallocation of capital. The firms with a marginal product of 50 percent and more are clearly too small, while other firms (the ones who bring the average down to 22 percent) must in some sense be too large.

Finally, De Mel, McKenzie, and Woodruff (2007) estimate the returns to small enterprises in Sri Lanka from a randomized experiment in which they offer a random sample of firms either SL Rs 10,000 or SL Rs 20,000 as capital infusion. They find average monthly returns in the 4–5 percent range, although this return does not correct for the cost of any additional work time put in by the owner or his or her family members (who are not directly paid) because of the inflow of the capital (probably not huge). This situation should be compared with the annual real return on bank loans, which was on the order of 3–7.5 percent in Sri Lanka at that time. Clearly, there is no evidence that the two returns were equalized.

**Evidence from Agriculture**

There is also direct evidence of very high rates of returns on productive investment in agriculture. In the forest-savannah area of southern Ghana, cocoa cultivation has been waning for many years because of swollen shoot disease. Cocoa is being replaced by a cassava-maize intercrop. Recently, pineapple cultivation for export to Europe has offered farmers in this area a new opportunity. In 1997 and 1998, more than 200 households in four clusters in this area, cultivating 1,070 plots, were surveyed every six weeks. Figure 4.2 reports the distribution of profits (in 1,000 cedis) for the traditional cassava-maize intercrop and for pineapples based on this survey (Goldstein and Udry 1999, figure 4). Pineapple production exhibits first-order stochastic dominance over the traditional intercrop, and the average return associated with switching from the traditional cassava-maize intercrop to pineapple is estimated to be in excess of 1,200 percent! Yet only 190 out of 1,070 plots were used for pineapple. According to Goldstein and Udry (1999, 38), "The virtually unanimous response to the question 'Why are you not farming pineapple?' provided by our respondents was 'I don't have the money,'" though some heterogeneity between those who have switched to pineapple and those who have not cannot be ruled out entirely.

---

9   The implicit assumption that the other factors of production are growing is probably reasonable for most developing countries, except perhaps those in Africa.

Figure 4.2 Distribution of Profits per Hectare

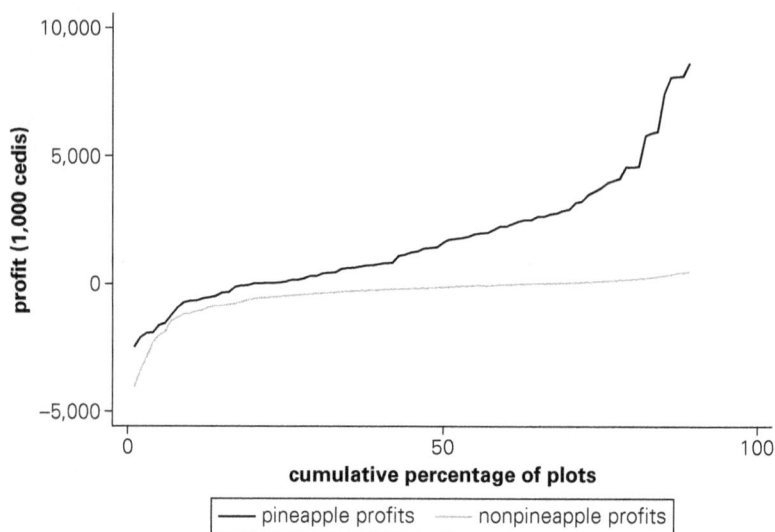

Source: Goldstein and Udry 1999, figure 4.

Evidence from experimental farms suggests that in Africa the rates of return from the use of chemical fertilizer (for maize) also would be high. However, this evidence may not be realistic if the ideal conditions of an experimental farm cannot be reproduced on actual farms. Foster and Rosenzweig (1995) show, for example, that the returns to switching to high-yielding varieties (HYVs) were actually low in the early years of the Green Revolution in India, and even negative for farmers without an education, despite the fact that these varieties had been selected for having high yields under the proper conditions. But they required complementary inputs of the correct quantities and timing. If farmers were not able or did not know how to supply those inputs, the rates of return were actually low.

Chemical fertilizer, however, is not a new technology, and the proper way to use it is well understood. To estimate the rates of return to using fertilizer in actual farms in Kenya, Duflo, Kremer, and Robinson (2008), in collaboration with a small nongovernmental organization (NGO), set up small-scale, randomized trials on people's farms. Each farmer in the trial delimited two small plots. On one randomly selected plot, a field officer from the NGO helped the farmer apply fertilizer. Other than that, the farmers continued to farm as usual. They found that their rates of return from using a small amount of fertilizer varied from 169 percent to 500 percent, depending on the year.

Evidence of a different type of underinvestment in agriculture is illustrated in table 4.3. In the so-called negative farm size–productivity relationship, the idea is that the smallest farms tend to be the most productive. The columns of the table compare the productivity of small and large farms in Brazil, Pakistan, and Malaysia (Berry and Cline 1979). The gap is enormous: a factor of 6.0 in Brazil and a factor of 2.75 in Pakistan. It is smaller

Table 4.3 Farm-Size Productivity Differences, Selected Countries

| Farm size[a] | Northeast Brazil[b] | Punjab, Pakistan[c] | Muda, Malaysia[d] |
|---|---|---|---|
| Small farm (hectares) | 563 (10.0–49.9) | 274 (5.1–10.1) | 148 (0.7–1.0) |
| Largest farm (hectares) | 100 (500+) | 100 (20+) | 100 (5.7–11.3) |

*Source:* Berry and Cline 1979.
a. 100 = largest farm size compared with second smallest farm size. Second smallest farm size used in calculations to avoid abnormal productivity results often recorded for the smallest plots.
b. Index taken using average gross receipts/areas for size group 2 (small) and 6 (large), averaged for all zones excluding zone F, where sugarcane and cocoa plantations skew productivity average for large farms.
c. Index taken using value added per cultivated acre for second smallest size group and largest.
d. Index taken from value added in agriculture/relong (0.283 ha = 1 relong).

(only 1.5) in Malaysia, but then the large farm in Malaysia is not very large. Taken together, the table provides strong *prima facie* evidence that markets are somehow not allocating the right amount of land to those who currently farm the smaller plots.

The problem with this kind of evidence is that it ignores the many reasons why the bigger farm may be inherently less productive—worse soil quality, for example. However, similar but somewhat less dramatic results show up even after I control for differences in land quality. Figure 4.3 shows the results of such an exercise. Each straight line in this figure represents the relationship between the profit-wealth ratio and a measure of underlying risk, the standard deviation of the date of monsoon onset, for four different size categories of farms (Rosenzweig and Binswanger 1993). The data were collected from the Indian ICRISAT villages. The first observation about the figure is that the profit-wealth ratio is highest for the smallest farms, and when risk is comparatively low, the gap is more than three to one. Because wealth includes the value of the land, the measure implicitly takes into account differences in the quality of the land, as long as land prices are a reasonable measure of land quality.

The second notable fact about this figure is that all the lines slope downward. When risk goes up, the average return goes down. In part this decline may be inevitable, but it also may reflect the fact that lack of insurance encourages people to avoid risky (but remunerative) choices.[10] This is consistent with the fact that profitability falls faster for the poorer farmers (who are less able to self-insure) as the risk goes up. Specifically, an increase of one standard deviation in the coefficient of variation of rainfall leads to a 35 percent reduction in the profit of poor farmers, a 15 percent reduction in the profit of median farmers, and no reduction in the profit of rich farmers. The study by Rosenzweig and Binswanger (1993) also finds that input choices are affected by variability in rainfall and that,

---

10 Some of the effects of lack of insurance may be quite subtle. Banerjee and Newman (1998) argue, for example, that the availability of insurance in one location (the village) and its unavailability in another (the city) may lead to inefficient migration decisions, because some individuals with high potential in the city may prefer to stay in the village to remain insured.

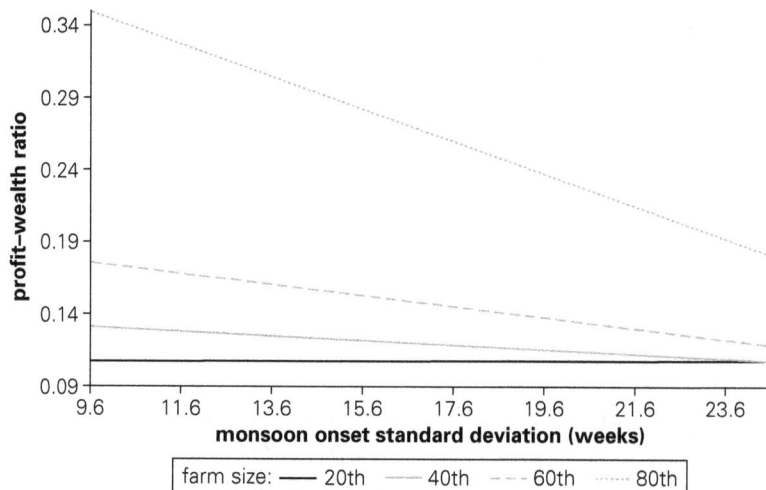

Figure 4.3 Profit-Wealth Ratios and Weather Variability, by Wealth and Class, Indian ICRISAT Villages

*Source:* Rosenzweing and Binswanger 1993.
*Note:* The onset date of the monsoon was the single most powerful of eight different rainfall characteristics to explain the gross value of farm output.

in particular, poor farmers make less efficient input choices in a risky environment.

In related work, Morduch (1993) investigates how the anticipation of credit constraint affects the decision to invest in HYV seeds. Specifically, he splits the sample into two groups: one group of landholders who are expected to have the ability to smooth their consumption, and one group that owns little land and is expected *a priori* to be constrained. He finds that the more constrained group devotes a considerably smaller fraction of its land to HYV seeds for rice and castor.

Another consequence of lack of insurance is that it may lead households to use productive assets as buffer stocks and consumption smoothing devices, resulting in inefficient investment. Rosenzweig and Wolpin (1993) argue that bullocks, an essential productive asset in agriculture, serve this purpose in rural India. Using the ICRISAT data covering three villages in semiarid areas in India, they show that bullocks, which constitute a large part of the households' liquid wealth (50 percent for the poorest farmers), are bought and sold quite frequently. Indeed, 86 percent of households had either bought or sold a bullock in the previous year, and a third of the household-year observations are characterized by a purchase or sale. They also find that sales tend to occur when profit realizations are high, whereas purchases take place when profit realizations are low. Because transactions in land are rare, bullocks are probably used for consumption smoothing. Recognizing that everybody needs bullocks at about the same time and that bullocks are hard to rent out, Rosenzweig and Wolpin estimate that, to maximize production efficiency, each household should own two bullocks at any given point in time. The data suggest that poor and midsize farmers considerably underinvest in bullocks, presumably because of the borrowing constraints and their inability to borrow and accumulate financial assets to smooth consumption. Almost half of the households in any given year own no bullock (most of the others own two).[11] Using the estimates derived from a structural model in which households use bullocks as a consumption smoothing device in an environment in which bullocks cannot be rented and no financial asset is available to smooth consumption, Rosenzweig and Wolpin simulate a policy in which farmers are given a certain nonfarm income of Rs 500 (which represents 20 percent of the mean household food consumption) every period. This policy would raise the average bullock holding to 1.56 and considerably reduce its variability because of two effects: the income is less variable, and, by increasing their income, "prudent" farmers (farmers with declining absolute risk aversion) become more willing to bear the agricultural risk.

There is also compelling evidence that sharecropping tenants are less productive than farmers who own their land. Binswanger and Rosenzweig (1986) and Shaban (1987) reveal that, controlling for farmers' fixed effect (that is, comparing the productivity of owner-cultivated and farmed land for farmers who cultivate both their own land and that of others) and for land characteristics, productivity is 30 percent lower in sharecropped plots. Shaban also shows that all the inputs are lower on sharecropped land, including short-term investments (fertilizer and seeds). He finds as well systematic differences in land quality (owner-cultivated land has a higher price per hectare), which could in part reflect long-term investment. In related work, Laffont and Matoussi (1995) use data from Tunisia to report that a shift from sharecropping to owner cultivation raises output by 33 percent, and moving from a short-term tenancy contract to a longer-term contract increases output by 27.5 percent.[12]

### Evidence from Human Capital

According to the report of the Commission for Macroeconomics and Health (WHO 2001), the returns to investing in health are on the order of 500 percent. However, this number is based on cross-country growth regressions and is not as easy to interpret as what would actually happen if someone invested an extra dollar in health. That being said, some specific health interventions clearly have had enormous private and social returns. For example, there is substantial experimental evidence that iron and vitamin A supplements increase productivity at relatively low cost.

---

11  The underinvestment on average and the situation in which one set of farmers owns too many bullocks and another owns too few is probably attributable to the fact that owning more than two bullocks is very inefficient for production—no small adjustment is possible at the margin.

12  Another piece of relevant evidence is the effects of titling nonagricultural land. Field (2003) provides evidence from a land titling program in the slums of urban Peru that suggests that the lack of a clear title to the land on which a household has built its home reduces the ability of the household members to work outside. Field hypothesizes that the reason is that someone has to be home to defend the untitled property from expropriation by others. However, she does not find any evidence that land titling improves access to credit.

Basta, Karyadi, and Scrimshaw (1979) studied an iron supplementation experiment conducted among rubber tree tappers in Indonesia. Baseline health measures indicated that 45 percent of the study population was anemic. The intervention combined an iron supplement and an incentive (for both treatment and control groups) to take the pill on time. Work productivity among those who received the treatment increased by 20 percent (or $132 a year) at a cost per worker-year of $0.50. Even taking into account the cost of the incentive ($11 a year), the intervention suggests extremely high rates of returns. Thomas et al. (2003) obtain lower, but still high, estimates in a larger experiment, also conducted in Indonesia. They find that iron supplementation experiments in Indonesia reduced anemia, increased the probability of participating in the labor market, and increased the earnings of self-employed workers. They estimate that for self-employed males the benefits of iron supplementation amount to $40 a year at a cost of $6 a year.[13]

A cost-benefit analysis of a deworming program in Kenya reports estimates of a similar order of magnitude (Miguel and Kremer 2004). Taking into account externalities (because of the contagious nature of worms), the program led to an average increase in school participation of 0.14 years. If one uses a reasonable figure for the returns to a year of education, this additional schooling will lead to a benefit of $30 over the life of the child at a cost of $0.49 per child per year. Not all interventions have the same rates of return, however. A study of Chinese cotton mill workers found that interventions led to a significant increase in fitness but no corresponding increase in productivity (Li et al. 1994).

Measured returns on private investment in education tend not to be quite so high. After our survey of the cross-country evidence on Mincerian returns, Banerjee and Duflo (2006) conclude that "using the preferred data, the Mincerian rates of returns seem to vary little across countries: The mean rate of returns is 8.96, with a standard deviation of 2.2. The maximum rate of returns to education (Pakistan) is 15.4 percent, and the minimum is 2.7 percent (Italy)." And yet most of the educational benefits of deworming would be captured by a child whose parents are willing to spend $0.50 on the deworming medicine. This investment clearly offers a return that is much higher than the measured Mincerian returns at affordable absolute cost, though they are not strictly comparable because deworming does not require the child to spend more years in school, but helps her get more out of the years she is already spending in school. However, when the deworming medicine was offered free to the children, the take-up was only 57 percent. In this sense, it is clear that at least some of the causes of underinvestment have to be sought in the way the family makes decisions rather than in the lack of resources.

---

13 This number takes into account the fact that only 20 percent of the Indonesian population is iron-deficient. The private returns of iron supplementation for someone who knows he or she is iron-deficient—which can be determined from a simple finger prick—would be $200.

All of this evidence suggests that markets are imperfect and wealth matters for investment. What do the data have to say about the relation between investment and the distribution of wealth? Several economists have tried to look at this question by examining the cross-country relation between inequality and growth (growth is presumably what investment is meant to achieve). Some have estimated a long-run equation, with growth between, say, 1960 and 1990 regressed on income in 1960, a set of control variables, and inequality in 1960 (see Benabou 1996 for a survey). Estimating these equations tended to generate negative coefficients for inequality. However, there are obvious concerns about whether such a relation could be driven entirely by omitted variables. To address this problem, Li and Zhou (1998) and Forbes (2000) use the Deininger and Squire data set to focus on the impact of changes in inequality over a five-year period on changes in growth over the next five years. The results change rather dramatically: the coefficient of inequality in this specification is positive and significant. Barro (2000) uses the same short-frequency data (he focuses on 10-year intervals), but does not introduce a fixed effect. He finds that inequality is associated negatively with growth in the poorer countries and positively in rich countries.

All of these results are based on linearly regressing growth on inequality. Banerjee and Duflo (2003b) regress growth (or changes in growth) nonparametrically on changes in inequality and find the relationship to be an inverted-U shape. In other words, both reductions and increases in inequality seem to be accompanied by a decline in growth. But we worry that this result might be driven either by omitted variables or by the fact that inequality is poorly measured.

On a more basic level, what can be made of this evidence is severely limited by problems of assigning causality. After all, although inequality might affect growth, growth also affects the distribution of wealth. Moreover, the policies or underlying economic conditions that drive one might very plausibly also drive the other. My view, therefore, is that it makes more sense to focus on specific causal mechanisms that connect the distribution of wealth to investment or growth outcomes and try to use the available evidence to assess the plausibility of these individual mechanisms.

**Effect on Aggregate Investment**

Inequality means that some people have more wealth than others. As already noted, at least some of these lucky people will end up overinvesting, while others, typically those who do not have enough money or the right social connections, will invest too little. Because some people overinvest and others underinvest, it is not obvious that aggregate investment needs to go down. For example, the economy could have a fixed supply of savings supplied inelastically. If the economy is closed, so that investment is always equal to savings in equilibrium, total investment will then be independent of the distribution of investments across the population.

By contrast, consider a scenario in which savings is interest-sensitive. An increase in wealth inequality would typically imply that there are more people who cannot invest as much as they want to, say, because they do not have enough credit or insurance. To compensate for the lack of investment demand from the poor, the rich, who are already in a position to invest as much as they want, would have to demand more capital. But this would happen only if the interest rate were lower, and a lower interest rate tends to discourage saving and thus investment.

When the investment, is not a financial investment but an investment of time or effort, there is no reason why underinvestment by one person will be matched by overinvestment by others. For example, consider a hypothetical setting in which initially land was equally distributed and every farmer farmed his own land. Then for some reason land becomes more unequally distributed. Now some farmers have more land than they want to farm, and some have less and want to work as tenants on the land that the big farmers do not want to farm. However, they are now too poor to feel comfortable with a fixed-rent contract, and so they become sharecroppers, with the concomitant loss in effort and productivity. This is a pure loss, not compensated by any gain elsewhere, because the land that continues to be owner-cultivated continues to have the previous (efficient) level of productivity.

In such an environment, a government intervention that forces the landlords to give their sharecroppers a higher share of the output than the market would give them should increase effort and productivity. This is exactly what happened in West Bengal, India, when a Left Front government came to power in 1977. Tenants' share of output was set at a minimum of 75 percent as long as the tenants provided all inputs, and tenants were guaranteed a large measure of security of tenure, which may have encouraged them to undertake more long-term investments in the land. According to the survey evidence, there was a substantial increase in both tenure security and the share of output going to the sharecroppers. The fact that the implementation of this reform was bureaucratically driven and proceeded at different speeds in different areas suggests the possibility of using variation in implementation of the reform to evaluate its impact. The data indicate that there was a substantial increase, 62 percent, in the productivity of the land (Banerjee, Gertler, and Ghatak 2002). More recent work on the impact of the same tenancy reform program using farm-level data finds similar though somewhat smaller results (Bardhan and Mookherjee 2007).

One reason why this particular redistributive reform worked so well is that agriculture, at least in labor-abundant countries, is an industry in which there seems to be diminishing returns to scale (though this situation might be changing with the introduction of high-value-added produce for export). To see what happens when one moves away from diminishing returns, it is worth going back to the opening example. There I said that moving to full equality would lead to the capital being used optimally, as long as all of the capital is invested. The caveat at the end is crucial. The problem is that if $K$ is a lot larger than mean wealth, then it is not clear that the interest rate can fall enough to permit someone with average wealth to borrow all the way up to $K$ (or rather if the interest rate were to fall that far, people would just keep the money in their mattresses). In that case, full equality is disastrous; no one will be able to invest. The only way to achieve some investment in this case is to make some people rich enough that they can borrow the necessary amount, and this would necessarily have to mean that others will end up much poorer (see Galor and Zeira 1993 for an early discussion of this point). However, even here one can have too much inequality: if some people are in a position to invest more than $K$, then taking wealth away from them and handing it to some of those who are too poor to invest will increase the total amount invested.

### Effect on the Scale of Investment

Returns to scale are also central to understanding the relationship between wealth inequality and the efficiency of investment. In particular, as long as there are diminishing returns to scale in the aggregate production function and the amount people can borrow (and therefore the maximum amount they can invest) is proportional to their wealth, greater inequality must lead to less effective investment. The reason is that, with diminishing returns, the smaller the firm or investor, the more productive it is (per dollar invested). More inequality makes the productive small firms even smaller and reallocates that capital to the unproductive large firms, which become even larger.

If the production technology exhibits increasing returns over some range, then it is no longer true that the smallest firms are the most productive, and redistributing capital from the smallest firms to somewhat larger firms might actually raise productivity. More generally, the effect of inequality will depend on the shape of the production function and the size of the investment potential of the average person relative to the fixed cost.

How good or bad is the assumption of decreasing returns in the production function of an individual firm? As mentioned earlier, McKenzie and Woodruff (2006) attempt to estimate a production function for small Mexican firms. Their estimates suggest that there are strong diminishing returns, while Mesnard and Ravallion (2001) find weak diminishing returns using Tunisian data. These results are reinforced by the evidence from the Sri Lankan experiment by De Mel, McKenzie, and Woodruff (2007) discussed earlier. The revenues of the firms that were randomly allocated SL Rs 20,000 in extra capital grew by less than twice as much as the growth in the revenue of the firms that received SL Rs 20,000.

And yet many economists argue that firms in developing countries suffer from being too small, and thus are unable to use the most effective technologies.[14] Certainly this would be consistent with our finding that the

---

14 See, for example, the McKinsey report on productivity in India cited in Banerjee and Duflo (2006).

return on capital in a set of very large firms in India is in the neighborhood of 80 percent (Banerjee and Duflo 2003a).

One way to square these two sets of claims is to assume that there are indeed diminishing returns to scale in the smallest firms, generated perhaps by the standard agency problem (as one expands one must hire labor, and hired labor is less efficient than family labor). However, once beyond a certain minimum efficient scale (which may be quite large, at least compared with the wherewithal of the average person in a developing country), the fact that one has access to much better technologies opens up the possibility of increasing returns, at least over some range.

What happens upon crossing into the zone of increasing return? Do the returns keep growing with investment, or does one eventually go back into diminishing returns? This question is obviously closely related to a question that comes up often: is it inequality that is of concern, or is poverty the main issue? Is the real problem that there are people who are too poor to achieve the minimum efficient scale, or are there also firms that are inefficiently large?

Although there is no good way to answer this question, it is worth noting that the very largest firms even in a country like India are traded on the stock market. The average stock market return is therefore a potential proxy for the return on capital in these firms. For the period 1991–2004, the average real return on the SENSEX (the index of the Indian stock market) was 11 percent. These returns probably understate the profitability of these firms, because some of the profits are likely diverted into the pockets of the controlling shareholders, but the gap between these numbers and the real returns that the firms in the Banerjee and Duflo (2003a) study were earning (more than 70 percent) is enormous. Of course, these are not random firms—indeed, it is possible they received the extra capital precisely because they are the most productive firms—but the firms in the study by De Mel, McKenzie, and Woodruff (2007) that were earning 4–5 percent per month were in fact chosen at random (albeit in Sri Lanka). There is at least some reason to believe that the largest firms are substantially less productive than many smaller firms.

### Effect on the Quality of the Investment

The logic of scrambling and its connection to wealth inequality have already been discussed. An interesting example of this phenomenon can be found in a study of the knitted garment industry in the southern Indian town of Tirupur (Banerjee and Munshi 2004). Two groups of people operate in Tirupur: the Gounders and the outsiders. The Gounders are members of a small, wealthy agricultural community in the area around Tirupur. They moved into the ready-made garment industry because there was not much investment opportunity in agriculture. Outsiders from various regions and communities began to move into the city in the 1990s. The Gounders, unsurprisingly, have much stronger ties to the local community and thus better access to local finance. But, as might be expected, they

Figure 4.4a Capital Stock—Net Cohort Effect, Gounders and Outsiders

Figure 4.4a Capital Stock—Net Cohort Effect, Gounders and Outsiders

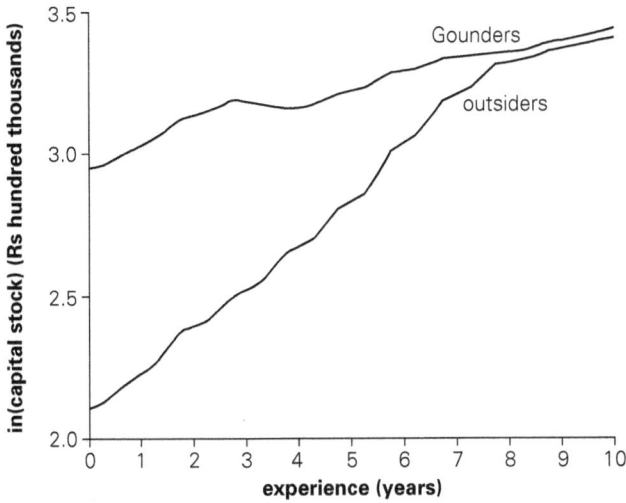

Figure 4.4b Capital-Export Ratio, Capital-Production Ratio—Net Cohort
Effects, Gounders and Outsiders

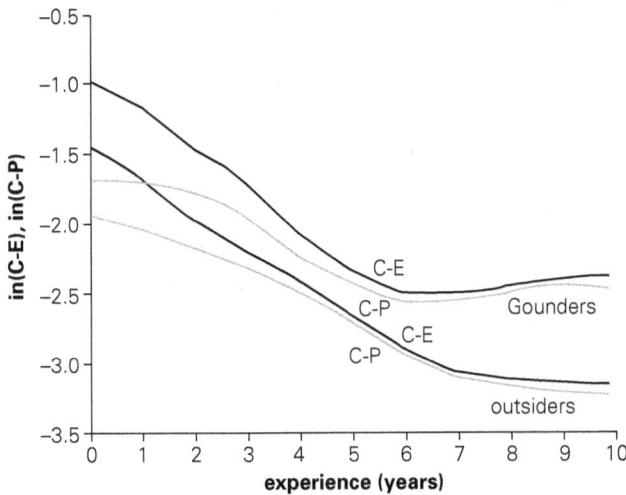

Source: Banerjee and Munshi 2004.

have less natural ability for garment manufacturing than the outsiders,
who came to Tirupur precisely because of its reputation as a center for
garment exports. The Gounders own about twice as much capital as the
outsiders on average. Figure 4.4a plots the capital stock of the Gounder
and outsider firms as a function of the age of the firm. It demonstrates that
Gounder firms of all ages own more capital, though there is a strong tendency toward convergence as the firms age. Figure 4.4b plots sales, once
again as a function of age. It is clear that the Gounders, despite owning
more capital, lose their early lead in sales by about year five and end up

selling less. The outsiders are clearly more able than the Gounders, but they nevertheless invest less[15] because they are less cash-rich and do not have the right connections.

## Conclusion

The relationship between the efficiency of investment and the distribution of wealth is anything but straightforward, and one purpose of this chapter is to bring out the various forces that contribute to that complexity. However, in response to at least a few important questions something more categorical can be said.

First, it is clear that the distribution of wealth is something that one needs to worry about, even if one has no normative preferences about the distribution of wealth. In developing countries, where financial markets often do not do what they are meant to, there is no presumption that the distribution of wealth is anywhere close to what it needs to be to induce efficient investment, and the loss in productivity is potentially very large.

Second, it is not true that there is no need to worry about the rich getting richer as long as the poor are also getting richer. The point is that the rich and the poor compete for resources, including capital, and when the rich become richer it is harder for the poor to compete with them. To see the exact logic behind this point, imagine a toy economy in which there are two technologies. One requires an investment of $K$ and yields $a$ per dollar invested. The other requires a minimum investment of $K^* > K$ and yields $a^* < a$ per dollar invested. Suppose that for starters neither the poor (who have wealth $W_1^1 < K$, say) nor the rich (who have wealth $W_2^1 > K$) can afford to invest in the more capital-intensive technology, but all of them can invest in the other technology. In other words, the initial equilibrium interest rate $r^1$ is such that

$$K < \left(1 + \lambda\left(r^1\right)\right) W_1^1 < \left(1 + \lambda\left(r^1\right)\right) W_2^1 < K^*. \tag{4.7}$$

The capital market clears by the rich lending to the poor and everyone investing in the less capital-intensive technology. Output per capita is $a W_{average}^1$. Now suppose $W_1^1$ goes up to $W_2^1$ while $W_1^2$ goes up to $W_2^2$ and

$$\left(1 + \lambda\left(r^1\right)\right) W_2^2 > K^* > \left(1 + \lambda\left(r^1\right)\right) W_1^2. \tag{4.8}$$

The rich can now try to invest in the capital-intensive technology as long as the interest rate remains the same. Will they want to do it? This depends on whether

$$a^* K^* - r^1 \left(K^* - W_2^2\right) \tag{4.9}$$

---

15 This is not because capital and talent happen to be substitutes. In these data, as it is generally assumed, capital and ability appear to be complements.

is larger or smaller than

$$aK - r^1\left(K - W_2^2\right),\qquad(4.10)$$

which translates into the condition

$$(a^* - r^1)K^* > (a - r^1)K\qquad(4.11)$$

for moving to the capital-intensive technology. Though $a^*$ is less than $a$, the fact that $K^*$ is larger than $K$ makes this possible.

Because the rich want to invest in the more capital-intensive project, they will now stop lending and start trying to borrow. This development will bid up the interest rate, which makes $\lambda$ go down. The net result can easily be that the poor can no longer reach up to $K$ and, as a result, turn into lenders. Only the less productive technology is now in use, and the total gross domestic product (GDP) is $a^* W^2_{average}$, which can easily be less than what it used to be despite the increased wealth.

This argument is reinforced if, as is likely, the fixed costs of investment go up when overall wealth goes up (because, say, the price of land or the wage rate goes up). If the technology of lending exhibits some increasing returns, as is plausible, this mechanism will apply with even greater force.

Third, as already emphasized, it is not true that the only real problem is that the poor are too poor to invest efficiently. It may also be that there is too much capital in the hands of the rich.

Fourth, there is reason to try to redistribute investible resources, not only toward the poor, but also toward specific groups of the nonpoor, including many established but smaller entrepreneurs. In this sense, more policy instruments than just microcredit may be needed. None of this, of course, takes into account the various costs of redistribution—incentive costs, tax collection costs, and the rest. But it does make clear that redistribution is not just about politics or some vision of a just society, though both of those are, of course, profoundly important. It is also about growth and the ability of societies to take best advantage of the available talent.

## References

Aleem, Irfan. 1990. "Imperfect Information, Screening, and the Costs of Informal Lending: A Study of a Rural Credit Market in Pakistan." *World Bank Economic Review* 4 (3): 329–49.

Banerjee, Abhijit V. 2000. "Prospects and Strategies for Land Reforms." In *Annual World Bank Conference on Development Economics 1999*, ed. B. Pleskovic and J. Stiglitz, 253–84. Washington, DC: World Bank.

Banerjee, Abhijit V., and Esther Duflo. 2003a. "Do Firms Want to Borrow More? Testing Credit Constraints Using a Directed Lending Program." Working Paper 2003-5, Bureau for Research in Economic Analysis of Development, Harvard University, Cambridge, MA.

_____. 2003b. "Inequality and Growth: What Can the Data Say?" *Journal of Economic Growth* 8: 267–99.

_____. 2006. "Growth Theory through the Lens of Development Economics." In *Handbook of Economic Growth*, Vol. 1a, ed. P. Aghion, and S. Durlauf, 473–552. Amsterdam: Elsevier.

_____. 2007. "The Economic Lives of the Poor." *Journal of Economic Perspectives* 21 (1): 141–67.

Banerjee, Abhijit V., Paul Gertler, and Maitreesh Ghatak. 2002. "Empowerment and Efficiency: Tenancy Reform in West Bengal." *Journal of Political Economy* 110 (2): 239–80.

Banerjee, Abhijit V., and Sendhil Mullainathan. 2008. "The Shape of Temptations: Implications for the Economic Lives of the Poor." Unpublished manuscript, Massachusetts Institute of Technology, Cambridge, MA.

Banerjee, Abhijit V., and Kaivan Munshi. 2004. "How Efficiently Is Capital Allocated? Evidence from the Knitted Garment Industry in Tirupur." *Review of Economic Studies* 71 (1): 19–42.

Banerjee, Abhijit V., and Andrew Newman. 1998. "Information, the Dual Economy and Development." *Review of Economic Studies* 65 (4): 631–53.

Bardhan, Pranab, and Dilip Mookherjee. 2007. "Land Reform and Farm Productivity in West Bengal." Unpublished manuscript, Boston University.

Barro, Robert J. 2000. "Inequality and Growth in a Panel of Countries." *Journal of Economic Growth* 5 (1): 5–32.

Basta, S., Soekirman D. Karyadi, and N. Scrimshaw. 1979. "Iron Deficiency Anemia and the Productivity of Adult Males in Indonesia." *American Journal of Clinical Nutrition* 32 (4): 916–25.

Benabou, Roland. 1996. "Inequality and Growth." In *NBER Macroeconomics Annual 1996*, ed. Ben Bernanke and Julio J. Rotemberg, 11–73. Cambridge, MA: MIT Press.

Berry, R. Albert, and William R. Cline. 1979. *Agrarian Structure and Productivity in Developing Countries*. Baltimore and London: John Hopkins University Press.

Besley, Timothy, and Robin Burgess. 2000. "Land Reform, Poverty and Growth: Evidence from India." *Quarterly Journal of Economics* 105 (2).

Binswanger, Hans P., Klaus Deininger, and Gershon Feder. 1995. "Power Distortions Revolt and Reform in Agricultural Land Relations." In *Handbook of Development Economics*, vol. 3, ed. J. Behrman and T. N. Srinivasan. Amsterdam: Elsevier Science.

Binswanger, Hans P., and Mark R. Rosenzweig. 1986. "Behavioural and Material Determinants of Production Relations in Agriculture." *Journal of Development Studies* 22 (April): 503–39.

Buera, Francisco. 2008. "Persistency of Poverty, Financial Frictions, and Entrepreneurship." Unpublished manuscript, Northwestern University, Evanston, IL.

Buera, Francisco, Joe Kaboski, and Yongshin Shin. 2008. "Finance and Development: A Tale of Two Sectors." Unpublished manuscript, Northwestern University, Evanston, IL.

Caballero, Ricardo, and Mohammed Hammour. 1998. "Improper Churn: Social Costs and Macroeconomic Consequences." Unpublished manuscript, Massachusetts Institute of Technology, Cambridge, MA, March.

Caselli, Francesco, and Nicola Gennaioli. 2005. "Credit Constraints, Competition, and Meritocracy." *Journal of the European Economic Association* 3 (2–3): 679–89.

Dasgupta, A. 1989. *Reports on Informal Credit Markets in India: Summary.* New Delhi: National Institute of Public Finance and Policy.

Davies, James, Susanna Sandström, Anthony Shorrocks, and Edward Wolff. 2006. "The Global Distribution of Household Wealth." *Wider Angle* (2): 4–7.

Deaton, Angus. 1997. *The Analysis of Household Surveys.* Washington, DC: World Bank.

De Mel, Suresh, David McKenzie, and Chris Woodruff. 2007. "Returns to Capital in Microenterprises: Evidence from a Field Experiment." Policy Research Working Paper 4230, World Bank, Washington, DC.

Djankov, Simeon, Rafael La Porta, Florencio López de Silanes, and Andrei Shleifer. 2003. "Courts." *Quarterly Journal of Economics* 118: 453–517.

Duflo, Esther, Michael Kremer, and Jonathan Robinson. 2008. "How High Are Rates of Return to Fertilizer? Evidence from Field Experiments in Kenya." *American Economic Review* 98 (2): 482–88.

Duflo, Esther, and Christopher Udry. 2004. "Intrahousehold Resource Allocation in Côte d'Ivoire: Social Norms, Separate Accounts, and Consumption Choices." NBER Working Paper 10498, National Bureau of Economic Research, Cambridge, MA, May.

Fafchamps, Marcel, and Susan Lund. 2003. "Risk-Sharing Networks in Rural Philippines." *Review of Economic Studies* 71 (2): 261–87.

Field, Erica. 2003. "Fertility Responses to Urban Land Titling Programs: The Roles of Ownership Security and the Distribution of Household Assets." Working paper, Harvard University, Cambridge, MA.

Fisman, Raymond. 2001. "Trade Credit and Productive Efficiency in Developing Countries." *World Development* 29 (2): 311–21.

Forbes, Kristin J. 2000. "A Reassessment of the Relationship between Inequality and Growth." *American Economic Review* 90 (4): 869–87.

Foster, Andrew D., and Mark R. Rosenzweig. 1995. "Learning by Doing and Learning from Others: Human Capital and Technical Change in Agriculture." *Journal of Political Economy* 103 (6): 1176–1209.

Galor, Oded, and Joseph Zeira. 1993. "Income Distribution and Macroeconomics." *Review of Economics Studies* 60: 35–52.

Gertler, Paul, and Jonathan Gruber. 2002. "Insuring Consumption against Illness." *American Economic Review* 92 (1): 51–76.

Ghate, Prabhu. 1992. *Informal Finance: Some Findings from Asia.* Oxford: Oxford University Press.

Goldstein, Markus, and Christopher Udry. 1999. "Agricultural Innovation and Resource Management in Ghana." Unpublished manuscript, Yale University, New Haven, CT.

Laffont, Jean-Jacques, and Mohamed Salah Matoussi. 1995. "Moral Hazard, Financial Constraints and Sharecropping in El Oulja." *Review of Economic Studies* 62 (3): 381–99.

Li, Hongyi, and Heng-fu Zhou. 1998. "Income Inequality Is Not Harmful for Growth: Theory and Evidence." *Review of Development Economics* 2 (3): 318–34.

Li, R., X. Chen, H. Yan, P. Deurenberg L. Garby, and J. G. Hautvast. 1994. "Functional Consequences of Iron Supplementation in Iron-Deficient Female Cotton Workers in Beijing, China." *American Journal of Clinical Nutrition* 59: 908–13.

McKenzie, David, and Christopher Woodruff. 2006. "Do Entry Costs Provide an Empirical Basis for Poverty Traps? Evidence from Mexican Microenterprises." *Economic Development and Cultural Change* 55 (October ): 3–42.

Mesnard, Alice, and Martin Ravallion. 2001. "Wealth Distribution and Self-Employment in a Developing Economy." CEPR Discussion Paper 3026, Centre for Economic Policy Research, London.

Miguel, Edward, and Michael Kremer. 2004. "Worms: Identifying Impacts on Education and Health in the Presence of Treatment Externalities." *Econometrica* 72 (1): 159–217.

Morduch, Jonathan. 1993. "Risk Production and Saving: Theory and Evidence from Indian Households." Unpublished manuscript, Harvard University, Cambridge, MA.

Olley, G. Steven, and Ariel Pakes. 1996. "The Dynamics of Productivity in the Telecommunications Equipment Industry." *Econometrica* 64 (6): 1263–97.

Rosenzweig, Mark R., and Hans P. Binswanger. 1993. "Wealth, Weather Risk and the Profitability of Agricultural Investment." *Economic Journal* 103 (January): 56–78.

Rosenzweig, Mark R., and Kenneth I. Wolpin. 1993. "Credit Market Constraints, Consumption Smoothing, and the Accumulation of Durable Production Assets in Low-Income Countries: Investments in Bullocks in India." *Journal of Political Economy* 101 (21): 223–44.

Shaban, Radwan. 1987. "Testing between Competing Models of Sharecropping." *Journal of Political Economy* 95 (5): 893–920.

Swaminathan, Madhura. 1991. "Segmentation, Collateral Undervaluation, and the Rate of Interest in Agrarian Credit Markets: Some Evidence from Two Villages in South India." *Cambridge Journal of Economics* 15 (2): 161–78.

Thomas, Duncan, Elizabeth Frankenberg, Jed Friedman, Jean-Pierre Habicht, Mohammed Hakimi, Nicholas Ingwersen, Jaswadi, Nathan Jones, Christopher McKelvey, Gretel Pelto, Bondan Sikoki, Teresa Seeman, James P. Smith, Cecep Sumantri, Wayan Suriastini, and Siswanto Wilopo. 2006. "Causal Effect of Health on Labor Market Outcomes: Experimental Evidence." CCPR Online Working Paper 070-06, Centre for Civil and Political Rights, Geneva.

Timberg, Thomas A., and C. V. Aiyar. 1984. "Informal Credit Markets in India." *Economic Development and Cultural Change* 33 (1): 43–59.

Townsend, Robert. 1994. "Risk and Insurance in Village India." *Econometrica* 62 (4): 539–91.

_____. 1995. "Financial Systems in Northern Thai Villages." *Quarterly Journal of Economics* 110 (4): 1011–46.

WHO (World Health Organization). 2001. *Macroeconomics and Health: Investing in Health for Economic Development*. Geneva: WHO.

# CHAPTER 5

# Gender Equality, Poverty Reduction, and Growth: A Copernican Quest

*Andrew Morrison, Dhushyanth Raju, and Nistha Sinha*

> To know that we know what we know, and to know that we do not know what we do not know, that is true knowledge.
>
> —Copernicus

This chapter surveys the empirical evidence linking gender equality with economic performance, with a particular focus on poverty reduction and economic growth. Specifically, it examines the instrumental case for gender equality as a potential contributor to poverty reduction and economic growth.

At the outset, it is important to recognize that the relationship between economic development/growth and gender equality is two-way. The general view is that economic development and growth are good for gender equality, and, conversely, that greater gender equality is good for development and growth. This view is reflected in most of the theoretical work on this relationship (e.g., Galor and Weil 1996).

The available empirical evidence on the link from development and growth to gender equality suggests that poverty and low levels of development perpetuate or exacerbate gender disparities and that economic growth and development can promote greater gender equality. For example, gender disparities in schooling outcomes are more severe among the poor, and this finding holds when one looks across as well as within countries. When individual developing countries have raised their living standards over time, key outcome measures of female well-being such as school participation, school attainment, life expectancy, and labor market earnings have generally increased, at times at faster rates than for males (World Bank 2001). In addition, evidence from panel cross-country regressions appears to show that an increase in per capita income has a robust positive effect on various measures of gender equality, with some studies finding that the effect is particularly pronounced among higher-income countries (Dollar and Gatti 1999; Forsythe, Korzeniewicz, and Durrant 2000; Oostendorp 2009). The nature of growth may also matter for whether and when gender disparities narrow. For example, if growth is ignited by trade liberalization, whether export sectors are male- or female-dominated will determine whether the initial effects of growth will yield greater gains for men or for women.[1]

Beyond this long-run relationship between growth and gender equality, short-term variations in output matter as well. There is evidence that households that experience sharp adverse changes in their economic circumstances are likely to compromise the nutritional, health, and educational status of girls more than that of boys (see, e.g., Rose 1999 for evidence from India). To the extent that economic development and growth afford households the means to lift themselves out of poverty or protect themselves from negative shocks, poverty (risk)-reducing growth may benefit girls more than boys.

The rest of this chapter examines the arguments for causality running in the other direction—from gender equality to growth and poverty reduction. Potential channels through which these effects could materialize include higher labor productivity via greater investments in human capital and greater allocative efficiency from equalizing access to productive assets and markets. The well-known evidence that returns on investments in educating girls are generally higher than returns on investments in educating boys points to the potential productivity gains of increasing gender equality (Schultz 2002). The available evidence also suggests weaker rights over productive assets for females. These weaker rights result in underinvestment, which, in turn, reduces productivity and earnings. If this underinvestment is systematic across households, this behavior could inhibit aggregate economic growth.

The next section of this chapter presents models and empirical evidence on the implications for technical and allocative efficiency of gender inequalities in four key markets: labor, credit, land, and agricultural technology.

---

1 Economic development and growth by themselves, however, may not eliminate gender disparities. A case in point is the persistent female disadvantage in political representation, occupational choices, and labor market earnings in developed countries, despite the human capital levels of females converging to those of males. One potential explanation is that societal and personal perceptions of lower female ability may be quite resistant to economic development and growth and can perpetuate a female disadvantage in outcomes even though rights and access to markets may be equalized across genders (Duflo 2005).

The central question is whether women face barriers that are not faced by men to participation in the labor, credit, and land markets, as well to the adoption of agricultural technology—and whether, as a consequence, their participation and adoption rates are below what they would have been without the presence of these constraints. Implicitly, we take a production function approach. If an economy has an aggregate production function in the form of

$$Q = q(A, K, L, R),$$

where A is technology, K is capital stock, L is (quality-adjusted) labor input, and R is (quality-adjusted) land input, gender inequalities can affect aggregate output directly if they result in lower technological adoption, lower capital stocks, or lower quality-adjusted land or labor inputs. Credit does not affect output directly, but could do so indirectly via an impact on optimal levels of A, K, L, and R. In this section, we pay particular attention to the credibility of evidence generated linking gender inequalities to technical and allocative efficiency in production, and to unanswered research questions that deserve more attention.[2]

The section that follows surveys the evidence on dynamic transmission mechanisms through which gender inequality today may affect output in the future. The principal channel through which this may occur is women's control over resources and the impact that this control has on resource allocation within the household, especially on investment in children's health and education.

The penultimate section of this chapter examines models and methodologies that attempt to model formally how suboptimal decisions at the micro level (individual, household, or firm) that result from gender inequalities can influence growth at the macro level. In practice, however, it is extremely difficult to attribute foregone growth or productivity to particular distortions. As Banerjee and Duflo (2004: 46) note, "Even where the prima facie evidence [of distortions] is strongest, we cannot automatically conclude that the particular distortion has resulted in a *significant* loss in productivity" (emphasis in original).

The final section of this chapter pulls together key themes and priorities for future research.

## Gender Equality and Participation in Labor, Land, Credit, and Technology Markets

This section presents models and empirical evidence on the implications for technical and allocative efficiency of gender inequalities in four key markets: labor, credit, land, and agricultural technology.

---

2   In summary, if gender inequality is found to be associated with technical and allocative inefficiency, it is necessarily also associated with lower output and income losses—and thus potentially with increased poverty at the household level. There is also a link to growth: persistent technical and allocative inefficiency potentially inhibits productivity growth.

## Labor

Measurement of female labor force participation rates is extremely sensitive to the definitions used, especially to whether home-based work and subsistence agricultural activities are captured (Assad, El-Hamidi, and Ahmed 2000; Bardasi et al. 2009). Despite these measurement challenges, there is substantial evidence that (1) female labor force participation rates have a U-shaped relationship with respect to national income levels across countries (Goldin 1995; Mammen and Paxson 2000); and (2) male-female gaps in labor force participation are a consistent feature of the economic landscape in both developed and developing countries.

Male-female participation differentials are attributable to a complex mix of individual choice, intrahousehold bargaining processes, and cultural norms that influence the division of labor between men and women. Although few would dispute that cultural norms affect female labor force participation rates, this does not make low female participation rates suboptimal. A more interesting question is whether women's labor force participation rates are indeed suboptimal (in the sense of leading to productivity losses) because of gender inequalities in earnings.[3]

There are two channels by which gender inequalities in wages or earnings might affect female participation rates. The first is a contemporaneous effect: given a positive wage elasticity of women's labor supply, lower expected earnings by women in relation to those by men are at least a partial explanation for women's lower labor force participation rates.[4] The second channel is an intergenerational effect. In view of the presence of male-to-female wage or earnings gaps, the private returns from educating girls may be lower than those from educating boys (Schultz 2002), and parents may respond by investing less in the education of girls. This response may or may not be productively inefficient, depending on the source of the wage gap. It is not inefficient if the returns from education are lower for girls simply because women are expected to spend less time in the labor force (Becker 1985; Polachek 1995).[5] It is inefficient if

---

3  Although one can speak of "suboptimal" levels of female labor force participation that arise from a *single* distortion in the labor market such as wage discrimination against women, the welfare impact of removing this distortion is uncertain in the presence of other distortions (theory of the second best). The discussion in this section uses *suboptimal* in the context of a single distortion: wage discrimination against women.

4  Two caveats are important here. First, these lower participation rates are only suboptimal to the degree that wage gaps do not reflect productivity differentials—that is, to the extent that they reflect discrimination and not differential human capital endowments. Second, no empirical work has been undertaken to estimate the magnitude of the impact of wage gaps associated with wage discrimination on female labor force participation rates.

5  But it does imply that the current division of labor between men and women (with women spending more time on household production) tends to reproduce itself through time via parents' optimizing decisions. As Elson (1999) notes, such a situation takes the "prevailing gender order" as a given. In the long run, changing this gender order would also change parental optimizing decisions.

differential educational investment in boys and girls is driven by a wage gap that has a discrimination component.

It is surprising, in view of the potential importance of future labor market outcomes in shaping parental investment in children, that relatively little research has been carried out on the topic.[6] The productivity effects of differential investment in girls and boys are magnified if—aside from the productivity and earnings effects just described—lower educational attainment by women also results in lower labor force participation rates. While a plausible hypothesis, the evidence on this is mixed (Ilahi 2000; Cameron, Dowling, and Worswick 2001).

Recent studies of Africa using detailed time-use surveys have generally found that women have higher levels of time poverty than men, where time poverty is defined as the amount of time spent on market work plus household responsibilities (see, e.g., Blackden and Wodon 2006; for a counterexample, see Lawson 2008). Time poverty limits the amount of time that can be allocated to increased market work. The link between the provision of infrastructure services (particularly water and electricity), lower levels of time poverty, and increased women's labor force participation is an accepted wisdom that has been the subject of surprisingly little empirical work. Three exceptions are papers on rural Pakistan (Ilahi and Grimard 2000), Nepal (Kumar and Hotchkiss 1988), and South Africa (Dinkelman 2008).

Beyond the question of labor force participation per se, is women's access to high-productivity, high-paying occupations limited, or do women suffer wage discrimination within occupations? The literature on occupational segregation by sex is voluminous, but until recently almost entirely descriptive.[7] Segregation is generally assumed to be a negative outcome, but little work has been done on links between segregation and inequality (Blackburn and Jarman 1997; Bridges 2003). An encouraging recent development has been new measures of occupational segregation that distinguish between segregation that is associated with income gaps (or some other measure of vertical differentiation such as skill level) and segregation that is not.[8] Occupational segregation may be associated with inefficiencies in the allocation of labor inputs. Using a simple model, Tzannatos (2008) estimates that the output gains associated with the elimination of occupational segregation and wage gaps would range from a low of 2 percent of gross domestic product (GDP) in the Nordic countries to a high of 6 percent in high-income East Asia.

A final source of inefficiencies in the labor market is associated with wage discrimination against women. Audit studies and nonparametric

---

6  Two papers on India from the 1980s —Rosenzweig and Schultz (1982) and Behrman (1986)— find inconsistent results. No research has been conducted on the topic since these papers.

7  There seems to have been little change in levels of occupational segregation in developing countries since the 1980s (Deutsch et al. 2004; Tzannatos 2008).

8  Although these new measures of occupational segregation do deal with the issue of whether segregation results in income losses for women, they do not address the issue of whether segregation is voluntary.

matching are two relatively new approaches—at least newly applied to developing countries—that offer more insight into discrimination in labor markets than the standard Oaxaca-Blinder decomposition. Audit studies were used recently to examine possible discrimination in Latin American labor markets based on gender, race, and class. They find no evidence of discrimination in Chile and Peru (Moreno et al. 2004; Bravo et al. 2007). Nonparametric matching has been used to fine-tune the comparison of male and female wages. Ñopo (2008) finds substantial wage gaps in Peru, ranging from 95 percent for individuals in the poorest decile of the income distribution to a low of 18 percent for those between the eighth and ninth deciles. Because of the greater importance of wage employment for women in Latin America than in most other regions of the world, it is not surprising that most work on wage discrimination has focused on this region.

### Areas for Future Research

Surprisingly little serious econometric work has been carried out on the impact of male/female wage or earnings gaps on women's labor force participation. A back-of-the-envelope approach to measuring the size of the contemporaneous disincentive effect would be to multiply the "unexplained" wage gap component arising from an Oaxaca-Blinder decomposition or matching exercise by the wage elasticity of female labor supply for a given location, but more sophisticated approaches could be used as well. Another challenge is updating and advancing the work on the intergenerational impacts of wage gaps that are transmitted through parental decisions on the nutrition and education of their children. Advances in experimental design and program evaluation provide opportunities to answer key questions: for example, do interventions that result in increased female labor participation (such as the Rural Employment Guarantee Scheme in India or gender-sensitive public works programs) also generate increases in girls' nutrition and education as perceptions change about the likelihood of women working outside the home?

The impact of infrastructure provision on female labor force provision is also an important area for new research. As noted earlier, there is a paucity of high-quality research documenting the effect of infrastructure provision on women's time use. Even scarcer are studies of labor force participation. The most attractive data sets for this research would be panel data that span the time period of provision of improved infrastructure, so that researchers can more effectively control for heterogeneity at different levels (community, household, and individual).

## Land

Apart from labor, land is the most important productive asset for households dependent on agriculture. It is also often the primary source of transferable and inheritable wealth for rural households (Deininger and Binswanger 1999). In many cases, access to water and other natural resources is contingent on households having access to land (FAO 2002).

The quantity and quality of land as well as the strength and extent of rights over land are likely to matter for the economic welfare of rural households. Evidence from across the developing world indicates that land ownership and land size are positively associated with household income and consumption levels.[9] Recent findings also demonstrate that access to and the size of land have significant poverty-reducing effects (Finan, Sadoulet, and de Janvry 2005). One channel that appears to be important in generating these effects is the increased productive efficiency engendered by well-defined and secure land rights (Besley 1995). According to the growing evidence, greater land tenure security promotes, among other things, increased agricultural investment and productivity, labor force participation, and investments in housing quality.[10]

In view of this evidence, a female disadvantage in land rights—particularly if it is not ameliorated by the sharing of output, income, and consumption within the household—is likely to affect adversely the socioeconomic welfare of women. Thus, a first question is: Are there systematic asymmetries in land rights between men and women?

In much of the developing world, women's land rights are significantly circumscribed, if not in principle then in practice. For example, under customary law in much of Sub-Saharan Africa, men hold permanent land rights. This state of affairs generally applies in both patrilineal and matrilineal systems. By contrast, women typically hold use rights over individual plots provided by men, though social norms often constrain the crop choices female farmers make (Kevane and Gray 1999). In South Asia, women typically do not own land, and when they do, such as under matrilineal and bilateral inheritance systems, men hold effective control rights (Agarwal 1994). In Latin America, despite the presence of parallel and bilateral inheritance systems, the gender division of labor that defines agriculture as a man's occupation often implies that men inherit land and women other assets (Deere and Leon 2003).

In general, the organization and functioning of the key modes of land acquisition—inheritance, marriage, land titling and registration initiatives, and market purchases—disadvantage women, perpetuating and sometimes exacerbating existing gender disparities in land ownership and accumulation. For example, evidence from Ethiopia and the Philippines shows that, by means of marriage and inheritance, assets of larger amounts and better quality are transferred to men, including land (Quisumbing 1994; Fafchamps and Quisumbing 2005).[11]

---

9  See, for example, Gunning et al. (2000) for Zimbabwe; Grootaert, Kanbur, and Oh (1997) for Côte d'Ivoire; Bouis and Haddad (1990) for the Philippines; and Carter and May (1999) for South Africa.

10 See, for example, Besley (1995) and Goldstein and Udry (2008) for Ghana; Banerjee, Gertler, and Ghatak (2002) for India; Do and Ayer (2008) for Vietnam; Galiani and Schargrodsky (2009) for Argentina; Field (2007) and Antle et al. (2003) for Peru; and de Laiglesia (2003) for Nicaragua.

11 Notwithstanding, inheritance appears to be the primary means through which women acquire land in general. See, for example, Deere and Leon (2003) for evidence from Latin America.

Land redistributive reforms and land titling/registration programs around the developing world have had mixed effects on women's land rights. For example, recent episodes of land titling in Latin America have strengthened women's land rights by explicitly targeting female-headed households, recognizing dual-headed households, and mandating joint land titling (Deere and Leon 2003). By contrast, in Sub-Saharan Africa formal titling and registration efforts have typically conferred full rights on the male household head, thereby undermining the traditional systems that offered men and women, at least in principle, overlapping rights to land. In South Asia, the person who "tills the land"—typically men (reinforced by perceptions of men as the main household breadwinners even where women work as farmers)—was designated the direct beneficiary of land reforms and land titling programs (Agarwal 1994, 2003).

Consistent with the stylized facts from the ethnographic literature, the limited evidence available indicates that the distribution of land ownership is skewed toward men. For example, in Latin America, depending on the country, 70–90 percent of formal owners of farmland are men, and, conditional on land ownership, men on average own more farmland than women (Deere and Leon 2003). In Ghana, 60–70 percent of landowners are men, and, conditional on ownership, the average monetary value of land is three times higher for men than for women (Doss 2006). In Burkina Faso, male-controlled plots are on average eight times larger than female-controlled plots (Udry 1996). In four other African countries, the average area cultivated by women ranges from one-third to two-thirds of the average area cultivated by men (Quisumbing, Estudillo, and Otsuka 2004).

So what are the socioeconomic effects of the female disadvantages in land rights and ownership? Only a few studies have examined this question. Goldstein and Udry (2008) find in Ghana that individuals in positions of power in the local political hierarchies have more secure land rights, which result in greater investments in land fertility through fallowing for longer periods and, in turn, higher yields and revenues. Because women are rarely in these positions of power, they face more insecure land rights, and leaving their plots fallow further undermines their limited rights. Consequently, women fallow their plots for shorter periods of time and therefore obtain significantly lower yields than men.

Strengthening titling also can have gender-differentiated effects. In Peru, increased tenure security for urban squatters through formal housing titles freed up time formerly devoted to ensuring housing and land security, thereby increasing the likelihood of market work outside the home and the number of hours worked. The labor supply effect was stronger for men than for women.

These studies are exceptions. Direct empirical evidence on the gender-differentiated effects of land tenure insecurity on investment and other economic behavior is largely nonexistent. Nevertheless, the fact that careful studies show that tenure insecurity impairs investment incentives in general, combined with independent evidence of higher levels of tenure insecurity for women in many settings, suggests that women's agricultural productivity and output are likely to be lower in relation to men's. One can then plausibly argue that weak tenure security is at least a partial explanation for the findings on gender differences in agricultural productivity.[12]

*Areas for Future Research*

The research agenda on the economics of gender and land is an open and fruitful one for two reasons. First, although there is extensive ethnographic evidence from the developing world on the gender distribution of land rights, there is limited systematic empirical evidence on the gender distribution of the ownership of land and other productive assets. Measuring the ownership and use of productive assets at the level of the individual rather than the level of the household should be a prerequisite for more insightful research in this area. Second, little is known about the gender-differentiated effects of land tenure security on intermediate outcomes such investment and productivity and on final outcomes such as income and consumption. For that matter, little is known about the economic effects of targeted efforts to strengthen the land rights of women.

## Credit

Access to credit is an important instrument for improving the present and long-term economic welfare of households. Credit can provide start-up or working capital for micro and small enterprises, support adoption of new technologies, and help households smooth consumption in the event of unanticipated shocks. Recent research has revealed that large shares of the population in developing countries do not use formal financial services, neither savings nor credit (Beck and Demirguc-Kunt 2008). Nonusers of credit services include those who do not want loans as well as those who do want loans but do not meet lenders' eligibility criteria. Are women overrepresented among those involuntarily excluded from the credit market?

Microfinance programs, one type of financial services available in many developing countries, typically target women under the assumption that women would like to borrow but are unable to do so (that is, they are credit-constrained). However, the actual empirical evidence on the extent of gender inequality in credit access is quite limited, largely because measuring access (or lack of access) is not straightforward (see Petrick 2005 for a review). The broader literature on credit access takes several approaches to measuring access. One approach is to look at borrowing behavior (uptake of credit services). Studies examining borrowing behavior of male and female entrepreneurs find that women are less likely to have ever applied for loans, and when they do, they are likely to use sources different from those

---

12 For example, evidence from Sub-Saharan Africa indicates that women have lower agricultural productivity conditional on several factors such as land size and crop selection (Quisumbing 1996). Other evidence from Africa shows male-female productivity differences within households as well, suggesting inefficiencies in the intrahousehold allocation of labor and other inputs between female- and male-controlled plots (Udry et al. 1995; Udry 1996).

used by men and receive smaller loans (Lycette and White 1989; Berger 1989; Buvinic and Berger 1994; Almeyda 1996). For example, Buvinic and Berger (1994) find that women form only a small percentage of all borrowers because fewer women apply and not because more female applicants are rejected. Akoten, Sawada, and Otsuka (2006) map different sources of credit used by firms in Kenya and then estimate the determinants of use of each source. They find significant gender differences in sources of credit used by their sample of garment producers, with female producers more likely to borrow from rotating savings and credit associations (ROSCAs) and microfinance institutions.

Women's borrowing behavior could differ from that of men for several reasons. Providers of financial services could consider women to be a lending risk because of their low incomes or limited access to collateral. Application procedures that often require a husband's or father's co-signature also could discourage prospective female borrowers (Berger 1989; Almeyda 1996). Lenders may discriminate against female borrowers, but the evidence reveals that, after controlling for various indicators of creditworthiness, there is little or no gender difference in loan denial rates or interest rates charged.[13]

Studies of the experience of borrowers provide only a partial picture of constraints to credit access because they exclude those who might have a demand for credit but do not apply for a loan or those who did apply but were rejected. Studies have used different approaches to defining and measuring constraints to credit access. One approach is to analyze qualitative information from borrowers and nonborrowers. Borrowers who say that they would have liked to borrow more at the prevailing interest rate and nonborrowers who say simply that they would have liked to borrow are classified as credit-constrained.[14] Most studies using this approach find that women are more likely to be credit-constrained. For example, Fletschner (2008), based on separate interviews with husbands and wives in Paraguay, finds that a higher percentage of women than men reported being credit-constrained.

Another approach to measuring credit constraints uses household survey–based techniques in which the respondent is asked about her optimal loan size and the maximum amount a lender is willing to lend her—that is, the credit access or credit limit (Diagne 1999; Diagne, Zeller, and Sharma 2000). A borrower is then defined as credit-constrained if her optimal loan size is effectively restricted by her credit limit. Based on an unconditional examination of credit limits and unused credit lines (the difference between the credit limit and amounts borrowed), Diagne, Zeller, and Sharma (2000) find that women in Bangladesh and Malawi are more likely to face a binding credit constraint than men.

---

13 See Buvinic and Berger (1994) for Peru, Storey (2004) for Trinidad and Tobago, and Raturi and Swamy (1999) for Zimbabwe.
14 See Baydas, Meyer, and Aguilera-Alfred (1994) for Ecuador; Barham, Boucher, and Carter (1996) for Guatemala; and Fletschner (2008) for Paraguay.

A related and interesting question is how male and female microentrepreneurs respond when they obtain better access to credit. De Mel, McKenzie, and Woodruff (2008) test the impact of small grants to randomly selected microenterprises in Sri Lanka and compare the returns by sex of the entrepreneur. Returns to capital are found to be markedly higher for men (about 9 percent) than for women; for female microentrepreneurs the returns are close to zero.[15] Dupas and Robinson (2009) test the effect of offering a savings instrument to male and female microentrepreneurs in Kenya. Savings accounts in a local village bank in rural Kenya were offered to a randomly selected sample of poor daily income earners such as market vendors. Despite the availability of informal saving sources such as ROSCAs, access to the savings account had a large and positive impact on productive investment levels and expenditures for women but not for men. Take-up of the savings accounts was high among women, even though these accounts paid no interest and imposed withdrawal fees.

*Areas for Future Research*

The pool of studies examining gender and access to credit is still limited, and more studies using a wider range of settings and samples of respondents (such as microentrepreneurs in different industries) are needed. The recent research on gender differences in the responses of entrepreneurs to injections of capital also raises questions about how male and female entrepreneurs use credit and is an interesting area for future research that could shape public policy for entrepreneurial development. Finally, there is emerging evidence that women benefit from savings instruments. Studies examining the underlying reasons for this finding and comparing the effects to that from offering credit would be useful from a policy perspective.[16]

**Agricultural Technology**

Adoption of improved seeds, fertilizer, soil management techniques, and other types of agricultural technology are critical for enhancing farm productivity. In developing countries, where adoption remains low, which farmers adopt technology remains an important policy question. Evidence suggests that many of the barriers to adoption are related not only to the characteristics of farmers but also to the characteristics of the markets relevant to the adoption decision: credit, information, and land. The evidence on the effect of farmer's gender comes mainly from regressions of adoption decisions, where a dummy for the sex of the farmer is included along with other determinants of technology adoption. A few studies go beyond the

---

15  The authors explore reasons for this surprising gender difference in firm behavior. They find that the gender difference in returns to the grants remains even after they control for measures of access to credit, wealth, risk aversion, and ability. Sectoral concentration by gender could explain some of the difference, but the gender difference in returns remains even when the analysis is restricted to industries in which both men and women are present.

16  Ashraf, Karlan, and Yin (2008), for example, find that the availability of commitment savings products in the Philippines improved women's control over decision making in the household.

adoption regression to unpack what drives differential adoption by male and female farmers.[17]

A key empirical challenge is to accurately identify who the key decision maker is in the farm household. Most studies assume that the household head is also the decision maker. But this assumption may not hold in parts of Africa where male and female family members farm individual plots. In adoption regressions, when the gender dummy is statistically significant, it is usually negative, indicating that female-headed households are less likely than male-headed households to adopt technology.[18] These regressions typically control for the household head's age and education, availability of labor (usually number of adult household members), village-level infrastructure, access to agricultural extension service, and land ownership.[19] Studies based on plot-level data find that female plot managers are less likely than male plot managers to adopt technology.[20] In addition, sex of the household head seems to matter; most studies find that female farmers in female-headed households are less likely to adopt technology than female farmers in male-headed households.

What underlies female farmers' lower probability of adopting technology? Reasons could be gender differences in risk aversion, investment behavior, or preferences in technology. Little research has been carried out on gender differences in farmers' investment behavior, and it is not clear that female farmers are more risk averse than male farmers (see, e.g., Duflo, Kremer, and Robinson 2009). There is some evidence, however, that male and female farmers may have different preferences in technology because of differences in the ultimate use of crop output (for marketing or for home consumption). For example, female farmers might prefer new seed varieties more suited to home use and storage than to marketing (see, e.g., Jha, Hojjati, and Vosti 1991).

Another reason for lower adoption by female farmers could be gender differences in the determinants of adoption such as farmer education, access to information about the benefits of new technology, access to labor, access to credit and land, and tenure security. Evidence suggests that there are gender-based differences in these determinants of adoption. For example, male- and female-headed households differ in the availability of family

---

17 Doss (2006) and Feder, Just, and Zilberman (1985) have reviewed the literature on determinants of technology adoption in general. Quisumbing (1995) and Doss (2001) review this literature from a gender perspective.

18 However, a few studies find that female-headed households are *more* likely than male-headed households to adopt new technology. For example, in their analysis of the adoption decision on a new crop (sunflower) in northern Mozambique, Bandiera and Rasul (2006) find that female-headed households are 36 percent more likely to adopt the new crop, even though such households are more likely to be poor. The authors attribute their finding to a lack of credit constraints in adopting the new crop.

19 The definition of headship varies across studies. Some studies include de facto female heads, and others do not.

20 See Doss and Morris (2001) for adoption of modern maize varieties in Ghana; Chirwa (2005) for Malawi; Evenson and Siegel (1999) for Burkina Faso; and Saito, Mekonnen, and Spurling (1994) for Kenya and Nigeria.

labor because female-headed households usually are smaller with no adult males.[21] In a study of adoption of modern varieties of maize and fertilizer in Ghana, Doss and Morris (2001) unpack what drives their finding that female-headed households are less likely to adopt modern maize varieties. They assess whether male and female farmers have equal access to each determinant of technology adoption, and they find gender-based differences. Female farmers (particularly those living in female-headed households) have significantly less access to extension services than male farmers do and are less likely to own land. And female farmers have fewer years of education than male farmers. Using a similar approach, Saito, Mekonnen, and Spurling (1994) find that male and female farmers in Kenya and Nigeria differ in the utilization of formal and informal sources of credit, with female farmers less likely to access formal financial services.

Intrahousehold dynamics that govern roles and norms about the allocation of inputs and output may also be important in shaping women's access to family labor, credit, and tenure security (Udry 1996; Udry et al. 1995). Within a farm household, the incentive of female plot managers to adopt productivity-enhancing technologies could depend on whether they have control over land and their output. The experience with the introduction of certain technologies aimed at improving the productivity of female-cultivated crops suggests that adoption can make the crop more attractive to men and thus weaken women's control over resources (von Braun and Webb 1989; Kumar 1994; Lilja and Sanders 1998). The interplay of gender inequality and technology adoption is visible even in settings where men and women farm jointly. For example, the adoption of high-yielding varieties of crops in India in the 1960s and 1970s is thought to have pushed women out of farm work because male farmers felt that men were more suited to working with the new technology (see review in Sudha and Rajan 1999). These results reveal the importance of taking into account intrahousehold dynamics when introducing new technologies.

*Areas for Future Research*
For effective policy design, it is important to understand what drives differential adoption by female farmers. More research that unpacks what drives gender differences in adoption is needed. Is it gender inequality in the determinants of adoption, gender differences in farmers' preference for risk, or the characteristics of the technology itself? If the main source of this difference lies in gender inequality in the markets that influence adoption, such as the information, credit, and land markets, then the appropriate policy response would be to address such inequalities. Research can identify whether gender inequality in these markets arises from discrimination in the markets or from intrahousehold decision-making processes that inhibit women's access to these determinants. Using this research, policymakers can then design the appropriate policy responses. One determinant of adoption that has received considerable attention is access to agricultural

---

21 This is an important constraint in settings in which households do not hire farm labor.

extension services. Based on research that showed that female farmers had limited contact with extension agents, several countries attempted to expand extension services to female farmers (see, e.g., Saito, Mekonnen, and Spurling 1994). Rigorous impact evaluations are needed to determine whether this expansion helped to encourage technology adoption by female farmers.

## Gender Equality and Productivity of the Next Generation

A growing literature links well-being during early childhood to productivity in adulthood (Behrman and Deolalikar 1988; Strauss and Thomas 1998; Glewwe, Jacoby, and King 2001; Alderman, Hoddinott, and Kinsey 2006; Orazem and King 2008). A substantial body of evidence also shows that, compared with fathers' characteristics, mothers' schooling and bargaining power in the household are significant determinants of children's well-being (Schultz 1997, 2002). Gender inequality that results in less investment in women and reduces their bargaining power in the household can therefore "transmit" low productivity to the next generation via low human capital accumulation among children.

Central to this dynamic transmission argument is the robustness of the finding that mothers' characteristics have a larger impact on children's outcomes than fathers' characteristics. How robust is this evidence?

One characteristic for which there is much empirical evidence is the effect of mothers' schooling on various measures of children's well-being; the effect of fathers' schooling tends to be smaller (see Schultz 1997 and 2002 for a discussion). It is difficult to disentangle the pathways through which women's education affects child well-being—it could be a combination of greater bargaining power in the household or improved ability to process information about child health and development (Caldwell, 1979; Cebu Study Team 1991; Thomas, Strauss, and Henriques 1991; Behrman et al. 1999; Glewwe 1999; Brown 2006). Unobserved ability and preferences could also play a role. In settings in which school enrollment is not universal, women with any schooling are likely those with higher ability. Another possibility is that better-educated men marry better-educated women, and so this effect of maternal education at least in part also reflects fathers' preferences (Basu 1999; Behrman et al. 1999; Schultz 2002).

Since the surge of interest in nonunitary models of the household, research has focused on identifying the impact of women's relative bargaining power on influencing decisions about children, such as the share of household expenditure devoted to child goods or child nutritional status, survival, and schooling. Measuring bargaining power within the household is the central empirical challenge. The challenge is to identify an exogenous source of relative control over resource allocation—one that is not itself an outcome of decision making within the household (see Lundberg and Pollak 1996 for a discussion). Early contributions to the literature used shares of income as a measure of relative control over resources (see, e.g., Phipps and Burton 1998). However, individual labor supply and earnings are likely an outcome of negotiation between husbands and wives as well as market wages and, thus, may not be an exogenous indicator of relative control over resources. Improving on this approach, a large number of studies use non-labor (unearned) income or asset ownership of each spouse as an indicator of bargaining power. Most studies using this approach find that mothers' ownership of assets is associated with better outcomes for children (Thomas 1990, 1997; Quisumbing and Maluccio 2003).

Using unearned income or asset ownership as a measure of bargaining also has limitations, because the assets owned today might have been financed using past earnings. A promising approach that gets around this issue is based on measuring the impact of programs that provide resources directly to households. Some recent studies examine the impact of conditional cash transfer programs in Latin America that provide transfers only to women. Because these programs do not give transfers to men, the relative effect of women's control over resources is measured by comparing expenditure shares between households with and without female transfer recipients. These studies find that transfer income increases households' investment in areas that women care about or areas generally considered to be in women's domain. Rubalcava, Teruel, and Thomas (2009) compare the marginal effect on household expenditure patterns of income received through the Oportunidades program in Mexico with the marginal effect of other sources of household income. They find that, controlling for total resources, cash transfers from the program resulted in higher shares of the household budget spent on education, children's clothing, and meat.

Schady and Rosero (2007) find similar effects in Ecuador for transfers made to women under Bono de Desarrollo Humano (BDH, Human Development Bond). Households receiving transfers spend more on food than nonparticipating households. A comparison of the impact of transfers among households with adult women and men and those with only adult women reveals that the impact of the program on food expenditure shares is higher in the former.[22] In addition, when they restrict their analysis to households with adult women and men, they find that program transfers have a significant impact on share of food expenditure mainly in those households in which women's initial (or pre-program) bargaining power is low (in which bargaining power is proxied for by educational attainment).

A limitation of the existing studies based on conditional cash transfer programs is that the programs give transfers only to women. Studies that examine programs that provide resources to women *and* men are able to compare the impact of a change in resources controlled by mothers and

---

22 If women have stronger preferences for spending on food, it is reasonable to expect higher food shares among BDH recipients in mixed-adult households in which transfers increased the bargaining power of women, but not among female-only households in which there are no men with whom to bargain.

fathers on children's well-being. Pitt and Khandker (1998) and Pitt et al. (2003) find that women's borrowing from microfinance programs in rural Bangladesh has a larger impact on children's well-being (their school enrollment and anthropometric measurements) than men's borrowing. In a study of the impact of pensions in South Africa, Duflo (2003) finds that girls who live with a grandmother who receives pensions weigh more and are taller than those who live with a grandmother who is not eligible to receive pension benefits. Pensions received by men have no effect on grandchildren's height or weight.

Because bargaining power depends not only on control over resources in the household but also on external conditions (such as the marriage market), changes in legislation that affect a woman's well-being were her marriage to dissolve provide an opportunity to analyze the impact of changes in bargaining power on household decision making (McElroy 1990). Such legislation includes rules governing settlement of marital property, child support, custody, and alimony. Studies examining the impact of the changes in divorce laws in the United States in the 1970s and 1980s find that these changes affected married women's labor supply (Stevenson 2007). In one of the few studies of a developing country, Rangel (2006) analyzes the impact of a 1994 change in Brazilian law that extended alimony rights to couples living in consensual unions or informal marriages; it did not change the rights of men or women living in formal unions. Combining Brazilian household survey data from before and after the law change and using formally married couples as a comparison group, Rangel finds that the extension of alimony rights resulted in an increase in cohabiting women's hours of leisure and to an increase in school attendance by their oldest daughters.

### Areas for Future Research

The evidence that mothers are a dynamic link to the productivity of the next generation is strong, but there is room to further refine this evidence. To this end, randomized experiments currently under way in Burkina Faso, Morocco, and Yemen plan to test the impact of giving transfers to mothers versus fathers, with and without conditions. These experiments will enable a rigorous assessment of the impact of giving resources to men and women on children's human capital.

## Gender Equality and Economic Development/Growth

The available microeconomic evidence suggests that improving the socioeconomic position of women (in relation to that of men) through greater access to economic resources and opportunities is likely to yield greater economic growth and development. Potential channels through which these effects could materialize include (1) greater investments in one's own human capital; (2) greater investments in children's human capital; and (3) allocative efficiency from equalizing access to productive assets and markets. The empirical evidence on these channels was discussed in earlier sections of this chapter.

Is the available macroeconomic evidence consistent with the growth implications from the microeconomic evidence? Generally yes, albeit with some methodological caveats. One source of such evidence is panel cross-country regressions. Because the relationship between growth and gender equality is two-way, this method has been used to examine the *ceteris paribus* effect of gender equality on the level of development and growth as well as vice versa, and the findings generally show positive effects in both directions.[23] Studies using this method, particularly the more recent ones, have attempted to be more careful in addressing the potential simultaneity between the level of economic development and gender equality—such as by using lagged values or instrumenting for the regressor of interest— as well as controlling for potential omitted variable bias by including an extensive set of relevant conditioning variables within a regression framework. Despite stronger studies, this empirical strategy is viewed as largely unpromising because identification remains problematic and, therefore, the interpretation of findings.

Another source of evidence is simulations based on country-level computable general equilibrium (CGE) models, constructed and calibrated using both national account and household survey data. In the economics of gender literature, these models have been used primarily to simulate the gender-differentiated effects of national pro-growth policy reform scenarios, such as trade liberalization and foreign direct investment (see, e.g, Arndt and Tarp 2000; Fontana and Wood 2000; Fofana, Cockburn, and Decaluwe 2005; Thurlow 2006; Cockburn et al. 2007).[24] These models have only recently begun to be used to examine the effects of pro-gender-equality policy reform scenarios on national economic growth prospects. Additional research is required before summary statements can be made on what the evidence shows.[25]

This approach has both pros and cons, but, on balance, it appears promising. An important strength is that it attempts to simulate the macroeconomic consequences of reforms, based to a large extent on the patterns, trends, and associations found in the microeconomic data. As such, these macro-micro simulation studies serve as a potentially useful complement to the purely microeconometric research discussed earlier. The performance of these models, of course, has to be validated against

---

23 For evidence on the effect of level of development or growth on gender equality, see, for example, Dollar and Gatti (1999), Klasen (2002), Abu-Ghaida and Klasen (2004), and Klasen and Lamanna (forthcoming). Esteve-Volart (2004) also examines this effect by looking within India at cross-state differences. For the reverse effect, see, for example, Dollar and Gatti (1999), Forsythe, Korzeniewicz, and Durrant (2000), and Oostendorp (2009).

24 See also Fontana (2003) for a review of the empirical literature on this issue.

25 An initial study of this type was carried out by the World Bank (2008). It finds that raising the level of female education generates greater growth. Reducing occupational segregation along gender lines and gender gaps in earnings also generates—albeit modest—increases in growth rates.

the real experiences of countries that undertake policy reforms of the types simulated. An important weakness of these models is that they are not designed to estimate the causal effect of gender equality on growth or vice versa. In our view, causality issues are best addressed via microeconometric studies—even if such studies cannot explicitly make the link to macro growth and distribution.

### Areas for Future Research

The growth consequences of greater gender equality and the gender equality consequences of growth and development should both be explored with equal vigor. Key questions include the following: What are the growth effects of reducing gender disparities in access to productive assets and income-generating activities? Which barriers to access, when relaxed, yield quantitatively large impacts on growth? How does the presence (or relaxation) of multiple barriers constrain (promote) growth? And how do the effects on gender equality differ, depending on the particular mechanism(s) behind growth? An additional pertinent question, especially given the current global economic climate, is how do economic growth slowdowns and contractions affect gender equality and through what channels?

## Future Research Agenda

Although the nature of research questions—as well as the strengths of the methods and data used to answer them—on the links between gender equality and economic development and growth within key markets, across generations, and at the aggregate level has improved over time, much more methodologically strong research is required to disentangle complex relationships and identify the main causal channels operating in both directions. Each of the earlier sections ended by pointing out important gaps in the existing literature and potentially promising empirical strategies to arrive at more compelling answers. This final section pulls together some of these points.

### Documenting Gender Disparities

Even though a fair amount is known about gender disparities in labor market outcomes such as participation, occupational distribution, and earnings across the developing world, much more needs to be learned about gender disparities in the nature of access to productive assets/inputs such as land, technology, and credit. A key constraint has been data collection efforts, which in the past have been largely limited to gathering general information on the ownership of productive assets from the household head or the main breadwinner, thereby implicitly treating the household as a monolithic unit. If potential intrahousehold differences in the ownership and use of productive assets are to be uncovered, survey questions must be able to capture more nuanced information and must be posed at the individual level rather than at the household level.

## Gender-Differentiated Effects of Increased Access to Economic Resources and Opportunities

More research is required to understand whether and how, for example, strengthening land tenure security or providing new productive technologies, basic community infrastructure such as water and energy supply, and credit/savings options in general affect economic decisions related to investment, production, income, and consumption, which differ systematically by gender. Rigorous impact evaluations—including, where feasible, prospective randomized designs—would aid in identifying the causal effects of the various interventions on these outcomes. Compelling evidence on gender-differentiated effects would clearly be useful to the policymakers designing future programs and projects that leverage these effects to maximize returns.

## Efficiency Gains

More rigorous evidence is needed on whether and how improving the socioeconomic position of mothers benefits children's welfare more than improving the same position of fathers, and whether improving gender equality, such as by reducing barriers to increasing human capital accumulation and accessing markets, translates into gains in national economic growth and development. On the first question, rigorous evidence is emerging as prospective randomized designs are being applied. On the second question, both microempirical methods and country-specific macrosimulations are promising strategies. These methods clearly benefit from the increasing availability of household survey data (over multiple points in time) in developing countries. They also benefit from the increasing availability (although at a slower rate) of panel household and individual survey data for longer periods and more developing countries. These data structures will greatly facilitate disentangling the relationship between gender equality and growth and development.

## References

Abu-Ghaida, Dina, and Stephan Klasen. 2004. "The Costs of Missing the Millennium Development Goal on Gender Equity." *World Development* 32: 1075–1107.

Agarwal, Bina. 1994. "Gender and Command over Property: A Critical Gap in Economic Analysis and Policy in South Asia." *World Development* 22: 1455–78.

———. 2003. "Gender and Land Rights Revisited: Exploring New Prospects via the State, Family and Market." *Journal of Agrarian Change* 3: 184–224.

Akoten J. E., Y. Sawada, and K. Otsuka. 2006. "The Determinants of Credit Access and Its Impacts on Micro and Small Enterprises: The Case of Garment Producers in Kenya." *Economic Development and Cultural Change* 54 (4): 927–44.

Alderman, H., J. Hoddinott, and B. Kinsey. 2006. "Long Term Consequences of Early Childhood Malnutrition." *Oxford Economic Papers* 58 (3): 450–74.

Almeyda, Gloria. 1996. *Money Matters: Reaching Women Microentrepreneurs with Financial Services*. Washington, DC: Inter-American Development Bank.

Antle, John, David Yanggen, Roberto Valdivia, and Charles Crissman. 2003. "Endogeneity of Land Titling and Farm Investments: Evidence from the Peruvian Andes." Department of Agricultural Economics Working Paper, Montana State University, Bozeman.

Arndt, Channing, and Finn Tarp. 2000. "Agricultural Technology, Risk, and Gender." *World Development* 28 (7): 1307–26.

Ashraf, Nava, Dean Karlan, and Wesley Yin. 2008. "Female Empowerment: Impact of a Commitment Savings Product in the Philippines." Poverty Action Lab, Massachusetts Institute of Technology, Cambridge, MA.

Assaad, Ragui, Fatma El-Hamidi, and Akhter U. Ahmed. 2000. "The Determinants of Employment Status in Egypt." FCND Discussion Paper 88, International Food Policy Research Institute, Washington, DC.

Bandiera, Oriana, and Imran Rasul. 2006. "Social Networks and Technology Adoption in Northern Mozambique." *Economic Journal* 116: 862–902.

Banerjee, Abhijit, and Esther Duflo. 2004. "Growth Theory through the Lens of Development Economics." Working Paper 05-01, Department of Economics, Massachusetts Institute of Technology, Cambridge, MA.

Banerjee, Abhijit, Paul Gertler, and Maitreesh Ghatak. 2002. "Empowerment and Efficiency: Tenancy Reform in West Bengal." *Journal of Political Economy* 110 (2): 239–80.

Bardasi, Elena, Kathleen Beegle, Andrew Dillon, and Pieter Serneels. 2009. "Assessing Labor Statistics in Sub-Saharan Africa: A Survey Experiment." Unpublished paper.

Barham, B., S. Boucher, and M. Carter. 1996. "Credit Constraints, Credit Unions, and Small-scale Producers in Guatemala." *World Development* 24 (5): 793–806.

Basu, Alaka Malwade. 1999. "Women's Education, Marriage, and Fertility in South Asia: Do Men Really Not Matter?" In *Critical Perspectives on Schooling and Fertility in the Developing World*, ed. Caroline H. Bledsoe, John B. Casterline, Jennifer A. Johnson-Kuhn, and John G. Haaga. Washington, DC: National Academy Press.

Baydas, Mayada M., Richard L. Meyer, and Nelson Aguilera-Alfred. 1994. "Discrimination against Women in Formal Credit Markets: Reality or Rhetoric?" *World Development* 22: 1073–82.

Beck, Thorsten, and Asli Demirguc-Kunt. 2008. "Access to Finance an Unfinished Agenda." *World Bank Economic Review* 22 (3): 383–96.

Becker, Gary. 1985. "Human Capital, Effort, and the Sexual Division of Labor." *Journal of Labor Economics* 3(1): S33–58.

Behrman, Jere. 1986. "Intrahousehold Allocation of Nutrients in Rural India: Are Boys Favored? Do Parents Exhibit Inequality Aversion?" *Oxford Economic Papers* 40 (1): 32–54.

Behrman, Jere R., and Anil B. Deolalikar. 1988. "Health and Nutrition." In *Handbook of Development Economics*, vol. 1, ed. Hollis Chenery and T. N. Srinivasan, 631–711. Amsterdam: Elsevier.

Behrman, Jere, Mark Rosenzweig, Andrew Foster, and Prem Vashishtha. 1999. "Women's Schooling, Home Teaching, and Economic Growth." *Journal of Political Economy* 107 (4): 682–714.

Berger, Marguerite. 1989. "Giving Women Credit: The Strengths and Limitations of Credit as a Tool for Alleviating Poverty." *World Development* 17: 1017–32.

Besley, Timothy. 1995. "Property Rights and Investment Incentives: Theory and Evidence from Ghana." *Journal of Political Economy* 193: 903–37.

Blackburn, R. M., and J. Jarman. 1997. "Occupational Gender Segregation." *Social Research Update* 16 (Spring).

Blackden, C. M., and Q. Wodon. 2006. *Gender, Time Use and Poverty in Sub-Saharan Africa*. Washington, DC: World Bank.

Bouis, Howard, and Lawrence Haddad. 1990. "Effects of Agricultural Commercialization on Land Tenure, Household Resource Allocation, and Nutrition in the Philippines." Research Report 79, International Food Policy Research Institute, Washington, DC.

Bravo, D. C., et al. 2007. "An Experimental Study about Labor Market Discrimination: Gender, Social Class and Neighborhood." Working paper, Inter-American Development Bank, Washington, DC.

Bridges, W. 2003. "Rethinking Gender Segregation and Gender Inequality: Measures and Meanings." *Demography* 40 (3): 543–68.

Brown, Philip H. 2006. "Parental Education and Investment in Children's Human Capital in Rural China." *Economic Development and Cultural Change* 54 (4): 759–89.

Buvinic, Mayra, and Marguerite Berger. 1994. "Sex Differences in Access to a Small Enterprise Development Fund in Peru." *World Development* 18: 695–705.

Caldwell, J. C. 1979. "Education as a Factor in Mortality Decline: An Examination of Nigerian Data." *Population Studies* 33 (3): 395–413.

Cameron, Lisa, J. Jalcolm Dowling, and Christopher Worswick. 2001. "Education and the Labor Market Participation of Women in Asia: Evidence from Five Countries." *Economic Development and Cultural Change* 49 (3): 461–77.

Carter, Michael, and Julian May. 1999. "Poverty, Livelihood and Class in Rural South Africa." *World Development* 27 (7): 1–20.

Cebu Study Team. 1991. "Underlying and Proximate Determinants of Child Health: The CEBU Longitudinal Health and Nutrition Study." *American Journal of Epidemiology* 133 (2): 185–201.

Chirwa, Ephraim. 2005. "Fertilizer and Hybrid Seeds Adoption among Smallholder Maize Farmers in Southern Malawi." *Development Southern Africa* 22 (1): 1–12.

Cockburn, John, Ismael Fofana, Bernard Decaluwe, Ramos Mabugu, and Margaret Chitiga. 2007. "A Gender-Focused Macro-Micro Analysis of the

Poverty Impacts of Trade Liberalization in South Africa." In *Research on Economic Inequality,* vol. 15, ed. P. J. Lambert. Stamford, CT: JAI Press.

Deere, Carmen Diana, and Magdalena Leon. 2003. "The Gender Asset Gap: Land in Latin America." *World Development* 31: 925–47.

de Mel, Suresh, David McKenzie, and Christopher Woodruff. 2008. "Are Women More Credit Constrained? Experimental Evidence on Gender and Microenterprise Returns." Policy Research Working Paper 4746, World Bank, Washington, DC.

Deininger, Klaus, and Hans Binswanger. 1999. "The Evolution of the World Bank's Land Policy: Principles, Experience, and Future Challenges. *World Bank Research Observer* 14: 247–76.

de Laiglesia, Juan R. 2003. "Investment Effects of Land Titling and Registration: Evidence from Nicaragua." Unpublished paper.

Deutsch, R., et al. 2004. "Working with Confines: Occupational Segregation by Gender in Three Latin American Countries." In *Women at Work: Challenges for Latin American Countries,* ed. C. Piras. Washington, DC: Inter-American Development Bank.

Diagne, A. 1999. Determinants of Household Access to and Participation in Formal and Informal Credit Markets in Malawi. FCND Discussion Paper 67, International Food Policy Research Institute, Washington, DC.

Diagne, Aliou, Manfred Zeller, and Manohar Sharma. 2000. "Empirical Measurements of Households' Access to Credit and Credit Constraints in Developing Countries: Methodological Issues and Evidence." FCND Discussion Paper 90, International Food Policy Research Institute, Washington, DC.

Dinkelman, Taryn. 2008. "The Effects of Rural Electrification on Employment: New Evidence from South Africa." Working paper, Department of Economics University of Michigan, Ann Arbor.

Do, Quy-Toan, and Lakshmi Ayer. 2008. "Land Titling and Rural Transition in Vietnam." *Economic Development and Cultural Change* 56: 531–79.

Dollar, David, and Roberta Gatti. 1999. "Gender Inequality, Income, and Growth: Are Good Times Good for Women?" Policy Research Report on Gender and Development Working Paper Series 1, World Bank, Washington, DC.

Doss, Cheryl R. 2001. "Designing Agricultural Technology for African Women Farmers: Lessons from 25 Years of Experience." *World Development* 29 (12): 2075–92.

———. 2006. "Analyzing Technology Adoption Using Microstudies: Limitations, Challenges, and Opportunities for Improvement." *Agricultural Economics* 34: 207–19.

Doss, Cheryl R., and Michael L. Morris. 2001. "How Does Gender Affect the Adoption of Agricultural Technologies? The Case of Improved Maize Technology in Ghana." *Agricultural Economics* 25: 27–39.

Duflo, Esther. 2003. "Grandmothers and Granddaughters: Old Age Pension and Intra-household Allocation in South Africa." *World Bank Economic Review* 17 (1): 1–25.

———. 2005. "Gender Equality in Development." Unpublished paper.

Duflo, Esther, Michael Kremer, and Jonathan Robinson. 2009. "Nudging Farmers to Use Fertilizer: Evidence from Kenya." Unpublished paper.

Dupas, Pascaline, and Jonathan Robinson. 2009. "Savings Constraints and Microenterprise Development: Evidence from a Field Experiment in Kenya." Working Paper 14693, National Bureau of Economic Research, Cambridge, MA.

Elson, Diane. 1999. "Labor Markets as Gendered Institutions: Equality, Efficiency and Empowerment Issues." *World Development* 27 (3): 611–27.

Esteve-Volart, Berta. 2004. "Gender Discrimination and Growth: Theory and Evidence from India." LSE STICERD Research Paper No. DEDPS42, Suntory and Toyota International Centres for Economics and Related Disciplines (STICERD) at the London School of Economics and Political Science (LSE).

Evenson, R., and M. Siegel. 1999. "Gender and Agricultural Extension in Burkina Faso." *African Affairs* 46 (1): 75–92.

Fafchamps, Marcel, and Agnes Quisumbing. 2005. "Assets at Marriage in Rural Ethiopia." *Journal of Development Economics* 77: 1–25.

FAO (Food and Agriculture Organization). 2002. "Gender and Access to Land." *FAO Land Tenure Studies* 4.

Feder, G., R. E. Just, and D. Zilberman. 1985. "Adoption of Agricultural Innovations in Developing Countries: A Survey." *Economic Development and Cultural Change* 33 (2): 255–98.

Field, Erica. 2007. "Entitled to Work: Urban Property Rights and Labor Supply in Peru." *Quarterly Journal of Economics* 122 (4): 1561–1602.

Finan, Frederico, Elisabeth Sadoulet, and Alain de Janvry. 2005. "Measuring the Poverty Reduction Potential of Land in Rural Mexico." *Journal of Development Economics* 77 (1): 27–51.

Fletschner, Diana. 2008. "Women's Access to Credit: Does It Matter for Household Efficiency?" *American Journal of Agricultural Economics.* 90 (3): 669–83.

Fofana, Ismael, John Cockburn, and Bernard Decaluwe. 2005. "Developing Country Superwomen: Impacts of Trade Liberalisation on Female Market and Domestic Work." Working Paper 05-19, Le Centre interuniversitaire sur le risque, les politiques économiques et l'emploi (CIRPÉE), Montreal.

Fontana, Marzia. 2003. "The Gender Effects of Trade Liberalization in Developing Countries: A Review of the Literature." Discussion Paper in Economics 101, University of Sussex, Brighton.

Fontana, Marzia, and Adrian Wood. 2000. "Modeling the Effects of Trade on Women, at Work, and at Home." *World Development* 28 (7): 1173–90.

Forsythe, Nancy, Roberta P. Korzeniewicz, and Valerie Durrant. 2000. "Gender Inequalities and Economic Growth: A Longitudinal Evaluation." *Economic Development and Cultural Change* 48: 573–617.

Galiani, Sebastian, and Ernesto Schargrodsky. 2009. "Property Rights for the Poor: Effects of Land Titling." Working Paper 7, Ronald Coase Institute, St. Louis.

Galor, Oded, and David N. Weil. 1996. "The Gender Gap, Fertility and Growth." *American Economic Review* 86 (3): 374–87.

Glewwe, Paul. 1999. "Why Does Mother's Schooling Raise Child Health in Developing Countries? Evidence from Morocco." *Journal of Human Resources* 34 (1): 124–59.

Glewwe, Paul, Hanan G. Jacoby, and Elizabeth M. King. 2001. "Early Childhood Nutrition and Academic Achievement: A Longitudinal Analysis." *Journal of Public Economics* 81 (3): 345–68.

Goldin, Claudia. 1995. "The U-Shaped Female Labor Force Function in Economic Development and Economic History." In *Investment in Women's Human Capital*, ed. T. P. Schultz. Chicago: University of Chicago Press.

Goldstein, Markus, and Christopher Udry. 2008. "The Profits of Power: Land Rights and Agricultural Investment in Ghana." *Journal of Political Economy* 116 (6): 981–1022.

Grootaert, Christiaan, Ravi Kanbur, and Gi-taik Oh. 1997. "The Dynamic of Welfare Gains and Losses: An African Case Study." *Journal of Development Studies* 33 (5): 635–57.

Gunning, Jan Willem, John Hoddinott, Bill Kinsey, and Trudy Owens. 2000. "Revisiting Forever Gained: Income Dynamics in the Resettlement Areas of Zimbabwe, 1983–96." *Journal of Development Studies* 36 (6): 131–54.

Ilahi, Nadeem. 2000. "Gender and the Allocation of Time and Tasks: What Have We Learnt from the Empirical Literature?" Background paper for *Engendering Development through Equality in Rights, Resources and Voice*. Washington, DC: World Bank.

Ilahi, N., and F. Grimard. 2000. "Public Infrastructure and Private Costs: Water Supply and Time Allocation of Women in Rural Pakistan." *Economic Development and Cultural Change* 49 (1): 45–75.

Jha, D., B. Hojjati, and S. Vosti. 1991. "The Use of Improved Agricultural Technology in Eastern Province." In *Adopting Improved Farm Technology: A Study of Smallholder Farmers in Eastern Province Zambia*, ed. R. Celis, J. T. Milimo, and S. Wanmali. Washington, DC: International Food Policy Research Institute.

Kevane, Michael, and Lesley C. Gray. 1999. "A Women's Field Is Made at Night: Gendered Land Rights and Norms in Burkina Faso." *Feminist Economics* 5: 1–26.

Klasen, Stephan. 2002. "Low Schooling for Girls, Slower Growth for All? Cross-country Evidence on the Effect of Gender Inequality in Education on Economic Development." *World Bank Economic Review* 16 (3): 345–73.

Klasen, Stephan, and Francesca Lamanna. Forthcoming. "Gender Inequality in Education and Employment and Economic Growth: New Evidence for Developing Countries." *Feminist Economics*.

Kumar, Shubh K. 1994. "Adoption of Hybrid Maize in Zambia: Effects on Gender Roles, Food Consumption, and Nutrition." Research Report 100, International Food Policy Research Institute, Washington, DC.

Kumar, Shubh K., and David Hotchkiss. 1988. "Consequences of Deforestation for Women's Time Allocation, Agricultural Production, and Nutrition in Hill Areas of Nepal." Research Report 69, International Food Policy Research Institute, Washington, DC.

Lawson, D. 2008. "Infrastructure and Time Poverty in Lesotho." *South African Journal of Economics* 76 (1): 77–88.

Lilja, Nina, and John H. Sanders. 1998. "Welfare Impacts of Technological Change on Women in Southern Mali." *Agricultural Economics* 19: 73–79.

Lundberg, Shelly, and Robert A. Pollak. 1996. "Bargaining and Distribution in Marriage." *Journal of Economic Perspectives* 10 (4): 139–58.

Lycette, M., and K. White. 1989. "Improving Women's Access to Credit in Latin America and the Caribbean." In *Women's Ventures: Assistance to the Informal Sector in Latin America*, ed. M. Berger and M. Buvinic, 19–44. West Hartford, CT: Kumarian Press.

Mammen, Kristin, and Christina Paxson. 2000. "Women's Work and Economic Development." *Journal of Economic Perspectives* 14 (4): 141–64.

McElroy, M. 1990. "The Empirical Content of Nash-Bargained House-Hold Behavior." *Journal of Human Resources* 25: 559–83.

Moreno, M., et al. 2004. "Gender and Racial Discrimination in Hiring: A Pseudo Audit Study for Three Selected Occupations in Metropolitan Lima." Discussion Paper 979, Institute for the Study of Labor (IZA), Bonn.

Ñopo, H. 2008. "Matching as a Tool to Decompose Wage Gaps." *Review of Economics and Statistics* 90 (2): 290–99.

Oostendorp, Remco H. 2009. "Globalization and the Gender Wage Gap." *World Bank Economic Review* 23 (1): 141–61.

Orazem, Peter F., and Elizabeth M. King. 2008. "Schooling in Developing Countries: The Roles of Supply, Demand and Government Policy." In *Handbook of Development Economics*, ed. T. P. Schultz and J. Strauss, chap. 5. Amsterdam: Elsevier.

Petrick, Martin. 2005. "Empirical Measurement of Credit Rationing in Agriculture: A Methodological Survey." *Agricultural Economics* 33 (2): 191–203, 209.

Phipps, Shelley, and Peter Burton. 1998. "What's Mine Is Yours? The Influence of Male and Female Incomes on Patterns of Household Expenditure." *Economica* 65: 599–613.

Pitt, Mark M., and Shahidur R. Khandker. 1998. "The Impact of Group-Based Credit Programs on Poor Households in Bangladesh: Does the Gender of Participants Matter?" *Journal of Political Economy* 106: 958–96.

Pitt, Mark M., Shahidur R. Khandker, Omar Haider Chowdhury, and Daniel L. Millimet. 2003. "Credit Programmes for the Poor and the Health Status of Children in Rural Bangladesh." *International Economic Review* 44 (1): 87–118.

Polachek, Solomon. 1995. "Human Capital and the Gender Earnings Gap: A Response to Feminist Critiques." In *Out of the Margin: Feminist Perspectives on Economics*, ed. Susan Feiner, Notburga Ott, and Zafiris Tzannatos. London and New York: Routledge.

Quisumbing, Agnes R. 1994. "Intergenerational Transfers to Philippine Rice Villages: Gender Differences in Traditional Inheritance Customs." *Journal of Development Economics* 43: 167–95.

———. 1995. "Gender Differences in Agricultural Productivity: A Survey of Empirical Evidence." FCND Discussion Paper 5, International Food Policy Research Institute, Washington, DC.

————. 1996. "Male-Female Differences in Agricultural Productivity: Methodological Issues and Empirical Evidence." *World Development* 24 (10): 1579–95.

Quisumbing Agnes R., and John A. Maluccio. 2003. "Resources at Marriage and Intrahousehold Allocation: Evidence from Bangladesh, Ethiopia, Indonesia, and South Africa." *Oxford Bulletin of Economics and Statistics* 65 (3): 283–327.

Quisumbing, Agnes R., Jonna P. Estudillo, and Keijiro Otsuka. 2004. *Land and Schooling: Transferring Wealth across Generations.* Baltimore: Johns Hopkins University Press.

Rangel, Marcos A. 2006. "Alimony Rights and Intrahousehold Allocation of Resources: Evidence from Brazil." *Economic Journal* 116 (July): 627–58.

Raturi, Mayank, and Anand V. Swamy. 1999. "Explaining Ethnic Differentials in Credit Market Outcomes in Zimbabwe." *Economic Development and Cultural Change* 47: 585–604.

Rose, Elaina. 1999. "Consumption Smoothing and Excess Female Mortality in Rural India." *Review of Economics and Statistics* 81 (1): 41–49.

Rosenzweig, M. R., and T. P. Schultz. 1982. "Market Opportunities, Genetic Endowments, and Intrafamily Resource Distribution: Child Survival in Rural India." *American Economic Review* 72 (4): 803–15.

Rubalcava, L., G. Teruel, and D. Thomas. 2009. "Investments, Time Preferences and Public Transfers Paid to Women." *Economic Development and Cultural Change* 57 (3): 507–38.

Saito, Katrine A., Hailu Mekonnen, and Daphne Spurling. 1994. "Raising the Productivity of Women Farmers in Sub-Saharan Africa," Discussion Paper 230, World Bank, Washington, DC.

Schady, Norbert, and Jose Rosero. 2007. "Are Cash Transfers Made to Women Spent Like Other Sources of Income?" Policy Research Working Paper 4282, World Bank, Washington, DC.

Schultz, T. P. 1997. "The Demand for Children in Low-Income Countries." In *Handbook of Population and Family Economics*, ed. M. R. Rosenzweig and O. Stark, 349–430. Amsterdam: North-Holland.

————. 2002. "Why Governments Should Invest More to Educate Girls." *World Development* 30 (2): 207–25.

Stevenson, Betsey, 2007. "Divorce-Law Changes, Household Bargaining, and Married Women's Labor Supply Revisited." Available at Social Science Research Network, http://ssrn.com/abstract=999679.

Storey, D. J. 2004. "Racial and Gender Discrimination in the Micro Firms Credit Market? Evidence from Trindad and Tobago." *Small Business Economics* 23: 401–22.

Strauss, John, and Duncan Thomas, 1998. "Health, Nutrition, and Economic Development." *Journal of Economic Literature* 36 (2): 766–817.

Sudha, S., and S. Irudaya Rajan. 1999. "Female Demographic Disadvantage in India 1981–1991: Sex-Selective Abortion and Female Infanticide." *Development and Change*, Special issue on gender, poverty and well-being 30: 585–618.

Thomas, Duncan. 1990. "Intrahousehold Resource Allocation: An Inferential Approach." *Journal of Human Resources* 25: 635–64.

———. 1997. "Incomes, Expenditures and Health Outcomes: Evidence on Intrahousehold Resource Allocation." In *Intrahousehold Resource Allocation in Developing Countries: Models, Methods, and Policy*, ed. Lawrence Haddad, John Hoddinott, and Harold Alderman. Baltimore: Johns Hopkins University Press.

Thomas, Duncan, John Strauss, and Maria-Helena Henriques. 1991. "How Does Mother's Education Affect Child Height?" *Journal of Human Resources* 26 (2): 183–211.

Thurlow, James. 2006. "Has Trade Liberalization in South Africa Affected Men and Women Differently?" IFPRI Development Strategies and Governance Discussion Paper 36, International Food Policy Research Institute, Washington, DC.

Tzannatos, Z. 2008. "Monitoring Progress in Gender Equality in the Labor Market." In *Equality for Women: Where Do We Stand on Millennium Development Goal 3?* ed. M. Buvinic et al. Washington, DC: World Bank.

Udry, Christopher. 1996. "Gender, Agricultural Production, and the Theory of the Household." *Journal of Political Economy* 104: 1010–46.

Udry, Christopher, John Hoddinott, Harold Alderman, and Lawrence Haddad. 1995. "Gender Differentials in Farm Productivity: Implications for Household Efficiency and Agricultural Policy." *Food Policy* 20 (5): 407–23.

von Braun, Joachim, and Patrick J. R. Webb. 1989. "The Impact of New Crop Technology on the Agricultural Division of Labor in a West Africa Setting." *Economic Development and Cultural Change* 50: 313–38.

World Bank. 2001. *Engendering Development through Gender Equality in Rights, Resources, and Voice.* Washington, DC: World Bank.

———. 2008. *Ethiopia: Unleashing the Potential of Ethiopian Women. Trends and Options for Economic Empowerment.* Washington, DC: World Bank.

# CHAPTER 6

# Inequality of Opportunity for Education: Turkey

*Francisco H. G. Ferreira and Jérémie Gignoux*

Questions about the relationship between equity and growth, which lie at the heart of every chapter in this volume, are at least as old as economics itself. In the preface to his *On the Principles of Political Economy and Taxation*, David Ricardo wrote:

> The produce of earth—all that is derived from its surface by the united application of labor, machinery and capital—is divided among three classes of the community, namely the proprietor of the land, the owner of the stock or capital necessary for its cultivation, and the laborers by whose industry it is cultivated.
>
> But in different stages of society, the proportions of the whole produce of the earth which will be allotted to each of these classes . . . will be essentially different. . . . To determine the laws which regulate this distribution is the principal problem in Political Economy.[1]

We are grateful to the editors, to Meltem Aran and Jesko Hentschel, and to workshop participants from the State Planning Organization, UNICEF, and TEPAV in Ankara for helpful comments on earlier drafts. All errors are our own. The views expressed in this chapter are those of the authors, and they should not be attributed to the World Bank, its executive directors, or the countries they represent.

1  David Ricardo, preface to *On the Principles of Political Economy and Taxation*, 1817 (1911 edition, p. 1), as cited by Atkinson and Bourguignon (2000) in their introduction to the *Handbook of Income Distribution*. Atkinson and Bourguignon already sound somewhat apologetic for failing to resist the temptation to begin with this well-known quotation. A similar apology is therefore even more clearly warranted here.

The quest to understand the links between development and distribution has remained central to modern economics as well. Lewis (1954), Kuznets (1955), and a long line of followers explored causation, running from economic growth and the patterns of structural change associated with it to the distribution of income. More recently, a thriving literature has explored the reverse direction of causality, operating from different degrees of inequality to the nature and rate of economic growth.[2]

But just as interest in the role of income inequality experienced something of a resurgence in mainstream economics in the 1990s (on this resurgence see Atkinson 1997), many social scientists, philosophers, and (even) economists appeared to become less certain that the inequality with which they should be fundamentally concerned was the one they observed in the income space—or indeed the one they might imagine in the space of utilities. Building on Rawls (1971), influential authors such as Sen (1980), Dworkin (1981), and Arneson (1989) challenged philosophers and economists to ask themselves what equality—or the equality *of what*—societies should really aim for? If individual outcomes, including incomes and well-being more generally, are at least in part the result of individual decisions, and if there is an ethical role for individual responsibility, then perhaps equity—understood as the form of equality that is socially just—requires equality in another space, in some sense logically prior to final outcomes. At the risk of greatly oversimplifying, the search for this prior space has taken us to concepts such as primary goods (Rawls 1971), capabilities (Sen 1980), equality of resources (Dworkin 1981), and equality of opportunity (Arneson 1989; Roemer 1998).

The conceptual literature on these different distributional domains is now both rich and well established, but its influence on applied economics has remained marginal. Despite Amartya Sen's Herculean efforts to move economists "from commodities to capabilities," the temptation to look for lost keys where the light shines has remained exceedingly powerful. Although incomes and consumption expenditures may be hard to measure accurately, they are immensely easier to observe and measure than concepts such as capabilities or opportunities.

This situation has, however, recently begun to change, in large part thanks to a particular formalization of the concept of equality of opportunities by Roemer (1998). His definition of the concept lends itself reasonably well to observation in the kind of household data that—even if somewhat more demanding than data on consumption or income alone—do exist in many countries.

Reduced to its essential core, Roemer's definition of equality of opportunity relies on a distinction between two normatively different kinds of determinants of a particular outcome of interest, which he calls *advantage*.

---

2   This literature has spanned economics, including the pioneering work of Loury (1981) and Galor and Zeira (1993), and economic history, including work by Engerman and Sokoloff (1997). The literature has now been reviewed so often that space is insufficient here for even a survey of surveys. One good recent survey is Voitchovsky (2005).

He calls those determinants over which individuals can exercise some discretion (i.e., those that are subject to some degree of individual choice or responsibility) *efforts*. Other determinants, over which individuals have no control, are called *circumstances*. Equal opportunities are said to exist in a society if circumstances are immaterial to the attainment of advantage. In such a situation, there will in general exist some inequality in advantages. But such differences will be attributable only to differences in efforts and not in circumstances.

Roemer's recent (and growing) influence over applied economists arises because such a definition has an immediate statistical implication: given the law of large numbers, equality of opportunity would imply that advantage should be distributed independently of circumstances. To the extent that some advantages (incomes, educational attainment, health status) and some circumstances (race, gender, family background, birthplace) can be observed in large enough samples, the hypothesis of stochastic independence can be tested statistically (e.g., see Lefranc, Pistolesi, and Trannoy 2008). In addition, to the extent to which inequalities between circumstance-homogeneous groups (which Roemer calls *types*) can be associated with inequality of opportunity, the latter concept can be measured cardinally, albeit in *consequential* terms. In other words, a certain amount (or share) of inequality in a particular advantage can be related to inequality of opportunity for the attainment of that particular outcome (e.g., see Bourguignon, Ferreira, and Menéndez 2007; Ferreira and Gignoux 2008).

By empirically identifying, describing, and quantifying inequality in a normatively more appropriate space for assessing social justice, we believe this incipient literature contributes to an economic understanding of equity. In due course, such empirical measures may even be related to the broader processes of growth and development in ways analogous to those in which income and wealth inequality have often been related.

In this chapter, we extend the cardinal approach to the measurement of inequality of opportunity to an advantage other than income, namely education. Because education has intrinsic value to individuals, it can certainly be considered an *advantage*, in Roemer's terms. Because it has such well-documented instrumental value for the achievement of other valued outcomes, such as health and incomes, it also reinforces an opportunity loop.

Education is itself difficult to measure, and this chapter investigates its distribution along two key dimensions: *quantity,* or attainment, which we capture through enrollment-age profiles, and *quality,* or achievement, which we measure through standardized test scores. Few countries are better suited for such an endeavor than Turkey—both for data availability and for intrinsic interest reasons. Turkey has good data on enrollment from the Turkish Demographic and Health Survey (TDHS) of 2003/2004 and on achievement from the Program for International Student Assessment (PISA) 2006 data set, both of which are described in more detail later in this chapter.

Analysis of these data reveals a complex pattern of inequality of opportunity. The profound differences in enrollment rates across genders, regions, and family backgrounds are generally compounded by additional differences in student achievement. But not all circumstances matter in the same ways, and exclusion patterns are not always as they at first appear. Gender is a dominant factor in explaining differences in enrollment, but not in achievement: once girls get to school, they tend to do no worse than boys (and better if one does not control for selection). Regional differences in enrollment, which are large in absolute terms, are not statistically significant once one controls for other circumstances. Differences in family background, whether measured in terms of parental education, father's occupation, or asset ownership, matter for all children, but much more so for girls. One can learn much about Turkish society, and the nature of its inequalities of opportunity, from applying these concepts to these rich data sources.[3]

The remainder of this chapter is organized as follows. The next section briefly describes the three data sets used in the analysis. The section that follows reports the pattern of correlations between individual circumstances and school enrollment. Next is a discussion of the measurement of inequality of opportunity applied to educational achievement in Turkey. The final section presents our conclusions.

## The Data

We use data from three surveys in our analysis. In the next section, we construct profiles of school enrollment rates by age using Turkey's latest Demographic and Health Survey, which was fielded between December 2003 and March 2004 by the Hacettepe Institute. The data were collected from a sample of 10,836 households, representative at the national level, but also at the level of the five major regions of the country (West, South, Central, North, and East). Information on the basic socioeconomic characteristics of the population was collected for all household members, and all ever-married women between the ages of 15 and 49 (8,075) further answered a detailed questionnaire on demography and health.

Information on enrollment was collected on all 18,376 household members from 6 to 24 years old. For all these children and young people, information also was collected on the following circumstance variables: gender, region of residence, type of area of residence, levels of education of mother and father, number of children in household, mother's native tongue, and household wealth. As noted, we classified region of residence into five broad categories—West, South, Central, North, and East; type of area into three categories—rural, small urban areas, and large

---

3   The recent literature on the determinants of school enrollment in Turkey includes Tansel (2002) and Kirdar (2007). We take a slightly different approach here, focusing on the description and measurement of inequality of opportunity for education rather than seeking to estimate the causal effects of specific circumstances on enrollment. Nevertheless, some of our descriptive results are close to findings in that literature.

cities;[4] parental education into three categories—no formal education or unknown level, primary education, and secondary or higher education; mother's native tongue into four categories—Turkish, Kurdish, Arabic, and Caucasian or missing; and number of children in the household into three categories—one or two, three to five, and six or more.[5] Household wealth was measured by means of a Filmer-Pritchett (2001) asset index, constructed by principal components analysis from information on household ownership of various durable goods, housing quality, and access to amenities. For this analysis, households were simply divided into quartiles of the distribution of this index.[6]

Later in this chapter we analyze information on scholastic achievement based on the standardized test scores reported in the 2006 Program for International Student Assessment data set for Turkey. The PISA survey was fielded at Turkish schools by the Organisation for Economic Co-operation and Development (OECD) between March and November 2006 (at the same time as in 56 other countries). The survey collected information on a sample of 4,942 15-year-olds enrolled in grades 7 and up. All children surveyed took tests in reading, math, and science. In addition to the test scores in these subjects, the PISA data set also reports the student's gender and some information on family background, including mother's and father's education, father's occupation, number of books owned by the household, durable goods ownership, and "cultural possessions."[7] School location variables also allow us to allocate the student to a geographic region of the country, as well as to rural or urban areas (including a disaggregation into large or small cities).[8]

The PISA sample is representative of the national population of 15-year-olds enrolled in grades 7 and up. However, because of the incomplete enrollment at age 15, repetition, and sample design issues, the sample coverage rate (the ratio of the population represented by the survey to the total population of 15-year-olds) is only 47 percent in Turkey. Particularly

---

4   In the TDHS, urban areas are defined as settlements with populations of more than 10,000, and large cities are Istanbul, Izmir, Bursa, Adana, and the capital, Ankara. Although information on area or region of residence is less consistent with an interpretation as an exogenous circumstance than is area of birth, this is the only information available for this age group in the TDHS. We assume that the two are very closely correlated for children.

5   We include all children (age 18 or younger) in our sample. Ninety percent of these are children of the household head and/or his or her spouse. For the 10 percent remaining, the data set does not permit an unambiguous identification of their parents. In these cases, we use the education levels of the household head and spouse in lieu of their parents' education levels.

6   Details of the construction of this asset index and of its distribution can be found in Ferreira, Gignoux, and Aran (2010).

7   Parental education was classified as in the TDHS, but secondary and higher education were coded separately. Father's occupation was coded into three groups, following the ISCO 88 classification: (1) legislators, senior officials, professionals, technicians, and clerks; (2) service workers, craft and related trade workers, plant and machine operators or assemblers, or unoccupied; and (3) skilled agricultural or fishery workers or workers with an elementary occupation. Durables include: dishwasher, VCR/ DVD, cell phone, car, computer, and TV. Cultural possessions refer to the household's ownership of works of literature, art, and poetry.

8   Because of differences in the sample frame, the regional breakdown for the PISA survey is coarser than that for the TDHS and includes only three main categories: West, Central, and East.

worrisome, of course, is the fact that selection into enrollment and repetition is clearly nonrandom. The analysis later in this chapter presents results mostly for the universe for which the sample is representative, in line with the literature based on PISA surveys. However, we also report two alternative attempts to correct for selection biases in estimating inequality of opportunity for educational achievement.

To correct for selection into the PISA sample, we use two-sample reweighting techniques and data from Turkey's 2006 Household Budget Survey (HBS). This survey has a nationally representative sample of about 8,500 households, which includes 683 individuals aged 15. A set of circumstance variables comparable to some of those in the PISA survey are available, including gender, area type,[9] parental education, and father's occupation. From the HBS sample weights, the total national population of the groups of 15-year-olds with each specific set of characteristics can be estimated. These estimates of the populations of the different "types" are used later in this chapter to provide two alternative estimates of the effects of selection on the measures of inequality of opportunity for educational achievement.

## Circumstances at Birth and School Enrollment

A natural way to begin an investigation of the distribution of opportunities for schooling is to consider how the age-enrollment profile varies by population subgroup, where the subgroups are defined by characteristics over which the students have no individual control—that is, by circumstance variables. Figure 6.1 presents this profile for the overall population of 6- to 24-year-olds in Turkey in 2004, as taken from the TDHS. The top panel presents the overall as well as the gender-specific profiles. Just over 50 percent of children are enrolled at age 6, and the other half are enrolled between the ages of 7 and 8. There is almost universal enrollment between the ages of 8 and 12, although 7 percent of girls and 2 percent of boys never make it to school even at those peak ages. A substantial drop in enrollment occurs from age 13 (roughly sixth grade), and it accelerates at age 16, after secondary school has begun. Only about a quarter of students are enrolled at age 18, when secondary school should be completed. Average enrollment in tertiary education is about 16 percent between the ages of 18 and 23. Throughout the enrollment decline range (ages 13–18), girls' enrollment falls earlier and faster than boys' enrollment. At age 15, for example, female enrollment is almost 20 percentage points below male enrollment.

The middle and bottom panels of figure 6.1 disaggregate boys' and girls' enrollment profiles by the five regions. The broad pattern of the profiles is similar across regions, with one striking exception: the profile for girls in

---

9 A few differences remain in the definition of the circumstances in the two surveys. In particular, in the HBS urban areas are identified as settlements with more than 20,000 inhabitants, whereas in the PISA the urban threshold is 15,000 inhabitants.

Figure 6.1 Enrollment-Age Profiles by Gender and Region

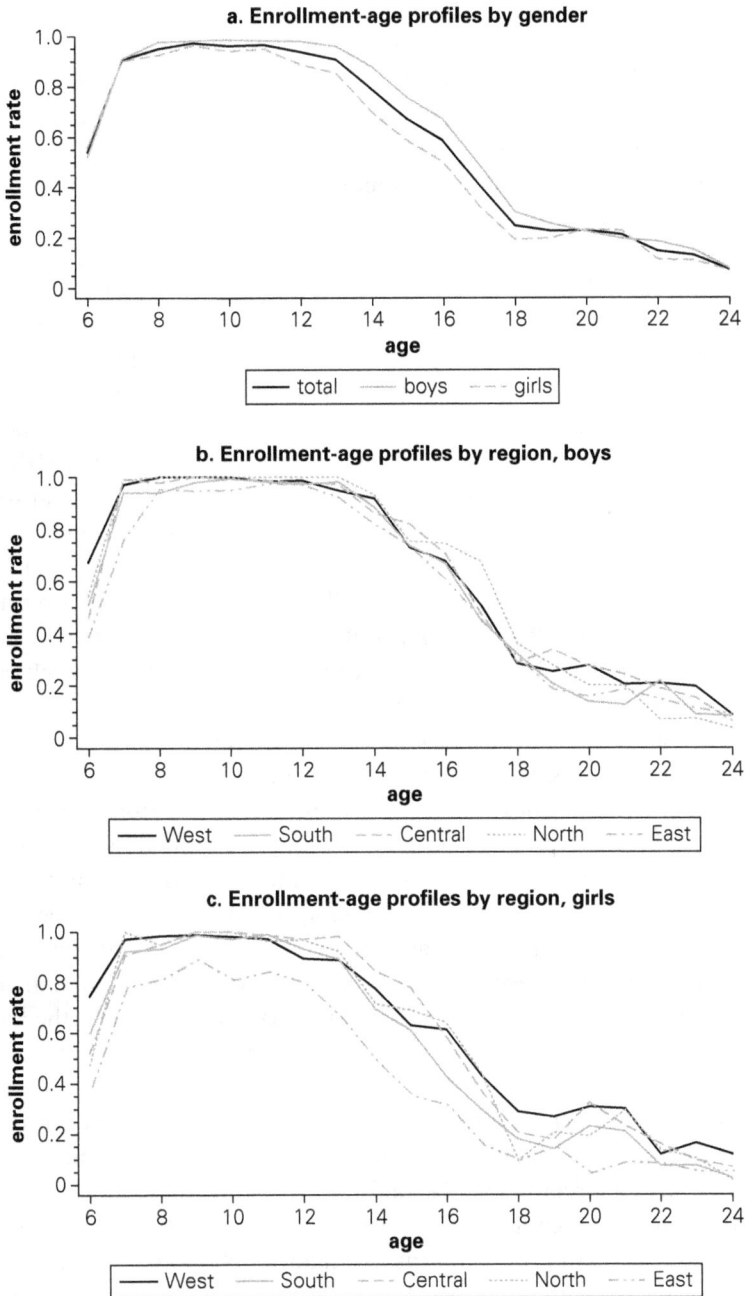

**a. Enrollment-age profiles by gender**

**b. Enrollment-age profiles by region, boys**

**c. Enrollment-age profiles by region, girls**

*Source:* Authors' calculations using data from the TDHS.
*Note:* The figure shows the enrollment-age profiles for the total population of girls and boys (top panel) and the enrollment-age profiles by region of residence for boys (middle panel) and girls (bottom panel). The distribution of the population of 6- to 24-year-olds by region is the following: West, 34.3 percent; South, 13.7 percent; Central, 21.1 percent; North, 7.3 percent; and East, 23.7 percent.

the East region lies entirely below the profiles for boys and girls in every other region of the country. Their enrollment rate peaks at just over 85 percent at age 9, and is below 40 percent by age 15. Although there are other cross-regional differences among girls (but almost none among boys), they pale in significance when compared with the gap between the East region and the rest of the country.

Figure 6.2 depicts enrollment in more detail by disaggregating profiles for urban (further classified into large cities and other towns) and rural areas. The top panel presents results for the country as a whole. Although there are small differences between large and smaller cities, the rural-urban enrollment deficit is more pronounced throughout, and becomes particularly substantial in the transition to secondary schooling. The middle and bottom panels focus on females and explore the differences between the East region (middle panel) and other regions (bottom panel). Residing in a rural area is a disadvantage for girls across the country, but *only for those age 13 and up outside the East region.* It is only in the East that some 20 percent of rural-area girls are excluded from schooling throughout the early primary years as well. By age 15, when about 80 percent of girls in urban areas in the rest of country are still enrolled, just over 50 percent of urban girls and fewer than 20 percent of rural girls are enrolled in the East.

Gender, region, and area of residence are not the only morally irrelevant, pre-determined circumstances correlated with educational attainment in Turkey. The educational background of one's parents is strongly associated with enrollment, as shown in figure 6.3 for mother's education. For both boys and girls, the profiles of those whose mothers have no formaleducation lie entirely below the profiles of those with more educated mothers. Once again, however, the gaps are considerably larger for girls than for boys. At age 16, 90 percent of boys with highly educated mothers are enrolled, and 60 percent of those with uneducated mothers. For girls, the corresponding rates are about 90 percent and 30 percent. At that age, the parental education gap is twice as large for girls as for boys, suggesting that the intergenerational persistence of educational inequality is more pronounced for women than for men.

This pattern of gender inequality in educational attainment is consistent across all other circumstances. Growing up in a household with many other children (also a circumstance beyond the control of the individual child) or in a poorer household is associated with lower enrollment across the age range[10] for both boys and girls (see figures 6.4 and 6.5, respectively). However, the strength of the negative correlation, say, between the number of children in the household and enrollment, is markedly greater for girls than for boys.

When the population of children is disaggregated by quartiles of the distribution of the household wealth index, such as in figure 6.5, the powerful effect of socioeconomic background on education is evident. This

---

10 Although the differences become less pronounced (and often statistically insignificant) above age 20.

Figure 6.2 Enrollment-Age Profiles by Type of Area

**a. Enrollment-age profiles by area, girls and boys**

**b. Enrollment-age profiles by area, girls in East region**

**c. Enrollment-age profiles by area, girls in other regions**

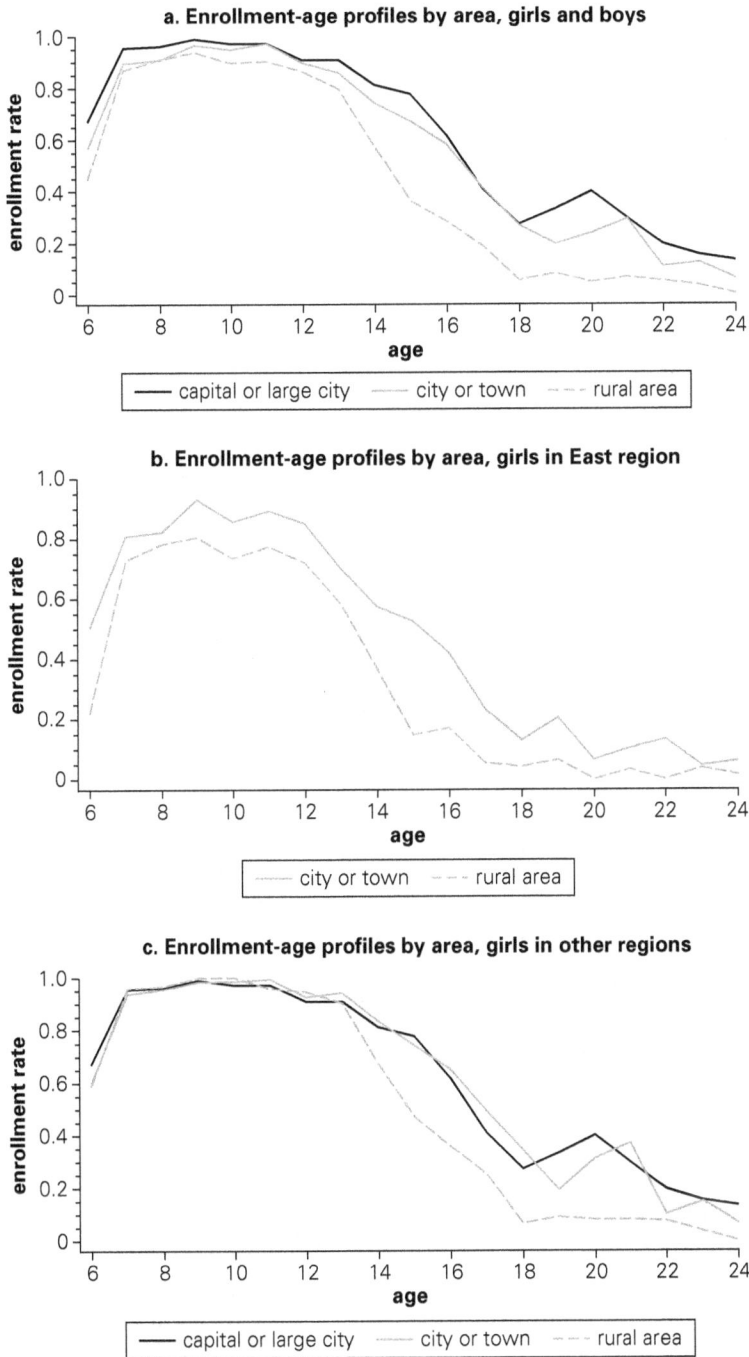

*Source:* Authors' calculations using data from the TDHS.

*Note:* Figure shows enrollment-age profiles for the total population of boys and girls by area type (top panel) and enrollment-age profiles by area type for girls in the East region (middle panel) and in other regions (bottom panel). Urban areas are defined as settlements with populations larger than 10,000. Large cities include Istanbul, Izmir, Bursa, and Adana, as well as the capital, Ankara. The distribution of the population of 6- to 24-year-olds by area type is the following: capital or large city, 26.5 percent; city or town, 40.3 percent; and rural area, 33.2 percent.

Figure 6.3 Enrollment-Age Profiles by Mother's Education

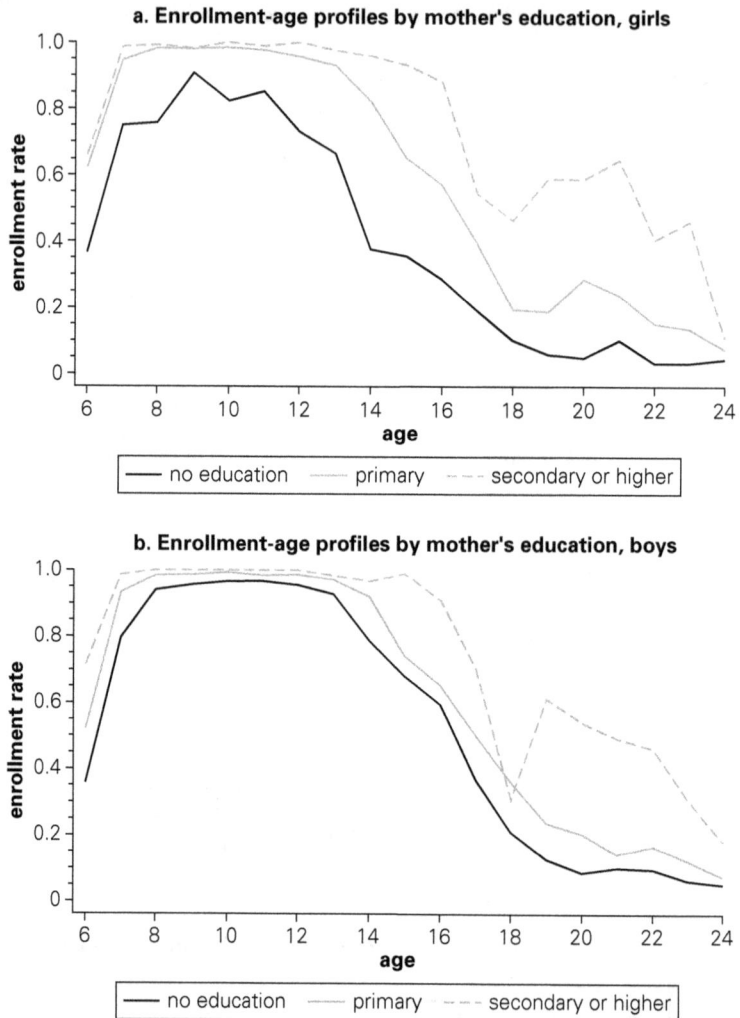

**a. Enrollment-age profiles by mother's education, girls**

**b. Enrollment-age profiles by mother's education, boys**

*Source:* Authors' calculations using data from the TDHS.
*Note:* Figure shows enrollment-age profiles by mother's education for girls (top panel) and boys (bottom panel). The distribution of the population of 6- to 24-year-olds by mother's education is the following: no education, 34.4 percent; primary, 50.5 percent; and secondary or higher, 15.0 percent.

is true for all age groups for girls (first-quartile girls never reach the 90 percent enrollment mark), and becomes pronounced for boys after ages 12–13. By age 20, more than half of the young men (and women!) hailing from the top quartile of the wealth distribution are attending college, but the same is true for less than 10 percent of men and women from the bottom quartile.

These various profiles document that school enrollment in Turkey is evidently *not* independent from circumstances at birth. Family background (in terms of wealth, parental education, and family size), gender, and place of residence (both the region and whether in a city or the countryside) are all statistically significantly associated with how long a

Figure 6.4 Enrollment-Age Profiles by Number of Children

**a. Enrollment-age profiles by number of children, girls**

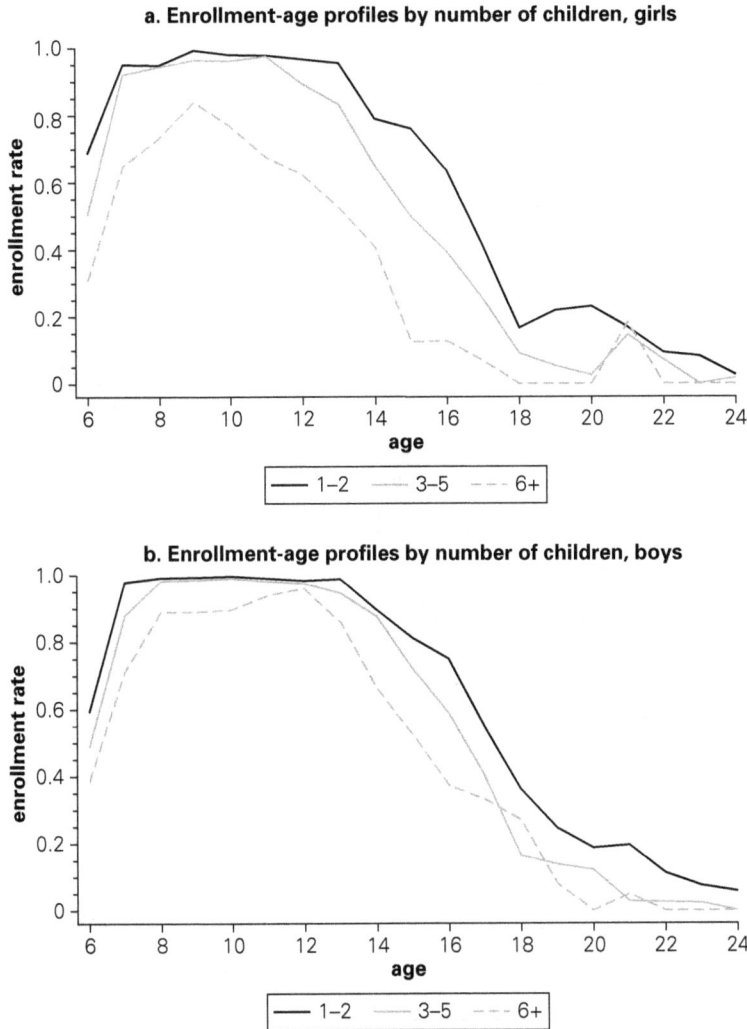

**b. Enrollment-age profiles by number of children, boys**

*Source:* Authors' calculations using data from the TDHS.
*Note:* Figure shows enrollment-age profiles by number of children under 18 years of age living in the household for girls (top panel) and boys (bottom panel). The distribution of the population of 6–24-year-olds by number of children is the following: one or two, 55.4 percent; three to five, 36.2 percent; and six or more, 8.5 percent.

Turkish child is likely to stay in school. And this amount of schooling, as we know from a copious international literature, is, in turn, causally related to future earnings and standard of living more broadly.

In the specific case of Turkey, no circumstance appears to be more important in influencing school-leaving than gender. But the disadvantage that girls experience in relation to boys is by no means uniform across the country. Spatially, this disadvantage is clearly more pronounced in the East and in rural areas. It is also more marked for girls born in poorer and larger families or to less educated mothers than it is for girls from a higher socioeconomic background or from smaller families.

Figure 6.5 Enrollment-Age Profiles by Quartiles of the Asset Index

**a. Girls**

**b. Boys**

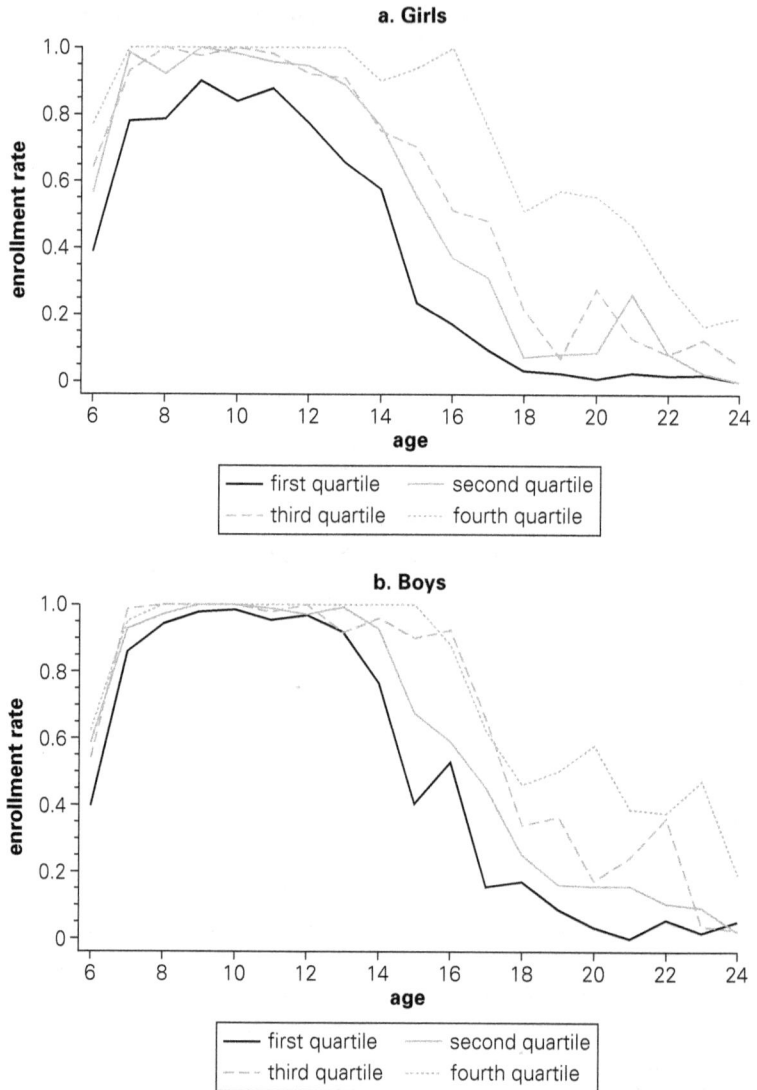

*Source:* Authors' calculations using data from the TDHS.
*Note:* Figure shows enrollment-age profiles by quartiles of the asset index, defined at the household level, for girls (top panel) and boys (bottom panel). The distribution of the population of 6- to 24-year-olds by quartiles of the household-level asset index is as follows: first quartile, 31.0 percent; second quartile, 25.6 percent; third quartile, 24.6; and fourth quartile, 18.9 percent.

Even though figures 6.1–6.5 are descriptively powerful, these various circumstances are obviously intercorrelated. Table 6.1 presents an attempt to disentangle their partial effects on enrollment by means of a simple probit regression of enrollment at age 15 on all of the previously discussed circumstances, as well as father's education and native tongue of the child's mother. These marginal effects are clearly not interpretable as causal, because many potentially relevant determinants are omitted

| Student characteristic | Probit marginal effects | | |
|---|---|---|---|
| | Total | Boys | Girls |
| Gender: Female | −0.170 | | |
| | [0.036]*** | | |
| Region of residence (omitted: West) | | | |
| South | 0.102 | 0.044 | 0.181 |
| | [0.057]* | [0.067] | [0.097]* |
| Central | 0.135 | 0.066 | 0.219 |
| | [0.057]** | [0.064] | [0.098]** |
| North | 0.133 | 0.054 | 0.246 |
| | [0.056]** | [0.066] | [0.089]*** |
| East | 0.126 | 0.104 | 0.168 |
| | [0.058]** | [0.060]* | [0.100]* |
| Area (omitted: large cities) | | | |
| Small urban areas | 0.040 | 0.088 | −0.070 |
| | [0.065] | [0.062] | [0.118] |
| Rural | −0.070 | 0.036 | −0.286 |
| | [0.069] | [0.068] | [0.114]** |
| Mother's education (omitted: no education) | | | |
| Primary education | 0.008 | −0.006 | 0.075 |
| | [0.045] | [0.049] | [0.084] |
| Secondary education | 0.209 | 0.192 | 0.267 |
| | [0.051]*** | [0.047]*** | [0.090]*** |
| Father's education (omitted: no education) | | | |
| Primary education | 0.113 | −0.023 | 0.315 |
| | [0.050]** | [0.062] | [0.085]*** |
| Secondary education | 0.200 | 0.051 | 0.400 |
| | [0.050]*** | [0.070] | [0.077]*** |
| Number of siblings (omitted: one to two children) | | | |
| Three to five children | −0.118 | −0.036 | −0.213 |
| | [0.046]** | [0.050] | [0.076]*** |
| Six or more children | −0.316 | −0.194 | −0.503 |
| | [0.086]*** | [0.110]* | [0.099]*** |
| Number of children missing | 0.055 | 0.121 | −0.070 |
| | [0.066] | [0.058]** | [0.117] |
| Asset quartile of the household (omitted: first quartile) | | | |
| Second quartile | 0.168 | 0.128 | 0.242 |
| | [0.041]*** | [0.043]*** | [0.073]*** |
| Third quartile | 0.268 | 0.243 | 0.279 |
| | [0.042]*** | [0.043]*** | [0.080]*** |

Table 6.1 (continued)

| Student characteristic | Probit marginal effects | | |
|---|---|---|---|
| | Total | Boys | Girls |
| Fourth quartile | 0.298 | 0.207 | 0.402 |
| | [0.039]*** | [0.045]*** | [0.065]*** |
| *Mother's native tongue (omitted: Turkish)* | | | |
| Kurdish | 0.044 | 0.066 | 0.077 |
| | [0.058] | [0.056] | [0.108] |
| Arabic | −0.079 | −0.209 | 0.025 |
| | [0.130] | [0.178] | [0.162] |
| Caucasian | −0.280 | −0.093 | −0.441 |
| | [0.270] | [0.270] | [0.230]* |
| Missing | −0.016 | 0.038 | −0.094 |
| | [0.053] | [0.055] | [0.092] |
| Observations | 924 | 466 | 458 |

*Source:* Authors calculations using data from the DHS 2003/2004, sample of 15-year-olds.
*Note:* Table shows probit estimates of enrollment at age 15. Marginal effects at sample mean reported. The excluded categories are West region, capital or large city, mother with no education or missing information, father with no education or missing information, one or two children, first quartile of the asset index, and mother's native tongue Turkish.
*** Significant at the 1 percent level; ** Significant at the 5 percent level; * Significant at the 10 percent level.

from the specification. They do, however, provide partial correlations that complement the description so far.

The probit regressions are estimated on the full sample of 15-year-olds as well as on samples of girls and boys separately. Gender remains a powerful correlate of enrollment even after controlling for the other observed circumstances, with girls appearing to be 17 percent less likely to be enrolled than boys at the sample mean. Family wealth also has a powerful partial correlation with enrollment, with marginal effects on all three asset quartiles being significantly higher than in the first, in the joint sample as well as in each gender-specific sample. Parental education is important, although father's education is only significant in the combined sample and in the girls' sample, suggesting that both less- and more-educated fathers try to send their sons to school. Children in larger households (or, more precisely, households with more children) are less likely to be enrolled at age 15, although this effect, too, is driven by girls. Similarly, girls in rural areas are significantly less likely to be enrolled in schools, whatever their family background. Interestingly, however, when we control for the entire set of circumstances, the coefficients on the region of residence acquire counterintuitive signs and mother's native tongue becomes insignificant.[11]

---

11 Some of these results do not generalize to wider age ranges. When we run the same probit specification for enrollment in the 12–15 age range, we find that a non-Turkish mother's native tongue is significantly associated with a lower enrollment rate for girls ages 12–15. Residence in the East region is still not significantly associated with the enrollment of 12- to 15-year-olds, but it is negatively associated with the probability of completing the four grades of the lower secondary level.

Figure 6.6 Enrollment-Age Profiles for One Highly Disadvantaged and One Highly Advantaged Group

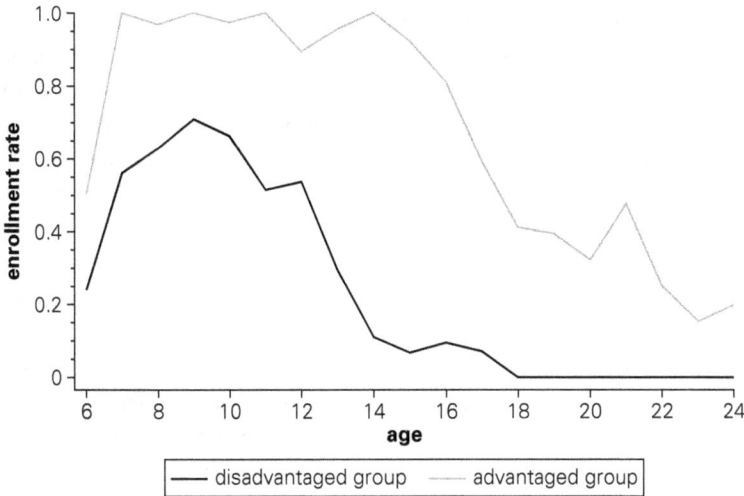

Source: Authors' calculations using data from the TDHS.
Note: Figure shows enrollment-age profiles for one highly disadvantaged and one highly advantaged group. The highly disadvantaged group consists of girls in rural areas of the East region whose mothers have no education and are not native speakers of Turkish living in a household with six or more children. This group encompasses 1.0 percent of the population of 6- to 24-year-olds. The highly advantaged group encompasses boys in urban areas of the Central region whose mothers have some education and are Turkish native speakers living in a household with one or two children. This group encompasses 2.5 percent of the population of 6- to 24-year-olds.

Another way to illustrate the interrelationship between the different circumstance variables and enrollment is to compare those who belong to many disadvantaged subgroups with those who belong to the most advantaged cells in the partition. This comparison provides a sense of the "cumulative effect" of belonging to subgroups with multiple sources of disadvantage (or advantage). Figure 6.6 depicts one possible comparison by plotting the enrollment-age profile of girls born in rural areas of the East region in households with six or more children to uneducated mothers whose first language was not Turkish (a group that accounts for roughly 1 percent of the population in the 6–24 age range). It also plots the profile for boys living in urban areas of central Turkey in households with two or fewer children with native Turkish-speaking mothers with some education (a group that accounts for some 2.5 percent of the population). The difference in enrollment rates is striking at every age. It is lowest at age 9, when enrollment for the disadvantaged group reaches a peak at about 70 percent. In absolute terms, it is highest at the crucial 14–15 age range, when children are making the transition from primary to secondary schooling. At this age, children in the advantaged group begin to fall back from 100 percent enrollment, whereas only some 10 percent of children in the disadvantaged group are enrolled.

The extent to which children accumulate human capital at school depends not only on how many years they attend classes but also (and among other things) on the quality of those classes. Although information on attainment is essential to understanding the distribution of educational opportunities in Turkey, it is not sufficient. It must be complemented by information on actual educational achievement. In this section, we use data from the 2006 PISA survey for Turkey, which contains standardized test scores for a sample of nearly 5,000 15-year-old students across the country in three subjects: Turkish (reading), math, and science. It also contains a rich information set on those children's circumstances, which, as described earlier in this chapter, includes gender, father's and mother's educational attainment, father's occupation, region and area of residence, language spoken at home, durable goods ownership, book ownership, and cultural possessions.

To the extent that we are prepared to treat each of these variables as representing true *Roemerian circumstances*—that is, characteristics that lie beyond the influence of the children themselves—then we can estimate a lower-bound measure of inequality of opportunity for educational achievement by calculating the share of the overall inequality in achievements attributable to these circumstances. In principle, this calculation can be done by means of either a standard (nonparametric) inequality decomposition or a parametric alternative, which relies on regression analysis.[12]

In an earlier work (Ferreira and Gignoux 2008), we describe each of these methods in some detail in the context of earnings, income, and consumption inequality and note the potential trade-off between parametric methods, which impose a functional form assumption on the relationship between advantage and circumstances, and the nonparametric decompositions, where conditional mean estimates become imprecise and small sample biases can be considerable for fine partitions of the sample. In the present context, the wealth of circumstances available in the data would be consistent with a partition of the sample into as many as 589,824 cells! Nonparametric inequality decompositions are therefore not an option, and we rely here on a regression-based decomposition.

Another feature of the data also makes the use of the regression-based decomposition the most natural. Because different items (or questions) in any test have different degrees of difficulty, a simple proportion of right answers is a poor measure of the latent variable of interest, which is the student's knowledge or achievement. PISA surveys everywhere (as well as many other applications) therefore use item response theory methods to adjust for these differences in item difficulty, under some assumption about

---

12  These are lower-bound estimates of the effect of circumstances because not all circumstances are observed. If additional circumstances were to become observable, they might raise (but could not lower) the between-group component of the inequality decomposition or the explanatory power of a regression. For a more detailed discussion that incorporates "effort" variables explicitly, see Ferreira and Gignoux (2008).

the underlying distribution of ability in the population. The process, which is described in detail in Mislevy (1991) and Mislevy et al. (1992), generates a set of scores with no inherent metric, which are then standardized around an arbitrary mean (typically 500) and with an arbitrary variance.

The arbitrary nature of the mean (which precludes the need for scale invariance as a property of the inequality index) and the normal distribution of the scores that results from standardization suggest the variance as the natural inequality indicator of choice. When the variance is used, the parametric estimate of the (lower-bound) share of inequality due to circumstances is given simply by the $R^2$ of a linear regression of the test score on circumstances. From such a regression, estimates of the additively decomposable partial effects of each circumstance can be calculated straightforwardly, as shown in Ferreira and Gignoux (2009).

Three separate regressions (for reading, math, and science scores, respectively) are reported in table 6.2. As in many other countries, girls perform significantly better than boys in reading, but worse in math. There is no significant gender difference in science scores. Children whose parents have a secondary or college education score higher in all three subjects, but the effect of primary education alone is not significant (as compared with the reference category of children whose parents have no formal education).[13]

Children whose fathers are employed as service workers, craft and related trade workers, or plant and machine operators or assemblers, or are unemployed, have significantly lower scores than children whose fathers work as legislators, senior officials, professionals, technicians, or clerks, even after controlling for parental education. A father's employment in agriculture, a fishery, or other elementary occupation, however, is not significant after controlling for urban-rural differences. These differences are both large and significant, with rural areas at a substantial achievement disadvantage. Scores from schools in the Central and West regions are significantly higher than those from the East region. This finding is in contrast with the result for the quantity of schooling reported in table 6.1, where, in the presence of a full set of controls, residence in the East region was not negatively associated with the probability of enrollment at age 15. In table 6.2, however, the coefficients for the area and region variables are both significant and quantitatively substantial, with absolute values of about half a standard deviation of the overall distribution of test scores, whereas the coefficients estimated for the father's occupation and parental education are between 20 percent and half of a standard deviation.

Before presenting our estimates of the lower-bound opportunity shares of inequality in educational achievement, we must describe how we have sought to address the important selection problem present in the Turkish (and in some other) PISA data. School enrollment at age 15 is 67 percent

---

13 For reading, secondary education is not significant for fathers, and tertiary education is not significant for mothers.

Table 6.2 Reduced-Form Regression of Standardized Test Scores on Circumstances

| Student characteristic | Reading | Math | Science |
|---|---|---|---|
| *Gender:* female | 33.24 | −13.85 | 2.16 |
| | [2.81]*** | [2.62]*** | [2.38] |
| *Father's education (omitted = no education)* | | | |
| Primary education | −7.68 | −4.06 | −4.80 |
| | [6.83] | [5.80] | [5.05] |
| Secondary education | 1.91 | 15.70 | 11.63 |
| | [7.33] | [6.60]** | [5.81]** |
| College education | 17.85 | 26.60 | 23.29 |
| | [8.40]** | [7.57]*** | [7.13]*** |
| *Mother's education (omitted = no education)* | | | |
| Primary education | −4.02 | 0.08 | −2.92 |
| | [4.83] | [4.01] | [3.66] |
| Secondary education | 11.05 | 15.50 | 12.53 |
| | [6.04]* | [5.42]*** | [5.06]** |
| College education | 9.09 | 38.73 | 25.88 |
| | [9.73] | [8.25]*** | [8.80]*** |
| *Father's occupation (omitted = legislator, senior official, professional, technician, and clerk)* | | | |
| Service worker, craft and related trade worker, plant and machine operator or assembler, or unemployed | −10.32 | −6.35 | −6.27 |
| | [3.26]*** | [3.07]** | [2.79]** |
| Skilled agricultural or fishery worker, or with an elementary occupation | −4.26 | −4.72 | −1.22 |
| | [4.23] | [3.80] | [3.65] |
| *Area (omitted = rural)* | | | |
| Town (< 100,000) | 32.81 | 19.49 | 28.99 |
| | [5.49]*** | [4.54]*** | [4.32]*** |
| City or large city (> 100,000 ) | 43.07 | 29.54 | 34.26 |
| | [5.29]*** | [4.39]*** | [4.24]*** |
| *Region (omitted = East)* | | | |
| Central | 35.45 | 41.31 | 37.72 |
| | [5.40]*** | [4.33]*** | [4.22]*** |
| West | 28.53 | 27.87 | 21.78 |
| | [4.83]*** | [4.07]*** | [3.82]*** |
| *Number of books at home* | | | |
| 11–25 | 14.09 | 16.34 | 11.22 |
| | [3.99]*** | [3.70]*** | [3.23]*** |
| 26–100 | 19.61 | 28.79 | 22.96 |
| | [4.05]*** | [3.79]*** | [3.36]*** |

Table 6.2 (continued)

| Student characteristic | Reading | Math | Science |
|---|---|---|---|
| More than 100 | 36.97 | 39.56 | 38.94 |
| | [5.00]*** | [4.81]*** | [4.34]*** |
| *Owned durables* | | | |
| Dishwasher | −4.34 | −2.28 | −4.82 |
| | [2.95] | [3.00] | [2.64]* |
| DVD/VCR | 0.61 | −0.16 | −1.58 |
| | [3.40] | [3.13] | [2.88] |
| Cell phone | 17.27 | 24.70 | 16.26 |
| | [9.74]* | [8.56]*** | [6.86]** |
| Television | 11.97 | 19.13 | 10.50 |
| | [23.01] | [13.82] | [12.99] |
| Computer | 13.65 | 19.07 | 16.56 |
| | [2.87]*** | [2.92]*** | [2.64]*** |
| Car | 4.34 | 7.72 | 2.75 |
| | [2.81] | [2.73]*** | [2.50] |
| *Cultural possessions* | | | |
| Literature | 37.09 | 28.22 | 32.67 |
| | [3.00]*** | [2.81]*** | [2.54]*** |
| Poetry | −11.46 | −13.63 | −14.04 |
| | [3.02]*** | [2.88]*** | [2.51]*** |
| Art | 4.22 | −1.30 | 4.00 |
| | [3.07] | [2.94] | [2.49] |
| Constant | 310.41 | 292.21 | 308.64 |
| | [25.35]*** | [15.40]*** | [14.05]*** |
| Observations | 4,942 | 4,942 | 4,942 |
| R-squared | 0.27 | 0.26 | 0.27 |

*Source:* Authors' calculations using data from the PISA survey, Turkey, 2006.
*Note:* Regression estimates of test scores in reading, math, and science. Only the first plausible values are used. The standard deviations for the test scores are 87.3 in reading, 88.9 in math, and 80.0 in science.
*** Significant at the 1 percent level; ** Significant at the 5 percent level; * Significant at the 10 percent level.

in Turkey. Repetition and nonresponses among those enrolled lowers the representativeness of the PISA data set to 47 percent of the country's population of 15-year-olds (OECD 2007). Thus, by restricting an assessment of educational inequality to PISA respondents, we would be excluding nearly half of the relevant population (which is clearly not randomly selected), and thus ignoring a potentially important share of the overall inequality.

The difficulty with addressing this problem, as with any correction for selection, is that the counterfactual test scores that nonparticipating 15-year-olds would have obtained if they had taken the test are not observed. Although standard Heckman correction procedures would help by controlling for selection on observables, many important likely determinants of participation in the exams are not observed. We therefore propose a nonparametric, two-sample procedure that generates plausible higher and lower alternative estimates for selection correction.

We exploit the fact that Turkey's Household Budget Survey, which is nationally representative, is also available for 2006. We partition the population of 15-year-olds in both the HBS and the PISA into groups with identical observable circumstances, using region, urban-rural status, and mother's education as the defining characteristics.[14] If the expanded population of 15-year-olds in cell $k$ of this partition $\{s_i^k\}$ in the PISA (HBS) survey is $\phi_{PISA}^k (\phi_{HBS}^k)$, then our "low alternative" estimate of the selection correction consists of reweighting each score $s_i^k$ by $\phi_{HBS}^k / \phi_{PISA}^k$.

This adjustment "corrects" for selection on observables, because it "reintroduces" the 15-year-olds who dropped out (or otherwise did not participate in the PISA exam), under the assumption that the distribution of test scores for nonparticipants would have been identical to the distribution for participants within each cell $k$. This assumption is, of course, the familiar assumption of no selection on unobservables.

But it is quite likely that selection did not depend only on the variables used to partition the population into $\{s_i^k\}$. In particular, it is plausible that within each cell nonparticipants would, on average, have had worse scores than participants. Under that assumption, a likely "higher alternative" effect of selection would be obtained by giving a proportion $\left( \phi_{HBS}^k - \phi_{PISA}^k \right) / \phi_{HBS}^k$ the lowest score in cell $k$, $\underline{s}^k$, after the reweighting process just described.[15]

Intuitively, this adjustment corresponds to counterfactually attributing to each and every nonparticipant the worst test score actually observed among participants within each cell $k$. Figure 6.7 shows the kernel density functions for the standardized PISA test scores in reading in 2006 under three different scenarios. The top panel depicts the observed sample distribution with no correction for selection. The middle panel depicts the counterfactual distribution with the "lower alternative" correction for selection. The bottom panel depicts the counterfactual distribution with the "higher alternative" correction for selection.

Table 6.3 summarizes our results on inequality of opportunity for educational achievement. For each of the three distributions of test scores (no correction, lower alternative correction for selection, and higher alternative correction for selection) and for each subject (reading, math, and science), the top half of the table reports both total variance and the lower bound on the share of this inequality, which corresponds to inequality

---

14 These three variables are defined identically in the two surveys, so that the partitions should be strictly comparable. A finer partition would have been possible, but would have generated statistically imprecise estimates of population weights in the HBS because of the sample size (683 15-year-olds).

15 In this procedure, the specific observations whose scores are modified are chosen randomly within each cell.

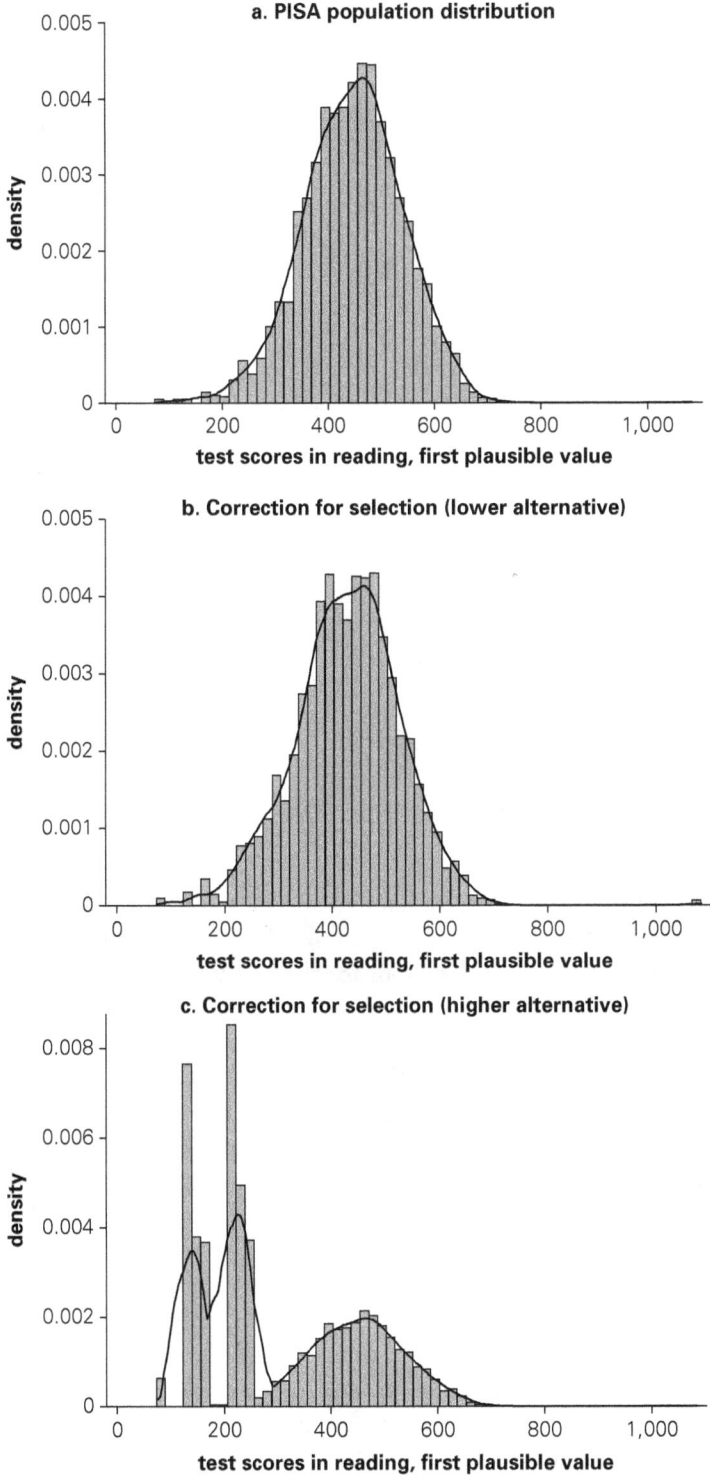

Figure 6.7 Distribution of Standardized Turkish Reading Test Scores under Three Alternative Assumptions about Selection into PISA Participation

**a. PISA population distribution**

**b. Correction for selection (lower alternative)**

**c. Correction for selection (higher alternative)**

*Source:* Authors' calculations using data from the PISA and HBS surveys.

| Measure of inequality | Reading | Math | Science |
|---|---|---|---|
| *No correction* | | | |
| Total inequality (variance) | 8,631.1 | 8,693.9 | 6,923.2 |
| Total share of inequality of opportunity | 0.262 | 0.260 | 0.269 |
| *"Lower alternative" correction* | | | |
| Total inequality (variance) | 9,678.0 | 8,360.1 | 6,819.9 |
| Total share of inequality of opportunity | 0.280 | 0.269 | 0.282 |
| *"Higher alternative" correction* | | | |
| Total inequality (variance) | 24,231.6 | 17,965.5 | 14,790.0 |
| Total share of inequality of opportunity | 0.327 | 0.322 | 0.327 |
| *Partial share of inequality of opportunity associated with each circumstance* | | | |
| Only gender | 0.041 | 0.003 | 0.001 |
| Only father's education | 0.022 | 0.042 | 0.040 |
| Only mother's education | 0.011 | 0.033 | 0.026 |
| Only father's occupation | 0.007 | 0.007 | 0.004 |
| Only area type | 0.036 | 0.020 | 0.030 |
| Only region | 0.022 | 0.028 | 0.026 |
| Only number of books | 0.037 | 0.050 | 0.055 |
| Only owned durables | 0.023 | 0.045 | 0.031 |
| Only cultural possessions | 0.063 | 0.033 | 0.055 |

*Source:* Authors' calculations using data from the PISA survey, Turkey, 2006.

of opportunity. This latter estimate is simply the $R^2$ of the regressions reported in table 6.2 (for the distribution with no correction for selection) and the $R^2$ of analogous regressions for the adjusted distributions.

The lower alternative selection correction increases the variance for the distribution of reading scores, but it has almost no effect on the other two variances. On the one hand, the higher alternative selection correction (as could be expected from an inspection of figure 6.7) increases the variances between two- and threefold. On the other hand, the opportunity shares of inequality do not vary much across subjects and turn out to be relatively insensitive to the alternative corrections for selection. With no selection correction, a minimum of 26 percent of the variance in reading and math scores and 27 percent of the variance in science scores are attributable to circumstances. These rise only very slightly, to 27–28 percent, under the more conservative selection correction procedure. Even under the higher alternative correction procedure, the lower-bound estimate of the opportunity share of inequality in educational achievement rises to some 32–33 percent.

The bottom half of table 6.3 reports the partial shares of inequality of opportunity associated with individual circumstances: gender, father's education, mother's education, father's occupation, type of area, and region. Socioeconomic background is also captured by the number of books owned by the household, durable goods owned, and cultural possessions. These shares are calculated so that they add up to the overall effect, in the manner described in Ferreira, Gignoux, and Aran (2010). The partial shares are reported only for the regression without selection correction, because the partition $\{s_i^k\}$ used for that correction is based on some but not all of the independent variables in the regression. This feature of the selection adjustment would make analysis of the partial effects in the corrected regression difficult to interpret.

When all circumstances are considered together and controlled for, family background seems to be the dominant source of inequality of opportunity for achievement in Turkey. For example, in math scores, mother's and father's education together account for 7.5 of the 26 percentage points in the overall share. Add father's occupation and the three "asset" indicators (numbers of books, durables, and cultural possessions), and these family background variables add up to 21 of the 26 percentage points. Interestingly, the largest part of this "family effect" shows up through material possessions—books, durables, and cultural possessions represent 12.8 percentage points. When these three variables are omitted from the regression, some (though by no means all) of their effect is picked up by mother's and father's education, with which they are collinear.[16] Although there are some small differences, the dominance of the family background variables is consistent across all three subjects.

Although area type and region in which schools are located are highly significant in the regression in table 6.2, their partial shares are relatively small in magnitude, generally accounting for between 5 and 6 percentage points of the 26–27 percentage points of the overall lower-bound circumstance share. Except in math, the rural-urban divide is more important than the broad regional location. As in enrollment, although spatial variables remain significant after controlling for other population characteristics, they account for much smaller variance shares than one might expect from the raw absolute regional differences. These absolute differences appear to be explained to a large extent by differences in the family background compositions across the residents of different regions and areas.

A student's gender, which was so important in explaining enrollment, is much less important in accounting for differences in achievement. It is largest in reading, where it accounts for 4.1 percent of total variance, and this is a subject in which girls do significantly better than boys. Although this difference may to some extent reflect differences in selection across genders—fewer girls are enrolled, so perhaps average ability is higher among enrolled girls than among enrolled boys—there is no evidence whatsoever to suggest that girls do worse than boys in school in Turkey.

---

16 In that specification, father's education and mother's education shares (for reading scores) are, respectively, 0.022 and 0.011. They are higher in the math and science decompositions.

Although the relationship between equity and growth has long been of concern to economists, recent developments in the conceptualization of inequality of opportunity have arguably made it easier for applied economists to measure and decompose the kinds of inequality that matter most rather than simply those on which data are more readily available. Following Roemer's 1998 definition of inequality of opportunity as that kind of inequality that is driven by morally irrelevant, predetermined circumstances, we have investigated the nature and magnitude of unequal opportunities for education in Turkey.

Using DHS data, we document large differences in enrollment by a student's gender and spatial location, across the whole relevant age range. In particular, we find that girls residing in the eastern provinces—and particularly (but not exclusively) in rural areas—are much less likely than their counterparts in other parts of the country and boys to attend school. Other circumstances associated with a lower probability of enrollment—or a higher probability of dropping out early—such as a lower household wealth index, a larger number of children, or lower levels of parental education appear to be systematically more important for girls than for boys. In other words, disadvantageous circumstances such as a poorer family background are more likely to lead girls than boys to drop out of school early, thereby potentially generating a more resilient inequality trap for Turkish women than for their menfolk.

Once the pattern of covariances between circumstances is taken into account by means of a simple probit model, a more nuanced picture emerges. Gender remains a key cleavage, with girls 17 percent less likely to be enrolled at age 15 than boys, at sample mean values of other correlates. Although family background variables such as household wealth, secondary or higher levels of parental education, and family size retain importance in the multivariate analysis, spatial variables become much less significant (or acquire counterintuitive signs). We interpret these results as suggesting that there is nothing inherent about the East as a region, or about smaller towns, that prevents children from going to school. They do have lower enrollment rates, but those rates reflect lower levels of advantage in family background; their households are larger and poorer, and their parents have less formal schooling. Once those factors are taken into account, the only spatial circumstance that retains its original sign and significance from the univariate analysis is rural residence for girls.

Broadly similar conclusions apply to educational achievement, as measured by PISA test scores, with the exception of the relative importance of school location after controlling for family background. Schools located in the East or in rural areas *are* significantly statistically associated with lower test scores, even controlling for all other circumstances. But quantitatively, spatial variables account for no more than a fifth of the overall opportunity share of inequality in achievement in Turkey. This overall share, estimated parametrically as a lower bound, is not trivial. Morally irrelevant circumstances account for over a quarter of total inequality in achievement, even when no correction for sample selection bias is attempted. When (a two-sample reweighting) correction for selection is implemented, the lower-bound share of the variance attributable to opportunities rises to between 27 and 33 percent.

Family background variables, including indicators for ownership of durable goods, books, and other cultural possessions, account for three-quarters to four-fifths of these shares. Parental education remains important, even controlling for those variables, but father's occupation is much less important. A prestigious occupation for one's father does not seem to contribute much to a child's achievement directly. Its contribution appears to operate primarily through the additional purchasing power that such an occupation generates, which can be used for buying inputs into a broadly defined "production function" of human capital.

Gender, which is of paramount importance as a circumstance determining access to education (via differences in enrollment and retention), is *not* an important determinant of achievement, conditional on being in school. In fact, possibly as a result of selection into enrollment, the one subject in which gender accounts for a sizable share of inequality (reading) is one in which the boys are disadvantaged. The policy lesson for those concerned with girls' education in Turkey seems to be: get— and keep—them in school. Once there, they seem to do well enough.

## References

Arneson, Richard. 1989. "Equality of Opportunity for Welfare." *Philosophical Studies* 56: 77–93.

Atkinson, Anthony B. 1997. "Bringing Income Distribution in from the Cold." *Economic Journal* 107 (441): 297–321.

Atkinson, Anthony, and François Bourguignon. 2000. "Income Distribution and Economics." Introduction to *Handbook of Income Distribution*, ed. Anthony Atkinson and François Bourguignon. Amsterdam: Elsevier.

Bourguignon, François, Francisco H. G. Ferreira, and Marta Menéndez. 2007. "Inequality of Opportunity in Brazil." *Review of Income and Wealth* 53 (4): 585–618.

Dworkin, Ronald. 1981. "What Is Equality? Part 2: Equality of Resources." *Philosophy and Public Affairs* 10 (4): 283–345.

Engerman, Stanley, and Kenneth Sokoloff. 1997. "Factor Endowments, Institutions, and Differential Paths of Growth among New World Economies: A View from Economic Historians of the United States." In *How Latin America Fell Behind*, ed. Stephen Haber. Stanford, CA: Stanford University Press.

Ferreira, Francisco H. G., and Jérémie Gignoux. 2008. "The Measurement of Inequality of Opportunity: Theory and an Application to Latin America." Policy Research Working Paper 4659, World Bank, Washington, DC.

Ferreira, Francisco H. G., Jérémie Gignoux, and Meltom Aran. 2010. "Measuring Inequality of Opportunity with Imperfect Data: The Case of Turkey." Unpublished paper, World Bank Development Research Group, Washington, DC.

Filmer, Deon, and Lant H. Pritchett. 2001. "Estimating Wealth Effects without Expenditure Data—or Tears: An Application to Educational Enrolments in States of India." *Demography* 38: 115–32.

Galor, Oded, and Joseph Zeira. 1993. "Income Distribution and Macroeconomics Income Distribution and Macroeconomics." *Review of Economic Studies* 60 (1): 35–52.

Kirdar, Murat. 2009. "Explaining Ethnic Disparities in School Enrollment in Turkey." *Economic Development and Cultural Change* 57 (2) 297–333.

Kuznets, Simon P. 1955. "Economic Growth and Income Inequality." *American Economic Review* 45 (1): 1–28.

Lefranc, Arnaud, Nicolas Pistolesi, and Alain Trannoy 2008. "Inequality of Opportunities vs. Inequality of Outcomes: Are Western Societies All Alike?" *Review of Income and Wealth* 54 (4): 513–46.

Lewis, Arthur W. 1954. "Economic Development with Unlimited Supply of Labour." *The Manchester School* 22 (2): 139–91.

Loury, Glenn C. 1981. "Intergenerational Transfers and the Distribution of Earnings." *Econometrica* 49: 843–67.

Mislevy, R. 1991. "Randomization Based Inference about Examinees in the Estimation of Item Parameters." *Psychometrika* 56: 177–96.

Mislevy, R., A. Beaton, B. Kaplan, and K. Sheehan. 1992. "Estimating Population Characteristics from Sparse Matrix Samples of Item Responses." *Journal of Educational Measurement* 29 (2): 133–61.

OECD (Organisation for Economic Co-operation and Development). 2007. *PISA 2006: Science Competencies for Tomorrow's World,* vol. 1. Paris: OECD.

Rawls, John. 1971. *A Theory of Justice.* Cambridge, MA: Harvard University Press.

Ricardo, David. 1817 (1911). *On the Principles of Political Economy and Taxation.* London: Dent.

Roemer, John E. 1998. *Equality of Opportunity.* Cambridge, MA: Harvard University Press.

Sen, Amartya. 1980. "Equality of What?" In *Tanner Lectures on Human Values,* ed. S. McMurrin. Cambridge: Cambridge University Press.

Tansel, Aysit. 2002. "Determinants of School Attainment of Boys and Girls in Turkey: Individual, Household and Community Factors." *Economics of Education Review* 21 (5): 455–70.

Voitchovsky, Sarah. 2005. "Does the Profile of Income Inequality Matter for Economic Growth?" *Journal of Economic Growth* 10 (3): 273–96.

# CHAPTER 7

# The (Indispensable) Middle Class in Developing Countries

*Nancy Birdsall*

Growth that is shared, broad-based, inclusive—there are various terms—is now widely embraced as the central economic goal for developing countries. A key contribution of the Commission on Growth and Development, chaired by Michael Spence, was its emphasis on shared growth.

But the concept of shared or inclusive growth is not well defined in the development economics literature. Since the early 1990s (and probably best marked by the influential 1990 *World Development Report* of the World Bank), the focus has been primarily on pro-poor growth, with the "poor" defined as people living on less than $1 a day, or in some regions $2 a day. The idea of pro-poor growth emerged in the early 1990s as a counterpoint to a singular concern with growth alone, measured in increases in per

I could not have written this chapter without the yeoman-like research assistance of Dan Hammer, who, for example, struggled with me over problems with recent updates of the purchasing power parity income/consumption numbers, and conceived of a way to incorporate the Demographic and Health Surveys data (on assets, not income or consumption) into the analysis. I am grateful to Michael Clemens, Ravi Kanbur, Mead Over, and Lant Pritchett and to participants in a seminar at the Center for Global Development for their comments on an earlier draft. I, however, take full responsibility for the shortcomings of this study.

capita income (World Bank 1990).[1] Pro-poor growth is generally defined as growth that benefits the poor at least as much or more than the rest of the population, and as the good outcome of policies and programs that are targeted at improving the lives and capacities of the very poor while not undermining growth itself. One example is donors' emphasis on primary over higher education during the last several decades as a way to ensure a benefit to the poor while investing in long-run growth through increases in human capital. Another is the successful implementation of conditional cash transfers, which have highly targeted the poor while minimizing the fiscal burden on the public sector and thus any trade-off with growth associated with a higher tax burden or reduced alternative growth-oriented public investment.

And yet these pro-poor, inclusive policies are not necessarily without trade-offs in fostering long-run growth.[2] In this chapter I argue that the concept of inclusive growth should go beyond the traditional emphasis on the poor and take into account changes in the size and economic command of the group conventionally defined as neither poor nor rich—that is, the middle class. My main rationale is that growth driven by and benefiting a middle class is more likely to be sustained—both economically, to the extent that the rent-seeking and corruption associated with highly concentrated gains to growth are avoided, and politically, to the extent that conflict and horizontal inequalities between racial and ethnic groups are easier to manage when not only is the overall size of the pie growing but also everyone is enjoying bigger slices.[3] On the positive side, sustained growth is arguably more likely where a politically salient middle class supports in its own economic interests sound and stable political and economic institutions. It is sound institutions that some argue are fundamental to sustained growth because they encourage investment by ensuring the rule of law and recognition of private property rights (Acemoglu, Johnson, and Robinson 2004). Both middle-income and low-income countries are far more vulnerable to various economic shocks (such as weather and terms of trade) than are industrialized economies (Perry 2009), and recent studies suggest that sustained growth for periods of 10 years and more has been more elusive in the developing world than shorter periods of "accelerated growth" (Hausmann, Pritchett, and

---

1  See also Ravallion (1998) and Ravallion and Chen (2001) for two of those authors' many contributions, as well as Kraay (2006).

2  The emphasis on primary over higher education ignores the lack of clear evidence that primary education has higher social returns than higher education once unmeasured positive externalities are properly taken into account (Birdsall 1996). This emphasis may have led to the underfunding of higher education in developing countries over the last three decades. Levy (2008) suggests that conditional cash transfers and other pro-poor programs in Mexico have not sufficiently taken into account trade-offs in how "social" programs and subsidies affect economy-wide incentives for investment and productivity.

3  I have reviewed and summarized the literature on the effects of income distribution on growth (Birdsall 2008). On inequality and managing policy trade-offs, see especially Stewart (2002) and Alesina and Rodrik (1994).

Rodrik 2004).[4] Short periods of growth often stem in fact from positive shocks such as a favorable but temporary shift in the terms of trade for a country (as in the commodity boom of 2002–08), the arrival of a skilled and committed leader, or the resolution of a war or internal conflict. Particularly in light of the 2008–10 global economic crisis, the question is whether a good-sized middle class, however defined, makes countries more resilient in the face of shocks—internal political shocks as well as external financial and weather shocks.

The purpose of this chapter is modest. I do not presume to make a larger and more economically commanding "middle class" an input to any model of growth.[5] In fact, as I will show, the emergence of a middle class using my definition is closely associated with growth, and is probably an outcome of growth as much or more than it is an input to growth. The same virtuous or reinforcing circle might be said of the middle class and democracy, the middle class and "sound" institutions, and so on.

Instead, I suggest a definition of the middle class in developing countries that emphasizes the alignment of its economic interests with sound economic policies and good governance—and thus its indispensability to sustainable economic growth—while allowing for the reality that it is subject to both the risks and the opportunities of a globally integrated economy.[6] In the sections that follow, I first set out and defend my definition of the middle class. I then provide some description of the size and economic command of the (indispensable) middle class across countries and over time. I conclude with some possible implications for domestic and international policy in view of the evidence of how small and fragile this class still is in developing countries.

This contribution to this volume complements a small but growing literature by development economists defining and exploring empirically the "middle class" in developing countries.[7] The literature is recent and small because of the laser-like focus in the donor community on reducing absolute poverty and its curses of ill health and poor access to education, and to some extent because of a prevailing assumption that the middle class in developing countries competes with the poor politically and economically, preferring to enhance its own access to state jobs and spending and preserve its limited privileges. This assumption may indeed be correct, particularly in countries in which the majority of households that appear to be "middle class" are highly dependent on the state. However, the prevailing assumption refers only vaguely to who middle-class households are in the first place.

---

4  Hausmann, Pritchett, and Rodrik (2004) report that "external shocks tend to produce growth accelerations that eventually fizzle out, while economic reform is a statistically significant predictor of growth accelerations that are sustained."

5  Easterly (2001) does so, defining the three middle quintiles, which in many countries will include people living below the poverty line, as the "middle class."

6  Because this notion of the indispensable nature of the middle class is a hypothesis and not a finding, or a presumption and not a conclusion, I hedge and put the term in parentheses in the title of this chapter.

7  This literature includes Birdsall, Graham, and Pettinato (2000); Milanovic and Yitzhaki (2002); Banerjee and Duflo (2007); Silber (2007); and Ravallion (2009).

But what about the absolute poor? An analytic focus on the middle class does not imply a lack of concern for the poor. To the contrary, in advanced economies the poor have probably benefited from the rule of law, legal protections, and, in general, the greater accountability of government that a large and politically independent middle class demands, as well as from the universal and adequately funded education, health, and social insurance programs a middle class wants and finances through the tax system.[8] Indeed, a focus on the middle class extends the focus on the poor, including on the grounds that growth that is good for the large majority of people in developing countries is more likely to be economically and politically sustainable for both economic and political reasons.[9] The political economy of targeted transfers is an example. Besley and Kanbur (1990) and Gelbach and Pritchett (2000), among others, argue that "leakier can be better"— that is, attempts to tighten targeting to reduce fiscal costs and reach only the truly poor can be counterproductive if the programs lose the political support of the middle class.

But if a focus on the middle class is merely a simple extension of caring about the poor, then the question arises of whether the distinction between pro-poor and middle-class growth has any implications for policy. Later in this chapter I argue that, in fact, it probably does. For cash transfers, the optimal degree of targeting depends structurally on the size and characteristics of the middle class. More generally, a singular focus on the poor may from a policy point of view ignore trade-offs that matter for the middle class, which, in turn, might undermine the macroeconomic stability and the social policies that the middle class tends to support—and that, in turn, may also benefit the poor (if perhaps less directly in the short run).

In the end, the possible tensions or trade-offs between strictly pro-poor and more inclusive and sustainable "middle-class" growth policies cannot be generalized. They must be assessed policy by policy in each country, and are likely to change over time as circumstances change. The implication is that policymakers in developing countries (and their international supporters and advisers) should be more systematic than they have been over the last several decades in considering distributionally weighted welfare outcomes when selecting and fine-tuning macropolicies rather than either unweighted growth outcomes or overly weighted poverty outcomes. A second implication is that where there are no obvious trade-offs between benefits for the poor versus the middle class, all the better. The real trade-off in many developing countries is probably not between benefits for the poor versus the middle class anyway but between benefits for the poor and the middle class together versus the rich. Put another way, the trade-off is probably between the short-term political benefits of policies that

---

8   This is one interpretation of Lindert's analysis (2004). See also Skopcol (1979). Provision of public goods is lower where there is inequality of income, especially between different ethnic or other groups (Alesina, Baqir, and Easterly 1999).

9   I summarized the evidence of this for Africa (Birdsall 2007), based on Hausmann, Pritchett, and Rodrik (2004), who present proof that many countries that have had long growth episodes subsequently have growth collapses.

preserve the status quo and benefit a small minority at the top of the income distribution, and the long-run growth associated with the financial, tax, business, and other policies that build a middle class and are, as it turns out, pro-poor as well.

## Defining the (Indispensable) Middle Class in Developing Countries

Inclusive growth implies an increase in the proportion of *people* in the middle class, attributable in part to some exit of people out of poverty[10] and an increase in the proportion of *total income those in the middle class command*. An increase in the total income the middle class commands (or an increase in the "economic command" of the middle class) implies gains in the middle at the "expense" of either the initially poor or the initially rich.[11] I define the "middle class" in the developing world to include people living on the equivalent of $10 a day or above in 2005 and at or below the 95th percentile of the income distribution in their own country.[12] This definition implies some absolute and *global* threshold ($10 a day) below which people are too poor to be middle class in any society in today's globally integrated economy, and some relative and *local* threshold (the 95th percentile of income/consumption) above which people are at least in their own society "rich." In this chapter I sometimes refer to the group as the politically potent or independent middle class to distinguish it from other definitions and to emphasize the logic behind this income/consumption definition.

### Why $10 a Day at the Bottom?

I suggest $10 a day (in 2005 purchasing power parity, or PPP, terms) as the absolute minimum income required for a person to have the economic security associated with middle-class status in today's global economy—and therefore the incentives and the potential to exercise political rights in his or her own interests.

Why have an absolute rather than a country-specific minimum level? Many conventional definitions assign to the "middle class" in each country

---

10 An increase in the proportion of people in the middle class can also result, of course, from movement of people out of the "rich" toward the middle, or reduced mobility from the middle to the rich.

11 These implications depend in part on the relative gains or declines in income and share of the initially rich. These statements assume that the rich are not losing in absolute terms. Silber (2007) suggests an alternative measure of the economic command of the middle class that does not depend on what happens to the incomes of the poor or the rich.

12 For other recent definitions, see Birdsall, Graham, and Pettinato (2000); Banerjee and Duflo (2007); and Ravallion (2009). Defining the top 5 percent of people in every country as "rich" implies that the following are "rich": the approximately 14 million people in the United States with a monthly income in 2002 at or above $9,504 (2005 purchasing power parity), the approximately 26 million in urban China with a monthly income in 2005 of just $372, and the 40 million in rural China with a monthly income in 2005 of just $168.

those in the middle of the income distribution in that country, whether the three middle quintiles or between 75 and 125 percent of median income (though where I have used the latter the discussion was primarily of the "middle stratum," not "middle class").[13] I propose an absolute minimum on the grounds that in the relatively open economies of most developing countries today, with economic security to some extent vulnerable to external as well as internal economic and political shocks (including weather and financial crises—consider the food and fuel price spikes in 2008) and some consumption standards set at the global level (a car, for example, is not everywhere a Lexus), some absolute minimum makes sense.

Why $10? Ten dollars a day is a high minimum compared with the conventional global absolute poverty line now used by the World Bank of $1.25 a day.[14] It is also high compared with the $2-a-day national poverty lines conventionally used in much of Latin America and in other middle-income regions and countries.

There is certainly no agreement among development economists on an income minimum for middle-class status in a developing country. Banerjee and Duflo (2007) designate as middle class in developing countries people who live on between $2 and $10 a day, thereby essentially assigning all those who have escaped the recognized poverty line of $2 a day (poverty but not extreme poverty) to middle-class status. Ravallion (2009) designates as middle class in developing countries all those people who live on between $2 and $13 a day. In doing so, he similarly defines the developing world's middle class as those who are not deemed "poor" by the standards of developing countries but who are poor by the standards of rich countries, and he caps the developing world middle class at a figure close to the poverty line in the United States. Thus by definition his middle class is meant to be non-Western and specific to developing countries.

There are good arguments, however, for rejecting the idea that anyone who escapes the absolute poverty associated with living on just $2 a day is a member of the "middle class" in his or her own country, let alone globally. Being a member of the middle class in the classic sense implies a reasonable level of economic security. Yet in most middle-income developing countries even living on $3 a day is not enough to be middle class. Ravallion, Chen, and Sangraula (2008) make the point that national poverty lines rise markedly across developing countries with average income. That rise reflects the reality that security in relation to basic needs is difficult to define in absolute terms (as Adam Smith famously noted, it is about the proper hat that makes a man feel presentable in his community). Moreover, there is considerable evidence that the number of people who live below the international

---

13 For an example using the three middle quintiles, see Easterly (2001). For those close to the median income, see Birdsall, Graham, and Pettinato (2000). Thurow (1987) also uses the latter definition.

14 Ravallion, Chen, and Sangraula (2008) explain the basis for this measure of poverty; it is close to the median of the national poverty lines of the 15 or so poorest countries in the world.

poverty lines of $1 or $2 a day is substantially greater over several months or years in developing countries than the number who are poor at any one moment. Pritchett, Suryahadi, and Sumarto (2000) use panel data to estimate, for example, that, although the headcount poverty rate may have been 20 percent in Indonesia in 1997, an additional 10–30 percent face an acute risk of poverty in the near future based on the past churning of households in and out of poverty. Similarly, Kanbur and Lustig (2000) record substantial increases in "poverty," conventionally defined, during crises, simply because a high proportion of the nonpoor live so close to the poverty line. They are vulnerable during a downturn, presumably because their permanent income is too low for them to have the precautionary savings or assets typically accumulated by middle-class households to ride out a downturn.

In fact, even $10 a day is low compared with the national poverty lines of member countries of the Organisation for Economic Development and Co-operation (OECD). Aiming for a more globally comparable income standard, Milanovic and Yitzhaki (2002) define the middle class as those living between the mean incomes of Brazil and Italy—that is, between about $12 and $50 a day (in 2000 PPP terms). With the exception of the United States, OECD countries define their poverty lines in relative terms, as 50 percent of median income.[15] That standard implies poverty lines, in PPP terms, of about $30 a day. The U.S. poverty line is based on the cost of a minimum nutritional basket and has not been updated in many years to reflect real increases in costs. However, even in the United States the poverty line for a single individual in 2008 was $29 a day and for each individual in a four-person household about $14 a day.[16]

Finally, it is likely that most people in developing countries living on $10 a day have surprisingly low (to many Western readers) social indicators. Infant mortality in the top quintile of households in Brazil (where daily income per capita is close to $10 or more among the least affluent) was more than 15 per 1,000 live births in the mid-1990s—similar to the rate among the notoriously underserved (and generally poor) African-American population of Washington, D.C., and twice the rate in the most "deprived" areas of Great Britain.[17] The "rich" in Bolivia and Ghana are even worse off—in 2003 infant mortality in households in the richest quintile in Bolivia was 32 per 1,000 live births and in Ghana 58 per 1,000. In the 1990s in Ghana, as many as 10 percent of children in the

---

15 Pritchett (2003, table 4) calculated that 50 percent of the median incomes of 13 OECD countries was in 2000 PPP terms. The unweighted average income of the countries he lists is $33.95 a day. Ravallion, Chen, and Sangraula (2008) object to this informal measure of poverty using half the median.

16 U.S. poverty lines are extracted from the 2008 Department of Health and Human Services guidelines.

17 As reported by Pritchett (2003). Pritchett also presents data showing that less than 25 percent of people in the richest quintile in India complete nine grades of school, compared with nearly universal completion of basic education in industrialized countries.

richest quintile were stunted, implying chronic malnutrition.[18] In fact, the low social indicators among the richest 20 percent of households in low-income countries such as Bolivia and Ghana are consistent with their income levels. It is just that, except for a tiny proportion of households in those countries (far tinier than the 20 percent in the top quintile), most people are income (or consumption) "poor" in the sense that their per capita daily income is far below $10.

In the end, $10 as a lower limit is admittedly ad hoc. It is in the right range—clearly on the low side by OECD standards but close to a minimum for a global standard. Behind this ad hoc number is the idea that at about $10 a day per person, household members are able to care about and save for the future and to have aspirations for a better life for themselves as well as their children because they feel reasonably secure economically (short of the kind of global recession under way today, a once-every-60-years event). Economic security implies that during downturns in the normal business cycle a household is unlikely to need to sell household or business assets or to take children out of school, and is insured through savings or formal insurance arrangements against such idiosyncratic risks as a family health catastrophe or a brief spell of personal unemployment. At an income level of about $10 a day per person, people in this middle class, feeling secure, are prepared to take reasonable business and other economic risks, and thus to be entrepreneurial capitalists. A measure of economic security also makes a household less vulnerable to patronage or clientelist political pressures and implies a greater likelihood of readiness to act politically to demand the economic policies that protect private property and encourage private investment.

And $10 a day has the advantage (like the original $1-a-day poverty line) of being a round number.

### Why the 95th Percentile at the Top?

Why define an upper bound of the middle class in relative (rather than absolute) terms? The relative maximum is meant to exclude that portion of a country's population in each country whose income is most likely to be from inherited wealth, or based on prior or current economic rents associated with monopoly or other privileges, and thus is less associated with productive and primarily labor activity than that of the nonrich.

In an earlier working paper I specified the 90th decile of income as the threshold above which a household would be defined as rich (Birdsall 2007). That level seemed reasonable because across almost all developing countries for which there is information on the distribution of income, the ratio of average income (household income per capita) of the 10th to the 9th deciles ranges from two to more than five, and is far greater than

---

18 Birdsall and Menezes (2004), as reported by the World Bank in online data based on the Demographic and Health Surveys (DHS). The child stunting statistics are taken from DHS data on Bolivia (1998) and Ghana (1993).

the ratio of income of the 9th to the 8th deciles. (For OECD countries the 10/9 ratio also exceeds the 9/8 ratio, but is usually below two.)

For two reasons, in this chapter I have modified the definition of the middle class to exclude only the top 5 percent of households. First, in most of the poorer developing countries (henceforth "low income," using the World Bank classification of countries[19]) household income per capita in 2005, even at the 90th decile, is below $10 a day. It seems unreasonable to assume that 10 percent of all households in Ghana, Guatemala, and India with income or consumption of below $10 day are relying primarily on nonproductive income. Second, further scrutiny of income distribution data for most developing countries suggests that the cumulative distribution has an inflection point (at which the second derivative becomes positive) not at or around the 90th decile, but at or even above the 95th decile (which in simplified form is evident by comparing the ratios in figure 7.1). At and above that inflection point income tends to be even more concentrated.

Meanwhile, the 95th percentile is as arbitrary a cutoff at the top as is $10 at the bottom in defining a country-based (indispensable) middle class. There is no empirical basis to assume in any particular country that a household at the 96th percentile of per capita income or consumption is more reliant on income from capital, privileges, or "rents," broadly speaking, than a household at the 94th percentile. In fact, in low-income countries the relevant cutoff at the top may be much higher, because income/consumption per capita even at the 95th percentile is still below $10 a day—for example, in Ghana and India. Ideally, the threshold above which a household is too "rich" to be "middle class" would be estimated for each country on the basis of information about financial and other assets, sources of income, and the nature of employment.[20] The advantage of choosing the percentile threshold is that it reflects the reality that within countries relative and not just absolute income matters, especially in the political context.

### Why an Income or Consumption Measure versus Education, Occupation, or Other Traditional Measures?

I use information from household surveys to "count" the middle class and its proportion of total income in various countries and years. The count is based on household income or consumption per capita between the early 1990s and 2005 or the most recent other year available. It would be better to "count" the middle class on the basis of a reliable measure of permanent income. But measuring permanent income is a task in itself, and no reasonable measures of permanent income (or of its breakdown between government transfers and independent sources—the latter being a preferred indicator) are available over time and across countries. Consumption is a

---

19 The World Bank income classification is based on 2007 gross national income (GNI) per capita. The low-income classification is assigned to countries with a GNI per capita of $935 or less; lower middle income, $936–3,705; upper middle income, $3,706–11,455; and high income, $11,456 or more.

20 Data on household wealth and its distribution are now available for a limited number of developing countries. See Davies et al. (2008).

**a. Consumption distribution**

**b. Income distribution**

Legend: (20/19)   (19/18)   (18/17)

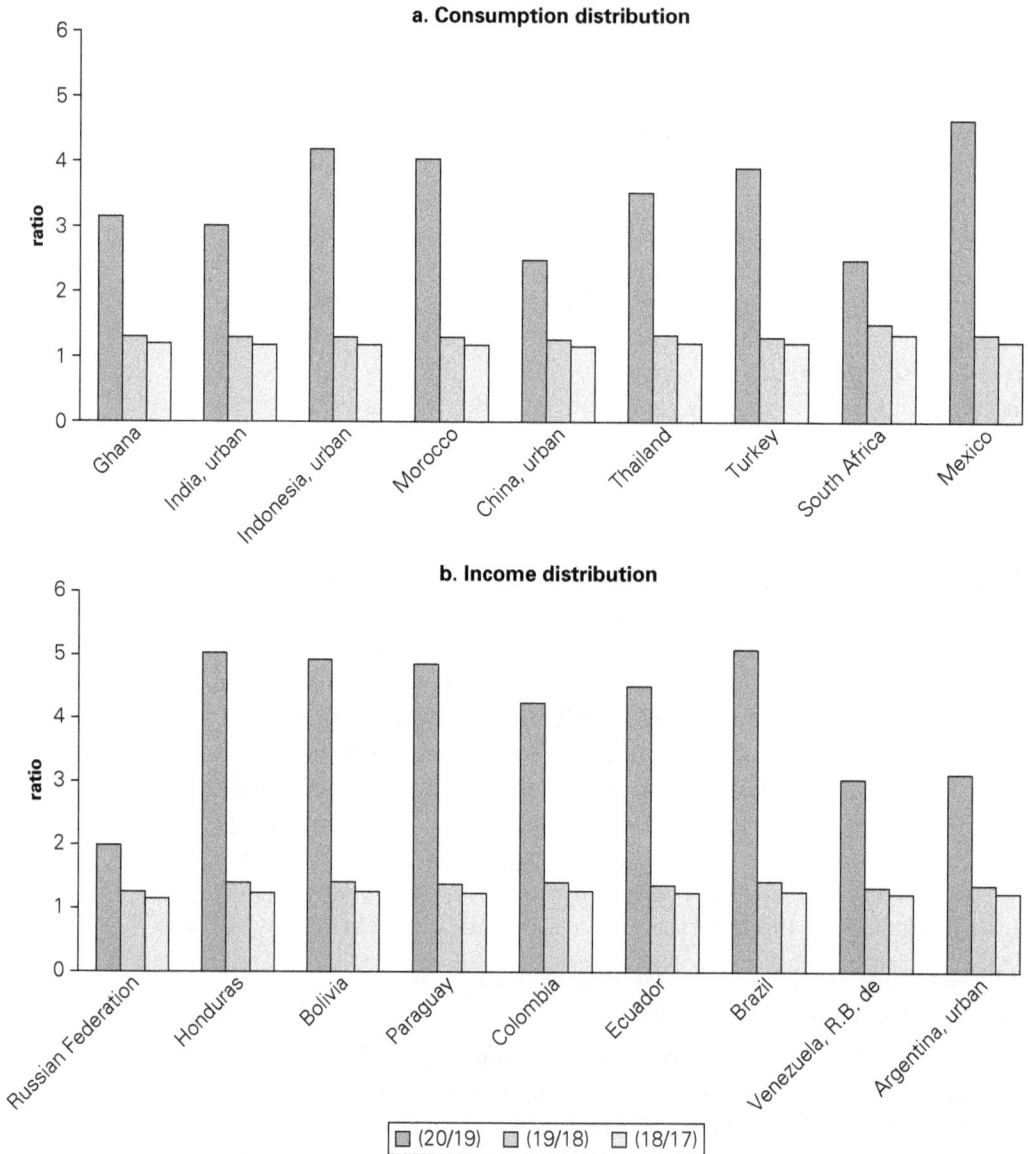

*Source:* Author's calculations using POVCAL data.

*Note:* The countries are ordered by World Development Indicators (WDI) mean income in 2005—lowest to highest, left to right. The legend entry "(20/19)" indicates the ratio of average household income of the 20th ventile (above the 95th percentile) to the 19th ventile (between the 90th and 95th percentiles), effectively showing the increasing slope of the top end of the POVCAL Lorenz curves. Data are from country household surveys in 2005 or closest available year.

better measure of permanent income than current income; generally the lower a household's consumption, the lower is its income. A still better measure may be education of the household head or all adults in the household.[21] But education of the household head is not sensitive to

---

21 Sociologists have traditionally identified the middle class in Western societies on the basis of education and occupation in a white-collar job.

changes in the economic environment, except over longer periods. An index of household assets such as that developed by Filmer and Pritchett (2001) would also be a better indicator of permanent income than current consumption/income. Table 7.1 lists some of the assets owned by households in Indonesia (urban), Turkey, and India (urban).[22] This approach does not solve the problem of using current income to define the middle class, but it does provide some indicator of its reasonableness.

## The Middle Class and Income-Based Identity

Members of the middle class are more likely to play a positive political role in accountable government—for example, by supporting the rule of law, property rights, and taxes to finance public goods such as education—to the extent that they identify with each other as the "middle class" with identifiable interests distinct from those of the rich and the poor. Measures of income polarization are based on the relevance of such "identification" (e.g., see Foster and Wolfson 1992 and Wolfson 1994). Economists' ideas about "identity," most notably those of George Akerlof (Akerlof and Kranton 2000), are discussed as well in the context of ethnic or gender identity, but there is also the concept of income identity, as in studies of the African American middle class.

A simple measure of potential income/consumption identity is the Gini coefficient of the middle class itself. A smaller value of the middle-class Gini, especially in relation to the overall Gini, suggests relative homogeneity within this middle class and a distinction between this group and those below and above it in the income distribution. Table 7.2 shows for selected countries for 1990 and 2005 the Gini coefficient of income/consumption inequality of members of the middle class using my definition. Except for several countries in Latin America, the Gini coefficients are generally between a very low 0.1 and 0.2 (and, as would be expected, are generally lower for the consumption-based survey countries). This finding suggests an extremely narrow range of income/consumption among the often small, in proportionate terms, middle classes in developing countries. The Gini coefficients are clearly correlated with the overall income range within a country for this group, which is, in turn, correlated with the absolute size of the group. The Gini for the U.S. middle class is, not surprisingly, much higher, at 0.38—indeed, it is higher than the Gini coefficient across all households in many countries. That finding reflects the fact that, along with the greater relative size of the middle class in the United States, $10 a day at the bottom of the class, as noted earlier, is actually well below what would be considered middle class in high-income countries, and $312, the daily income per capita at the top of the class, is 30 times greater than $10. Differences between the bottom and top income/consumption households

---

22 I identified the "middle class" in these countries by imposing the income/consumption distributions based on the World Bank's POVCAL estimates and my income/consumption cutoffs on the asset distributions developed by Filmer and Pritchett (2001) using the Demographic and Health Surveys data.

Table 7.1 Assets of Income/Consumption Groups, Selected Countries
(percentage of classified population owning a particular asset)

| Asset | Indonesia, urban | | | Turkey | | | India, urban | | |
|---|---|---|---|---|---|---|---|---|---|
| | Poor | Middle | Rich | Poor | Middle | Rich | Poor | Middle | Rich |
| Refrigerator | 14 | 86 | 100 | 92 | 99 | 100 | 15 | 89 | 99 |
| Car | 1 | 22 | 98 | 8 | 41 | 85 | 1 | 16 | 75 |
| Bicycle | 40 | 49 | 69 | 11 | 26 | 46 | 43 | 47 | 55 |
| Telephone | 8 | 73 | 100 | 68 | 95 | 100 | 10 | 68 | 97 |

*Source:* Author's calculations based on DHS data and POVCAL distributions.

Table 7.2 Gini Coefficients of Income/Consumption of Middle Class, Selected
Countries, 1990 and 2005

| Country | Income (I) / consumption (C) | | Pseudo-Gini for middle class | |
|---|---|---|---|---|
| | 1990 | 2005 | 1990 | 2005 |
| Ghana | C | C | — | — |
| India, urban | C | C | — | — |
| Indonesia, urban | C | C | — | — |
| Morocco | C | C | 0.047 | 0.039 |
| China, urban | C | C | — | 0.034 |
| Thailand | C | C | — | 0.082 |
| Turkey | C | C | 0.080 | 0.109 |
| South Africa | C | C | 0.127 | 0.103 |
| Mexico | I | C | 0.142 | 0.168 |
| Russian Federation | C | C | 0.146 | 0.141 |
| Honduras | I | I | — | 0.080 |
| Bolivia | I | I | 0.076 | 0.122 |
| Paraguay | I | I | 0.048 | 0.144 |
| Colombia | I | I | 0.101 | 0.131 |
| Ecuador | I | I | 0.090 | 0.123 |
| Brazil | I | I | 0.168 | 0.162 |
| Venezuela, R.B. de | I | I | 0.131 | 0.040 |
| Argentina, urban | I | I | 0.199 | 0.185 |
| Chile | I | I | 0.162 | 0.201 |
| Sweden | I | I | 0.235 | 0.231 |
| United States | I | I | 0.325 | 0.380 |

*Source:* Author's calculations, using POVCAL data.
— = no middle class in that year for that country.

are probably too great to pretend that the group as a whole represents a
single class. Indeed, in the United States the terms *lower* and *upper middle
class* are now widely used. The Gini for the middle class in Sweden is lower,
at 0.23, but still higher than in most developing countries.

## This (Indispensable) Middle Class and Growth

Defined in this manner, an increase in the size and economic command of the middle class is likely to signal that the underlying growth is based on wealth creation and productivity gains in private activities. That growth is thus self-sustaining and transformative (politically as well as economically, because the more powerful middle class demands government policies conducive to wealth creation), as opposed to being driven largely by exploitation of natural resources, by remittances, or by infusions of external aid.

## Country Estimates: Economic Size and Share of the Global Middle Class in Developing Countries

Figure 7.2 shows the economic command of the middle class so defined for selected countries, and the change in that indicator between 1990 (or years close to 1990) and 2005. (In the discussion that follows, I refer mostly to the economic command variable, which is generally higher and shows a greater increase or decline compared with the size variable.[23]) The estimates are based on household surveys in developing countries of income or consumption in purchasing power terms for various years around 1990 and 2005, using the most recent (2005) PPP updates. Estimated distributions of household income or consumption for each country and year are available from the World Bank's online poverty analysis tool, PovcalNet.[24] The resulting income/consumption country averages are lower than the gross domestic product (GDP) per capita estimates, which include nonhousehold production (and associated nonhousehold income), and the overall estimates are systematically lower for countries in which the data are for consumption rather than income. For these reasons alone, it is not possible to compare the resulting country averages to standard measures of GDP per capita, or to make comparisons across countries—including of the size of the middle classes between the consumption-based and income-based country estimates. Perusal of the survey-based estimates also indicates less growth in household income/consumption than would be expected based on average measured GDP per capita growth over the relevant periods in some countries. In short, although the resulting estimates allow useful description in the broad sense, they are best viewed as illustrative, not dispositive.

Several observations are in order. The first is the lack of an (indispensable) middle class in some countries[25] and its relatively small size

---

23 Table 7.3 later in this chapter includes the size of the middle class and the change in size between the two years.

24 PovcalNet provides the estimated distribution parameters and the survey-based average monthly income/consumption data for each survey, allowing calculation of the size and the share of income/consumption for the middle class as defined here, with its lower absolute and upper relative bounds.

25 How can a class that is indispensable be virtually nonexistent in many countries? The reader is reminded that the term *indispensable* refers (admittedly loosely) to a notion of political indispensability, or of indispensability in assuring a government that is accountable to its citizens.

**a. Consumption distribution**

**b. Income distribution**

☐ 1990   ☐ 2005

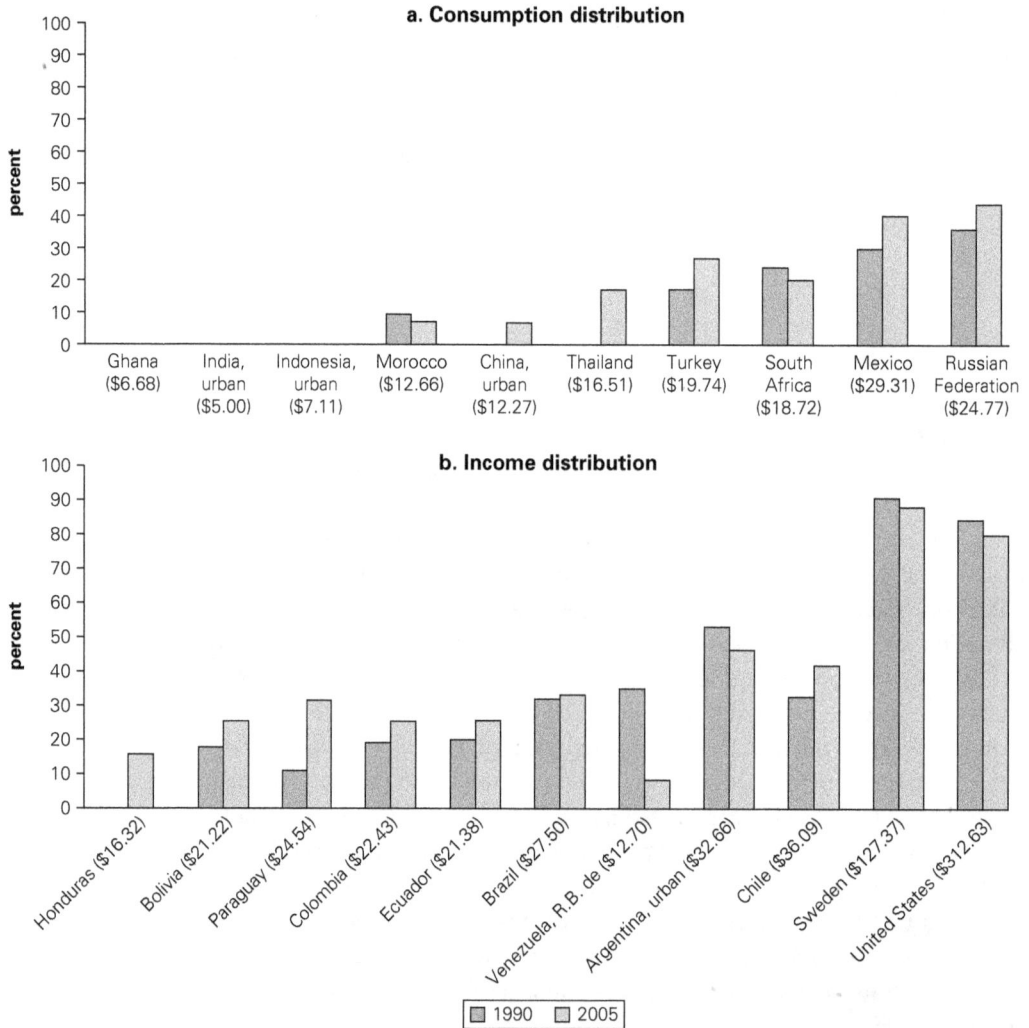

*Source:* Author's calculations using POVCAL data.

*Note:* The countries are ordered by WDI mean income in 2005—lowest to highest, left to right. The dollar amount in parentheses indicates daily per capita income of individuals at the 95th percentile of the country's income/consumption distribution, as reported by PovcalNet, in 2005. The survey data used are from the closest available survey year to 1990 or 2005.

and economic command in low-income compared with middle-income developing countries.

Figure 7.2 shows the daily per capita consumption/income of households in each country at the 95th percentile. By my definition, Thailand and urban China in 1990 and urban India, Ghana, and Indonesia in 1990 and (about) 2005 have no middle class at all. In other words, all households in those countries in those years with consumption at or greater than $10 a day are in the top 5 percent of all households and are thus in this context "rich." (Figure 7.3 provides a dramatic illustration of the missing middle class in many developing countries and its small size where it is present.)

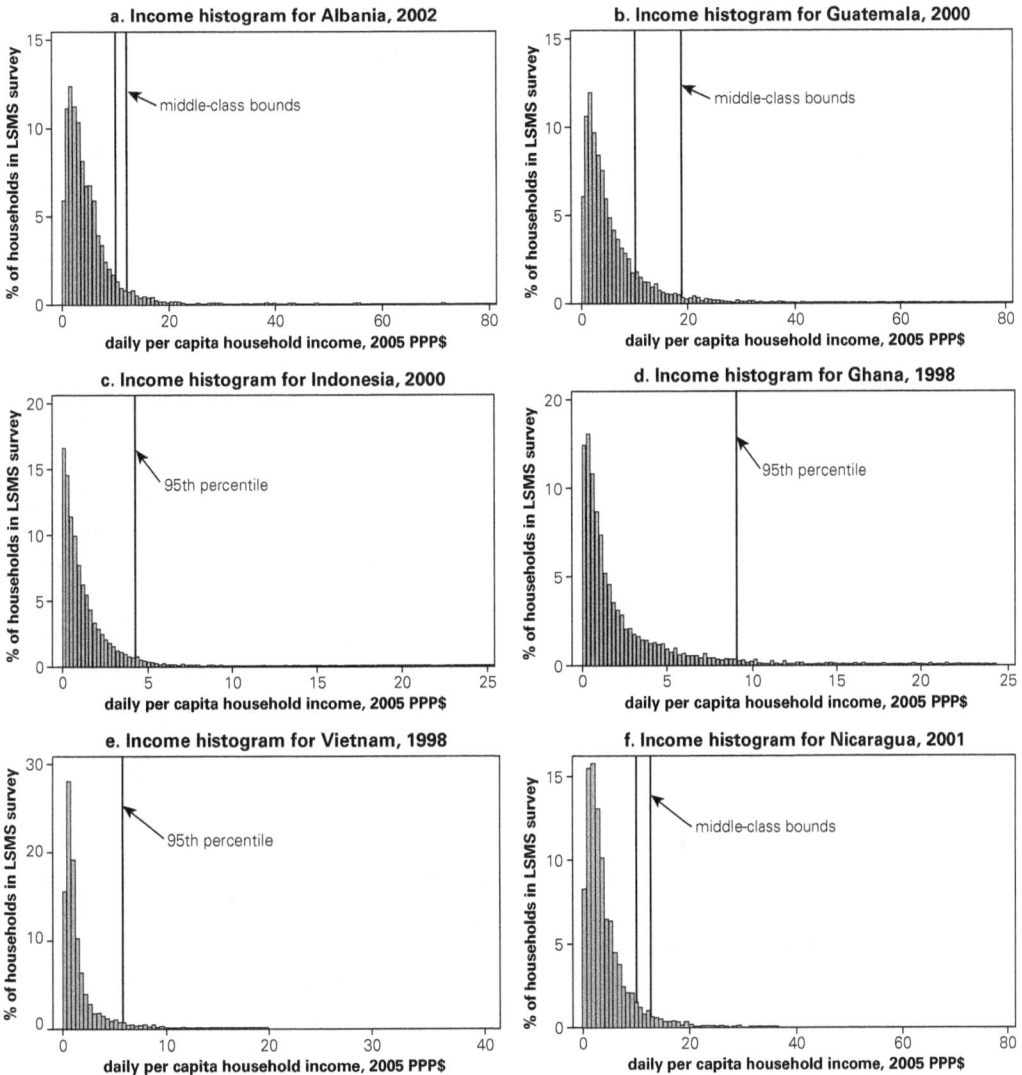

Figure 7.3 Income Histograms for Selected Countries and Years

a. Income histogram for Albania, 2002

b. Income histogram for Guatemala, 2000

c. Income histogram for Indonesia, 2000

d. Income histogram for Ghana, 1998

e. Income histogram for Vietnam, 1998

f. Income histogram for Nicaragua, 2001

*Source:* LSMS data via FAO compilation.
*Note:* Average daily per capita household incomes are normalized to match the POVCAL 2005 PPP figures. The income figures are generated based on the question in the agricultural production section of the household questionnaire that asks about household consumption of agricultural production. Note, also, that if the upper bound of the middle class is below $10 per day, there will be no middle class, indicated by only one vertical line. LSMS = Living Standards Measurement Survey.

But what about India? Some of the numbers in figure 7.2 will strike some readers as too low—for example, for Thailand in 1990 and especially for urban India. Any definition of the middle class that suggests there was no middle class at all in urban India in 2005 is not credible. How can this be?

First, it is likely that a large portion of people conventionally viewed as "middle class" in India are among the most affluent 5 percent of people whom I have defined as "rich." The McKinsey Global Institute (2007) reports a "middle class," defined as people with disposable annual incomes from about $4,200 to $21,000, or about $11–$55 a day, of about 50 million people in India, which is less than 5 percent of India's total population of about 1.3 billion. Second, the survey data for India record consumption, not income; in most households, particularly affluent households, consumption is consistently below income, which helps explain some of the shortfall in measured numbers of middle-class people. Third, the distribution of income in India is relatively less concentrated than that of many developing countries with larger middle classes such as those in Latin America. This finding suggests that the appropriate cutoff for "rich" households is above the 95th percentile in India (and other South Asian countries). Indeed, as noted earlier, ideally the threshold for "rich" would be country-specific.[26]

Among countries for which estimates are based on income, not consumption, data, Honduras in 1990 also had no middle class. Honduras and Bolivia are among the richest of those countries, most of which are in Sub-Saharan Africa. These countries are classified by the World Bank as "low-income"—that is, income per capita is less than about $800 a year at market exchange rates. Most still had no (indispensable) middle class in 2005. As in India, it is likely in Sub-Saharan Africa that virtually all households in urban areas with apparent middle-class status (many working as civil servants or with the aid community or international nongovernmental organizations) are among the 5 percent most affluent in their countries. In a country in which 40–60 percent of all people are living below the international poverty line of $1.25 a day, this is not as surprising as it seems at first glance. It does suggest something about the political challenge inherent in creating and maintaining accountable government, particularly where a high proportion of the richest 5 percent of the nation's population are members of the political class—that is, they are directly or indirectly dependent on government for their income, whether as civil servants or as employees of parastatals or formal institutions highly dependent on public policies such as banks and natural resource producers.[27]

The (indispensable) middle class is larger in most middle-income countries. Where it does exist in the developing world (leaving out the former socialist economies of Eastern Europe), its command of income or consumption in many countries is still small compared with the command of the "rich": 7 percent compared with 18 percent in China (urban), 20 percent

---

26 As shown in figure 7.2, per capita consumption for India at the 95th percentile is $5 a day. It is only at the 99th percentile that, using my estimates, per capita consumption reaches $10. Above the 98th percentile, the functional form used to estimate the entire distribution probably dominates what are likely to be very noisy survey data at the top of the consumption distribution. In addition, my numbers reflect the recent large downward adjustments in average dollar income in purchasing power parity terms for India (and China) based on 2005 price data that have only just been incorporated. The new Penn World Tables with these PPP adjustments have not yet received the kind of scrutiny earlier adjustments are now getting (Johnson et al. 2009).

27 Elsewhere I have presented data suggesting that the top quintile in low-income countries heavily relies on employment by the state or state-owned enterprises (Birdsall 2007). This may be more characteristic of small countries (in economic size and in population), assuming that the number of public employees rises less than proportionally with the population of a country. That would imply that the independent middle class is even smaller in many African countries than in India for any given measure.

compared with 30 percent in South Africa, and 26 percent compared with 35 percent in Colombia (see table 7.7 later in this chapter). Brazil, Chile, Mexico, the Russian Federation, and Turkey are interesting exceptions in which the middle-class economic command is equal to or greater than that of the "rich." They may be the countries in which in political terms it is possible to distinguish three classes: the poor, the middle, and the rich. Elsewhere in the developing world, the relevant political economy might better distinguish between the rich—with political salience—and the rest.

Second, from 1990 to 2005, a period of healthy growth almost everywhere and the growing integration of developing countries into the global economy, the economic command of the (indispensable) middle class increased in most middle-income countries, notably in urban China. Exceptions include urban Argentina, República Bolivariana de Venezuela (income data), and Morocco and South Africa (consumption data). Although over the relevant period overall household consumption in South Africa grew at 2.35 percent and in Morocco at 3.39 percent (based on the household survey data), the size and economic command of the middle class declined in those countries. Both the United States and Sweden also saw a decline in the economic command of the middle class—a phenomenon widely observed for the United States in the context of the 2008 presidential campaign and often blamed on "free trade" and "globalization." The increase in income inequality and the stagnation of median wages in the United States since the early 1980s have been attributed to, among other things, the decline in access to good education (Goldin and Katz 2007). The decline in Sweden may be more of a surprise. The proportion of income commanded by the middle class in Sweden is higher than in the United States, despite Sweden's lower per capita income. In 2005 average per capita income was about $32,000 in Sweden and about $42,000 in the United States.[28]

Third, the overall command of the middle class in all the developing countries is far lower than in Sweden and the United States, mostly because of the lower average income across the entire distributions. The extent to which the middle class more than the poor or the rich constitutes the bulwark of accountable government and sustained economic growth suggests the nature of the challenge in developing countries. Only in Chile, Russia, and Mexico is the middle class command of total income/consumption close to or greater than 40 percent, compared with about 80 percent in the United States and almost 90 percent in Sweden (the figures for Mexico and Russia are for consumption and would be higher in income terms).

Table 7.3 summarizes my middle-class indicators, which supplement information embedded in the more traditional measures of income distribution such as the Gini coefficient and the Theil index. For example, the change over the periods studied in the economic command of the middle class is not necessarily in the expected opposite direction from the change in

28 The quoted incomes are GNI per capita, PPP (current international dollars), as given in the World Bank's *World Development Indicators 2008* (World Bank 2008).

Table 7.3 Distribution Statistics, Selected Countries, 1990 and 2005

| Country | I/C | Middle-class size (proportion of population) | | Middle-class share (proportion of income/consumption) | | Gini | | Theil | | Difference from 1990 to 2005 | | |
|---|---|---|---|---|---|---|---|---|---|---|---|---|
| | | 1990 | 2005 | 1990 | 2005 | 1990 | 2005 | 1990 | 2005 | Middle-class size | Middle-class share | Gini |
| Ghana | C | 0.000 | 0.000 | 0.000 | 0.000 | 0.381 | 0.428 | 0.24 | 0.31 | 0.000 | 0.000 | 0.046 |
| India, urban | C | 0.000 | 0.000 | 0.000 | 0.000 | 0.356 | 0.376 | 0.21 | 0.24 | 0.000 | 0.000 | 0.020 |
| Indonesia, urban | C | 0.000 | 0.000 | 0.000 | 0.000 | 0.347 | 0.399 | 0.20 | 0.25 | 0.000 | 0.000 | 0.053 |
| Morocco | C | 0.044 | 0.035 | 0.098 | 0.073 | 0.392 | 0.411 | 0.26 | 0.23 | -0.009 | -0.025 | 0.019 |
| China, urban | C | 0.000 | 0.034 | 0.000 | 0.070 | 0.256 | 0.347 | 0.10 | 0.20 | 0.034 | 0.070 | 0.091 |
| Thailand | C | 0.000 | 0.087 | 0.000 | 0.174 | 0.438 | 0.425 | 0.33 | 0.31 | 0.087 | 0.174 | -0.014 |
| Turkey | C | 0.101 | 0.159 | 0.176 | 0.274 | 0.441 | 0.432 | 0.16 | 0.30 | 0.058 | 0.098 | -0.008 |
| South Africa | C | 0.096 | 0.076 | 0.243 | 0.203 | 0.595 | 0.580 | 0.63 | 0.59 | -0.019 | -0.040 | -0.016 |
| Mexico | C | 0.177 | 0.280 | 0.299 | 0.405 | 0.553 | 0.483 | 0.35 | 0.35 | 0.103 | 0.107 | -0.070 |
| Russian Federation | C | 0.244 | 0.298 | 0.363 | 0.439 | 0.486 | 0.375 | 0.27 | 0.23 | 0.055 | 0.076 | -0.111 |
| Honduras | I | 0.000 | 0.068 | 0.000 | 0.157 | 0.575 | 0.569 | 0.47 | 0.50 | 0.068 | 0.157 | -0.006 |
| Bolivia | I | 0.082 | 0.122 | 0.176 | 0.254 | 0.420 | 0.582 | 0.29 | 0.56 | 0.039 | 0.078 | 0.162 |
| Paraguay | I | 0.048 | 0.180 | 0.109 | 0.315 | 0.397 | 0.541 | 0.26 | 0.44 | 0.132 | 0.206 | 0.143 |
| Colombia | I | 0.105 | 0.135 | 0.191 | 0.255 | 0.576 | 0.590 | 0.20 | 0.43 | 0.030 | 0.063 | 0.014 |
| Ecuador | I | 0.097 | 0.139 | 0.198 | 0.257 | 0.505 | 0.538 | 0.40 | 0.40 | 0.042 | 0.059 | 0.034 |
| Brazil | I | 0.164 | 0.194 | 0.317 | 0.331 | 0.606 | 0.566 | 0.65 | 0.47 | 0.030 | 0.013 | -0.040 |
| Venezuela, R.B. de | I | 0.206 | 0.032 | 0.348 | 0.081 | 0.441 | 0.482 | 0.33 | 0.39 | -0.174 | -0.267 | 0.041 |
| Argentina, urban | I | 0.391 | 0.305 | 0.532 | 0.464 | 0.454 | 0.500 | 0.35 | 0.42 | -0.086 | -0.068 | 0.047 |
| Chile | I | 0.206 | 0.327 | 0.325 | 0.419 | 0.557 | 0.551 | 0.35 | 0.26 | 0.121 | 0.095 | -0.006 |
| Sweden | I | 0.950 | 0.950 | 0.904 | 0.879 | 0.240 | 0.257 | 0.09 | 0.11 | 0.000 | -0.025 | 0.017 |
| United States | I | 0.938 | 0.909 | 0.844 | 0.812 | 0.372 | 0.448 | 0.22 | 0.33 | -0.029 | -0.032 | 0.077 |

Source: Author's calculations using POVCAL data.

the Gini coefficient[29]—that is, an increase in the middle class is not always associated with a decline in overall inequality. In India and Brazil, a rising middle class is not associated with a declining Gini. However, for urban China (treated here as a country) the notable increase in middle-class command (from zero in 1990) is associated with a substantial *increase* in the overall Gini, and that is also true for Ecuador. In South Africa, the decline in middle-class command is associated with a *decrease* in the overall Gini. The same is true for other measures of inequality (not shown).[30]

## Characteristics of the Global Middle Class

Table 7.4 provides information for selected countries on the education of household heads for the three groups: poor, middle class, and rich. The information for the first set of countries is based on the World Bank's Living Standards Measurement Surveys (LSMS), most of which were conducted in the 1990s, and thus do not reflect the increases since then in the size and command of the middle class shown in figure 7.2. Other than the high levels of education for Indonesia and Ecuador, the information is consistent with my priors about the levels and differences in education across the three groups. Except for Nicaragua and Guatemala, the middle class in most countries has close to or more than 10 years of education (measured in most surveys as grade completed). The information for the second set of countries is based on Demographic and Health Surveys (DHS) conducted more recently. The DHS includes good data on education as well as a measure of household wealth based on household assets, but does not include data on household income. However, it is possible to use the data on household assets combined with World Bank distributions (based on other surveys that do include income) to define the three groups (low-income, middle class, and rich).[31] To take one example, in Turkey in 2005, 65 percent of household heads in middle-class households had 11 or more years of education and 32 percent had 16 years or more, compared with 26 percent and 5 percent, respectively, of adults in lower-income households. These averages are below but approaching those for the middle class in the more affluent OECD countries, where a high school education, about 12 years, is more of a minimum for middle-class status.

By contrast, adults in "middle-class" households, defined as those above the international poverty line of $2 (based on the definition of Banerjee and Duflo [2007] of income of between $2 and $10 a day), are far less educated. They are likely to have attained educational levels no greater than

---

29 The Ginis shown in the table are calculated from the same data (POVCAL) used to identify the middle class. The Ginis match reasonably well the Ginis published in *World Development Indicators*.

30 For India, South Africa, and Russia, the comparison is between an income-based Gini and changes in middle-class command based on consumption survey data.

31 I applied the World Bank's POVCAL distributions to the countries shown to define the three income groups (poor, middle, rich). The matching of wealth and income is imperfect, but it does broadly distinguish among the three income groups.

Table 7.4 Average Education of Household Head, by Class, Selected Countries and Years

| Country | Year | Source | Middle- class size | Education of household head | | |
|---|---|---|---|---|---|---|
| | | | | Poor | Middle | Rich |
| Malawi | 2004 | LSMS | 0.000 | 4.58 | | 9.64 |
| Madagascar | 1993 | LSMS | 0.000 | 3.50 | | 4.05 |
| Nigeria | 2004 | LSMS | 0.000 | 2.72 | | 4.60 |
| Indonesia | 2000 | LSMS | 0.000 | 8.19 | | 14.45 |
| Bangladesh | 2000 | LSMS | 0.000 | 3.29 | | 7.06 |
| Vietnam | 1998 | LSMS | 0.000 | 6.72 | | 7.62 |
| Pakistan | 2001 | LSMS | 0.000 | 4.10 | | 8.87 |
| Nepal | 2003 | LSMS | 0.000 | 3.20 | | 9.61 |
| Ghana | 1998 | LSMS | 0.000 | 4.71 | | 8.21 |
| Nicaragua | 2001 | LSMS | 0.035 | 4.01 | 7.43 | 8.33 |
| Albania | 2005 | LSMS | 0.060 | 8.91 | 11.37 | 12.17 |
| Ecuador | 1998 | LSMS | 0.027 | 7.00 | 12.03 | 9.50 |
| Guatemala | 2000 | LSMS | 0.119 | 3.33 | 7.32 | 9.80 |
| Bulgaria | 2001 | LSMS | 0.090 | 9.97 | 12.06 | 11.21 |
| Panama | 2003 | LSMS | 0.280 | 6.65 | 9.94 | 12.92 |
| Morocco | 2004 | DHS | 0.035 | 3.06 | 9.24 | 11.73 |
| Colombia | 2005 | DHS | 0.135 | 7.37 | 10.95 | 13.62 |
| Peru | 2004–08 | DHS | 0.137 | 6.75 | 11.23 | 13.47 |
| Dominican Republic | 2007 | DHS | 0.167 | 7.88 | 11.29 | 14.43 |
| Turkey | 2003 | DHS | 0.159 | 5.98 | 10.01 | 13.28 |

Note: For countries with no middle class, the education measure is left blank; the "poor" represent households below the 95th percentile on the income/consumption distribution.

and possibly below the averages for their countries of just 4.2 years for countries of South Asia, 5.7 years for Latin America, and 6.5 years for East Asia, compared with the average of 9.8 years in advanced countries (Barro and Lee 2000). Based on scores on internationally comparable tests, those levels of education imply illiteracy in many low-income countries (Filmer, Hasan, and Pritchett 2006), so that, whether in terms of income security or sufficient literacy to acquire information relevant to voting decisions, the Banerjee and Duflo middle class is not likely to be a relevant group in terms of its economic interests or political ability to support the institutions and policies associated with good governance, the rule of law, property rights, and, more generally, a level playing field.

Table 7.5 shows the average number of people in poor, middle-class, and rich households. Poor households are generally larger, to some extent reflecting the definition of income/consumption of household income per capita.

Table 7.6 shows the employment status of the middle class, compared with that of the poor and the rich, for the Dominican Republic and Turkey. In Turkey, the poor are more likely than the middle class to be self-employed

| Country | Year | Average per capita household income | Middle-class size (%) | Number of household members | | |
|---------|------|-------------------------------------|----------------------|------|--------|------|
| | | | | Poor | Middle | Rich |
| Malawi | 2004 | $1.12 | 0.00 | 4.58 | | 2.88 |
| Madagascar | 1993 | $1.19 | 0.00 | 5.11 | | 2.68 |
| Nigeria | 2004 | $1.30 | 0.00 | 5.06 | | 3.29 |
| Indonesia | 2000 | $1.36 | 0.00 | 5.40 | | 2.79 |
| Bangladesh | 2000 | $1.40 | 0.00 | 5.23 | | 4.23 |
| Vietnam | 1998 | $1.64 | 0.00 | 4.73 | | 4.28 |
| Pakistan | 2001 | $1.80 | 0.00 | 7.33 | | 4.48 |
| Nepal | 2003 | $1.85 | 0.00 | 5.24 | | 3.67 |
| Ghana | 1998 | $2.06 | 0.00 | 4.38 | | 2.29 |
| Nicaragua | 2001 | $4.21 | 3.50 | 5.56 | 3.47 | 3.03 |
| Albania | 2005 | $5.33 | 6.00 | 4.33 | 3.38 | 3.46 |
| Ecuador | 1998 | $6.00 | 2.70 | 4.56 | 3.08 | 4.26 |
| Guatemala | 2000 | $6.08 | 11.90 | 5.48 | 3.94 | 2.81 |
| Bulgaria | 2001 | $6.81 | 9.00 | 3.14 | 2.34 | 2.42 |
| Panama | 2003 | $9.54 | 28.00 | 4.71 | 3.16 | 2.26 |

*Source:* LSMS household survey data.
*Note:* The average income measure is daily. For countries with no middle class, the number of household members is left blank.

or receiving daily/seasonal wages than salaried workers. The difference between the middle class and the rich in percentages of "regular" wage or salaried workers is relatively small, reflecting the middle-income status of the diversified Turkish economy. In the Dominican Republic, the poor are more likely than the middle class to be self-employed or domestic workers. Surprisingly, the distinction in "employee" status between the poor and the middle class is small, suggesting that many households with income/consumption above the conventional $2-a-day line but below my $10-a-day minimum threshold enjoy regular if low-wage participation in the formal sector.

It is unfortunate that typical household surveys of income and consumption do not include information on public- versus private-sector employment. For that reason, it is impossible to assess the extent to which the income/consumption-based middle class, as I have defined it, is highly dependent directly or indirectly on the state for employment.

Finally returning to table 7.1, at least for urban Indonesia and urban India, the items owned that appear to distinguish between low-income and middle-class households are a refrigerator and a telephone. However, the choice of assets for this table was largely arbitrary (for one thing, the information on assets is not common across the country surveys), and the number of countries shown is limited. It would be convenient to have a single, globally traded consumption good that would reliably "mark" the indispensable middle class, but the refrigerator and telephone are not necessarily

Table 7.6 Household Characteristics for Occupation/Pay Period, Selected Countries (proportion of total population)

| Turkey (2003) Occupation category | Poor | Middle | Rich |
|---|---|---|---|
| Employer (10+ employees) | 0.007 | 0.026 | 0.080 |
| Employer (1–9 employees) | 0.050 | 0.139 | 0.219 |
| Waged worker (regular) | 0.320 | 0.362 | 0.310 |
| Salaried, government official (regular) | 0.096 | 0.268 | 0.266 |
| Daily wage (seasonal/temporary) | 0.092 | 0.014 | 0.004 |
| Self-employed (regular) | 0.330 | 0.165 | 0.106 |
| Self-employed (irregular) | 0.084 | 0.020 | 0.011 |
| Unpaid family worker | 0.021 | 0.005 | 0.004 |
| Dominican Republic (2007) Pay period | | | |
| Hour | 0.003 | 0.001 | 0.000 |
| Day | 0.269 | 0.111 | 0.045 |
| Week | 0.171 | 0.131 | 0.096 |
| By week | 0.100 | 0.102 | 0.069 |
| Month | 0.457 | 0.656 | 0.790 |
| Dominican Republic (2007) Occupation category | | | |
| Employee | 0.491 | 0.581 | 0.568 |
| Employer | 0.070 | 0.115 | 0.192 |
| Self-employed | 0.353 | 0.260 | 0.222 |
| Member of cooperative | 0.002 | 0.002 | 0.000 |
| Work for family member | 0.011 | 0.006 | 0.007 |
| Domestic work | 0.074 | 0.037 | 0.011 |

Source: Author's calculations using DHS data.

the right ones (especially the telephone in view of the declining cost and increased use of mobile phones among the poor in many countries).

Does the absolute size of the middle class matter? As an indispensable political class for its likely alignment of its own economic interests with sustainable economic policy and reasonable governance, perhaps what matters within countries is not the relative size or income/consumption share of the middle class, but rather the absolute size of the middle-income population and its absolute dollar command of income or consumption goods and services. In most developing countries, the middle class by my definition is small in absolute terms. Among the countries studied, only Russia, Mexico, and Brazil have more than 25 million people in the middle class; urban China has not quite 20 million (table 7.7). By this measure, Brazil and Mexico have larger middle classes than China, and Russia is the largest among all the countries analyzed. If all of Sub-Saharan Africa is treated as a single country, the numbers in table 7.7 imply that of its some

Table 7.7 Absolute Size of Middle Class and Middle Class plus Rich

| Country (year) | I/C | Middle-class population | Middle class plus rich population | Middle-class share of national income | Rich share of national income |
|---|---|---|---|---|---|
| Ghana (2005.5) | C | 0 | 1,126,751 | 0.00 | 0.22 |
| India, rural (2004.5) | C | 0 | 39,000,000 | 0.00 | 0.18 |
| India, urban (2004.5) | C | 0 | 15,700,000 | 0.00 | 0.20 |
| Indonesia, rural (2005) | C | 0 | 5,723,481 | 0.00 | 0.16 |
| Indonesia, urban (2005) | C | 0 | 5,304,420 | 0.00 | 0.22 |
| Morocco (2007) | C | 1,044,183 | 2,551,319 | 0.07 | 0.23 |
| China, rural (2005) | C | 0 | 38,900,000 | 0.00 | 0.19 |
| China, urban (2005) | C | 17,800,000 | 44,100,000 | 0.07 | 0.18 |
| Thailand (2004) | C | 5,490,658 | 8,640,803 | 0.17 | 0.23 |
| Turkey (2005) | C | 11,400,000 | 15,000,000 | 0.27 | 0.23 |
| South Africa (2000) | C | 3,574,911 | 5,919,533 | 0.20 | 0.30 |
| Mexico (2006) | C | 28,900,000 | 34,000,000 | 0.41 | 0.27 |
| Russian Federation (2005) | C | 42,700,000 | 49,900,000 | 0.44 | 0.18 |
| Honduras (2005) | I | 461,337 | 803,043 | 0.16 | 0.32 |
| Bolivia (2005) | I | 1,115,742 | 1,574,843 | 0.25 | 0.32 |
| Paraguay (2005) | I | 1,060,418 | 1,355,351 | 0.32 | 0.30 |
| Colombia (2003) | I | 6,083,750 | 8,331,040 | 0.26 | 0.35 |
| Ecuador (2005) | I | 1,815,542 | 2,468,592 | 0.26 | 0.31 |
| Brazil (2005) | I | 36,300,000 | 45,700,000 | 0.33 | 0.33 |
| Venezuela, R.B. de (2003) | I | 857,582 | 2,186,432 | 0.08 | 0.24 |
| Argentina, urban (2005) | I | 10,600,000 | 12,400,000 | 0.46 | 0.25 |
| Chile (2003) | I | 5,321,656 | 6,136,412 | 0.42 | 0.34 |
| Sweden (2002) | I | 8,572,838 | 9,024,040 | 0.88 | 0.14 |
| United States (2000) | I | 269,000,000 | 284,000,000 | 0.81 | 0.19 |

*Source:* Population data taken from World Development Indicators.
*Note:* "Middle class plus rich" includes all households with per capita daily income of over $10 a day and above the 95th percentile on the income/consumption distribution.

300 million people, just 3.6 million in South Africa are "middle class" in the political sense. Of the 15 million I have called "rich" because they are in the top 5 percent of households in their own countries, perhaps another 5–10 million should be counted as middle class, suggesting at the moment a maximum of 20 million middle-class people in the region, similar to the number for urban China (treated as a country) but below the numbers in Mexico and Brazil.

From the point of view of the consumer market and for some aspects of economic policy such as openness to foreign direct investment on which the interests of the rich and the middle class are likely to be aligned, it may be that the absolute size of the middle class combined with the absolute size of the "rich" within a country is the most salient. Table 7.7 shows the absolute size of the middle class plus the rich in countries around 2005. India's 55 million and China's 83 million (combining urban and rural in both cases) stand out.

The last two columns of table 7.7 allow a comparison in countries with absolutely large middle-class or rich populations, or both, of the relative economic command of the two groups. This comparison serves as a kind of counterpoint to the view that it is their combined absolute income that matters for the politics of economic policy. As noted earlier, in only a few developing countries does the middle class share exceed that of the rich.

## Implications for Policy, Domestic and International

Does making a distinction between pro-poor growth and growth that increases the size and command of the middle class have any implications for policy? Are there any trade-offs between policies that favor the middle class and those that favor the poor, or is a focus on the middle class merely a simple extension of caring about the poor?

### Macroeconomic Policy

At the most basic level—in terms of sensible macroeconomic policy—the distinction is not important. Inflation, high interest rates, and overvalued exchange rates (increasingly a thing of the past) hurt the poor and the middle class alike.[32] The increases from 1990 to 2005 in the size and economic command of the middle class in Chile, Mexico, and Turkey suggest that eventually—and sometimes with a long lag time—better macropolicy, combined with a benign external environment and a commodity boom, brings growth that is inclusive in both reducing poverty and increasing the size of the middle class. At the same time, during a period in which the general trend across the developing world has been improved macroeconomic fundamentals, it is not possible at this level of crude analysis to distinguish across developing countries between the effect of good policy and the effect of overall economic growth (due in part to good policy), because the size of the middle class over the period and across countries is highly correlated with average per capita income for the countries and years studied (figure 7.4). In short, growth is not only "good for the poor" (Dollar and Kraay 2002), but also apparently good for building the indispensable middle class.

More to the point, for most low-income countries, the distinction between the poor and near-poor, living on less than $10 a day, and the nonexistent middle class is by definition irrelevant. All but the very rich, if not the absolutely poor by the international standard of $1.25 a day, are in income terms living at levels well below poverty lines in the OECD countries.

---

32 I discuss macroeconomic policy and its effects on the middle class in Birdsall (2009).

Figure 7.4 Middle-Class Size versus Income (Alternate), 1990 and 2005

**a. Income distribution, 1990 and 2005**

average daily income per capita, 2005 PPP$

**b. Consumption distribution, 1990 and 2005**

average daily income per capita, 2005 PPP$

○ middle-class size; proportion of population
—— linear fit, 1990   - - - linear fit, 2005

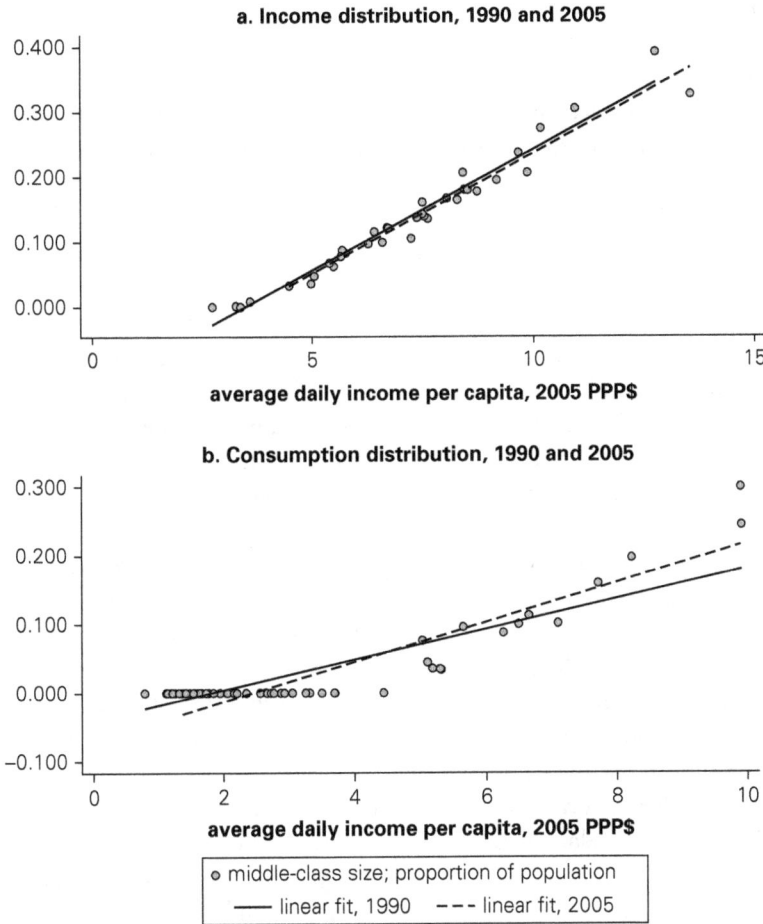

*Source:* Author's calculations using POVCAL data.

## Volatility and Vulnerability

In welfare terms, the poor suffer most when negative shocks derail an economy, whether negative external financial and economic conditions or internal political upheaval or unfavorable terms of trade or catastrophic weather events. Analysts do not know much about the extent to which such shocks set back an increase in the size and economic command of an independent middle class—in part because there is little consensus and therefore little systematic data on who or what that middle class is. Ravallion (2009) shows convincingly that from 1990 to 2002 almost a billion people moved from income of just below $2 a day to just above $2 a day—mostly in Asia (half in China). They are obviously vulnerable to the ongoing global recession. I define the indispensable middle class in terms of its members' relative sense of economic security compared with those in the lower-income group, but that sense of security is in the face of typical cyclical downturns, not in the face of a global recession. The total size of this middle class in the developing world, including Russia, is roughly 200 million of the almost 6 billion people in the developing world (see table 7.7). To the extent that they are heavily dependent for their security on formal sector employment (table 7.6), particularly in tradable sectors, those numbers are likely to decline. And there are likely to be considerable trade-offs between protecting their jobs and incomes during the downturn versus extending in time and scope safety net programs for those already at lower incomes.

*The trade-off may be about politics, especially in low-income and oil economies.* However, in the absence of this middle class, the question is where does good governance (and sensible economic policy) come from? The relatively small size of the group in many low-income countries (including rural India and rural China were they to be countries) suggests considerable vulnerability to bad politics, including during periods of economic growth, that over time is likely to undermine what, in retrospect, will have been unsustainable growth. Zimbabwe and Côte d'Ivoire come to mind, and perhaps Pakistan. Put another way, for low-income countries there is a considerable premium on honest and competent leadership and in general on whatever it takes to sustain good government from the top in the absence of the pressure for accountability from below. Alternative sources of accountability include market pressures for countries dependent on foreign investment and trade (in very small economies private foreign investors have considerable leverage, often untapped, in demanding the rule of law). Countries at higher average income levels that are heavily dependent on oil or other natural resources are similarly vulnerable—República Bolivariana de Venezuela, where the middle class has shrunk (figure 7.2), comes to mind. For the low-income countries heavily dependent on aid, primarily in Sub-Saharan Africa and Central America, this vulnerability suggests the logic of donors favoring those countries in which the evidence of effective and honest leadership is clear—be it in terms of proportion of budgets spent on education and health, minimal corruption, fair elections, or other measures.[33]

### Microeconomic Policies: Taxes, Spending, Trade and Jobs, and Foreign Aid

At the same time, in most developing countries a singular focus on the poor is likely to ignore trade-offs that matter for the incipient or small and fragile middle class. Choices on the expenditure side are the most obvious. One example is loss of political support for narrowly targeted cash transfer programs.[34] Less studied but equivalent is the likely withdrawal of middle-class support for spending overall on education in Latin America in response to the reduction in the implicit subsidies at the higher education level from

---

33 The U.S. Millennium Challenge Account program is an example of where this basis for aid is the most explicit.

34 Gelbach and Pritchett (2000) introduce their analysis with an anecdote from Sri Lanka, where the switch from a broad food subsidy to a targeted program was associated over several years with a dramatic reduction in expenditures on the latter.

which the middle class has benefited, even though the truly rich have no doubt benefited far more. Perhaps the biggest trade-off occurs when the middle class loses trust in government's ability to spend effectively at all and withdraws support for tax collection in general.[35] There are also obvious trade-offs on the revenue side, between taxes on labor and trade (the latter is usually a last resort for lack of administrative capacity) and taxes on capital and property (which may hurt most small businesses) and on how progressive the overall tax structure is.

Finally, for countries that have become heavily dependent on aid there is the risk that aid intended to finance services for the poor keeps upward pressure on the exchange rate, hurting prospects for small businesses. Although those pressures can be managed at the macroeconomic level by intelligent fine-tuning, that requires a steady hand at the top, which is something that is already at a premium in low-income countries.

In the end, as noted earlier, it is not possible to generalize about the possible tensions or trade-offs between strictly pro-poor and more inclusive "middle-class" growth policies. They need to be assessed policy by policy in each country, and they are likely to change over time as circumstances change. The implication is that policymakers in developing countries (and their international supporters and advisers) should be more systematic than they have been over the last several decades in considering distributionally weighted welfare outcomes when selecting and fine-tuning economic policies rather than relying either on unweighted growth outcomes or on overly weighted poverty outcomes.

A systematic approach, however, will not be possible until far better information is available on the characteristics of the middle class in developing countries—and, before that, a consensus among economists on the concept itself.

My own conclusion, based in part on the combination of small numbers with their growth in the boom years since 1990, is that in developing countries the real trade-off in policy design is far better thought of as a trade-off between the rich and the rest rather than, as has been the mindset of the international community for several decades, the absolute poor and the rest. The small size of what I have presumptively called the (indispensable) middle class in the developing world should be a telling reminder that the overwhelming majority of people in the developing world are poor by Western standards, and that in most developing countries only the truly rich by local standards enjoy what Westerners think of as middle-class living standards. The trade-off in most countries is therefore usually between policies that preserve short-term stability and benefit a small minority at the top of the income distribution versus financial, tax, social insurance, land market, and other policies that are conducive to building a middle class and are, it turns out, pro-poor as well.

---

35 Birdsall, de la Torre, and Menezes (2008) provide a detailed discussion of this trade-off for Latin American countries.

Table A7.1 Summary Statistics and Income Ratios for Selected Countries, 2005

| Country | I/C | Mean income ($, 2005 PPP) | Income at 95th percentile | Middle class share of population | Middle class share of income/ consumption | Ventile ratios | | | Decile ratios | | |
|---|---|---|---|---|---|---|---|---|---|---|---|
| | | | | | | (20/19) | (19/18) | (18/17) | (10/9) | (9/8) | (8/7) |
| Ghana | C | 78 | 203 | 0 | 0 | 3.15 | 1.31 | 1.19 | 4.16 | 1.34 | 1.24 |
| India, urban | C | 62 | 152 | 0 | 0 | 3.03 | 1.29 | 1.18 | 3.94 | 1.32 | 1.21 |
| Indonesia, urban | C | 89 | 216 | 0 | 0 | 4.18 | 1.30 | 1.18 | 5.56 | 1.33 | 1.22 |
| Morocco | C | 161 | 385 | 0.035 | 0.073 | 4.03 | 1.29 | 1.18 | 5.34 | 1.32 | 1.22 |
| China, urban | C | 162 | 373 | 0.034 | 0.07 | 2.48 | 1.25 | 1.16 | 3.10 | 1.27 | 1.19 |
| Thailand | C | 190 | 502 | 0.087 | 0.174 | 3.51 | 1.33 | 1.20 | 4.75 | 1.37 | 1.25 |
| Turkey | C | 235 | 600 | 0.159 | 0.274 | 3.89 | 1.30 | 1.19 | 5.17 | 1.34 | 1.23 |
| South Africa | C | 153 | 569 | 0.076 | 0.203 | 2.50 | 1.49 | 1.33 | 3.73 | 1.64 | 1.45 |
| Mexico | C | 330 | 891 | 0.280 | 0.405 | 4.64 | 1.35 | 1.22 | 6.46 | 1.40 | 1.27 |
| Russian Federation | C | 301 | 753 | 0.298 | 0.439 | 1.99 | 1.27 | 1.17 | 2.50 | 1.31 | 1.22 |
| Honduras | I | 164 | 496 | 0.068 | 0.157 | 5.02 | 1.39 | 1.25 | 7.29 | 1.47 | 1.34 |
| Bolivia | I | 204 | 645 | 0.122 | 0.254 | 4.94 | 1.41 | 1.26 | 7.25 | 1.50 | 1.36 |
| Paraguay | I | 257 | 746 | 0.180 | 0.315 | 4.86 | 1.38 | 1.24 | 6.95 | 1.45 | 1.32 |
| Colombia | I | 232 | 682 | 0.135 | 0.255 | 4.25 | 1.41 | 1.26 | 6.20 | 1.50 | 1.35 |
| Ecuador | I | 229 | 650 | 0.139 | 0.257 | 4.51 | 1.37 | 1.24 | 6.41 | 1.44 | 1.31 |
| Brazil | I | 279 | 836 | 0.194 | 0.331 | 5.09 | 1.41 | 1.26 | 7.48 | 1.49 | 1.35 |
| Venezuela, R.B. de | I | 136 | 386 | 0.032 | 0.081 | 3.04 | 1.33 | 1.21 | 4.08 | 1.38 | 1.27 |
| Argentina, urban | I | 333 | 993 | 0.305 | 0.464 | 3.10 | 1.36 | 1.23 | 4.27 | 1.43 | 1.30 |
| Chile | I | 412 | 1,097 | 0.327 | 0.419 | 3.20 | 1.38 | 1.24 | 4.48 | 1.45 | 1.31 |
| Sweden | I | 2,020 | 3,872 | 0.950 | 0.879 | 2.18 | 1.19 | 1.11 | 2.56 | 1.19 | 1.13 |
| United States | I | 3,348 | 9,504 | 0.909 | 0.812 | 1.62 | 1.28 | 1.19 | 2.02 | 1.36 | 1.27 |

Source: Author's calculations using POVCAL data.
Note: The first column indicates whether data are based on household consumption or income data. Surveys are from 2005 or closest available year.

# References

Acemoglu, Daron, Simon Johnson, and James Robinson. 2004. "Institutions as the Fundamental Cause of Long-Run Growth." NBER Working Paper 10481, National Bureau for Economic Research, Cambridge, MA.

Akerlof, George, and Rachel Kranton. 2000. "Economics and Identity." *Quarterly Journal of Economics* 115 (3): 715–53.

Alesina, Alberto, and Dani Rodrik. 1994. "Distributive Politics and Economic Growth." *Quarterly Journal of Economics* 109: 465–90.

Alesina, Alberto, Reza Baqir, and William Easterly. 1999. "Public Goods and Ethnic Divisions." *Quarterly Journal of Economics* 114 (4): 1243–84.

Banerjee, Abhijit, and Esther Duflo. 2007. "What Is Middle Class about the Middle Classes around the World?" CEPR Discussion Paper DP6613, Centre for Economic Policy Research, London.

Barro, Robert J., and Jong-Wha Lee. 2000. "International Data on Educational Attainment: Updates and Implications." http://www.cid.harvard.edu/ciddata/ciddata.html.

Besley, Timothy, and Ravi Kanbur. 1990. "The Principles of Targeting." Working Paper 385, World Bank, Washington, DC.

Birdsall, Nancy. 1996. "Public Spending on Higher Education in Developing Countries: Too Much or Too Little?" *Economics of Education Review* 15 (4): 407.

———. 2007. "Do No Harm: Aid, Weak Institutions and the Missing Middle in Africa." *Development Policy Review* 25 (5): 575–98.

———. 2008. "Income Distribution: Effects on Growth and Development." In *International Handbooks of Development Economics*, Vol. 2, ed. Amitava Krishna Dutt and Jaime Ros. Cheltenham: Edward Elgar Publishing.

———. 2009. "The Macroeconomic Foundations of Inclusive Middle-Class Growth." In *The Poorest and Hungry*. Washington, DC: International Food Policy Research Institute.

Birdsall, Nancy, and Rachel Menezes. 2004. "Toward a New Social Contract in Latin America." *Center for Global Development Policy Brief* 3 (2).

Birdsall, Nancy, Augusto de la Torre, and Rachel Menezes. 2008. *Fair Growth*. Washington, DC: Center for Global Development.

Birdsall, Nancy, Carol Graham, and Stefano Pettinato. 2000. "Stuck in the Tunnel: Is Globalization Muddling the Middle Class?" Working Paper No. 14, Brookings Institution Center on Social and Economic Dynamics, Washington, DC.

Davies, James B., Susanna Sandström, Anthony Shorrocks, and Edward N. Wolff. 2008. "UNU-WIDER World Distribution of Household Wealth." WIDER Discussion Paper 2008/3, World Institute for Development Economics Research, Helsinki.

Dollar, David, and Aart Kraay. 2002. "Growth Is Good for the Poor." *Journal of Economic Growth* 7 (3): 195–225.

Easterly, William. 2001. "The Middle Class Consensus and Economic Development." *Journal of Economic Growth* 6 (4): 317–35.

Filmer, Deon, and Lant Pritchett. 2001. "Estimating Wealth Effects without Expenditure Data—or Tears: An Application to Educational Enrollments in States of India." *Demography* 38: 115–32.

Filmer, Deon, Amer Hasan, and Lant Pritchett. 2006. "A Millennium Learning Goal: Measuring Real Progress in Education." Working Paper 97, Center for Global Development, Washington, DC.

Foster, James E., and Michael C. Wolfson 1992 . "Polarization and the Decline of the Middle Class: Canada and the U.S." Unpublished paper, Vanderbilt University, Nashville.

Gelbach, Jonah, and Lant Pritchett. 2000. "Indicator Targeting in a Political Economy: Leakier Can Be Better." *Journal of Policy Reform* 4: 113–45.

Goldin, Claudia, and Lawrence F. Katz. 2007. "The Race between Education and Technology: The Evolution of U.S. Educational Wage Differentials, 1890 to 2005." NBER Working Paper 12984, National Bureau for Economic Research, Cambridge, MA.

Hausmann, Ricardo, Lant Pritchett, and Dani Rodrik. 2004. "Growth Accelerations." NBER Working Paper W10566, National Bureau for Economic Research, Cambridge, MA.

Johnson, Simon, William Larson, Chris Papageorgiou, and Arvind Subramanian. 2009. "Is Newer Better: The Penn World Table Revisions and the Cross-Country Growth Literature." Working Paper 191, Center for Global Development, Washington, DC. http://www.cgdev.org/content/publications/detail/1423224.

Kanbur, Ravi , and Nora Lustig. 2000. "Why Is Inequality Back on the Agenda?" In *Annual World Bank Conference on Development Economics, 1999.* Washington, DC: World Bank.

Kraay, Aart. 2006. "When Is Growth Pro-Poor? Cross-Country Evidence." *Journal of Development Economics* 80 (1): 198–227.

Levy, Santiago. 2008. *Good Intentions, Bad Outcomes*. Washington, DC: Brookings Institution Press.

Lindert, Peter. 2004. *Growing Public: Social Spending and Economic Growth Since the Eighteenth Century, Volume I: The Story*. New York: Cambridge University Press.

McKinsey Global Institute. 2007. "The 'Bird of Gold': The Rise of India's Consumer Market." Washington, DC.

Milanovic, Branko, and Shlomo Yitzhaki. 2002. "Decomposing World Income Distribution: Does the World Have a Middle Class?" *Review of Income and Wealth* 48 (2): 155–78.

Perry, Guillermo. 2009. *Beyond Lending: How Multilateral Banks Can Help Developing Countries Manage Volatility*. Washington, DC: Center for Global Development.

Pritchett, Lant. 2003. "Who Is *Not* Poor? Proposing a Higher International Standard for Poverty." Working Paper 33, Center for Global Development, Washington, DC. http://www.cgdev.org/content/publications/detail/2758/.

Pritchett, Lant, Asep Suryahadi, and Sudarno Sumarto. 2000. "Quantifying Vulnerability to Poverty : A Proposed Measure, Applied to Indonesia." Policy Research Working Paper 2437, World Bank, Washington, DC.

Ravallion, Martin. 1998. "Poverty Lines in Theory and Practice." Living Standards Measurement Study Working Paper 133, World Bank, Washington, DC.

———. 2009. "The Developing World's Bulging (but Vulnerable) 'Middle Class.'" Policy Research Working Paper 4816, World Bank, Washington, DC.

Ravallion, Martin, and Shaohua Chen. 2001. "How Did the World's Poor Fare in the 1990s?" *Review of Income and Wealth* 47 (3): 283–300.

Ravallion, Martin, Shaohua Chen, and Prem Sangraula. 2008. "Dollar a Day Revisited." Policy Research Working Paper 4620, World Bank, Washington, DC.

Silber, Jacques. 2007. "Measuring Poverty: Taking a Multidimensional Perspective." *Hacienda Pública Española, IEF* 182 (3): 29–74.

Skopcol, Theda. 1979. *States and Social Revolutions.* New York: Cambridge University Press.

Stewart, Frances. 2002. "Horizontal Inequality: A Neglected Dimension of Development." WIDER Annual Lecture, World Institute for Development Economics Research, Helsinki, March.

Thurow, Lester. 1987. "A Surge in Inequality." *Scientific American* 256: 30–37.

Wolfson, Michael. 1994. "When Inequalities Diverge." *American Economic Review* 84 (2): 353–58.

———. 2008. *World Bank Indicators 2008.* Washington, DC: World Bank.

# CHAPTER 8

# Outlining a Research Agenda on the Links between Globalization and Poverty

*Ann Harrison and Margaret McMillan*

More than 1 billion people live in extreme poverty, which is defined by the World Bank as subsisting on less than $1 a day.[1] In 2001, fully *half* of the developing world lived on less than $2 a day. And yet if Sub-Saharan Africa and Eastern Europe are excluded, extreme poverty rates are lower today than they were 20 years ago. In the last two decades, the percentage of the world's population living in extreme poverty has fallen from 33 percent to 17 percent. While poverty rates were falling, developing countries were becoming increasingly integrated into the world trading system. If analysts use the share of exports in the gross domestic product (GDP) as a measure of "globalization," then developing countries are now more "globalized" than high-income countries (see Harrison and Tang 2005).

Does globalization reduce poverty? Will ongoing efforts to eliminate protection and increase world trade improve the lives of the world's poor?

---

Previously published as Ann Harrison and Margaret McMillan. "On the Links between Globalization and Poverty." *Journal of Economic Inequality* (Springer Netherlands) 5, no. 1 (April 2007): 123–34. Reprinted with permission from Springer Science and Business Media.

1   All the poverty estimates in this paragraph are taken from the World Bank's official poverty Web site, http://iresearch.worldbank.org/PovcalNet/jsp/index.jsp. The $1 a day poverty line is actually $1.08 in 1993 purchasing power parity dollars.

---

There is surprisingly little evidence on this question. Winters, McCulloch, and McKay (2004), Goldberg and Pavcnik (2004), and Ravallion (2004) survey the recent evidence. But in all three surveys the authors acknowledge that they review only the *indirect* evidence on the linkages between globalization and poverty. Almost no studies have tested for the *direct* linkages between the two.[2]

Yet one of the biggest concerns of globalization's critics is its impact on the poor. This chapter begins by summarizing some key findings from the 2007 book *Globalization and Poverty* (Harrison 2007).[3] The 15 studies and accompanying discussions that make up the book are part of a National Bureau of Economic Research (NBER) project that asks the following questions: How has global economic integration affected the poor in developing countries? Does trade reform that reduces import protection improve the lives of the poor? Has increasing financial integration led to more or less poverty? How have the poor fared during currency crises? Do agricultural support programs in rich countries hurt the poor in developing countries? Or do such programs in fact provide assistance by reducing the cost of food imports? Finally, does food aid hurt the poor by lowering the price of the goods they sell on local markets?

What do we mean by "globalization"? We focus on two aspects: first, the international trade in goods and, second, the international movements of capital, including foreign investment, portfolio flows, and aid. The "orthodox" perspective on trade and poverty, based on the writings of David Dollar, Anne Krueger, and others, is that openness to trade is good for growth, and growth is good for the poor. According to the orthodox view, it follows that openness to trade should reduce poverty. But what if openness to trade is associated with increasing inequality? If so, then average income may increase, while those at the bottom of the income distribution become poorer. Krueger and Dollar argue that increased globalization will in fact reduce inequality in poor countries. The reason is

---

2   Winters, McCulloch, and McKay (2004) write in their insightful and comprehensive survey that "there are no direct studies of the poverty effects of trade and trade liberalization." Goldberg and Pavcnik's (2004) excellent review points out that "while the literature on trade and inequality is voluminous, there is virtually no work to date on the relationship between trade liberalization and poverty." The few studies that do examine the links between globalization and poverty typically use computable general equilibrium models to disentangle the linkages between trade reform and poverty. Although such research provides an important contribution to understanding the channels through which globalization could affect poverty, it is extremely important to be able to look at actual ex post evidence of the impact of trade and investment reforms on the poor. See the studies cited in Winters, McCulloch, and McKay (2004), Ravallion (2004), and Hertel and Winters (2005).

Recent studies of globalization and inequality focus primarily on the distributional consequences of globalization rather than on poverty. The exceptions are, for example, Bhagwati's *In Defense of Globalization* (2004). Bardhan's publications on this topic include his 2000 International Labour Organization Nobel Peace Prize Lecture, published as "'Social Justice in a Global Economy," as well as two texts by Bardhan (2003, 2004). See also the 2005 book by Hertel and Winters, *Poverty and the WTO: Impacts of the Doha Development Agenda*.

3   Chapters may be downloaded from http://www.nber.org/books/glob-pov/index.html.

that these countries have a comparative advantage in producing goods that use unskilled labor.

The most important lesson that emerges from the NBER volume is that orthodox perspectives on the linkages between globalization and poverty are misleading, if not downright wrong. Results from the 15 studies that make up the volume suggest that the gains from trade are highly unequal and that the poor do not always benefit from globalization. This chapter begins by summarizing five lessons that emerge from *Globalization and Poverty*. The second part of the chapter turns to some unresolved issues and topics for further research.

## Six Lessons on the Linkages between Globalization and Poverty

The chapters that make up the NBER volume are creative but careful attempts to find answers to the questions just listed. Although the topics and countries of analysis vary widely, they all seek to provide insight into the impact of globalization on poverty. Thus, it is possible to draw some general lessons from these studies.

*The poor in countries with an abundance of unskilled labor do not always gain from trade reform.* One of the most famous theorems in international trade derived from the Heckscher-Ohlin (HO) model of international trade is the Stolper-Samuelson (SS) theorem. In its simplest form, this theorem suggests that the abundant factor should see an increase in its real income when a country opens up to trade. If the abundant factor in developing countries is unskilled labor, then this framework suggests that the poor (unskilled) in developing countries have the most to gain from trade. Krueger (1983) and Bhagwati and Srinivasan (2002) have used this insight to argue that trade reform in developing countries should be pro-poor, because these countries are most likely to have a comparative advantage in producing goods made with unskilled labor.

In their contribution to the NBER volume, Don Davis and Prachi Mishra (2007) challenge the assumptions behind Stolper-Samuelson. Davis and Mishra argue that applying trade theory to suggest that liberalization will raise the wages of the unskilled in unskilled-abundant countries is "worse than wrong—it is dangerous." They show that such arguments are based on a very narrow interpretation of the Stolper-Samuelson theorem. In particular, SS holds only if all countries produce all goods, if the goods imported from abroad and produced domestically are close substitutes, or if comparative advantage can be fixed in relation to all trading partners.

In addition, the country studies on India and Poland show that labor is not nearly as mobile as the HO trade model assumes; for comparative advantage to increase the incomes of the unskilled, they need to be able to move out of contracting sectors and into expanding ones. Davis and Mishra, as well as the empirical case studies in the volume, suggest that the real world is not consistent with an HO world. The assumptions necessary for HO to work in reality are simply not present; there are too many barriers to entry and exit for firms and too many barriers to labor mobility for workers.

Another reason the poor may not gain from trade reform is that developing countries have historically protected sectors that use unskilled labor, such as textiles and apparel. This pattern of protection, although at odds with simple interpretations of HO models, makes sense if standard assumptions (such as factor price equalization) are relaxed. Trade reform may result in less protection for unskilled workers, who are most likely to be poor. Finally, penetrating global markets even in sectors that traditionally use unskilled labor requires more skills than the poor in developing countries typically possess.

*The poor are more likely to share in the gains from globalization when complementary policies are in place.* The studies on India and Colombia suggest that globalization is more likely to benefit the poor if trade reform is implemented in conjunction with reducing impediments to labor mobility. In Zambia, poor farmers are expected to benefit from greater access to export markets only if they also have access to credit, technical know-how, and other complementary inputs. The studies also point to the importance of social safety nets. In Mexico, if poor corn farmers had not received income support from the government, their real incomes would have been halved during the 1990s. In Ethiopia, if food aid had not been well targeted, globalization would have had little impact on the poor. The fact that other policies are needed to ensure that the benefits of trade are shared across the population suggests that relying on trade reform alone to reduce poverty is likely to be disappointing.

*Export growth and incoming foreign investment can reduce poverty.* In the countries studied, poverty has fallen in regions where exports or foreign investment is growing. In Mexico, the poor in the most globalized regions have weathered macroeconomic crises better than their more isolated neighbors. In India, opening up to foreign investment has been associated with a decline in poverty. The study on Zambia suggests that poor consumers gain from falling prices for the goods they buy, while poor producers in exporting sectors benefit from trade reform through higher prices for their goods. In Colombia, increasing export activity has been associated with an increase in compliance with labor legislation and a fall in poverty. In Poland, unskilled workers—who are the most likely to be poor—have gained from Poland's accession to the European Union.

*Financial crises are costly to the poor.* In Indonesia, poverty rates increased by at least 50 percent after the currency crisis in 1997. Although recovery in Indonesia has been rapid, the Mexican economy has yet to recover fully from its 1995 peso crisis. In 2000, poverty rates in Mexico were higher than they had been 10 years earlier. Cross-country evidence also suggests that financial integration leads to higher consumption and output volatility in low-income countries. One implication is that low-income countries are more likely to benefit from financial integration if they also create reliable institutions and pursue macroeconomic stabilization policies, including the use of flexible exchange rate regimes. However, foreign investment flows have very different effects from other types of capital flows. Unrestricted capital flows are associated with a higher likelihood of poverty, whereas foreign direct investment (FDI) inflows are associated with a reduction in poverty. The poverty-reducing effects of FDI are clearly documented in the case studies on India and Mexico.

*Globalization produces both winners and losers among the poor.* The heterogeneity in outcomes associated with poverty-globalization linkages is one theme that emerges from various country case studies in the NBER volume. Even within a single region, two sets of farmers producing the same good may be affected in opposite ways. In Mexico, some small and most medium corn farmers saw their incomes fall by half in the 1990s, whereas large corn farmers gained. Across different countries, poor wage earners in exporting sectors or in sectors with incoming foreign investment gained from trade and investment reforms. Conversely, poverty rates increased in previously protected sectors that were exposed to import competition. Within the same country or even the same region, trade reform may lead to income losses for rural agricultural producers and income gains for rural or urban consumers of those same goods.

*Different measures of globalization are associated with different poverty outcomes. How* globalization is measured determines *whether* globalization is good for the poor. Measures of export activity and foreign investment are generally associated with poverty reduction, while removal of protection (an ex ante measure of globalization) or import shares (an ex post measure) are frequently associated with rising poverty. These different effects are consistent with short-run models of international trade (such as the specific sector model) in which factors of production cannot move easily from contracting or import-competing sectors to expanding or export-oriented ones.

The case study on Colombia prepared by Penny Goldberg and Nina Pavcnik (2007) illustrates this heterogeneity of outcomes. Goldberg and Pavcnik investigate the impact of a large reduction in average tariffs in Colombia between 1984 and 1998 on a variety of urban labor market outcomes: the probability of becoming unemployed, minimum wage compliance, informal sector employment, and the incidence of poverty. The Colombian experience suggests that individuals in sectors with increasing import competition are likely to become poorer, while those in sectors in which exports are growing are less likely to be poor.

This is exactly the conclusion reached by Petia Topalova (2007), who estimates the impact of trade reform in India on poverty. In the 1990s, India embarked on remarkable trade reform, reversing decades of protectionist policies that had led to average tariffs in excess of 90 percent. Using household data that spans the period before and after reform, Topalova relates changes in tariffs to changes in the incidence of poverty. She finds that the rural poor gained less from the trade reform than other income groups or the urban poor. Topalova also discusses why the rural poor gained less than other groups from liberalization: restrictions on labor mobility in rural areas have impeded adjustment. She finds that the negative impact of trade policy on poverty is reduced or eliminated in regions with flexible labor laws.

## Unresolved Issues: A Research Agenda

The series of papers in the NBER volume present the most comprehensive evidence to date on the linkages between globalization and poverty. However, this is a relatively new area of research for economists, and many questions remain unanswered. In this section, we draw on the new evidence uncovered in the NBER project and describe what we believe to be the most important areas for further research.

**How can countries integrate the poorest of the poor into the world trading system?** One-sixth of the world's population lives in extreme poverty. Figuring out how to lift these people out of that poverty is arguably the most pressing issue. But it also is the most difficult. The poorest of the poor tend to be untouched by globalization. This is evident among the poorest Mexican corn farmers, who report that they never sell corn, and among the poorest Ethiopian farmers, who are net buyers of food. The number of the extreme poor in Sub-Saharan Africa has nearly doubled over the last two decades, growing from about 170 million to 310 million. Roughly half of Sub-Saharan Africa lives in extreme poverty, and this number has *increased* over the last two decades. This region has seen very little in the way of foreign investment and still exports primarily unprocessed agricultural products.

More research is needed to identify the critical interventions required to lift these poor out of poverty. What are the key constraints? How important is outside intervention? In light of the scarcity of resources available, creating a ranking of which complementary investment or reform is needed most to allow the poor to access world markets would be very useful.

**What are the central issues in measuring poverty?** As acceptable definitions of poverty shift over time, one question that must be addressed by poverty researchers is why they are focusing primarily on one aspect of the entire distribution of income. Presumably, focusing on the entire distribution of income—and thus income inequality—should become increasingly important. Once one focuses on the fact that poverty lines are constantly changing across countries and also within the same country over time, it becomes puzzling why poverty researchers do not focus more on broader measures of income distribution as well.

In addition to explicitly focusing on the entire distribution of income, researchers should focus on issues related to measuring the absolute numbers of poor versus the incidence of poverty. As discussed by Emma Aisbett (2007) in her chapter in the NBER volume, the incidence of poverty has generally declined, but the number of individuals who are living on less than $2 a day has actually increased. Elsewhere, Ravi Kanbur (2001, 2004) discusses this issue in more detail. He also emphasizes the need to use other outcome measures, such as health and mortality, in assessing the lives of the poor (Kanbur 2004). Those issues are also emphasized by Duncan Thomas and Elizabeth Frankenberg (2007) in the NBER volume.

**Why hasn't increasing financial integration helped the poor more?** One avenue through which globalization could affect the welfare of the poor is financial liberalization, which has increased the scope for capital to flow to developing countries. In theory, openness to capital flows could alleviate poverty through several channels. If greater financial integration contributes to higher growth by expanding access to capital, expanding access to new technology, stimulating domestic financial sector development, reducing the cost of capital, and alleviating domestic credit constraints, then such growth should reduce poverty. Access to international capital markets should also allow countries to smooth consumption shocks, reducing output or consumption volatility.

However, Eswar Prasad et al. (2007) in their NBER volume contribution suggest that the impact of financial integration on poverty—via possible growth effects—is likely to be small. They argue that because there are no clear linkages between financial integration and growth in the aggregate cross-country evidence, direct linkages between financial integration and poverty are likely to be difficult to find. They also explore another link: whether financial integration has smoothed or exacerbated output and consumption volatility. Because the poor are likely to be hurt in periods of consumption volatility, income smoothing made possible by global financial integration could be beneficial to the poor. However, Prasad et al. find that the opposite is true—financial globalization in developing countries is associated with higher consumption volatility.

Why has international financial integration not helped the poor more? Prasad et al. (2007) suggest that there is a threshold effect: beyond a certain level of financial integration (50 percent of GDP), financial integration significantly reduces volatility. However, most developing countries are well below this threshold. Further research is necessary to understand why such a threshold might exist. What prevents lower-income developing countries from exploiting the benefits of international financial integration? Is the answer that financial globalization must be approached with the right set of complementary policies such as flexible exchange rates, macroeconomic stabilization policies, and the development of strong institutions? Prasad et al. suggest that if there is institutional development and good governance—including transparency in business and government transactions, control of corruption, rule of law, and financial supervisory capacity—then poor countries may also gain from financial integration. Yet more evidence is needed on this question.

**How have the poor weathered the currency crises of the last two decades?** Evidence from the 1997 Indonesian currency crisis shows that in the first year of the crisis poverty rose by between 50 and 100 percent, real wages declined by about 40 percent, and household per capita consumption fell by about 15 percent (Thomas and Frankenberg 2007). Yet remarkably, in 2002 poverty in Indonesia was below what it was at the start of the crisis. By contrast, between 1990 and 2000 poverty in Mexico increased. Although poverty increased less in northern Mexico—the part of the country most exposed to the forces of globalization—nevertheless poverty in Mexico was higher in 2000 than in 1990.

These contrasting experiences suggest two questions for research. First, why was Indonesia able to recover so much more quickly than Mexico? Were the special transfer programs in Indonesia—targeted at consumption and education of poor households—responsible for the different experiences in addressing poverty during this decade? Or is it because Mexico entered into the North American Free Trade Agreement (NAFTA) just before the peso crisis? Second, are there long term-consequences from the Indonesian financial crisis for the poor? Although recovery was rapid, households adjusted in the short run by cutting expenditures on durables, health care visits, and school attendance. Will there be long-term consequences from this behavior, despite the fact that poverty rates quickly reverted back to precrisis levels?

**Who among the poor are the winners from globalization?** A number of the case studies in the NBER volume point to winners among the poor from globalization. These include the poor wage earners in export-competing sectors and in sectors or regions that are recipients of foreign direct investment. Particularly in light of the vocal criticism leveled at globalization, these beneficiaries should be identified and emphasized in any future research agenda on the relationship between globalization and poverty. Of particular interest would be research that could further identify the impact of foreign investment inflows and export growth on poverty reduction in India and China.

Although research on China is constrained by the lack of micro data sets in the public domain, the relationship between rising inequality, falling poverty, and globalization deserves further investigation. Some researchers, notably Kanbur and Zhang (2005), have found that increasing globalization is associated with higher inequality in China, whereas others have found no relationship (Ravallion 2004). In Prasad et al. 2007, Shang-Jin Wei reports evidence suggesting that trade is associated with falling inequality. Differences in the approaches can be traced to different uses of openness measures (Kanbur uses aggregate data on tariffs and trade shares, while Wei uses city-level data on exports) and different approaches.

Although access to Chinese data is fairly restricted, the Indian Ministry of Statistics is quite open to researchers who wish to purchase data. Data are typically available before and after the 1991 Indian reforms, which would allow researchers to more carefully assess the effects of those reforms on the poor. The debate on the impact of the 1991 trade reform in India on welfare outcomes is by no means resolved. Although Topalova (2007) suggests that the trade reform hurt the poor in import-competing sectors in states with rigid labor laws, others dispute her findings. Even the evidence on the productivity effects of these reforms is not consistent across the different studies available.

**Can analysts better identify the complementarities between measures of globalization and other policies?** It is increasingly evident that the poor are more likely to gain from openness to trade if other complementary policies are in place. Some recent studies emphasize the importance of complementary policies in determining the benefits or costs of trade reform for developing countries. For example, Bolaky and Freund (2004) show that trade reform actually leads to income losses in highly regulated economies.

However, much more work is needed to identify which types of policies should accompany trade reform. There has been little analysis to show, for example, that financial globalization would be beneficial to developing countries if it is accompanied by flexible exchange rate regimes or better institutions. Additional work is needed to identify whether trade reform introduced in conjunction with labor market reform is more likely to reduce poverty, and how to properly design social safety nets to accompany trade reform. Mexico has been successful in targeting some of the poorest hurt by reform, but these programs are expensive and additional research could determine whether this approach is realistic for the poorest countries.

Further research is needed to identify the source of the immobility of labor. Although studies on India and Colombia show that some of these sources are artificial—stemming from labor market legislation, which inhibits hiring and firing—Goh and Javorcik (2007) argue that much of the immobility of labor in Poland stems from societal factors that discourage workers from relocating. Further evidence identifying the relationship between gross labor inflows and outflows and trade reform would be useful in this regard.

The fact that the gains or losses from trade reform for the poor may hinge on the mobility (or immobility) of labor needs to be more explicitly addressed in existing models of international trade. Some models adopt assumptions of perfect factor mobility (HO), while others assume no factor mobility (specific sector). Neither assumption is consistent with reality. In addition, many of globalization's critics perceive the world through the lens of imperfect competition. Yet most trade economists assume perfect competition or zero profits, which is not consistent with reality in at least some sectors of developing economies.

The need for labor mobility is emphasized here, but does this mean that protection of workers should be scrapped? Clearly, the answer is no. Although workers need to be able to move from contracting to expanding sectors, dropping measures that provide rights for workers does not seem to be the answer either. Workers in many developing countries still do not benefit from basic health and safety regulations, and the right to organize is frequently not recognized by governments. In many countries, workers seeking to form unions are fired or jailed, or even worse. Striking the right balance between safeguarding worker rights and ensuring labor mobility in order to create new jobs is difficult but necessary.

**Can analysts identify the dynamic effects of industrial country trade and aid policies on developing country agriculture?** Several issues explored in the NBER volume include how industrial country policies affect the incidence of poverty in developing countries. Those studies suggest that, at least in the short run, subsidies and food aid from member countries of the Organisation for Economic Co-operation and Development (OECD) have probably helped the poor in other countries. In their study of Ethiopian rural grain producers, James Levinsohn and Margaret McMillan (2007) explore the impact of food aid on both the consumption and production of the rural poor. They address the concern that food aid further exacerbates poverty by depressing the incomes of rural producers. Even though Levinsohn and McMillan confirm that a more optimal arrangement would be to buy food from local producers and distribute it to poor consumers,[4] they also show that the net impact of food aid on the poor in Ethiopia has been positive, because the poor in Ethiopia are primarily net consumers rather than net producers of food and thus food aid has alleviated poverty.

However, further research is needed to identify whether there are longer-term dynamic effects. For example, even if the poor in Ethiopia are currently net beneficiaries from food aid, there exists the possibility that over the long run food aid has discouraged poor farmers from planting or investing, transforming them from net producers into net consumers.

Another issue that deserves further research is the impact of OECD agricultural subsidies on poverty. Although the research presented in the NBER volume suggests that the poorest countries have been net beneficiaries of OECD agricultural subsidies because these poor countries are net food importers, decades of OECD subsidies may have discouraged poor countries from producing agricultural goods in the first place. Figure 8.1 shows that though some poor countries were net food importers even in the 1970s, a shift over time has led these countries to become even more dependent on food imports. That shift may have been caused by OECD agricultural subsidies.

Far-reaching reforms across developing countries have reduced barriers to trade, but agriculture remains protected in many countries. Both China and India have protected agricultural sectors. In the coming decade, agriculture is likely to open up more to competition in both developed and developing countries. Yet the highest incidence of poverty in developing

---

4 Such an arrangement assumes that local purchase does not drive prices up for some poor people.

Figure 8.1 Average Income and Net Food Exports by Decade in Repeated Cross-Section of Developing Countries

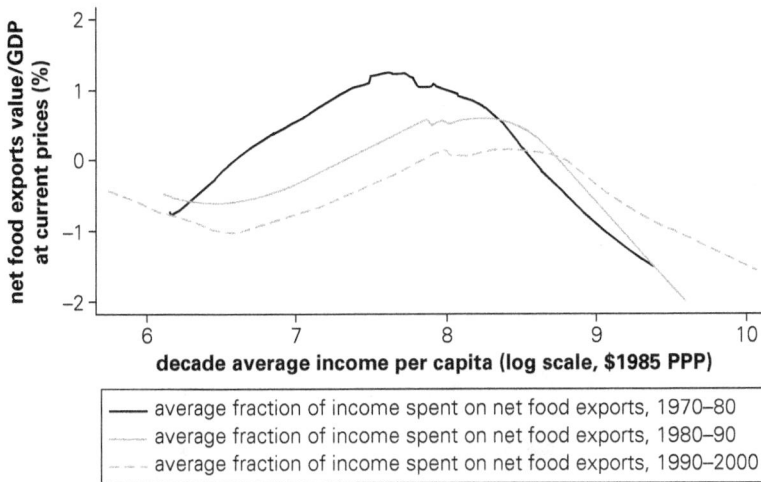

Source: McMillan 2007.
Note: Graph depicts average fraction of income spent on net food exports for three periods.

countries is in rural areas. What will be the impact of trade reform targeted at the agricultural sector on the rural poor? How can complementary measures be introduced to cushion the negative impact? This remains an important area for future research.

**Why is there no relationship between globalization and poverty in the aggregate cross-country data?** The evidence in figure 8.2 suggests that there is no significant relationship between globalization (measured using average import tariffs) and poverty. What could explain the lack of any robust association between globalization and poverty reduction in the aggregate data? One strong possibility, which is clearly revealed in the country case studies that use microdata for households or firms, is that there is too much heterogeneity in the effects of trade reform on the poor. Because poor workers in import-competing sectors lose from reform, while poor workers in export-oriented sectors gain—according to the studies by Goldberg and Pavcnik (2007) on Colombia and Topalova (2007) on India— it is not surprising that in the aggregate these different effects are lost.

Another possibility, related to the many heterogeneous effects of globalization on the poor, could be that cross-country data on poverty are too poor in quality to yield meaningful results. Angus Deaton (2003) has argued that relying on national income data to impute poverty yields very different results from estimates based on household data. If analysts rely only on World Bank estimates of poverty, which are based on household surveys, the number of observations is very small. The World Bank poverty estimates provide only two or at most three data points over time for any one country. Consequently, it is not surprising that cross-country estimates using these data are so fragile.

Figure 8.2 Correlation between Poverty and Protection (Tariffs)

**correlation between fraction of households living on $1 per day and average import tariff controlling for country fixed effects**

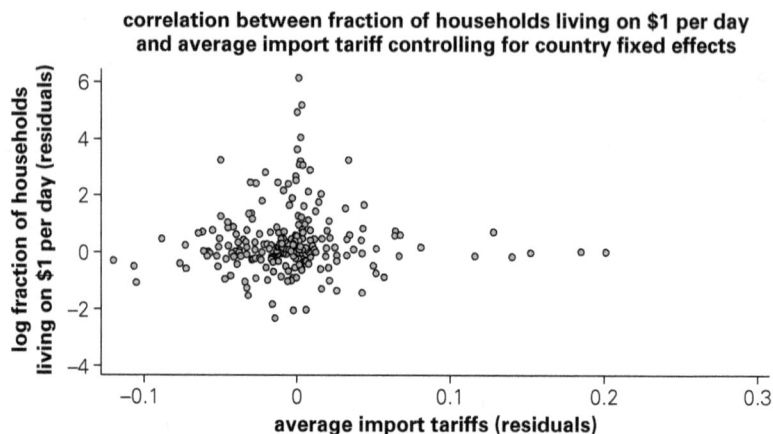

*Source:* World Bank (poverty data); Gwartney and Lawson 2009 (tariffs).
*Note:* Poverty is measured as the percentage of households in a country living on less than US$1 a day, calculated in 1993 purchasing power parity dollars.

A third possibility is that the aggregate relationship between globalization and poverty is not significant because the costs of trade reform have fallen disproportionately on the poor. In light of the knowledge that openness to trade is generally associated with growth, and that sectors hit by import competition in countries such as India and Colombia have gained less from trade reform, the gains from trade in the aggregate have not been big enough to offset some of the adverse distributional consequences for the poor. The lack of any robust positive association between trade and poverty reduction could indicate that the growth gains from trade have failed to trickle down to the poor because they simply do not participate in the benefits. This interpretation of the results is consistent with the fact that some studies find that globalization is associated with increasing inequality. In the NBER volume, for example, Branko Milanovic and Lyn Squire (2007) and William Easterly (2007) find that increasing globalization is associated with increasing inequality. Consequently, as noted, the third possibility, which is consistent with the evidence so far at the aggregate level, is that the growth gains from trade have been wiped out by the adverse distributional outcomes for the poor. Identifying whether increasing inequality associated with globalization completely offsets any gains to the poor from the growth effects of trade should be an important priority.

## Conclusion

In a recent lecture at a World Bank conference on poverty measurement, François Bourguignon pointed out that although economists have made tremendous strides in understanding how to measure poverty, they still have a limited understanding of the impact of different economic policies on poverty outcomes. The NBER book, *Globalization and Poverty*, seeks to address this gap by exploring the relationship among trade, foreign investment, and poverty outcomes. Nevertheless, many questions remain unanswered.

Although significant progress has been made in identifying linkages between globalization and poverty outcomes, much is still not known. In this chapter, we describe the lack of any correlation between globalization measures and poverty measures in the aggregate cross-country data, which is consistent with the possibility that aggregate growth gains from trade have bypassed the poor. Several other issues important for policy are identifying key complementary policies that could cushion the adverse effects of globalization on the poor and the causes of the lack of labor mobility identified in many of the country studies. The fact that workers cannot easily relocate from contracting, import-competing sectors to expanding export sectors means that the short-run costs of reform can be quite high. Identifying why workers cannot easily move in the wake of reform remains a pressing issue for further research.

## References

Aisbett, Emma. 2007. "Why Are the Critics So Convinced that Globalization Is Bad for the Poor?" In *Globalization and Poverty*, ed. Ann Harrison. Chicago: University of Chicago Press for National Bureau of Economic Research.

Bardhan, Pranab. 2000. "Social Justice in a Global Economy." International Labour Organization, Geneva. http://www.ilo.org/public/english/bureau/inst/papers/sopolecs/bardhan.

———. 2003. "International Economic Integration and the Poor." In *Global Governance: An Architecture for the World Economy,* ed. H. Siebert. New York: Springer.

———. 2004. "The Impact of Globalization on the Poor." In *Brookings Trade Forum: 2004,* ed. Susan Collins and Carol Graham. Washington, DC: Brookings.

Bhagwati, Jagdish. 2004. *In Defense of Globalization.* New York: Oxford University Press.

Bhagwati, J., and T. N. Srinivasan. 2002. "Trade and Poverty in the Poor Countries." *AEA Papers and Proceedings* 92 (2): 180–3.

Bolaky, B., and C. L. Freund. 2004. "Trade, Regulations, and Growth." Working Paper, World Bank, Washington, DC.

Davis, Don, and Prachi Mishra. 2007. "Stolper-Samuelson Is Dead and Other Crimes of Both Theory and Data." In *Globalization and Poverty*, ed. Ann Harrison. Chicago: University of Chicago Press for National Bureau of Economic Research.

Deaton, Angus. 2003. "How to Monitor Poverty for the Millennium Development Goals." RPDS Working Paper 221, Princeton University, Princeton, NJ. DOI: 10.2139/ssrn.393240.

Easterly, William. 2007. "Globalization, Prosperity, and Poverty." In *Globalization and Poverty,* ed. Ann Harrison. Chicago: University of Chicago Press for National Bureau of Economic Research.

Goh, Chor-Ching, and Beata Smarzynska Javorcik. 2007. "Trade Protection and Industry Wage Structure in Poland." In *Globalization and Poverty,* ed. Ann Harrison. Chicago: University of Chicago Press for National Bureau of Economic Research.

Goldberg, Penny, and Nina Pavcnik 2004. "Trade, Inequality, and Poverty: What Do We Know?" In *Brookings Trade Forum: 2004,* ed. Susan Collins and Carol Graham. Washington, DC: Brookings

———. 2007. "The Effects of the Colombia Trade Liberalization on Urban Poverty." In *Globalization and Poverty,* ed. Ann Harrison. Chicago: University of Chicago Press for National Bureau of Economic Research.

Gwartney, James, and Robert Lawson. 2009. *Economic Freedom of the World: 2009 Annual Report.* With the assistance of Joshua Hall. Economic Freedom Network. http://www.freetheworld.com.

Harrison, Ann, ed. 2007. *Globalization and Poverty.* Chicago: University of Chicago Press for National Bureau of Economic Research.

Harrison, Ann, and Helena Tang. 2005. "Trade Liberalization: Why So Much Controversy." In *Growth in the 1990s: Learning from a Decade of Reform,* ed. N. Roberto Zagha. Washington, DC: World Bank.

Hertel, Thomas W., and L. Alan Winters, eds. 2005. *Poverty Impacts of a WTO Agreement: Putting Development Back into the Doha Agenda.* New York: Palgrave Macmillan.

———. 2006. *Poverty and the WTO: Impacts of the Doha Development Agenda.* Hampshire, UK: Palgrave Macmillan and World Bank.

Kanbur, Ravi. 2001. "Economic Policy, Distribution, and Poverty: The Nature of Disagreements." *World Development* 29 (6): 1083–94.

———. 2004. "Growth, Inequality, and Poverty: Some Hard Questions." Unpublished manuscript, Cornell University, Ithaca, NY.

Kanbur, Ravi, and Xiaobo Zhang. 2005. "Fifty Years of Regional Inequality in China: A Journey through Central Planning, Reform, and Openness." *Review of Development Economics* 9 (1): 87–106.

Krueger, A. 1983. *Trade and Employment in Developing Countries, 3: Synthesis and Conclusions.* Chicago: University of Chicago Press.

Levinsohn, James, and Margaret McMillan. 2007. "Does Food Aid Harm the Poor? Household Evidence from Ethiopia." In *Globalization and Poverty,* ed. Ann Harrison. Chicago: University of Chicago Press for National Bureau of Economic Research.

McMillan, M. 2007. "Food Aid and Poverty." With Barrett Kirwan. *American Journal of Agricultural Economics* 89 (5).

Milanovic, Branko, and Lyn Squire. 2007. "Does Tariff Liberalization Increase Inequality? Some Empirical Evidence." In *Globalization and Poverty,* ed. Ann Harrison. Chicago: University of Chicago Press for National Bureau of Economic Research.

Prasad, Eswar S., Kenneth Rogoff, Shang-Jin Wei, and M. Ayhan Kose. 2007. "Effects of Financial Globalization on Developing Countries: Some Empirical

Evidence." In *Globalization and Poverty*, ed. Ann Harrison. Chicago: University of Chicago Press for National Bureau of Economic Research.

Ravallion, Martin. 2004. "Competing Concepts of Inequality in the Globalization Debate." In *Brookings Trade Forum: 2004*, ed. Susan Collins and Carol Graham. Washington, DC: Brookings.

Thomas, Duncan, and Elizabeth Frankenberg. 2007. "Financial Crises and Poverty: The Case of Indonesia." In *Globalization and Poverty*, ed. Ann Harrison. Chicago: University of Chicago Press for National Bureau of Economic Research.

Topalova, Petia. 2007. "Trade Liberalization, Poverty and Inequality: Evidence from Indian Districts." In *Globalization and Poverty*, ed. Ann Harrison. Chicago: University of Chicago Press for National Bureau of Economic Research.

Winters, Alan L., Neil McCulloch, and Andrew McKay. 2004. "Trade Liberalization and Poverty: The Evidence So Far." *Journal of Economic Literature* 42 (March): 72–115.

# CHAPTER 9

# Global Wage Inequality and the International Flow of Migrants

*Mark R. Rosenzweig*

Although it is well known that global income inequality is high, the extent to which wage rates differ across persons with the same skill but located in different countries is not well understood. Because of data limitations, in practice measures of income inequality across countries are usually based on the per capita gross domestic product (GDP). Until recently, for many countries no data providing comparable cross-country information on worker earnings and their characteristics were available. Yet information on cross-country wage inequality for workers with a given skill is useful for three reasons. First, it helps to identify the sources of inequality. Average earnings differ across workers located around the world for two reasons: workers differ in average skill levels, and the rewards to skill—skill prices—differ across countries. If the difference in average skill levels is the major reason for global wage or earnings inequality, a focus on upgrading skills might be a suitable remedy. If, however, wage inequality is mainly due to the different pricing of skills across countries, the remedies might be quite different.

Labor force surveys providing wages by occupation such as that by Free-man and Oostendorp (2000) indicate that in 1995 a construction carpenter's wage in India was $42 a month. A worker in the same occupation in Mexico earned $125 a month, while his counterparts in the Republic of Korea and the United States earned $1,113 and $2,299 a month, respectively. These are enormous differences in earnings. But economists do not know how much of these observed wage differentials are due to differences in skill and how much to the different prices of skill across countries. Surely the average construction carpenter in India has a lower level of schooling than, for example, a carpenter in the United States, and that may account for some part of the difference.[1]

A second reason that information on rewards to skill across countries is useful is that it helps analysts understand the magnitudes and patterns of the global migration of labor. Basic models of migration depict the choice of location of a worker with a given skill. Thus, the relevant set of variables is the wages a worker with a given skill would earn at different locations. Country-specific skill prices are central to understanding the individual gains from migration, and thus the quantity and the selectivity—that is, which workers of what skill levels move to which country. Whether a construction carpenter in India would want to move to, say, Korea depends on how much of the observed wage gap is a result of Koreans in the same occupation having more skill than their counterparts in India. If most of the difference stems just from a gap in skills, then for a typical low-skill Indian carpenter the incentives to migrate are low.

Yet as in the literature on global inequality, studies of the determinants of international migration do not use any cross-country wage data. Instead, they almost always rely on differences in country-specific levels of per capita GDP to explain, along with some other nonwage aggregate variables, cross-border migration. Per capita GDP is related to skill price, as discussed later in this chapter, but per capita GDP also differs across countries because of differences in the average domestic levels of human capital and because of differences in the proportion of the population that is employed because of differences, for example, in the labor force participation of women and in the proportion of the population of labor force age (dependency ratio). Variations in these cross-country factors for given skill prices do not have a strong direct bearing on individual migration decisions. Income also affects the ability to finance migration, so per capita income will imperfectly pick up both skill price and income effects, which may go in opposite directions.

A third reason it is important to have information on how skills are priced across countries is that inequality in skill prices indicates how well or how badly skill, or human capital, is allocated around the world. Large differences in skill prices imply there is a large global misallocation of labor (and perhaps other factors of production such as capital), and

---

1   These wages are not corrected for purchasing power parity.

thus that total world income is substantially lower than it could be if labor were reallocated across countries. From a global efficiency point of view, if inequality in country-specific skill prices is high, then one might view statistics on the "brain drain"—the proportion of highly skilled persons born in "poor" countries who reside in "rich" countries—as a measure of the contribution of international migration to the alleviation of world income inequality. This would be particularly so if poor countries reward skills meagerly and rich countries reward skill with a high price. Thus, from the perspective of global efficiency, the statistic that, for example, 43 percent of tertiary-educated Ghanaians live in member countries of the Organisation for Economic Co-operation and Development (OECD), would be seen not as alarmingly high but as alarmingly low, if the skill price in Ghana is still substantially lower than the average OECD skill price.[2]

In this chapter, I first set out a framework for understanding the determinants in the variation in the pricing of skills across countries and describe the model underlying the Mincer specification of wages that is used widely to estimate the relationship between schooling and wages. I then show how, using wages and the human capital attributes of workers located around the world, skill prices can be identified and the Mincer model can be tested. After describing the data sets that can be used to obtain estimates of skill prices, I estimate a global wage equation that is more general than the Mincer specification and provides estimates of skill prices for 140 countries. The estimates reject the Mincer model, implying that factors affecting the supply of schooling as well as schooling productivity need to be taken into account to understand the pricing of skill across countries.

The skill price estimates indicate that, as a first-order approximation, variation in skill prices substantially dominates the cross-country variation in schooling levels or rates of return to schooling in accounting for the global inequality in the earnings of workers around the world. I also show that the variation in skill prices and GDP across countries has opposite and significant effects on the number and quality of migrants to the United States, including employment migrants with permanent visas and persons with student visas. Skill prices also matter for which students return to their home countries. The migration findings indicate that among countries with the same GDP, low–skill price countries experience larger per capita outflows of total human capital—numbers of migrants multiplied by their average years of schooling—despite outmigration being more positively selective in higher–skill price countries. By contrast, countries with lower skill prices have, on net, larger populations of higher-educated persons trained outside their country, despite experiencing lower return rates of foreign students, which offsets the permanent outflow of "brains."

---

2   This statistic was obtained from the database on stocks of educated foreign-born around the world assembled by Beine, Docquier, and Rapoport (2001, 2006).

## Framework for Understanding the Proximate Determinants of Wages and Skill Prices across Countries

To understand the proximate determinants of the rewards to skills across countries, it is useful to consider three functions. First, the aggregate production technology relates the total output of a country $Y_j$ to the vector of aggregate skills of its labor force $X_j$ and its capital stock and natural resources $K_j$ to yield

$$Y_j = Y(X_j, K_j, \Phi_j), \qquad (9.1)$$

where $\Phi_j$ are technology parameters, which may be country-specific. For purposes of exposition, I assume initially that there is one skill type (the different types of skills are considered later in this chapter). The country-specific skill price $\omega_j$ is just the marginal value product of skill $\partial Y_j/\partial X_j$. The wage $W_{ij}$ of a worker $i$ in country $j$ is then given by

$$W_{ij} = \omega_j x_{ij}, \qquad (9.2)$$

where $x_{ij}$ is the number of skill units of worker $i$ in country $j$. Thus, wage inequality within a country is due solely to differences in skills across workers. Differences in wages across workers in different countries stem from both differences in their skill levels and in the country-specific prices of skill. Skills are usually not measured directly or provided in most data sets. However, inputs to the production of skill, such as years of formal schooling $S_{ij}$, are measured. Therefore, the skill production function for a country is

$$x_{ij} = S_j(S_{ij}, H_{ij}, I_{ij}), \qquad (9.3)$$

where $H_{ij}$ is a vector of school inputs other than years of schooling attended, and $I_{ij}$ is a vector of other human capital inputs, including training and work experience. A large literature has attempted to characterize (estimate) the skill production function, examining the effects of school inputs such as class size, textbooks, and teacher attributes. Substituting (9.3) into (9.2), one would get a wage function relating a worker's wage to his or her skill inputs and the skill price. Cross-country wage inequality would then be proximately determined by differences in cross-country skill prices, the technology of skill production, and differences in years of schooling, schooling inputs, and work experience across individuals.

The most popular wage function used in empirical studies of wage determination is the Mincer wage function, which is

$$log\ W = w_j + \beta_j S_{ij} + I_{ij}\gamma_j, \qquad (9.4)$$

where $w_j$ is an intercept, perhaps specific to country $j$, and $\beta_j$ is the rate of return to schooling in each country. If this is the correct wage function, then to completely characterize global wage inequality one would need to know just three parameters: the intercepts and the country-specific rates of return to schooling $\beta_j$ and work experience $\gamma_j$. Conspicuously absent from the Mincer specification are school quality variables—that is, the inputs to schooling. Is this just a misspecification? And what is the relationship between variation in skill prices across countries and the parameters of the Mincer wage function? For example, if the rate of return to schooling is higher in country A compared with country B, does that mean that skill is more rewarded in country A?

The original specification of the wage function derived by Jacob Mincer (1958) was based on the assumption that individuals discount future income and that there are no nonmarket barriers to schooling—that is, the amounts of schooling chosen by individual workers are not constrained by school availability or by access to finance (credit constraints). In particular, lifetime income $y$ for an infinitely lived agent $i$ who spends $S_{ij}$ years in school is by definition

$$y(S_{ij}) = \int_S W(S_{ij})e^{-r(j)t}dt \, , \qquad (9.5)$$

where $r(j)$ is the subjective discount rate in $j$. Relationship (9.5) embodies the assumption that earnings are zero when schooling is being acquired— the only cost to schooling is thus the foregone wage. With no barriers to schooling, lifetime wages must be equal for all workers no matter what their schooling level—that is, for example, if college graduates had higher lifetime earnings, then more persons would go to college, driving down the wages of college graduates until lifetime incomes are the same. This arbitrage assumption means that

$$y(S'_j) = y(S'_j) \, , \qquad (9.6)$$

for any $S$, $S'$, including $S = 0$. Moreover, because agents would compare the returns to schooling with the returns to capital, the discount rate would be equated to the cost of capital. Thus, in the Mincer earnings function (9.4), the parameters have a structural interpretation in terms of the model: the intercept is the wage a worker who had no schooling would earn in country $j$; $w_j = W(0)_j$, the base wage for country $j$; and the rate of return to schooling is actually the rate of return to capital in the economy, $\beta_j = r_j$.

Thus, in the Mincer model the rate of return to schooling says nothing about the scarcity of skill, just the scarcity of capital! And variables reflecting the quality of schooling do not belong in the specification, even if inputs to schools vary a lot across countries or even individuals. The reason is that the Mincer wage equation is an equilibrium condition that always holds no matter what happens to school quality or in labor markets, so long as the return to capital or the base wage is not affected. Consider, for example, a country in which the government raises the quality of its universities. This higher quality, by definition, increases the wages of university graduates compared with the wages earned by them in the past, but the higher wages of graduates then attract more students to the universities (remember that there are no entry barriers to schooling in the model), and thus eventually the wages of the university graduates are driven down, until the return to schooling for everyone again equals the discount rate and the return to capital.

If the actual world conformed to the Mincer model, analysts would need to know the country-specific heterogeneity in base wages, returns to capital, and schooling to fully account for world wage inequality. Existing data sets provide information on average years of schooling across countries (e.g., Barro and Lee 2001). The average years of schooling for the population aged 15 and over vary from about 3 to 14 years across countries. Estimates of returns to schooling (capital) from Mincer wage regressions estimated from labor force data from 52 countries, as reported in Bils and Klenow (2000), suggest a range from 0.024 to 0.28. Interestingly, Bils and Klenow do not report the intercepts (base wages) from those regressions. However, it would be a straightforward exercise to back out the intercepts (base wages) given the information on average wages, average schooling levels, and the estimated $\beta_j$'s for the 52 countries.

That said, this imputation exercise is not worth carrying out for three reasons. First, it is not at all clear that the data used for each of the 52 countries are comparable. They were obtained by different researchers, who may have dealt differently with the thorny problem of attributing wages to, for example, the self-employed (a large part of low-income-country labor forces), or who are using data sets that differentially exclude certain workers such as part-time or informal. Second, this sample of 52 countries represents less than one-third of countries. Third, and perhaps most important, the Mincer model may be inappropriate to characterize the determinants of wages around the world.

Putting aside the issue of data for the moment, two alternative approaches to the highly restrictive Mincer model exploit the relationships given in equations (9.1), (9.2), and (9.3). The first approach uses aggregate data on outputs $Y$, the labor force $L$, and schooling $S$ across countries. For example, assume that the aggregate production function (9.1) is Cobb-Douglas, so that

$$Y_j = A_j L_j{}^a \prod K_{nj}{}^\gamma, \tag{9.7}$$

where $A_j$ characterizes the technology level (TFP) of the country, $K_{nj}$ is the vector of capital stock and natural resources, and $L_j = N_j \left( s(x_{ij}) \right)$, where $N_j$ is the total number of workers in country $j$ and the $s$ function relates the average skills of the work force in $j$ to observables such as schooling years and school inputs—the inverse of (9.3). The skill price for country $j$, the marginal product of a unit of skill, is then

$$\omega_j = \alpha Y_j / N_j \left( s(x_{ij}) \right). \tag{9.8}$$

Taking logs of (9.8) yields

$$\log(\omega_j) = \log \alpha + Ln(Y_j / N_j) - Ln(s(x_{ij})). \tag{9.9}$$

Thus, assuming the popular Cobb-Douglas functional form, all that is needed to compute skill prices across countries are data on output *per worker*, estimates of the coefficients $\alpha$ (labor share) from aggregate production function estimates, and information on schooling, given assumptions about the *s* function.

Equation (9.9) is also useful in showing how skill prices are related to per capita GDP, which is typically used to characterize both global income inequality and the determinants of migration. As can be seen, the skill price of a country is positively associated with its GDP per worker, which is only imperfectly correlated with its GDP per capita. More important, the skill price, given GDP per worker, is negatively associated with its average level of human capital. Thus, high-GDP countries with unusually high levels of schooling will have a relatively low skill price. Conversely, poor countries that have unusually low levels of schooling will have high returns to skill. Differences in per capita GDP across countries are therefore not very informative about the efficiency of the distribution of skilled workers around the globe, nor are they good measures, used alone, of the gains from international migration for workers of different skill levels.

A second approach to estimating global, country-specific skill prices uses individual worker data from different countries on wages and human capital inputs, including schooling years and schooling quality variables. For example, assume that the skill production function has the form

$$x_{ij} = \mu_{ij} exp(\beta_j S_{ij} + I_{ijk}\gamma_k + H_{ijn}\delta_n),\qquad(9.10)$$

where $\mu_{ij}$ is an unobserved component of skill for a worker *i* in country *j*. Note that the coefficient $\beta_j$ is not the return to schooling (capital) as in the Mincer model, but expresses how a unit increase in schooling years augments skill. Replacing (9.10) in (9.2) and taking logs yields

$$log(W_{ijz}) = log\,\omega_j + \beta_j S_{ij} + I_{ijk}\gamma_{jk} + H_{ijn}\,\delta_n + log\,\mu_{ij}.\qquad(9.11)$$

The estimated country-specific intercepts from wage relationship (9.11) estimated across individual workers from different countries yield directly the (log) skill prices, one for each country represented. With multiple workers for each country, it is also possible to allow the coefficients on schooling and the other human capital variables to vary across countries. Note that in this one skill case, the wage equation (9.11) looks identical to the Mincer wage equation (9.4) except that inputs to schooling appear in the specification. Of course, if the skill production function had a different functional form, the specification would look very different. With the specific functional form for the skill production function chosen in (9.10), the Mincer model is then nicely nested within the specification (9.11). If the Mincer model is correct, the coefficient vector $\delta$ associated with the vector of school quality inputs $H_{ijn}$ should be zero (school quality does not matter in the Mincer model). Using appropriate comparable data on wages of workers around the world one can thus also test the Mincer model.[3]

It is also possible to obtain estimates of the relationships between skill prices and aggregate country variables and test the Cobb-Douglas functional form of the aggregate production function. Substituting (9.9), the skill price relationship with aggregate income, into (9.11), yields

$$log(W_{ijz}) = log\,\alpha + Ln(Y_j/N_j) - Ln(s(x_{ij})) + \beta_j S_{ij}$$
$$+ I_{ijk}\gamma_k + H_{ijn}\delta_n + log\,\mu_{ij}. \qquad (9.12)$$

This hybrid equation contains both individual worker variables, characterizing the worker's own schooling years and school quality, and country-level variables, characterizing output and the quality of the country's aggregate work force. If the Cobb-Douglas functional form is true, the coefficient on per worker GDP should be equal to one in this global wage regression. More important, estimates of equation (9.12), obtained from a subsample of countries for which there is both individual wage and human capital information as well as aggregate income and labor force variables, can be used to predict skill prices for countries in which there are no individual worker wages but only the aggregates, which are more generally available. Up to this point, I have assumed that there is only one type of skill. In the Mincer model it does not matter, again, how many different types of skill there are; the equilibrium relationship between years of schooling and wages characterized by the Mincer wage equation remains the same. For any integrated domestic economy, as assumed in the model, there is only one rate of return, that to capital. In the more agnostic approach in which markets can be imperfect, one can easily incorporate multiple skill types, but for empirical applications it is necessary to take a stand on how many skill types there are and which laborers fit into which category of skill. For example, with suitable data it is possible to distinguish skill prices for, say, those workers with less than a high school education and those with at least some college. Then the parameters of equations (9.11) and (9.12) would have to be estimated for each of the two groups.[4]

## Global Wage Data Sets

To quantify the global inequality in wages and to account for how much of world wage inequality is due to variations across countries in skill prices and how much to differences in human capital, data are needed that provide comparable wage and human capital information for representative workers for most countries—that is, a global wage data set that is comparable,

---

3   There are other tests: the returns to capital should equal the Mincer schooling return and the Mincer schooling return should be the same for every schooling level.

4   This discussion ignores how heterogeneity in unobservable skills might affect schooling choices, which has implications for how the relevant parameters are estimated.

comprehensive, and representative in countries and workers. Only three data sets, all of which have become available in recent years, can be used to obtain estimates of world skill prices and their determinants and to carry out tests of the Mincer model. They are the New Immigrant Survey Pilot, Occupational Wages Around the World, and the New Immigrant Survey.

The New Immigrant Survey Pilot (NISP) is a random sample of new permanent resident aliens in the United States who obtained the permanent visa (green card) in 1996 (Jasso et al. 2000). The relevance of this sample for gauging global inequality in wages is that the survey obtained information on the earnings of these new immigrants in their last jobs in their home countries before coming to the United States and on their complete employment histories. Thus, information on wages worldwide is taken from a common questionnaire, which also provides information on workers' schooling, including the location of schooling, and work experience. The disadvantage of the data set is that it is a small sample—it consists of only 332 workers who worked prior to coming to the United States (the total number of respondents is 800), and these workers represent only 54 countries. However, the subsample of countries with wage data on migrants and aggregate information on incomes and the labor force can be used to estimate hybrid equation (9.11), enabling predictions of skill prices for those countries on which information on per worker GDP and aggregate schooling measures is available. This procedure was carried out in Jasso and Rosenzweig (2009), and the predicted skill prices for 125 countries were used to examine the determinants of immigration in both Australia and the United States. The other drawback of this sample is that it is selective, including only workers who were able to emigrate to the United States.

The data set Occupational Wages Around the World (OWW) is based on International Labor Organization (ILO) labor force surveys, put together and made more comparable by Freeman and Oostendorp (2000). Many years are covered, and a large number of observations are made in any given year—for example, 4,942 observations in 1995. Each survey is meant to represent the workers in each country. The main shortcoming of this database is that the observations are average wages in an occupation. There are no other variables characterizing human capital—that is, there is no information on age, work experience, or schooling. The number of countries represented in any given year is also small; the maximum number is 67. However, there is an incomplete overlap in country coverage across years, so that one can, combining years, achieve a larger set of countries. Again, using the hybrid equation relating aggregate country variables to wage data, it is possible to estimate skill prices for many more countries, but it is necessary to assume that the one occupational variable captures all of a worker's human capital attributes.

The New Immigrant Survey (NIS) baseline data set is a larger and more comprehensive version of the NISP. It contains information on a probability sample of new immigrants to the United States in 2003. Home country wages, adjusted for purchasing power parity (PPP) and inflation, for over

4,000 workers representing 140 countries are contained in these data, along with comprehensive migration and schooling histories. Thus, it is possible to use the NIS data to estimate skill prices, without any information on aggregate country variables, for as many as 140 countries.

Table 9.1 provides descriptive statistics for the three data sets. The average annualized earnings of the sampled immigrants is predictably higher than the earnings of those respondents represented in the OWW data set, given that immigrants to the United States have higher schooling levels than the average person in the world—in the NISP and NIS samples average years of schooling are 14.4 and 13.8, respectively. This compares with the population-weighted world average, based on the Barro-Lee data of 6.3 years. That immigrants are positively selected for schooling is an implication of most standard migration models (see later discussion), because the United States has a higher skill price than most countries of the world (Jasso and Rosenzweig 2009). When estimating country-specific skill prices from these data, as noted, schooling and other human capital variables are controlled.

## Estimates of Worldwide Skill Prices and Tests of the Mincer Model

Using the three global wage data sets, it is possible to estimate country-specific skill prices. In this section I report results from estimating skill prices using the NIS data. Country-specific skill prices were obtained based on a specification of the log wage equation (9.11) in which each country is allowed to have a unique intercept (the skill price) and a unique coefficient

Table 9.1 Characteristics of Global Earnings Data Sets

| Data set/variable | NISP home country workers | OWW, 1995 | NIS home country workers |
|---|---|---|---|
| Mean annualized earnings of respondents ($) | 14,719[a] (2,602) | 10,208[b] (13,289) | 17,803[a] (29,410) |
| Mean age of respondents | 34.6 (8.53) | – | 39.7 (11.5) |
| Mean years of schooling of respondents | 14.4 (4.5) | – | 13.8 (3.82) |
| Number of industries | – | 49 | – |
| Number of occupations | – | 161 | – |
| Number of countries | 54 | 67 | 140 |
| Number of workers | 332 | 4,924 | 4,455 |

Source: NISP, OWW, and NIS data.
Note: NISP = New Immigrant Survey Pilot; OWW = Occupational Wages Around the World; NIS = New Immigrant Survey.
a. PPP-adjusted.
b. Exchange rate–adjusted, country-specific calibration with lexicographic imputation.

on the individual schooling ($\beta_j$) and labor force experience variables (the $\gamma_{jk}$). Working within the constraints of missing variables, I obtain 139 estimated skill prices. The estimates indicate that, unsurprisingly, I can soundly reject the hypothesis that skill prices are the same across countries, but I cannot reject the hypothesis that the schooling and work experience coefficients are identical across countries. Bils and Klenow (2000) do not carry out a statistical test of whether the schooling coefficients estimated for each of the 52 countries were not statistically significantly different, so it is not clear whether the global variance in schooling returns is essentially zero or my estimates of schooling returns by country lack precision.

The NIS data can also be used to test whether the Mincer model is the appropriate model for specifying and interpreting the relationship between wages and schooling. To carry out the test, I allow the country-specific schooling coefficient $\beta_j$ to vary with measures of school quality in each country. Eight measures are used: average class sizes, average teacher salaries, and pupil/teacher ratios in primary and secondary schools and the number of ranked universities and the average rank of the ranked universities based on the Times Higher Education survey. As noted, in the Mincer equilibrium model, school quality should be unrelated to the returns to schooling, which are anchored by the return to capital. Table 9.2 reports estimates of the log wage equation. In the first column, a bare specification is used in which the coefficient on schooling is assumed to be the same across countries and no school quality variables are included, but intercepts differ by country. Interestingly, in this Mincer specification the global coefficient on schooling of 0.095 is almost identical to the average of the 52 country schooling returns in the Bils and Klenow collection of estimates—0.096. However,

Table 9.2 Test of Mincer Model: Fixed-Effects-Country Log Wage Regression Coefficients from NIS Using Bartik School Quality Data and Log of Hourly Wage for Men at Last Job before Coming to the United States

| Origin country variable | (1) | (2) |
|---|---|---|
| Total years of schooling completed | 0.0948 (6.12)[a] | 0.0721 (3.30) |
| Work experience | 0.0298 (2.24) | 0.0339 (2.30) |
| Work experience squared ($\times 10^{-3}$) | −0.0697 (2.59) | −0.0664 (2.19) |
| Interactions with Bartik school quality variables?[b] | No | Yes |
| F-test: $\grave{\mathbf{E}} = 0$ [p-value] (d.f., d.f.) | – | 2.50 [0.006] (10, 1,226) |
| Number of sending countries | 112 | 112 |

*Source:* New Immigrant Survey (NIS) and Bartik 2008.
a. Absolute value of t-ratio is in parentheses.
b. The school quality measures are pupils per teacher, spending per pupil, and average teacher salaries in primary and secondary schools; the number of ranked universities; and the average rank of ranked universities, if any.

based on the second column of the table, I strongly reject the hypothesis that the schooling coefficients do not vary by schooling quality. The Mincer model, assuming perfectly functioning labor, credit, and capital markets, is thus rejected.

Rejection of the Mincer model means that the country-specific intercepts can be interpreted as skill prices and that it is necessary to account for schooling quality variables in estimating the determinants of wages. However, by estimating one skill price per country I am assuming there is only one type of skill. To see whether ignoring skill-type heterogeneity will seriously affect inferences about either world inequality or incentives for migration, I reestimated wage equation (9.11) separately for two groups of workers, those with 12 years of education or less and those with 16 years of education or more—yielding two sets of country-specific skill prices. Figure 9.1 shows the correlation between the college graduate skill prices and the skill prices obtained assuming one skill. As can be seen, the two series co-move strongly; the correlation is over 0.74. Given this high correlation, it is not possible to assess the contribution of variations in the pricing of skills across countries by skill type. As will become clear, however, cross-country differences in skill prices in the one-skill-price framework account for a large component of the variance in earnings across countries as well as the quantity and human capital intensity of cross-border labor flows.

## Proximate Determinants of Global Earnings Inequality

It is useful to compare the cross-country variation in estimated skill prices from the NIS with the global variation in average years of schooling from

Figure 9.1 Relationship between Log Skill Price (One Skill) and Log of College Plus Skill Price

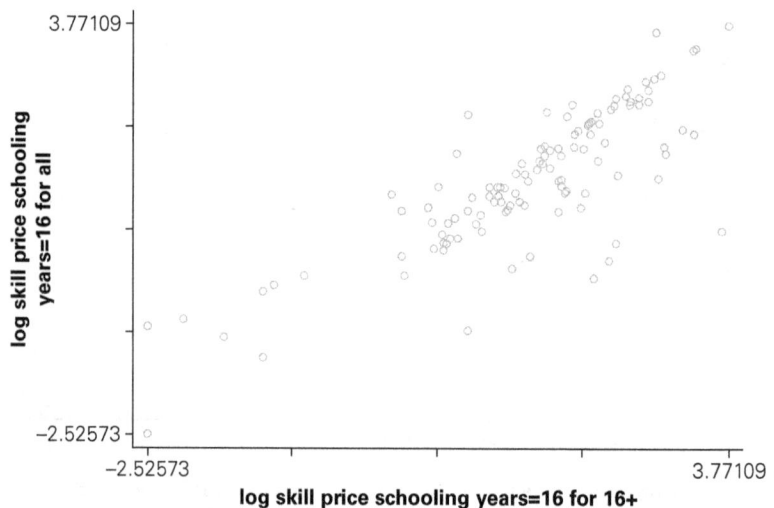

Source: NIS data.

Barro and Lee (2001), the schooling returns from the 52-country table in Bils and Klenow (2000), and the GDP per adult equivalent in order to understand the proximate determinants of world inequality in incomes.[5] Because differences in GDP across countries reflect differences in schooling levels and the rewards to skills as well as the variability in labor force participation, it is expected that the global variation in GDP will exceed that of the other variables, unless there are strong negative covariances across human capital levels, skill prices, and returns.[6]

Table 9.3 reports three inequality statistics for each variable: the coefficient of variation (CV), the span (ratio of highest to lowest value), and the ratio of highest to lowest value in the interquartile range (IR). The three statistics generally show the same patterns across the four global variables: GDP per adult equivalent and country-specific skill prices exhibit the most global variation, and schooling levels and returns the least. Indeed, the coefficient of variation of schooling is less than 60 percent of that for GDP, whereas the CV for skill prices is over 85 percent of the CV for GDP. Thus variability in schooling levels across countries is 44 percent of the variability in country-specific skill prices. The span statistic, in which the variation in skill prices exceeds the variation in incomes across countries, suggests that despite trimming there may be outliers in the set of skill price estimates, which will in part contaminate the CV comparisons. The IR measure is insensitive to outliers in any of the variables. However, the patterns are similar for this inequality measure—the IR statistic for average schooling is only 44 percent of the IR of GDP, while the IR for skill prices is 73 percent of the IR of GDP. For this statistic, then, the cross-country variability in skill prices is 66 percent higher than the intercountry variability in schooling attainment.

Using equation (9.11), the set of estimated worldwide skill prices can be used to compute the hourly wage of any worker of given schooling for any rate of return ($\beta$). Thus, for example, the earnings of high school or college graduates for 140 countries could be constructed. To illustrate the importance of skill price variability in world wage inequality relative to both variability in schooling levels and schooling returns (the coefficient on schooling), I use the skill price estimates to predict earnings for persons with both 12 and 16 years of education for a given schooling return, using equation (9.11), for a subset of countries. I then alter the schooling coefficient differentially across countries to assess how this would affect cross-country earnings gaps by schooling level. For this comparison, I select five countries with low and intermediate levels of skill prices: Nigeria, India, Indonesia, Mexico, and Korea. Figure 9.2 reports the predicted annualized earnings for high school and college graduates for each of these countries based on their estimated skill prices and an assumed schooling return of 0.07.

---

5  Nine outliers were removed from the set of skill price estimates. The formula was to remove the topmost and bottommost values obtained from countries with only one person represented in the data. Thus, my estimate of the global variation in skill prices is conservative.

6  Both the schooling level and the schooling return variables are positively correlated with skill prices.

Table 9.3 Global Inequality: Comparisons of the Global Variation in Schooling, Schooling Returns, Per Capita GDP, and Skill Prices

| | Number of countries | Coefficient of variation | Span (ratio) | Interquartile range (ratio) |
|---|---|---|---|---|
| Average years of schooling, 15+ population | 106 | 0.474 | 14.4 | 2.2 |
| Mincer schooling return | 52 | 0.494 | 11.7 | 1.7 |
| GDP per adult equivalent | 139 | 0.948 | 76.7 | 4.9 |
| Skill price | 130 | 0.807 | 108.9 | 3.6 |

*Source:* Average years of schooling: Barro and Lee 2001; Mincer schooling return: Bils and Klenow 2001; GDP: World Tables 2003; skill price: estimated by the author using the New Immigrant Survey.

Figure 9.2 Predicted 1996 Annual Earnings of High School and College Graduates Based on NISP Skill Prices, Selected Countries (r = 0.07)

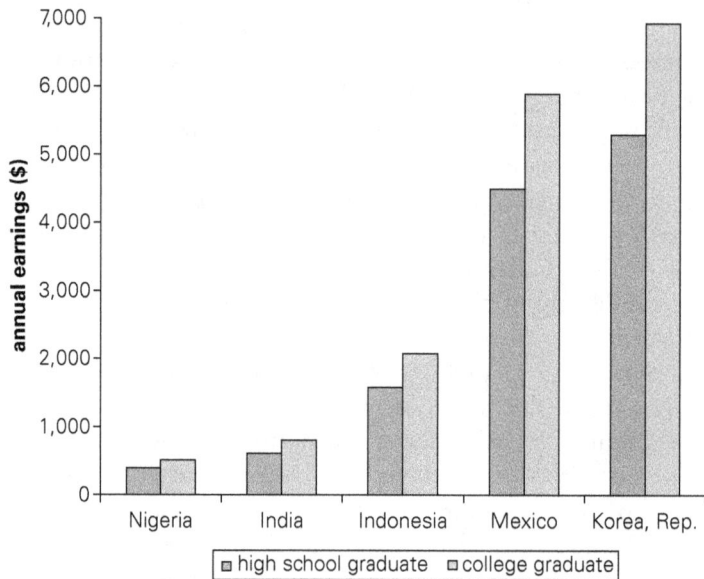

*Source:* New Immigrant Survey Pilot.

Four features of figure 9.2 are notable. First, earnings differences across the countries, for either schooling level, are enormous. For example, a Korean high school graduate earns 10 times more than a high school graduate in India, a college graduate in Mexico earns almost three times more than a college graduate in Indonesia, and so on. The cross-country misallocation in skill is evidently very high. Second, a pattern evident in figure 9.2 is that differences in earnings across countries within each schooling level dominate differences in earnings within countries across schooling levels. Providing a Nigerian high school graduate with a college education (with a

7 percent return), for example, raises his or her earnings by $200 a year. If that high school graduate migrates to Indonesia or Mexico, his or her earnings rise by $1,200 or $5,400 a year. Put another way, if everyone in the world obtained a college degree but stayed in place, even ignoring standard within-country general equilibrium effects that would depress the return to schooling, world wage inequality would not be substantially altered. The gaps in wages between persons in poor (low–skill price) and rich (high–skill price) countries would not be affected significantly by improvements in schooling attainment in poor countries, unless such improvements affected skill prices positively.

A third feature of figure 9.2 is that the higher the skill price, the larger the absolute gains from increasing schooling. In India, for example, the annual gain in earnings from obtaining a college degree over a high school diploma is just $190. The same additional four years of schooling yields a gain of $1,600 a year in Korea and $500 a year in Indonesia, but only $120 a year in Nigeria. Yet the rate of return to schooling is the same in all four countries. These cases illustrate the point that rates of return to schooling provide no information on differences in the productivity or value of schooling across countries. It is necessary to know how skills are priced in each country—skill prices.

Finally, figure 9.2 shows that the absolute differences in earnings across the countries are always larger for the college graduates compared with the high school graduates. The gap between what a high school graduate earns in Korea and Indonesia is $3,700 a year; the cross-country earnings gap for the same two countries for a college graduate, however, is $4,850 a year. Similarly, a high school graduate working in Mexico earns $2,900 more a year than one working in Indonesia; a college graduate would earn $3,800 more. Put another way, the absolute gains from migration are higher for the more educated. As I discuss and test more formally shortly, as long as schooling is not strongly positively correlated with migration costs, international migration will tend to be positively selective—that is, the more educated in a population are more likely to emigrate to a country with a higher skill price.

The patterns of earnings by country and schooling level depicted in figure 9.2 were constructed based on the assumption that the return to schooling was identical across countries. How is intercountry inequality, and the gains from crossing borders by schooling level, affected if heterogeneity in schooling returns is increased, leaving skill price differences the same? Figure 9.3 reports the results of this counterfactual for two countries, Bangladesh and Korea, again based on their estimated skill prices. However, in this case earnings are computed for the two schooling groups within each country for two rates of return to schooling, 0.07 (as before) and 0.10. For both rates of return the patterns in figure 9.2 are apparent in figure 9.3—the differences in earnings across the two countries within schooling groups dominate strongly differences in earnings across schooling groups within each country; the gains from schooling investment are higher in the higher–skill

Figure 9.3 Predicted 1996 Earnings Based on NISP Skill Prices by Schooling
Level and Schooling Return, Bangladesh and the Republic of Korea

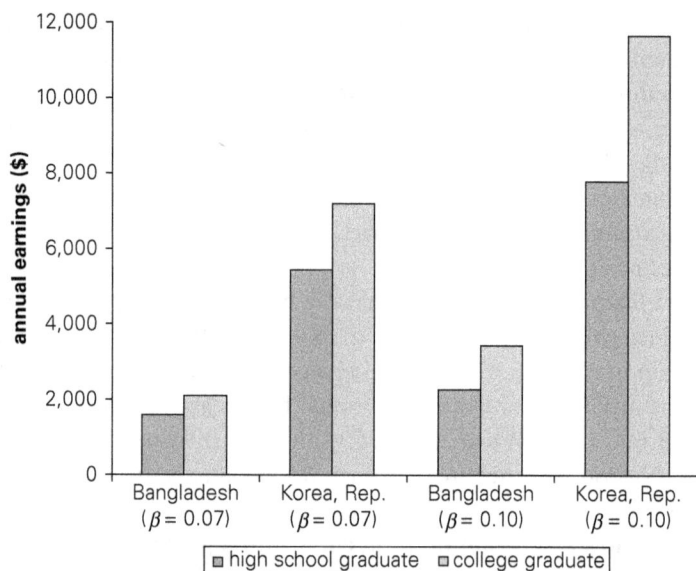

Source: New Immigrant Survey Pilot.

price country; and the gains from moving to the higher–skill price country
are higher for the more educated.

The most interesting experiment is one in which the return to schooling
in the lower–skill price country, in this case Bangladesh, is increased, while
leaving the return at the same (lower) level for the higher–skill price country, Korea. Does this experiment alter any of the conclusions made under
the assumptions of equal returns? First, the figure reveals that the increase
in the return to schooling increases both high school and college graduate
earnings in Bangladesh and lowers the earnings gap between the two countries for both groups. However, despite the relatively larger increase in the
earnings of college graduates, the gap in earnings between Korean and Bangladeshi college graduates is still larger than the gap between high school
graduates across the two countries. And despite the fact that the return
to schooling is 43 percent higher in Bangladesh than in Korea, the gains
from migration are still higher for the college graduates than for the high
school graduates.

## Skill Prices, GDP, and International Migration

In this section I use the estimated skill prices, combined with other country-
specific information, to examine the determinants of international migration. This exercise is useful from two perspectives. First, if one accepts the
estimates of skill prices as being accurate, they can be used to appropriately

test models of migration and to assess how differing prices of skill across countries affect the quality and amount of migration. Or, accepting models of migration, one can view this exercise as validating the skill price estimates, which should significantly affect the choices of migrants.

## A Framework

The simplest framework for understanding the forces affecting migration and that incorporates skill prices begins with agent $i$ residing in country $j$ with a given number of skill units $x_i$. That agent earns $W_{ij} = \omega_j x_i$ at home, from (9.2), but can earn $W_{iu} = \omega_u x_i$ in country $u$. The net gain from migration $G_{ij}$, ignoring issues of skill transferability, is then

$$G_{ij} = [\omega_u - \omega_j]x_i - C_{ij}, \qquad (9.13)$$

where $C_{ij}$ is the direct cost of migration. The agent migrates from $j$ to $u$ if $G_{ij} > 0$.

Equation (9.13) has several testable implications for both the quantity and selectivity of migration. Given a distribution of private costs within a country, it can be shown easily that, first, the larger the skill price gap $\omega_u - \omega_j$, the greater the gain from migration and thus the more migration. Countries with the lowest skill prices will experience the highest rates of outmigration. Second, agents with more skill units have greater gains from migration, as was seen in figure 9.2. As a consequence, for given fixed costs of migration, as the skill price gap narrows, migration becomes more positively selective—only those agents with the highest levels of skills still experience a gain from migration net of costs. Migrants from countries with the highest skill prices will be highly skilled, but there will be fewer of them. Third, increases in the cost of migration will lower the number of migrants, but also increase the average skill levels of those who migrate, because only those with the highest levels of skill will experience a net gain from migration. Migrants from nearby countries will be numerous and relatively low skill. A key point is that changes in the skill price gap and in the costs of migration will have opposite effects on the quantity and quality of migration flows.

A more elaborate model would incorporate country-specific amenities in a utility-maximizing framework, but the basic implications from (9.13) would still hold (see Jasso and Rosenzweig 2009). In an empirical study of international migration, (9.13) suggests that variables are needed that measure skill prices at destination and origin, the determinants of human capital production, as in (9.3), as well as migration costs. A major issue in examining the determinants of international migration is that, unlike domestic migration in most countries, international migration is heavily regulated, subject, for example, to quotas by country of origin and restrictions based on family relationships to destination country citizens. Characterizing the costs and opportunities of international migration is thus complex. In addition, the model ignores uncertainty and thus the costs of search. One related important aspect of migration is that it tends to depend on networks, which play an important role in reducing search and other migration costs. Therefore, migration is a dynamic phenomenon, with today's migration costs related to past migration histories to particular destinations.

U.S. immigration is an example of a heavily regulated system. More than 90 percent of U.S. immigrants qualify for a visa because of a family relationship. To minimize the complexities associated with international migration, I look at two types of international migrants to the United States: migrants who obtain an employment visa and migrants who obtain a student visa. Migrants who obtain an employment visa are not required to have family members in the United States to qualify, and visa qualification in this category is based on the human capital characteristics of the potential migrant and the willingness of a U.S. employer to hire the migrant. Jobs that qualify in this category are the kinds in which the role of networks is minimal. Those who qualify can also bring their immediate relatives (children and spouses). The appropriate category that comes closest to the "economic" migrant to which the model pertains is the "principal applicant"—that is, the person who receives the job offer as opposed to the relative of someone who does. Principal applicant visas make up less than 5 percent of all U.S. permanent resident visas. Fortunately, the NIS oversampled immigrants in this category, so that sufficient numbers represent most countries. Moreover, country quotas were not binding in the period covered by the NIS for this category of immigrant. Because the NIS provides the number of employment principal immigrants by country and their schooling, it is possible to look at the determinants of both the quantity and quality of immigrants in this category.

U.S. student visas are relatively unregulated and not subject to country quotas. Generally, all that is necessary to qualify for a student visa is to have obtained admission to one of the thousands of qualifying U.S. educational institutions. The two sources of annual information on foreign students by country of origin are (1) the student visas issued by the State Department each year and (2) the number of foreign students studying in the United States by both U.S. institution and country of origin, which is provided in the Student and Exchange Visitor Information System (SEVIS). The United States is the most popular destination for foreign students; approximately 250,000 came to the United States to study in 2004.

A somewhat different model is required to examine student migration decisions—that is, the decisions on where to acquire schooling. The model incorporates, besides the attributes of the schools at both the origin and the potential destinations, the skill prices at home and in potential destinations because of the possibility that acquiring schooling abroad increases the probability of obtaining a job offer where one is studying (this model is set out in Rosenzweig 2007, 2008). If so, part of the gain from acquiring schooling in destination country $u$ as opposed to in home country $j$ will be determined by the gap in skill prices between the two countries, as in (9.13). Based on the NIS information on the prior visas held by immigrants and the SEVIS data on stocks of foreign students, I constructed country-specific measures of the fraction of foreign students who were able to stay permanently in the United States (Rosenzweig 2008). On average, 20 percent of students stayed, suggesting that studying in the United States hugely increases the probability of immigrating there. Stay rates, however, differed greatly across countries. It is possible to use these measures of student stay rates to also examine determinants of the fraction of U.S. foreign students returning to their home countries.

To estimate the determinants of migration to the United States incorporating country skill prices, I use two measures of migration costs: distance of each country's capital to the nearest port of entry to the United States and GDP per adult equivalent. I expect that the distance from origin to destination is positively associated with the costs of migration. For GDP, I expect that wealthier households are more able to bear the immediate costs of migration, so that richer countries, among those with the same skill prices, will experience higher rates of outmigration. I also include as determinants the school quality variables used in the tests of the Mincer model and the size of the home country population. To extend the number of countries beyond the 139 for which I have direct estimates of skill prices in order to minimize country selectivity, I estimated an auxiliary equation predicting skill prices based on equation (9.12), using information on each country's per worker GDP, its average schooling levels, and the school quality variables. Based on these estimates, I predicted skill prices for 168 countries.

### Estimates

Table 9.4 reports the estimates of the effects of origin country skill prices per adult-equivalent GDP and distance, all in logs, on the log of the number of employment visa principal migrants to the United States in 2003 and the log of the average years of schooling of those migrants.[7] The coefficient signs conform perfectly to the model: skill prices are negatively related to the number of migrants but positively related to their average schooling; distance reduces migration but raises the quality of those who do migrate; and GDP is positively associated with outmigration but negatively associated with the schooling of the outmigrants. Thus, GDP and skill prices have opposite effects on the quantity and quality of migration. Studies that use only origin country GDP as a determinant of migration are thus confounding the effects of financial constraints with the gains associated with increased wages.

What do these estimates imply for a brain drain by low- and high-skill price countries? One measure of skill outflow is the total number of

---

7   The number of countries in the analysis of the schooling of the employment migrants is reduced because some countries did not have any employment migrants. A more sophisticated analysis would take into account the selectivity associated with nonmigration. However, it is an implication of the model that factors affecting the decision to migrate also affect who migrates (selectivity).

| | Log number of employment visa principal immigrants | Log average schooling of employment visa principal immigrants |
|---|---|---|
| Log skill price (NIS, 2003) | −0.827 | 0.499 |
| | (1.23)[a] | (2.83) |
| Log GDP per adult equivalent | 0.604 | −0.108 |
| | (2.74) | (1.60) |
| Log distance of country to the United States | −0.248 | 0.0377 |
| | (4.98) | (4.43) |
| R-squared | 0.611 | 0.112 |
| Number of sending countries | 168 | 94 |

Source: New Immigrant Survey.
Note: The specification also includes whether there is a military base in the home country, the log of the home country labor force size, and measures of the quality of primary and secondary schools.
a. Absolute values of bootstrapped t-ratios in parentheses are based on the multiple imputation method.

years of schooling of the migrants—the number of migrants multiplied by their average schooling. Although the point estimate of the skill price on the number of employment migrants is not estimated with precision, the magnitude is high in absolute value, suggesting that a doubling of the skill price would reduce outmigration by 83 percent. The average schooling of the outmigrants, column (2), would increase by 50 percent, however. The net effect of increasing the origin country skill price on the total outflow of human capital, measured by the total years of schooling of all migrants, is thus negative. Doubling the skill price reduces the total human capital outflow by 33 percent. Thus, less human capital flows out of high–skill price countries compared with low–skill price countries. Put another way, even though outmigration is more skill-intensive in high– than in low–skill price countries, because far more migrants leave from low–skill price countries, the total loss in human capital is greater. From the perspective of poor countries that subsidize education, this is a loss. From the perspective of global efficiency, however, that more human capital flows out of places where skill is rewarded less to places where it is more valuable is good news.

What about the flows of foreign students to rich countries and back? Table 9.5 reports estimates from Rosenzweig (2008) that look at the effects of skill prices (estimated from the NISP and OWW), per capita GDP, and distance on the number of foreign students who migrate to the United States and their return rates. The first two columns indicate that higher skill prices at origin, whether estimated from the NISP or the OWW world wage data sets, reduce the number of students who seek schooling abroad. Because these estimates control for measures of school quality, the estimates suggest that foreign schooling is in part a job-seeking phenomenon. The estimates also suggest, parallel to those obtained for permanent migrants, that for given skill prices countries that are richer experience greater outflows of

Table 9.5 Effects of Home Country Skill Price, GDP, and Distance on Log of Number and Exit Rate of Foreign University Students in the United States, 2004

| Dependent variable | Log number of U.S. foreign students | | Log exit rate of foreign students | |
|---|---|---|---|---|
| Basis for skill price | NISP | OWW | NISP | OWW |
| Log skill price | −0.259 (2.17)[a] | −0.730 (2.14)[a] | 0.0152 (2.31) | 0.0193 (3.61) |
| Log GDP per adult equivalent | 0.516 (2.85) | 1.06 (2.71) | 0.00145 (0.56) | −0.00137 (0.42) |
| Log distance of country to United States | −0.298 (4.30) | −0.309 (4.44) | 0.00163 (0.52) | 0.00237 (0.75) |
| R-squared | 0.766 | 0.766 | 0.183 | 0.202 |
| Number of sending countries | 125 | 125 | 125 | 125 |

Source: New Immigrant Survey.
Note: The specification also includes the log of the home country population and measures of the number and quality of home country universities. NISP = New Immigrant Survey Pilot; OWW = Occupational Wages Around the World.
a. Absolute values of bootstrapped t-ratios in parentheses are based on the multiple imputation method.

migrants. Countries with lower skill prices experience more student out-migration. Moreover, the students from these countries are also less likely to return. As seen in the third and fourth columns of table 9.5, student return rates are higher to countries that have higher skill prices that reward skill.

Outsourcing of schooling may be a benefit for poor countries, which cannot afford to supply a sufficient quantity of high-quality schools, but only if students return. Is foreign schooling relatively beneficial for poorer countries? The point estimates suggest that a doubling of the skill price lowers the outflow of students by from 26 to 73 percent and also increases their return rates by from 1.5 to 1.9 percent. The net effect is that the total number of students who receive their higher levels of schooling abroad are significantly greater in low–skill price countries. Although such countries lose a greater fraction of their best and brightest because they "outsource" far more students compared with high–skill price countries, the total numbers that return are higher. Outsourcing higher education thus appears to benefit, on net, poorer countries.

## Conclusion

Global inequality in incomes can be viewed from various perspectives—for example, as an indicator of global unfairness, as a measure of the challenge for development policy, or as a measure of the inefficient global allocation of labor or capital. Understanding the proximate determinants of income inequality is useful for all of these perspectives. In this chapter, I used newly available data on the wages and human capital of workers across the countries to shed light on how much of inequality in incomes across countries is due to inequality in human capital and how much is from differential rewards to the same skills—that is, the cross-country variation in skill prices. I showed how the global wage data can be used to identify skill prices worldwide and to test the Mincer model of schooling and wages that has been used pervasively to specify and interpret wage functions estimated within countries. I also used estimates of the set of country-specific skill prices to quantify the relative importance of skill and skill price variation in explaining income inequality and to assess how variation in the rewards to skill across countries affects the quantity and quality of cross-border migrant flows, including permanent employment and student migrants to the United States from around the world.

The data reject the model underlying the Mincer wage specification, which assumes perfect capital and labor markets and no barriers to schooling acquisition (and no permanent differences in lifetime earnings), suggesting that a framework incorporating the determinants of the supply and pricing of skills is better suited to accounting for wage inequality. My estimates also indicate that domestic rates of return to schooling across countries are relatively uninformative about differences in the rewards to skill across countries. To fully characterize the global wage distribution, one needs to know how schooling affects wages, levels of schooling, and skill prices for each country. My estimates indicate that the global variation in skill prices is significantly greater in magnitude than either the variation in schooling levels or schooling returns. In particular, my estimates of country-specific skill prices suggest that global inequality in the price of skill exceeds global inequality in either average per country schooling levels or returns by as much as 70 percent, depending on the measure. That most of global inequality in incomes is due to intercountry differences in the prices of skills suggests that greater equalization of schooling levels arising from domestic schooling policies will have only marginal effects on global inequality, that domestic development policies in poor countries should focus on the underlying reasons skills are less valued, and that, given the structure of skill prices, labor is poorly distributed across countries based on global efficiency criteria.

My estimates based on patterns of migration to the United States indicate that skill price variation is an important determinant of the variation in the number and schooling levels of migrants. In conformity with a simple model of migration choice, the estimates indicate that among countries with similar levels of per capita income, countries with low skill prices experience greater rates of outmigration than countries with high skill prices, but the average schooling levels of those leaving low–skill price countries are lower than those from high–skill price countries. Despite this selectivity, the estimates suggest that the total amount of human capital—the total schooling years of migrants—exiting countries is greater per capita in low– than in high–skill price countries. By contrast, low–skill price countries appear to gain more from the migration of persons to acquire schooling abroad. Although more students from low–skill price countries study abroad and the return rates of those students are also lower for such countries compared with those for countries in which skills are more favorably rewarded, on net larger stocks of foreign-trained, tertiary-educated persons are in low–skill price countries than in high–skill price countries. Existing estimates of the brain drain from low-income countries thus need to take into account both phenomena—the permanent outflow of those who have acquired their schooling in the home country and the numbers of persons in home countries who received their subsidized schooling elsewhere. Finally, my estimates indicate that rising incomes accompanied by stagnant skill prices will lead to greater outmigration. Thus, for example, humanitarian aid, which increases incomes in poor countries but does little to increase the rewards to skills, can worsen the brain drain, although it would also increase global efficiency and therefore output. How individual countries increase incomes will then significantly affect the global mobility of workers and total world output.

## References

Barro, Robert J., and Jong-Wha Lee. 2001. "International Data on Educational Attainment: Updates and Implications." *Oxford Economic Papers* 53 (3): 541–63.

Bartik, Alex. 2008. "New International Data on Schools." Senior thesis, Yale University, New Haven, CT.

Beine, Michel, Frédéric Docquier, and Hillel Rapoport. 2001. "Brain Drain and Economic Growth: Theory and Evidence." *Journal of Development Economics* 64 (1): 275–78.

———. 2006. "Measuring International Skilled Migration: New Estimates Accounting for Age of Entry." Research Report, World Bank, Washington, DC.

Bils, Mark, and Peter J. Klenow. 2001. "Does Schooling Cause Growth?" *American Economic Review* 90 (5): 1160–83.

Freeman, Richard B., and Remco Oostendorp. 2000. "Wages round the World: Pay across Occupations and Countries." NBER Working Paper 8058, National Bureau of Economic Research, Cambridge, MA, December.

Jasso, Guillermina, Doug Massey, Mark Rosenzweig, and James Smith, 2000. "The New Immigrant Survey Pilot: Overview and New Findings about Legal Immigrants at Admission." *Demography* (February).

Jasso, Guillermina, and Mark Rosenzweig. 2009. "Selection Criteria and the Skill Composition of Immigrants: A Comparative Analysis of Australian and US Employment Immigration." In *Skilled Immigration Today*, ed. Jagdish Bhagwati and Gordon Hanson. New York: Oxford University Press.

Mincer, Jacob. 1958. "Investment in Human Capital and Personal Income Distribution." *Journal of Political Economy* 66 (4): 281–302.

Rosenzweig, Mark R. 2007. "Global Wage Differences and International Student Flows." In *Brookings Trade Forum: Global Labor Markets*, ed. Susan Collins and Carol Graham. Washington, DC: Brookings.

————. 2008. "Higher Education and International Migration in Asia: Brain Circulation." In *ABCDE World Bank Conference*, ed. François Bourguignon. New York: Oxford University Press.

Times Higher Education survey. http://www.timesonline.co.uk/tol/news/uk/education/article4910798.ece.

# CHAPTER 10

# International Migration and Development

*Gordon H. Hanson*

A decade ago, trade and investment liberalization dominated the global economic policy agenda. The World Trade Organization (WTO) had recently opened its doors; the United States, Mexico, and Canada were implementing the North American Free Trade Agreement (NAFTA); and much of Southeast Asia and South America were nearing the peak of an economic boom driven in part by greater openness to inflows of foreign capital. In bilateral and multilateral discussions of economic integration, global migration was often missing from the agenda entirely.

Today, international labor flows are viewed as an integral part of the process of globalization. Between 1990 and 2005, the number of people residing outside of their country of birth grew from 154 million to 190 million, reaching a level equivalent to 3 percent of the world population (United Nations 2005). In many developing countries, emigration rates have increased dramatically. Between 1990 and 2000, the fraction of the adult population who had emigrated to member countries of the Organisation for Economic Co-operation and Development (OECD) rose from 30 percent to 35 percent in Jamaica, 14 percent to 20 percent in El Salvador, 8 percent to

The author thanks Roberto Zagha and Ravi Kanbur for helpful comments on this chapter.

13 percent in the Dominican Republic, 8 percent to 12 percent in Mexico, 7 percent to 12 percent in Haiti, 4 percent to 8 percent in Honduras, and 2 percent to 6 percent in Ecuador.[1]

The growth in labor flows from low-income to high-income countries has not been greeted with universal enthusiasm, either by policy makers or academics. In theory, international migration increases economic efficiency by shifting labor from low-productivity to high-productivity environments. As workers move from Central America to the United States, North Africa to Europe, or Southeast Asia to Australia, the global labor supply shifts from labor-abundant to labor-scarce economies, compressing international differences in factor prices and raising the global gross domestic product (GDP). Migrants enjoy large income gains (Rosenzweig 2007), family members at home share in these gains through remittances (Ozden and Schiff 2006; Fajnzylber and Lopez 2007), and nonmigrating workers in the sending country enjoy higher wages thanks to a drop in the local labor supply (Aydemir and Borjas 2007). What is there not to like?

One source of dissension is that international migration redistributes income within and between countries. It thus comes as no shock that inflows of foreign labor provoke political conflict and have become a frequent topic of debate in labor-importing countries. More surprising, perhaps, is that economists are often among those criticizing migration. In the literature, one finds two broad complaints. In low-income sending countries the concern has long been that the wrong individuals leave (e.g., see Bhagwati and Hamada 1974). In most of the developing world, those more highly skilled have the highest propensity to emigrate. If positive spillovers are associated with accumulating human capital (Lucas 1988) or if education is public and financed through taxes (Bhagwati and Rodriguez 1975), then the emigration of skilled labor can undermine economic development (Benhabib and Jovanovic 2007). Possible corrections include taxing the emigration of skilled labor (McHale 2007) or having receiving countries admit more unskilled workers from the developing world (Pritchett 2006).

In high-income receiving countries, the complaint is that the wrong immigrants are arriving (Borjas 1999b). In the United States and Europe, the average immigrant has much less schooling than the average native worker (Boeri, McCormick, and Hanson 2002). If immigrants receive lower income than the natives, increased labor inflows may exacerbate distortions created by social insurance programs or means-tested entitlement programs (Borjas and Hilton 1996; Wellisch and Walz 1998), fueling political opposition to immigration (Hanson, Scheve, and Slaughter 2007). Most rich receiving countries tightly restrict immigrant admissions in contrast to their pro-liberalization stances on trade and investment (Hatton and Williamson 2004).

To be sure, the claims made by both the emigration pessimists and the immigration pessimists are controversial. On the brain drain, the recent

---

1   See Docquier and Marfouk (2006). Adults are those 25 years and older.

literature counters earlier arguments by suggesting that opportunities for emigration may increase the incentive to acquire human capital by enough to create a brain gain (Stark, Helmenstein, and Prskawetz 1997; Stark and Wang 2002). In receiving countries, especially the United States, some economists see the consequences of immigration for native workers as benign or even positive (Card 2005; Cortes 2005; Ottaviano and Peri 2006). Still, the literature leaves one with the impression that the workers whom sending countries would most like to see go are the ones whom receiving countries would least like to see come. It is no wonder, then, that there has never been a Washington consensus on international migration. If economists do not agree on the benefits of open borders, surely policymakers will not either.

A further complication is that control over international migration is largely in the hands of the receiving countries. Labor flows between rich and poor nations tend to be unidirectional, from the rich to the poor. In 2005 just 12 higher-income nations were host to 51 percent of the global stock of international migrants (United Nations 2005).[2] The United States alone is home to 20 percent of the global migrant stock, but sends few migrants to developing countries. Because high-income countries are able to set global migration policy unilaterally, they have little incentive to address sending-country concerns.

The disconnect between sending- and receiving-country perspectives on international migration raises a host of important policy questions. Is emigration a viable strategy for developing countries to use in raising living standards? Are there environments in which emigration may be particularly helpful or harmful?

In this chapter I selectively review academic literature on the causes and consequences of emigration from developing countries. My aim is to identify facts about international migration that are relevant to those concerned about why labor moves between countries and how these movements affect sending-country economies.[3] Empirical work on global labor flows is still in an early state. And, as is often the case, the literature provides incomplete answers to some of the most urgent questions. Nevertheless, recent work yields some robust results and is helpful for identifying where future research should be directed.

In the next section I describe the current trends in international migration. Developing countries that are small, densely populated, and middle-income tend to have the highest emigration rates. In the section that follows I discuss the relationship between skill and migration. In nearly

---

2   The 12 were the United States; Russian Federation; Germany; France; Canada; United Kingdom; Spain; Australia; Hong Kong, China; Israel; Italy; and Japan.

3   Although there are labor flows between low- and middle-income countries, data constraints require me to focus on the flows into high-income countries. There appear to be sizable flows from the former Soviet republics to Russia; Bangladesh to India; Egypt, India, Pakistan, and the Philippines to the Gulf states; Afghanistan to Iran; Iraq to Syria; other southern African states to South Africa; Indonesia to Malaysia; Malaysia to Singapore; Guatemala to Mexico; and Nicaragua to Costa Rica (Ratha and Shaw 2007).

all countries, those more highly skilled are those most likely to emigrate. The positive selection of emigrants is consistent with international differences in labor productivity—rather than international differences in inequality—being the primary determinant of which types of workers leave. Emigrants sort themselves across destination countries according to the reward to skill, in a manner consistent with income maximization. This section is followed by one devoted to a discussion of the contribution of migrant networks to lowering migration costs, which for many countries appear to be substantial.

I follow this discussion with a section that examines the research on the impact of emigration on sending countries.[4] In the few cases that have been studied, labor outflows appear to help raise sending-country wages while having little impact on fiscal accounts. Although there has been recent progress in the literature, the question of whether the opportunities for emigration produce a brain drain or a brain gain remains unresolved. Economists still do not know how opportunities for emigration affect the stock of human capital in sending countries. Recently, migrant remittances have grown rapidly, and their positive correlation with household consumption has led some analysts to ascribe a causal role to remittances in development. A more reasoned view is that remittances are simply a by-product of intrahousehold specialization. There is some evidence that labor outflows promote trade, technology diffusion, and political openness, although the econometric identification of these impacts is not problem-free.

By way of conclusion, I summarize in the final section what appear to be the more empirically robust findings (or nonfindings) in the literature.


## Dimensions of International Migration

International migration appears to be on the rise. Only recently have cross-country data on emigrant stocks become available. As a result, research on international migration is still emerging. In this section I discuss data sources on the stock of international migrants, and then move on to examine emigration rates in sending countries, the distribution of migrants across receiving countries, the correlates of bilateral migration flows, and the emigration of skilled labor.

### Data and Recent Trends

Recently, analysts have made several attempts to measure international migration. Carrington and Detragiache (1998) estimate emigration rates in 1990 for individuals with a tertiary education from 61 source countries to OECD countries. Adams (2003) applies a similar methodology to estimate

---

4  The literature on the impacts on receiving countries is much more developed—see Borjas (1999a, 2007).

emigration rates for 24 large labor-exporting countries in 2000. The OECD (2006) lists for each member country the foreign-born population 15 years and older in 2000 by source country and education level (primary, secondary, tertiary, or unknown). Although these sources are welcome additions to the literature, each has gaps in coverage for sending countries, migrant skill levels, or time (Docquier and Marfouk 2006; Hanson 2007).

In useful recent work, Docquier and Marfouk (2006) extend the OECD data by constructing more complete estimates of the stocks of international migrants. They use the population censuses for 30 OECD countries in 1990 and 2000 to obtain the count of adult immigrants (25 years and older) by source country and level of education (primary, secondary, or tertiary). They combine these counts with the counts of the size of adult populations and the fraction of adult populations with different levels of schooling from Barro and Lee (2000) to obtain emigration rates by education level and source country. Their work yields 174 source countries in 1990 and 192 in 2000. Although the set of source countries is comprehensive, the coverage of destination countries excludes those countries not in the OECD as of 2000.

Low-income countries are an increasingly important source of migrants to high-income countries. Table 10.1 shows the share of the immigrant population in OECD countries by sending-country region.[5] In 2000, 67 percent of immigrants in OECD countries were from a developing country, up from 54 percent in 1990. This gain came almost entirely at the expense of Western Europe, whose share of OECD immigrants fell from 36 percent to 24 percent. Among developing sending regions, that made up of Mexico, Central America, and the Caribbean is the most important, accounting for 20 percent of OECD immigrants in 2000, up from 15 percent in 1990. Half of this region's migrants come from Mexico, which in 2000 was the source of 11 percent of OECD immigrants, making it by far the world's largest supplier of international migrants.[6] The next most important developing source countries of OECD immigrants are Turkey, with 3.5 percent of OECD immigrants; China, India, and the Philippines, each with 3 percent; Vietnam, the Republic of Korea, Poland, Morocco, and Cuba, each with 2 percent; and Ukraine, Serbia, Jamaica, and El Salvador, each with 1 percent.

Destination regions tend to draw more heavily on migrants from particular source countries. Mexico, Central America, and the Caribbean are the largest source region for North America, but they do send a few migrants to other parts of the world. Eastern Europe is the most important developing source region for OECD Europe. And Southeast Asia is the most important developing source region for Australia and Oceania. It is not surprising that geographic distance plays an important role in migration.

---

5   Tables and figures are based on calculations using raw data from Docquier and Marfouk (2006).

6   As recently as 1990, the United Kingdom was the largest source country for immigrants in the OECD.

Table 10.1 Share of OECD Immigrants by Sending Region, 2000
(percent)

| | Share of immigrants by OECD receiving region | | | | |
|---|---|---|---|---|---|
| | All OECD | North America | Europe | Asia, Oceania | Change in OECD share, 1990–2000 |
| **Low-income sending region** | | | | | |
| Mexico, Central America, Caribbean | 20.2 | 37.4 | 2.5 | 0.2 | 5.3 |
| Southeast Asia | 10.2 | 13.7 | 3.9 | 16.0 | 1.6 |
| Eastern Europe | 9.9 | 4.9 | 16.1 | 11.6 | 4.2 |
| Middle East | 6.3 | 3.2 | 11.3 | 2.9 | 0.1 |
| South Asia | 5.2 | 5.2 | 5.5 | 3.6 | 1.1 |
| North Africa | 4.4 | 0.9 | 9.8 | 1.8 | −0.6 |
| South America | 4.1 | 5.0 | 3.1 | 3.5 | 1.0 |
| Central, South Africa | 3.6 | 2.1 | 6.1 | 2.1 | 0.7 |
| Former Soviet Union | 2.9 | 2.3 | 4.2 | 1.0 | −0.2 |
| Pacific Islands | 0.4 | 0.3 | 0.1 | 2.7 | 0.0 |
| Total | 67.2 | 75.0 | 62.6 | 45.4 | 13.2 |
| **High-income sending region** | | | | | |
| Western Europe | 24.4 | 15.2 | 33.6 | 36.8 | −11.1 |
| Asia, Oceania | 5.5 | 6.2 | 1.8 | 15.6 | −1.0 |
| North America | 2.9 | 3.7 | 2.0 | 2.3 | −1.1 |
| Total | 32.8 | 25.1 | 37.4 | 54.7 | −13.2 |

*Source:* Author's calculations using raw data from Docquier and Marfouk (2006).
*Note:* Table shows data for 2000 on the share of different sending regions in the adult immigrant population of the entire OECD membership and three OECD subregions. High-income North America includes Canada and the United States, and high-income Asia and Oceania include Australia; Hong Kong, China; Japan; Korea; New Zealand; Singapore; and Taiwan.

The growing importance of lower-income countries in the supply of international migrants has contributed to an overall increase in labor flows into rich countries. Table 10.2 shows the share of the population that is foreign-born in select OECD member countries. The size of the immigrant population varies across destinations, reflecting differences in both their attractiveness and openness to international migrants. Aside from Luxembourg, the countries with the largest immigrant presence in 2004 are Australia (24 percent), Switzerland (24 percent), New Zealand (19 percent), and Canada (18 percent). Next in line are the large economies of Germany (13 percent), the United States (13 percent), France (10 percent), and the United Kingdom (9 percent), with the United States hosting 40 percent of immigrants living in OECD countries.

There is strong evidence that a rising share of labor inflows in rich countries are made up of illegal entrants. The data for the United States are the most extensive on this aspect of immigration. In 2005, illegal immigrants accounted for 35 percent of the U.S. foreign-born population, up

**Table 10.2 Share of Foreign-Born Population in Total Population, Select OECD Countries, 1995–2004**
(percent)

| | 1995 | 2000 | 2002 | 2004 | Change, 1995–2004 |
|---|---|---|---|---|---|
| Australia | 23.0 | 23.0 | 23.2 | 23.6 | 0.6 |
| Austria | | 10.5 | 10.8 | 13.0 | |
| Belgium | 9.7 | 10.3 | 11.1 | | |
| Canada | 16.6 | 17.4 | 17.7 | 18.0 | 1.4 |
| Czech Republic | | 4.2 | 4.6 | 4.9 | |
| Denmark | 4.8 | 5.8 | 6.2 | 6.3 | 1.6 |
| Finland | 2.0 | 2.6 | 2.8 | 3.2 | 1.2 |
| France[a] | | 10.0 | | | |
| Germany[b] | 11.5 | 12.5 | 12.8 | 12.9 | 1.4 |
| Greece[c] | | 10.3 | | | |
| Hungary | 2.8 | 2.9 | 3.0 | 3.2 | 0.4 |
| Ireland[d] | 6.9 | 8.7 | 10.0 | 11.0 | 4.0 |
| Italy[c] | | 2.5 | | | |
| Luxembourg | 30.9 | 33.2 | 32.9 | 33.1 | 2.2 |
| Mexico | 0.4 | 0.5 | | | |
| Netherlands | 9.1 | 10.1 | 10.6 | 10.6 | 1.6 |
| New Zealand[d] | 16.2 | 17.2 | 18.4 | 18.8 | 2.6 |
| Norway | 5.5 | 6.8 | 7.3 | 7.8 | 2.3 |
| Poland | | | 1.6 | | |
| Portugal | 5.4 | 5.1 | 6.7 | 6.7 | 1.3 |
| Slovak Republic[c] | | 2.5 | | 3.9 | |
| Spain[c] | | 5.3 | | | |
| Sweden | 10.5 | 11.3 | 11.8 | 12.2 | 1.7 |
| Switzerland | 21.4 | 21.9 | 22.8 | 23.5 | 2.2 |
| Turkey | | 1.9 | | | |
| United Kingdom | 6.9 | 7.9 | 8.6 | 9.3 | 2.3 |
| United States | 9.3 | 11.0 | 12.3 | 12.8 | 3.5 |

*Source:* OECD 2006.
*Note:* Empty cells indicate that data were missing in the source.
a. Value for 2000 is from 1999.
b. Value for 2004 is from 2003.
c. Value for 2000 is from 2001.
d. Value for 1995 is from 1996.

from 28 percent in 2000 and 19 percent in 1996. Of the 2005 population of illegal immigrants, 56 percent were from Mexico, implying that 60 percent of the population of Mexican immigrants in the United States was unauthorized (Hanson 2006).

Countries vary widely in the propensity of their populations to emigrate. As of 2000, 22 developing nations had seen 10 percent or more of

Figure 10.1 Persistence in Emigration Rates, 1990 and 2000

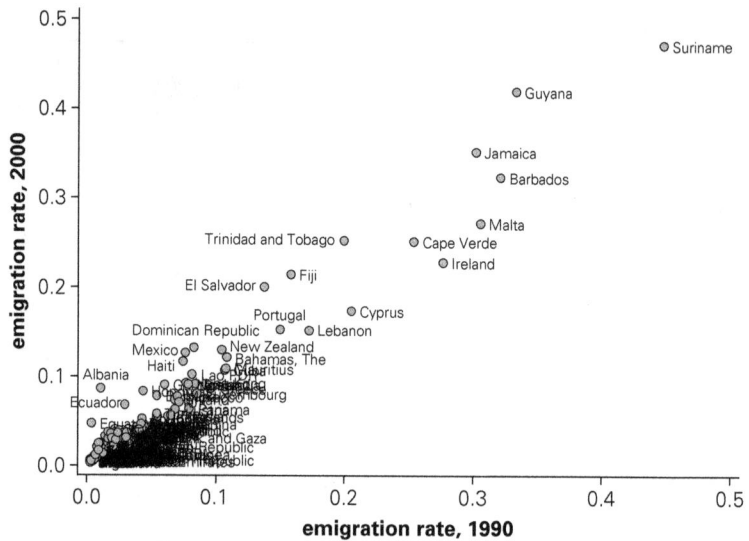

Figure 10.1 Persistence in Emigration Rates, 1990 and 2000

*Source:* Author's calculations using raw data from Docquier and Marfouk (2006).

their adult populations migrate to OECD countries, and 16 developing countries had emigration rates above 5 percent. At the other extreme, 52 developing countries had emigration rates below 1 percent.

Emigration is rising persistently over time (see figure 10.1, which plots emigration rates in 1990 and against those in 2000). The countries with the largest increases in emigration rates from 1990 to 2000 include neighbors of the United States (the Caribbean, Central America, and Mexico) and former eastern bloc countries (Albania and Bulgaria). The countries experiencing the largest decrease in emigration rates are Ireland, Lebanon, Panama, and Greece. Interestingly, war-torn countries do not have particularly high emigration rates to the OECD countries overall or large increases in emigration rates over the 1990s.

Income is an obvious driver of emigration. In figure 10.2, it appears that the relation between emigration rates and income is nonmonotonic. There is a threshold level of per capita GDP of about $3,000 in 2000 purchasing power parity (PPP)–adjusted terms, below which emigration rates are very low. Above this threshold, emigration falls as average income rises. This nonmonotonicity is consistent with recent literature on the relationship between international migration and income. Clark, Hatton, and Williamson (2007) correlate emigration flows to the United States with a large number of sending-country characteristics for a panel of 81 countries over the period 1971–1998.[7] They find an inverted U in the relationship between sending-country average income and emigration. Emigration rates

---

7  They calculate the emigration flow as the log ratio of U.S. legal immigrants admitted to the source-country population, a measure that is problematic (see Hanson 2007).

Figure 10.2 Emigration Rates and Per Capita GDP, 2000

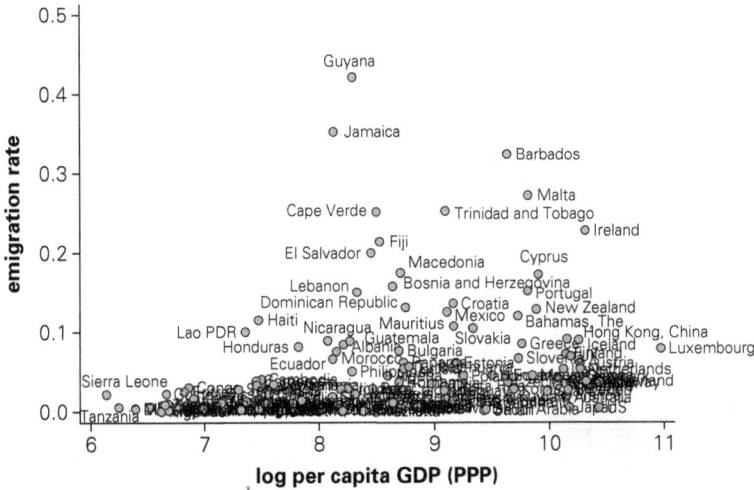

*Source:* Author's calculations using raw data from Docquier and Marfouk (2006).
*Note:* PPP = purchasing power parity.

increase as income rises for countries at low income levels and decreases as income rises at higher income levels. They also find that migration flows to the United States are higher for countries that speak English, are geographically closer to the United States, and have large existing populations of U.S. immigrants. The elasticity of emigration flows for distance is –0.20 to –0.28, which would imply that in moving from El Salvador (3,400 kilometers from the United States) to Brazil (7,700 kilometers from the United States) emigration to the United States would fall by 20 percent. Other research is consistent with this finding (Hanson 2007).

In related work, Mayda (2005) examines bilateral migration between a large number of source countries and 14 OECD destination countries over the period 1980–1995. She regresses bilateral migration rates on income per capita in the source and destination countries and average income per capita in other OECD destinations, among other control variables. Bilateral migration increases as destination-country income rises and decreases as the income of other destinations rises, consistent with the idea that better economic conditions in third countries deflect migration away from a given destination.

**Brain Drain**

Much of the literature on international migration focuses on the movement of skilled labor, whose departure may drain poor economies of scarce supplies of human capital. Figure 10.3 plots the emigration rate for adults with a tertiary education against the emigration rate for all adults. In 2000, 41 developing countries had emigration rates for the tertiary educated of above 20 percent.

The brain drain is a concern where there are distortions in the decision to acquire human capital. Absent distortions, moving labor from a

Figure 10.3 Emigration Rates for the More Educated, 2000

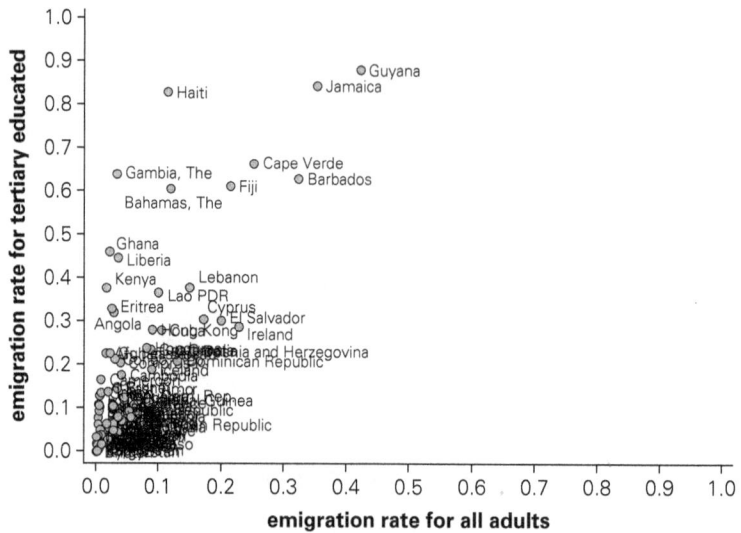

Source: Author's calculations using raw data from Docquier and Marfouk (2006).

low-productivity to a high-productivity economy unambiguously raises global income (Benhabib and Jovanovic 2007). However, if positive externalities are associated with learning (e.g., Lucas 1988), then the social product of human capital exceeds its private product and the exodus of skilled labor from a country may have adverse consequences for its economic development (Bhagwati and Hamada 1974). Another negative impact of the brain drain is that those states that subsidize the educations of many of their citizens would be deprived of the tax contributions that those citizens who emigrated would have made to offset the cost of their schooling (McHale 2007).

Recent literature explores the possibility that the opportunity for emigration may actually increase the supply of human capital in a country, creating a brain gain (Stark and Wang 2002). With high incomes for skilled labor in rich countries and uncertainty about who will succeed in emigrating, the option of moving abroad induces individuals to accumulate enough additional human capital to compensate for the loss in skill to labor outflows (Beine, Docquier, and Rapoport 2001).[8] For this argument to take root, the probability of emigrating must be large enough to affect the expected return to investing in skill. It also must be true that many people believe they have a good chance of moving abroad. If, for most people, the expected probability of emigrating is small, the brain gain logic collapses. One environment in which this might occur is in countries in which the distribution of wealth is highly unequal, so that few people are able to afford the upfront costs of either acquiring human capital

---

8   See Docquier and Rapoport (2007) for a survey of the theoretical literature on the brain drain.

(which may involve both direct costs for schooling and indirect costs of time out of the labor force) or moving abroad (which may involve direct costs to acquire a visa and indirect time costs).

Only a handful of empirical papers examine the relationship between emigration and human capital accumulation. For a cross section of countries, Beine, Docquier, and Rapoport (2006a) report a positive correlation between emigration to rich countries (measured by the fraction of the tertiary-educated population living in OECD countries in 1990) and the increase in the stock of human capital (measured as the change from 1990 to 2000 in the fraction of adults who have tertiary education). Although this finding is consistent with emigration increasing the incentive to acquire education, the cross-section correlation between emigration and schooling is not well suited for causal inference about the impact of a brain drain on educational attainment. Education and migration decisions are likely to be jointly determined, making each endogenous to the other. Valid instruments for migration are very difficult to find. Despite four decades of research, economists still do not know how the opportunity to emigrate affects the supply of human capital in sending countries, leaving the debate on the brain drain unresolved.

Finally, it is worth considering how emigration rates for the highly educated have changed in recent decades. Figure 10.4 plots emigration rates for the tertiary educated across countries in 1990 and 2000. The countries with the largest increase in emigration rates for the highly educated are primarily those that have experienced civil conflict, such as Afghanistan, Angola, Congo, Haiti, Mozambique, Rwanda, Sierra Leone, and Somalia. Thus, even though civil conflict does not provoke a general flight to OECD

Figure 10.4 Persistence in Emigration of the Highly Educated, 1990 and 2000

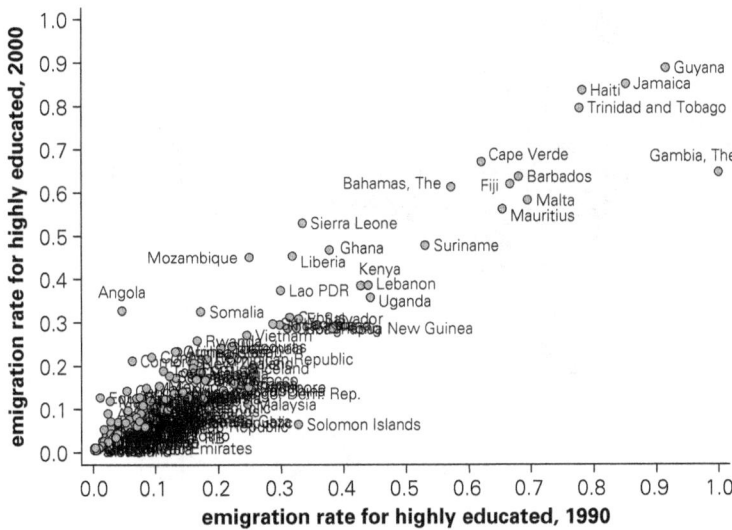

Source: Author's calculations using raw data from Docquier and Marfouk (2006).

countries, it does appear to provoke the flight of the more highly skilled. It has long been recognized that the induced emigration of skilled labor may be an important cost of civil war. Figure 10.4 is consistent with this perception, although careful research quantifying these costs is difficult to find in the literature.

## Selection into Migration

Who migrates from poor to rich countries is the subject of a growing empirical literature. The high propensity of the highly educated to migrate abroad is seen clearly in figure 10.5, which plots the share of emigrants with tertiary education against the share of the general population with tertiary education in 2000. Nearly all points lie above the 45° line, indicating that in the large majority of countries emigrants are positively selected in terms of schooling—that is, with the exception of a few countries (e.g., Canada, Turkey, United States), the more highly educated are overrepresented among emigrants relative to their presence in the population as a whole.

Positive selection of emigrants is at odds with much of the recent empirical literature on international migration. In an influential line of work, Borjas (1987, 1991) uses the Roy (1951) model to show how migration costs and international variation in the premium for skill affect the incentive to migrate. In countries with low average wages and high wage inequality, which appears to be the case in much of the developing world, there is negative selection of emigrants. Those with the greatest incentive to relocate to rich countries (which tend to have high average wages and

Figure 10.5 Selection of Emigrants in Terms of Education, 2000

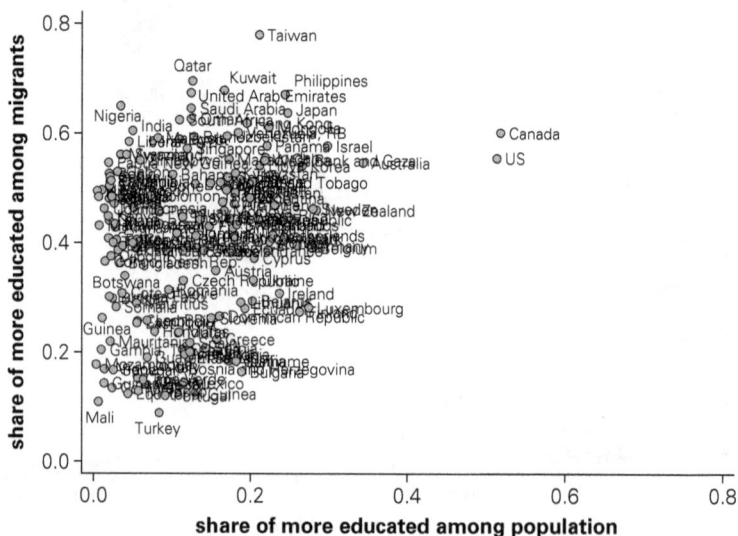

Source: Author's calculations using raw data from Docquier and Marfouk (2006).

low wage inequality) are individuals with below-average skill levels in their home countries.

Much of the recent empirical research on Borjas's negative-selection hypothesis examines labor movements either from Mexico to the United States or from Puerto Rico to the U.S. mainland. Puerto Rican outmigrants tend to have low education levels relative to those of nonmigrants (Ramos 1992; Borjas 2006), consistent with migrants being negatively selected in terms of skill. Mexican emigrants, however, appear to be drawn more from the middle of the country's schooling distribution, consistent instead with intermediate selection. Feliciano (2001), Chiquiar and Hanson (2005), Cuecuecha (2005), Orrenius and Zavodny (2005), and McKenzie and Rapoport (2006) find that emigrants from Mexico are drawn from the middle of the wage or schooling distribution, while Ibarraran and Lubotsky (2007) and Fernandez-Huertas (2006) find that Mexican emigrants are drawn from the lower middle of the wage or schooling distribution.

Based on figure 10.5, Mexico and Puerto Rico (and Turkey) appear to be exceptional cases. Positive selection of emigrants is a nearly universal phenomenon. Despite strong evidence that emigrants are positively selected in terms of schooling, there is confusion in the literature over the relationship between income inequality and the incentive to emigrate. An empirical approach made popular by Borjas (1987) is to explain bilateral migration using sending-country per capita GDP and income inequality (e.g., as measured by the Gini coefficient) relative to the receiving country (e.g., see Mayda 2005; Clark, Hatton, and Williamson 2007). A positive parameter estimate on the Gini coefficient indicates that migrants are negatively selected in terms of skill. However, this approach characterizes selection into migration only under restrictive conditions.

To characterize the relationship between income inequality and migration, it is useful to develop a simple model of the migration decision. Let the wage for individual $i$ from sending country $s$ in receiving country $r$ be

$$W_{isr} = \exp{(\mu_r + \delta_r z_i)}, \qquad (10.1)$$

where $\mu_r$ is the return to raw labor in $r$, $\delta_r$ is the return to an additional year of schooling level in $r$, and $z_i$ is an individual $i$'s years of schooling. Let the cost of migrating from country $s$ to country $r$ be given by

$$C_{isr} = f_{sr} + \varepsilon_{isr}, \qquad (10.2)$$

where $f_{sr}$ is a fixed monetary cost common to all individuals that migrate from $s$ to $r$, and $\varepsilon_{isr}$ is an idiosyncratic migration cost term that has mean zero and an extreme value distribution. Finally, let the utility associated with migrating from country $s$ to country $r$ be a linear function of wages and migration costs, such that

$$U_{isr} = W_{isr} - C_{isr}, \qquad (10.3)$$

where utility from not migrating equals the sending-country wage. If individuals make the migration decision in order to maximize utility, then, given the error is extreme value, the model is a logit. Consider the log odds of an individual with a college education migrating from $s$ to $r$, which, given the logit structure, can be written as

$$\ln \frac{E_{sr}^c}{E_s^c} = \left(W_r^c - W_s^c\right) - f_{sr},$$

(10.4)

where $E_{sr}^c$ is the share of the college-educated in $s$ that migrate to $r$, $E_s^c$ is the share of college-educated that remain in $s$, and $W_h^c$ is the wage to college-educated labor in country for $h = r, s$.] Equation (10.4) expresses the logic of the Roy model, in which income maximization is the motivation for migration. More individuals will move from country $s$ to country $r$ the larger is the wage differential between the two countries and the smaller are the fixed migration costs. Grogger and Hanson (2007) show how this setup can be generalized to allow for migration costs specific to skill and correlation in idiosyncratic migration costs across receiving countries.

To use this model to evaluate migrant selection in terms of skill, I follow Grogger and Hanson (2007) and compare the log odds of emigrating for those with a college education $c$ relative to those with a primary education $p$, which from (10.4) is given by

$$\ln \frac{E_{sr}^c}{E_s^c} - \ln \frac{E_{sr}^p}{E_s^p} = \left(W_r^c - W_s^c\right) - \left(W_h^p - W_s^p\right),$$

(10.5)

where fixed migration costs are differenced out of the expression. If the net gain from emigrating for the college-educated exceeds that for the primary-educated, the expression in (10.5) would be positive and emigrants from $h$ would be positively selected in terms of education. Using (10.1), this would require that

$$e^{\mu_r - \mu_s} > \frac{e^{\delta_s z_c} - 1}{e^{\delta_r z_c} - 1},$$

(10.6)

where $z_c$ indicates years of schooling for a college-educated worker and the return to primary-educated labor is normalized to equal $\mu$. Under the convenient approximation that $\exp(x) - 1 = x$ for small $x$, I can rewrite equation (10.6) as

$$\frac{W_r^p}{W_s^p} > \frac{\delta_s}{\delta_r}.$$

(10.7)

On the left of (10.7) is the ratio of *wages paid to raw labor* (proxied here by the wage for primary-educated labor) in the *receiving country relative to the sending country,* which can be thought of as the ratio of raw labor productivity in the two countries. On the right of (10.7) is the ratio of the Mincerian *return to schooling* (the log wage gain from an additional year of schooling) in the *sending country relative to the receiving country.*[9]

---

9　See Grogger and Hanson (2007) for more details on this derivation.

According to equation (10.7), emigrants from sending country $s$ will be positively selected in terms of schooling as long as the gain in the productivity of raw labor from moving abroad more than compensates educated workers for the loss in the return to schooling.[10] One can think of the ratio of the return to schooling on the right of (10.7) as capturing wage inequality, because, all else being equal, higher returns to schooling in country $s$ will imply greater wage inequality. Apparent in (10.7) is that higher wage inequality in a country by no means guarantees more negative selection of emigrants. Other factors come into play, such as labor productivity. Differences in labor productivity matter for selection because more skilled workers have more productivity-equivalent units of labor to supply than unskilled workers. All else being equal, higher labor productivity increases the incentive to emigrate more for those more highly skilled. One way to explain the positive selection of emigrants in figure 10.5 is that international differences in labor productivity are large relative to international differences in the Mincerian return to schooling.

To interpret the condition in (10.7), note that when comparing poor sending countries with rich receiving countries, it is usually true that the raw wage is higher in the receiving country and the return to schooling is higher in the sending country. Suppose that in Nigeria someone with a primary education would earn $1,000 a year and someone with a college education would earn $5,000 a year, whereas in the United States the comparable sums are $20,000 and $40,000. Clearly, the implied return to schooling in Nigeria (log return to schooling of 0.16) is higher than in the United States (log return to schooling of 0.07). And yet the higher productivity of raw labor in the United States (the U.S./Nigerian raw wage ratio is 20) more than compensates, making the net gain from emigrating from Nigeria greater for more educated workers. Thus, when there are large differences in raw labor productivity between countries, emigrants will tend to be positively selected in terms of skill.

Negative selection of workers by skill will emerge either where differences in labor productivity across countries are small or where migration costs are increasing in skill. The latter feature is adopted by Borjas (1987), who assumes that migration costs are fixed in units of time, so that the more highly skilled workers pay more to migrate. As a result, in his model, at least in its most simplified form,[11] the pattern of migrant selection is determined entirely by the relative return to skill across countries. However, once one introduces large productivity differences between countries or migration costs that are fixed in monetary units, the pattern of selection cannot be determined. Selection may be positive or negative, depending on relative labor productivity, relative returns to skill, and skill-specific migration costs. Even in the simple model of migration I develop here,

---

10 A similar implication is present in Rosenzweig (2007), who derives a Roy model of migration with moving costs that include components that are fixed in monetary units and time-equivalent units.

11 See Borjas (1991) for more elaborate models with negative and positive selection.

migration selection in terms of skill is not robust. Although this may seem obvious once one inspects the theory, it is perhaps a result that is underappreciated in the literature.

Credit constraints in sending countries could lead to migration costs *decreasing* in skill, which would strengthen the pressure for positive selection. Suppose, for example, that education and migration are subject to a fixed monetary cost and that credit market imperfections make wealthier individuals subject to lower borrowing costs (e.g., Rapoport 2002). The wealthier, then, are more likely to become educated and more likely to migrate abroad (Assunção and Carvalho forthcoming). For Mexico, McKenzie and Rapoport (2007) find an inverted U-shaped relationship between migration and wealth, consistent with low-wealth individuals being too poor to afford migration and high-wealth individuals having an incentive not to leave.

Rosenzweig (2007) examines migrant selectivity using data from the New Immigrant Survey (NIS). The NIS reports the wage an individual earned in his last job before coming to the United States, which Rosenzweig uses to estimate the marginal product of labor by source country. A country's overall emigration rate to the United States is decreasing in the marginal product of labor, suggesting that countries with higher labor productivity send fewer migrants to the United States. Rosenzweig estimates that raising a country's marginal product of labor by 10 percent relative to the United States would reduce the number of emigrants obtaining U.S. employment-based visas by 8 percent. The average schooling of emigrants to the United States is increasing in the marginal product of labor, indicating that in countries with higher labor productivity it is the more educated migrants who are most likely to leave.[12]

Any analysis of migrant selection based on observed characteristics leaves open the question of how migrants are selected on unobservables. McKenzie, Gibson, and Stillman (2006) examine this issue using data on Tonga. Citizens of Tonga can enter a lottery to obtain a visa to move to New Zealand. Comparing visa applicants who lost the lottery (meaning they stayed in Tonga) with nonapplicants, McKenzie and his colleagues find that those desiring to migrate have higher earnings, controlling for observed characteristics, which suggests that prospective migrants from Tonga are positively selected in terms of unobserved skill. They also find that failing to account for selection on unobservables leads to substantial overstatement of the gains to migration.

What does the simple model of income maximization in (10.5) imply about how emigrants sort themselves across destination countries? Suppose the expression is rewritten as

---

12 In related work, Rosenzweig (2006) finds that the numbers of students who come to the United States for higher education and who stay in the United States after completing their education are each decreasing in the marginal product of labor in the source country, suggesting that low rewards for skill in a country induce students seeking university training to pursue their schooling abroad.

$$\ln\frac{E_{sr}^c}{E_s^c} - \ln\frac{E_{sr}^p}{E_s^p} = \left(W_r^c - W_r^p\right) + \alpha_s + \eta_{sr}, \qquad (10.8)$$

where $\alpha_s$ is a country fixed effect that absorbs sending-country wages, and $\eta_{sr}$ is a disturbance term capturing measurement error in migration flows. Equation (10.8) is a regression specification that predicts that more skilled workers will flow in greater numbers to receiving countries that have larger rewards for skill, expressed here by the level difference in wages between high- and low-educated labor. Grogger and I (2007) develop a fixed-effects specification similar to 10.8) and, using data from Beine, Docquier, and Rapoport (2006b), find that the bilateral flow of more educated migrants relative to less educated migrants is increasing in the destination-country earnings gap between high-income and low-income workers.

Their results can account for the observed pattern of emigrant sorting across destinations, as seen in table 10.3. The United States is by far the largest destination country for international migrants, and Canada is the second largest. In 2000, 53 percent of the foreign-born population in OECD countries resided in North America, while 36 percent resided in the European Union and 10 percent resided in Asia and Oceania. The draw of the United States and Canada is strongest for the more educated. Although North America attracts only 35 percent of emigrants with a primary education, it attracts 66 percent of emigrants with tertiary education. In Europe, the shares are flipped, because it attracts 24 percent of emigrants with tertiary schooling and 56 percent of emigrants with primary schooling.

The pattern of emigrant sorting in table 10.3 is consistent with observed differences in the reward for skill. Among OECD destinations, the level difference in income between high-skill and low-skill labor is largest in the United States. Canada has the fourth-largest difference (and the United Kingdom and Australia are second and third, respectively). By contrast, continental Europe has a relatively low income gap between high- and low-skill labor, consistent with relatively low income inequality. The consequence of these income differences appears to be that North America and Australia

Table 10.3 Share of OECD Immigrants, by Receiving Region and Education, 2000 (percent)

| Destination region | All | Education group | | |
|---|---|---|---|---|
| | | Primary | Secondary | Tertiary |
| North America | 51.4 | 35.2 | 54.0 | 65.5 |
| European Union | 38.4 | 56.0 | 34.9 | 23.6 |
| Asia and Oceania | 10.2 | 8.8 | 11.1 | 10.9 |
| All OECD | | 35.5 | 29.2 | 35.3 |

*Source:* Grogger and Hanson 2007.

attract a more highly skilled mix of immigrants, whereas continental Europe attracts a less skilled mix.

## Networks and Migration Costs

Although the evidence in table 10.2 points to growth in international migration, the global stock of emigrants remains small, at about 3 percent of the world population. This figure is surprising, because the gains in international migration appear to be huge. In earlier work (Hanson 2006), I report that in 2000 the average hourly wage for a male with nine years of education was $2.40 in Mexico and $8.70 for recent Mexican immigrants in the United States in PPP-adjusted prices. Based on an average work week for U.S. adult male workers of 35 hours, these wages would amount to an annual income gain of $12,000.

One way in which to reconcile large and persistent cross-country income differences with small global labor movements is to recognize that receiving countries are successful in restricting labor inflows. Although the long queues for immigration visas in receiving countries reflect the legal admission restrictions, the rising levels of illegal immigration suggest that the borders are porous. Furthermore, the observed costs of illegal entry are small when compared with the estimated income gains. In a sample of high-migration communities in Mexico over the period 2002–2004, Cornelius (2005) finds that migrants paid on average $1,700 to be smuggled across the U.S. border, or one-seventh the apparent income gain.

Another explanation for small global labor flows is the existence of large unobserved migration costs associated with credit constraints in financing migration, uncertainty over economic opportunities abroad, the psychological cost of leaving home, or other factors. There is considerable academic interest in the role of migration networks in lowering such costs. Survey evidence suggests that transnational migration networks provide prospective migrants with information about economic conditions in destination countries, support in managing the immigration process, and help in obtaining housing and finding a job (Massey, Goldring, and Durand 1994; Massey and Espinosa, 1997). Much of the research on migration networks focuses on Mexico. On the process of crossing the border, Orrenius and Zavodny (2005) report that among young males in Mexico the probability of migrating to the United States is higher for those whose fathers or siblings have emigrated. Gathmann (2004) documents that migrants with family members in the United States are less likely to hire the services of a professional smuggler, and that those who do are likely to pay lower prices. Finally, McKenzie and Rapoport (2006) find that average schooling is lower among migrants from communities in Mexico with a stronger U.S. presence. These results are each consistent with the notion that networks lower migration costs.

Although economists still know little about the magnitude of migration costs, research on networks suggests that migrant flows are sensitive to changes in these costs. Other evidence of the sensitivity of migration to migration costs is found in the illegal crossings at the Mexico-U.S. border. For illegal migration, the intensity of border enforcement is an important determinant of entry costs, which take the form of fees paid to smugglers. Cornelius (2005) reports that smuggler prices to enter the United States illegally increased by 37 percent between 1996–1998 and 2002–2004, which spans the period during which the United States stepped up border enforcement efforts in response to the terrorist attacks of September 11, 2001.

Gathmann (2004) examines the consequences of expanded border enforcement for migration. She identifies the correlates of smuggler prices paid by migrants from Mexico to the United States and estimates the impact of smuggler prices on migrant demand for smuggler services. The price a migrant pays to a smuggler is higher in years when border enforcement is higher, but the elasticity of smuggler prices with respect to enforcement is small, in the range of 0.2–0.5. During the sample period, a one-standard-deviation increase in enforcement would have led to an increase in smuggler prices of less than $40. The demand for smuggler services and the probability of choosing to migrate to the United States are both responsive to changes in smugglers' prices. However, because of the small enforcement elasticity of smugglers' prices, the increase in U.S. border enforcement from 1986 to 1998 (during which real spending on border enforcement increased by four times) would have reduced the average migration probability in Mexico by only 10 percent.

In many destination countries, migrants reinforce networks by forming hometown associations that help members of their home communities make the transition to living in a new location. By creating links between the destination country and a specific community in the source country, these associations may lower migration costs for individuals linked by kinship or birthplace to migrants living abroad. Of the 218 hometown associations formed by Mexican immigrants and enumerated in a 2002 survey in California, 87 percent were associated with one of the nine central and western states in Mexico that have dominated migration to the United States since the early 20th century (Cano 2004), indicating that migrant networks in Mexico are organized along regional lines.

Regional variation in migration networks creates regional variation in migration dynamics. McKenzie and Rapoport (2007) reveal that in Mexican communities with historically weak migration networks, moderately wealthier individuals are more likely to migrate, though very high-wealth individuals are not. Migrants are thus drawn from the middle of the wealth distribution, meaning that migration increases inequality. In communities with strong migration networks, however, lower-wealth individuals can afford to migrate, so that in these locations migration lowers inequality.

Emigration changes a country's supply of labor, skills mix, and exposure to the global economy. These effects may have important consequences for a sending country's aggregate output, structure of wages, fiscal accounts, and trade and investment flows, among other outcomes. In this section, I discuss recent empirical research on the impact of emigration on developing economies.

### Labor Markets and Fiscal Accounts

Most research on the labor market impacts of emigration focuses on Mexico. Mishra (2007) examines the correlation between emigration to the United States and decadal changes in wages for cohorts in Mexico defined by their years of schooling and labor market experience. She estimates that over the period 1970–2000 the elasticity of wages for emigration in Mexico is 0.4, implying that a 10 percent reduction in the labor supply because of emigration would raise wages by 4 percent. Using a similar approach, Aydemir and Borjas (2007) estimate a wage elasticity for emigration in Mexico of 0.6. Wage elasticities of this magnitude suggest that emigration has had a substantial impact on Mexico's wage structure. Based on her estimation results and that fact that 13 percent of Mexico's labor force emigrated to the United States between 1970 and 2000, Mishra (2007) calculates that emigration has raised average wages in the country by 8 percent. Upward wage pressure has been strongest for young adults with above-average education levels (those with 9–15 years of schooling), who in the 1990s were those most likely to emigrate (Chiquiar and Hanson 2005).

In response to changes in the labor supply associated with emigration, one might expect the supply of capital in Mexico to adjust, with the country becoming less attractive to inward foreign direct investment. Alternatively, higher wages could erode Mexico's comparative advantage in labor-intensive industries, reducing the net exports of labor services embodied in goods as a consequence of emigration-induced Dutch disease. Either change would tend to offset the effects of emigration on wages in the country. Because the estimation approaches in Mishra (2007) and Aydemir and Borjas (2007) are reduced form, they capture the wage impact of emigration, *net* of these and other adjustments. Their results suggest that any response of capital accumulation or trade to emigration is too slow or too small to undo the wage consequences of labor outflows, at least over 10-year time intervals. Such a finding is not all that surprising. Factor price differences between the United States and Mexico create an incentive for trade in goods, north-to-south flows of capital, and south-to-north flows of labor. Despite dramatic reductions in barriers to trade and investment between the two countries over the last two decades, U.S.-Mexico wage differences remain large. Because trade and investment are insufficient to equalize factor prices within North America, theory would predict that migration from Mexico to the United States would affect wages in both countries, consistent with the evidence.

The Mexican emigration experience differs from those of other countries in the absence of positive selection, the high fraction of those leaving who enter the destination country as illegal migrants, and the sheer scale of the exodus. The positive selection of emigrants in most source countries raises the prospect of important fiscal impacts from international migration. In countries with progressive income taxes, the loss of skilled emigrants could adversely affect public budgets through a loss of future tax contributions. These lost contributions are, in part, the returns to public investments in the education of emigrating workers, which, after emigration, accrue to the destination countries.

Although there is a large body of theoretical literature on the taxation of skilled emigration (e.g., Bhagwati and Hamada 1974; Bhagwati and Wilson 1989; Docquier and Rapoport 2007), empirical research on the subject is sparse. One recent contribution is that by Desai, Kapur, and McHale (2003), who examine the fiscal effects of the brain drain from India. In 2000, individuals with tertiary education made up 61 percent of Indian emigrants, but just 5 percent of India's total population. Between 1990 and 2000, the emigration rate for the tertiary-educated rose from 2.8 percent to 4.3 percent, compared with an increase of just 0.3 percent to 0.4 percent for the population as a whole. Desai, Kapur, and McHale find in their examination of Indian emigration to the United States that in 2000 it was host to 65 percent of India's skilled emigrants (and 49 percent of all Indian emigrants). They begin by producing a counterfactual income series that gives emigrants the income they would have earned in India based on their observed characteristics and the returns to these characteristics in India (using a Mincer wage regression). On the tax side, they calculate income tax losses by running the counterfactual income series through the Indian income tax schedule and indirect tax losses by using estimates of indirect tax payments per unit of gross national income. On the spending side, they calculate expenditure savings by identifying categories for which savings would exist—which are most categories except interest payments and national defense—and then estimating savings per individual. The results suggest that Indian emigration to the United States cost India net tax contributions of 0.24 percent of GDP in 2000, which were partially offset by the tax take on remittances (coming off of the sales tax revenue generated by the extra spending that remittances make possible) of 0.1 percent of GDP. For India, then, the tax consequences of skilled emigration appear to be modest. For small countries with very high emigration rates (figure 10.4), the tax consequences would obviously be larger.

The research discussed so far addresses the static consequences of emigration for an economy, ignoring the dynamic considerations that may arise if skilled emigration raises the incentive of unskilled workers to acquire human capital. In theory, feedback effects from emigration to human capital accumulation may change a country's rate of economic growth. According to Mountford (1997), in the presence of human capital externalities an emigration-induced increase in the incentive to acquire skill can help an economy escape a poverty trap, characterized by low investment in education and low growth, and move to an equilibrium with high investment and high growth. Yet it is entirely possible for feedback effects to work in the opposite direction. Miyagiwa (1991) develops a model in which, because of human capital spillovers, the migration of skilled labor from a low-wage, skill-scarce economy to a high-wage, skill-abundant economy reinforces the incentive for a brain drain, depleting the low-wage country of skilled labor. In Wong and Yip (1999), the negative effects of a brain drain on the stock of human capital reduce the growth rate of the labor-exporting country.

Because plausible theoretical models offer very different predictions for the long-run consequences of skilled emigration, the effect of a brain drain on an economy is ultimately an empirical question. As mentioned in the second section of this chapter, the literature on how emigration affects the incentive to acquire skill has yet to produce conclusive results, making it impossible to say whether the consequences of a brain drain for growth are likely to be positive or negative. Case study evidence is similarly inconclusive. In China; India; and Taiwan, China, the migration of skilled labor to Silicon Valley in the United States—where Indian and Chinese immigrants account for one-third of the engineering labor force—has been followed by increased trade with and investment from the United States, helping to foster the creation of local high-technology industries (Saxenian 2002). The recent rise in educational attainment in those three economies may, in part, be the result of the lure of working in the United States and the domestic expansion of sectors intensive in the use of skilled technicians.[13] In Africa, however, the exodus of skilled professionals, many of whom work in health care, may adversely affect living standards.

### Remittances and Return Migration

In a static setting, if the only effect of international migration were to move labor from one country to another, welfare in the sending country would decline (Hamilton and Whalley 1984). Although the average incomes of migrants and destination-country natives would rise, the average income in the sending country would fall. Migrants, however, often send a portion of their income to family members at home, possibly reversing the income loss in the sending country associated with the depletion of labor. In the last several years, there has been substantial academic and policy interest in the consequences of remittances for economic activity in sending countries.

Table 10.4 shows workers' remittances received from abroad as a share of GDP by geographic region. Remittances have increased markedly in East Asia and the Pacific, Latin America and the Caribbean, South Asia, and Sub-Saharan Africa. As of 2004, remittances exceeded official development

---

13 Between 1990 and 2000, the share of the adult resident population (i.e., net of the brain drain) with a tertiary education rose from 2.0 percent to 2.7 percent in China; 4.1 percent to 4.8 percent in India; and 12.2 percent to 19.1 percent in Taiwan, China.

Table 10.4 Workers' Remittances and Compensation of Employees, 1992–2005 (percentage of GDP)

| Region | 1992 | 1996 | 2000 | 2002 | 2004 | 2005 |
|---|---|---|---|---|---|---|
| East Asia and Pacific | 0.56 | 0.71 | 1.00 | 1.47 | 1.48 | 1.50 |
| Europe and Central Asia | | 1.02 | 1.42 | 1.27 | 1.28 | 1.44 |
| Latin America and Caribbean | 0.70 | 0.79 | 1.04 | 1.67 | 2.06 | 1.98 |
| Middle East and North Africa | 8.31 | 3.69 | 3.07 | 3.76 | 4.31 | 4.13 |
| South Asia | 1.76 | 2.42 | 2.85 | 3.72 | 3.57 | 3.53 |
| Sub-Saharan Africa | 0.76 | 1.04 | 1.49 | 1.67 | 1.60 | 1.57 |

*Source:* Various issues of the World Bank's *World Development Indicators.*
*Note:* Empty cells indicate that data were missing in the source.

assistance in all regions except Sub-Saharan Africa and were greater than 65 percent of foreign direct investment inflows in all regions except Europe and Central Asia. Among the smaller countries of Central America, the Caribbean, and the South Pacific, remittances account for a large share of national income, ranging from 10 percent to 17 percent of GDP in the Dominican Republic, Guatemala, El Salvador, Honduras, Jamaica, and Nicaragua, and representing an astounding 53 percent of GDP in Haiti (Acosta, Fajnzylber, and Lopez 2007).

Reported remittances reflect those captured by the balance of payments, which Freund and Spatafora (2007) suggest may understate actual remittances. Formal remittance channels include banks and money transfer operators (e.g., Western Union) for which service fees average 11 percent of the value of remittances. Informal remittances, which are moved by couriers, relatives, or migrants themselves, tend to have lower fees, but presumably higher risk. Formal remittances correlate negatively with service charges; a 10 percent increase in fees associated with a 1.5 percent reduction in transfers. Fees are lower in economies that are dollarized and more developed financially (as measured by the ratio of bank deposits to GDP).

Theoretical literature on migration models remittances as the outcome of a dynamic contract between migrants and their families. A family helps finance migration costs for one of its members in return for a share of future income gains associated with having moved to a higher-wage location. Remittances are, then, the return on investments the family has made in the migrant. The prediction is that remittances rise after an increase in emigration and decline as existing emigrants age and pay off debts to their families.

Having migrants abroad may also provide insurance for a family. To the extent that income shocks are imperfectly correlated across countries, migration helps families smooth consumption over time by keeping remittances high when sending-country income is low relative to that of the destination country and low when sending-country income is relatively high (Rosenzweig and Stark 1989). Yang (2008) examines changes in remittances to households in the Philippines before and after the Asian financial crisis, which he uses as a natural experiment to examine the impact of remittances on household behavior. As of 1997, 6 percent of Philippine households had a member who had migrated abroad. Some had moved to countries in the Middle East, whose currencies appreciated sharply against the Philippine peso in 1997–1998, while others emigrated to countries in East Asia, whose currencies appreciated less sharply or even depreciated. Consistent with consumption smoothing, remittances increased more for households whose migrants resided in countries that experienced stronger currency appreciation against the peso. Because the income shocks associated with movements in exchange rates are largely transitory in nature, the responses of remittances reveal the extent to which migrants share transitory income gains with family members at home. Yang finds that a 10 percent depreciation of the Philippine peso is associated with a 6 percent increase in remittances.

Contrary to Yang's results, remittances appear to be unresponsive to changes in government transfers. In Mexico (Teruel and Davis 2000) and Honduras and Nicaragua (Olinto 2007), remittances are not correlated with changes in rural household receipts from conditional cash transfer programs, which were introduced into communities on a randomized basis, permitting experimental analysis of their impact on household behavior. Were remittances a vehicle for consumption smoothing among rural households, one would expect them to decline for a sending-country household following an exogenous increase in government income support.

In his look at the impact of remittances on education in the Philippines before and after the Asian financial crisis, Yang (2008) finds that households with migrants in countries experiencing stronger currency appreciation in relation to the Philippine peso had larger increases in spending on child education, spending on durable goods (televisions and motor vehicles), children's school attendance, and entrepreneurial investments. In these households, the labor supply of 10- to 17-year-old children fell by more than that in households without migrants, particularly for boys. In Mexico, Woodruff and Zenteno (2007) also find a positive correlation between migration and sending-country business formation. For a sample of small-scale enterprises, capital investment and capital output ratios are higher in firms where the owner was born in a state with higher rates of migration to the United States. Woodruff and Zenteno instrument for current state migration rates using proximity to the railroads along which Mexico's initial migration networks became established (Durand, Massey, and Zenteno 2001). Their results are consistent with two different mechanisms for business formation: (1) remittances relax credit constraints on the creation of small enterprises, or (2) return migrants—who may have accumulated valuable work experience in the United States—are more likely to launch new businesses upon returning to Mexico.

Remittances indicate that migrants maintain contacts with family members at home. They may do so, in part, because they anticipate eventually returning home, and so return migration may depend on their foreign earning opportunities. Yang (2006) finds that an exchange rate shock that raises the peso value of foreign earnings reduces the likelihood that a Philippine emigrant returns home; 10 percent real appreciation is associated with a one-year return rate that is 1.4 percent lower.

One potential negative consequence of remittances is an increase in the demand for nontraded goods and services, driving up their prices and contributing to real exchange rate appreciation. Concerns about Dutch disease would be particularly acute for small countries experiencing large labor outflows, including many economies in Central America, the Caribbean, and the Pacific. Research into the consequences of emigration for real exchange rates is still in its early stages.

## Information and the Flow of Ideas

The positive correlation between bilateral trade and migration has been interpreted as evidence of a "diaspora externality," in which previous waves of migration create cross-national networks that facilitate exchange. Gould (1994) finds that bilateral trade involving the United States is larger with countries that have larger immigrant populations in the United States. Head, Reis, and Swenson (1998) reveal that a 10 percent increase in Canada's immigrant population from a particular country is associated with a 1 percent increase in bilateral Canadian exports and a 3 percent increase in bilateral Canadian imports. More recent immigration has an even stronger correlation with trade. It is difficult to draw causal inferences from these results, because immigration may be correlated with unobserved factors that also affect trade, such as the trading partners' cultural similarity or bilateral economic policies (e.g., preferential trade policies or investment treaties that raise the return to both migration and trade).

Pushing the analysis a step further, Rauch and Trindade (2002) focus specifically on networks associated with overseas Chinese populations. Successive waves of emigration from southeastern China have created communities of ethnic Chinese throughout Southeast Asia, as well as in South Asia and on the east coast of Africa. Rauch and Trindade find that bilateral trade is positively correlated with the interaction between two countries' Chinese populations (expressed as shares of the national population), which is similar to the findings in Gould (1994) and Head, Ries, and Swenson (1998). More interesting, the correlation between Chinese populations and trade is stronger for differentiated products than it is for homogeneous goods. To the extent that differentiated products are more subject to informational problems in exchange (Rauch 1999), these are the goods one would expect to be the most sensitive to the presence of business networks.

Still unclear is whether greater trade is the natural outcome of increased migration or a reflection of the types of people who select into migration. If those who are more highly skilled are more likely to migrate abroad and to exploit opportunities for commercial exchange, then the correlation between trade and migration may be a by-product of migrant self-selection.

Subsequent policies to liberalize immigration in destination countries would not necessarily increase trade with sending countries, unless they allowed for the admission of individuals with a propensity to engage in trade. Head, Ries, and Swenson (1998) find that immigrants admitted as refugees or on the basis of family ties with Canadian residents have a smaller effect on trade than immigrants admitted under a point system that values labor market skills.

More controversial is the impact of emigration on political outcomes in sending countries. When individuals live and work in another country, they are exposed to new political ideologies and alternative systems of government. This exposure may be the most important for students who go abroad to obtain a university degree, because they are at an impressionable age and often travel on visas that require them to return to home after completing their studies. Spilimbergo (2006) suggests that there is an association between a country's democratic tendencies and the political systems of the countries under which its students did their university training. He finds a positive correlation between the democracy index in a sending country and the average democracy index in the countries in which a country's emigrant students have studied. Unknown is whether the political system of the sending country influences the types of countries in which its students choose to study. Kim (1998), for example, finds that the bilateral flow of foreign students is larger between countries that share a common religion.

## Summary and Conclusions

Over the last decade and a half, migration flows from low- and middle-income countries to high-income countries have been increasing. This phenomenon is just beginning to be understood, because cross-country data on international migration have only recently become available. Another factor hindering research is that migration is jointly determined with many other outcomes, complicating causal inference from the impact of migration on economic development. With these concerns in mind, I summarize what appear to be the more robust findings (or nonfindings) in the literature:

1. *Bilateral migration flows are negatively affected by migration costs, as captured by the geographic or linguistic distance between countries, the absence of migration networks, or the stringency of border enforcement against illegal entry.* That migration is negatively correlated with migration costs is not surprising. What is surprising is that migration flows are so small in relation to observed migration costs, suggesting that the unobserved costs—broadly defined—must be substantial.
2. *Emigration rates are highest for those in the middle-income group of developing countries and for developing countries with higher population densities.* The inverted U-shaped relationship between average income and migration is suggestive of credit constraints that prevent

individuals with very low incomes from being able to finance migration through borrowing.

3. *In most developing countries, the more educated are the most likely to emigrate.* In the large majority of sending countries, emigrants are positively selected in terms of observable skill. In theory, positive selection would result from large international differences in labor productivity, small international differences in the return to skill, or migration costs that do not increase in skill too strongly. In Australia, Europe, and North America, high labor productivity attracts the more educated immigrants from low-income countries, despite the fact that many of these individuals could earn a higher annual percentage return on their schooling at home.

4. *Emigrants sort themselves across destinations according to income-earning possibilities, and the countries that have the highest incomes for skilled labor attract the most educated mix of immigrants.* The ability of a country to attract more highly skilled emigrants appears to depend on its reward to skill relative to that of other destinations. Thus, Australia, Canada, the United Kingdom, and the United States, where high-skilled workers enjoy relatively high earnings, attract a more highly skilled mix of emigrants than continental Europe.

5. *Empirically, the impact of opportunities for skilled emigration on the stock of human capital in a country is unknown.* Over the last decade, the new theoretical literature that has emerged has taken a more sanguine view of the brain drain. Although the notion that skilled emigration raises the incentive of those left behind to acquire skills is plausible, the literature is missing well-identified econometric estimates of how human capital accumulation and economic growth respond to labor outflows. Economists still do not know whether opportunities for skilled emigration create a brain drain or a brain gain.

6. *There is some evidence that emigration puts upward pressure on wages in sending countries.* Economic theory suggests that, in the short run, the exodus of labor from a country would raise wages. Evidence from Mexico indicates that emigration has increased wages for the skill groups and regions with the highest emigration rates. The preponderance of relatively highly educated individuals among emigrants suggests that labor outflows may have adverse consequences on sending countries' public finances. However, for India the fiscal effects of skilled emigration appear to be small. If emigration affects the wage structure, one would expect it also to affect housing prices, but research on how labor outflows affect real estate values is scant.

7. *Migrant remittances tend to positively correlate with household consumption and investments in education and entrepreneurial activities in sending countries.* For households sending migrants abroad, remittances may largely replace the income lost from the lower labor supply on the national labor market. Because remittances appear to decline with a migrant's time abroad, the sending-country income boost from emigration may not be long-lived.

Despite recent advances in the theoretical and empirical analysis of international migration, a great deal is still not known about global labor movements. Much of the individual-level data on international migration covers Mexico and the United States, which are the subject of a large literature. But there is still more to learn about these largest sending and receiving countries. And yet the highest payoff to research is likely to be in the many understudied parts of the world. Since 1990, Central and Eastern Europe have become major sending regions; the Gulf States, the Russian Federation, and Spain have become an important receiving regions; and emigration from China, India, Indonesia, Pakistan, and the Philippines have accelerated—and these are only a few of the recent developments in global labor flows.

Among the many questions about international migration that deserve further study, I would emphasize the following:

- Analysts know little about the magnitude of international migration costs. What is the relative importance of uncertainty, credit constraints, and destination-country admission policies in keeping the poor from migrating to rich economies?
- Although there is evidence that migration networks play an important role in reducing moving costs, the dynamics of networks are poorly understood. Are there diminishing returns in the impact of network size on migration costs? Or does the existence of networks imply that the spatial opportunities for emigration will only become more unequal over time?
- Analysts still know little empirically about the factors that determine who leaves different countries. What are the contributions of international differences in labor productivity, returns to schooling, and migration costs to migrant selection? How does the exodus of skilled labor affect the wage structure, housing values, and the real exchange rate?
- Because of the importance of human capital in economic development, how skilled emigration affects a country's relative supply of skills is a question of first-order policy importance. How do changes in the education, tax, or other policies of developing countries affect skilled emigration, the domestic supply of skills, or remittances from skilled emigrants?
- Because the sending and receiving countries are still far from having equal factor prices, trade, migration, and foreign direct investment may happen concurrently, even reinforcing one another. How does migration interact with international trade and foreign direct investment?
- The inflow of remittances has been a welcome financial boon for many labor-exporting countries. Do remittances help deepen domestic financial markets as households use banks or other intermediaries to manage lumpy income receipts from abroad?

Some members of the development policy community are calling for rich countries to open their economies more widely to labor inflows from poor countries (see, e.g., Prichett 2006). Completely open borders are off the table politically. Were the developed world to propose an increase in immigration quotas, should developing countries take it up on the offer? The answer would depend on how destination countries structure the additional labor inflows. An increase in immigration quotas that targets workers with higher levels of skill could raise global income, even as it hurts the less skilled majority in source countries (Benhabib and Jovanovic 2007). Quotas targeted to less skilled workers could raise global welfare. The adoption of such a policy would surely face opposition in receiving countries because of concerns about fiscal and labor market consequences. Convincing sending and receiving countries to coordinate on international migration is a difficult task. A helpful first step would be to determine whether the interests of the two groups of countries are really as far apart as they seem.

## References

Acosta, Pablo, Pablo Fajnzylber, and Humberto Lopez. 2007. "How Important Are Remittances in America?" In *Close to Home*, ed. Pablo Fajnzylber and Humberto Lopez. Washington, DC: World Bank.

Adams, Richard. 2003. "International Migration, Remittances, and Brain Drain: A Study of 24 Labor Exporting Countries." Policy Research Working Paper 2972, World Bank, Washington, DC.

Assunção, Juliano J., and Leandro S. Carvalho. Forthcoming. "Financial Constraints, Migration, and Inequality." *Journal of Development Economics*.

Aydemir, Abdurrahman, and George J. Borjas. 2007. "A Comparative Analysis of the Labor Market Impact of International Migration: Canada, Mexico, and the United States." *Journal of the European Economic Association* 5 (4): 663–708.

Barro, Robert J., and Jong-Wha Lee. 2000. "International Data on Educational Attainment: Updates and Implications." Working Paper 42, Weatherhead Center for International Development, Harvard University, Cambridge, MA.

Beine, Michel, Frédéric Docquier, and Hillel Rapoport. 2001. "Brain Drain and Economic Growth: Theory and Evidence." *Journal of Development Economics* 64 (1): 275–89.

———. 2006a. "Brain Drain and Human Capital Formation in Developing Countries: Winners and Losers." IRES Working Paper 2006-23, Institute for Resources, Environment and Sustainability, University of British Columbia, Vancouver.

———. 2006b. "Measuring International Skilled Migration: New Estimates Accounting for Age of Entry." Research Report, World Bank, Washington, DC.

Benhabib, Jess, and Boyan Jovanovic. 2007. "Optimal Migration: A World Perspective." Working Paper 12871, National Bureau of Economic Research, Cambridge, MA.

Bhagwati, Jagdish N., and Koichi Hamada. 1974. "The Brain Drain, International Integration of Markets for Professionals, and Unemployment." *Journal of Development Economics* 1 (1): 19–42.

Bhagwati, Jagdish N., and Carlos Rodriguez. 1975. "Welfare Theoretic Analyses of the Brain Drain." *Journal of Development Economics* 2 (3): 195–221.

Bhagwati, Jagdish N., and John Wilson, eds. 1989. *Income Taxation and International Mobility*, Cambridge, MA: MIT Press.

Boeri, Tito, Barry McCormick, and Gordon H. Hanson. 2002. *Immigration Policy and the Welfare State*. Oxford: Oxford University Press.

Borjas, George J. 1987. "Self-Selection and the Earnings of Immigrants." *American Economic Review* 77 (4): 531–53.

———. 1991. "Immigration and Self-Selection." In *Immigration, Trade, and the Labor Market*, ed. John Abowd and Richard Freeman, 29–76. Chicago: University of Chicago Press.

———. 1999a. "The Economic Analysis of Immigration." In *Handbook of Labor Economics*, ed. Orley C. Ashenfelter and David Card, 1697–760. Amsterdam: North-Holland.

———. 1999b. *Heaven's Door: Immigration Policy and the American Economy*. Princeton, NJ: Princeton University Press.

———. 2006. "Labor Outflows and Labor Inflows in Puerto Rico." Unpublished paper, Harvard University, Cambridge, MA.

———. ed. 2007. *Mexican Immigration*. Chicago: University of Chicago Press; Cambridge, MA: National Bureau of Economic Research.

Borjas, George J., and Lynette Hilton. 1996. "Immigration and the Welfare State: Immigrant Participation in Means-Tested Entitlement Programs" *Quarterly Journal of Economics* 111 (2): 575–604.

Cano, Gustavo. 2004. "Organizing Immigrant Communities in American Cities: Is This Transnationalism, or What?" Working Paper 103, Center for Comparative Immigration Studies, University of California, San Diego.

Card, David. 2005. "Is the New Immigration Really So Bad?" *Economic Journal* 115 (507): 300–23.

Carrington, William J., and Enrica Detragiache. 1998. "How Big Is the Brain Drain?" Working Paper 98/102, International Monetary Fund, Washington, DC.

Chiquiar, Daniel, and Gordon Hanson. 2005. "International Migration, Self-Selection, and the Distribution of Wages: Evidence from Mexico and the United States." *Journal of Political Economy* 113 (April): 239–81.

Clark, Ximena, Timothy Hatton, and Jeffrey Williamson. 2007. "Explaining U.S. Immigration, 1971–1998." *Review of Economics and Statistics* 89 (2): 359–73.

Cornelius, Wayne A. 2005. "Impacts of U.S. Immigration Control Policies on Migratory Behavior: The View from Mexican Sending Communities." Unpublished paper, University of California, San Diego.

Cortes, Patricia. 2005. "The Effects of Low-Skilled Immigration on US Prices: Evidence from CPI Data." Unpublished paper, Massachusetts Institute of Technology, Cambridge, MA.

Cuecuecha, Alfredo. 2005. "The Immigration of Educated Mexicans: The Role of Informal Social Insurance and Migration Costs." Unpublished paper, Instituto Tecnológico Autónomo de México (ITAM), Mexico City.

Desai, Mihir, Devesh Kapur, and John McHale. 2003. "The Fiscal Impact of High Skilled Emigration: Flows of Indians to the U.S." Working Paper 03–01, Weatherhead Center for International Affairs, Harvard University, Cambridge, MA.

Docquier, Frederic, and Abdeslam Marfouk. 2006. "International Migration by Educational Attainment, 1990–2000." In *International Migration, Remittances, and the Brain Drain,* ed. Caglar Ozden and Maurice Schiff, 151–200. Washington, DC: World Bank; New York: Palgrave Macmillan.

Docquier, Frederic, and Hillel Rapoport. 2007. "Skilled Migration: The Perspective of Developing Countries." Unpublished paper, Bar-Ilan University, Ramat-Gan, Israel.

Durand, Jorge, Douglas S. Massey, and Rene M. Zenteno. 2001. "Mexican Immigration in the United States." *Latin American Research Review* 36 (1): 107–27.

Fajnzylber, Pablo, and Humberto Lopez, eds. 2007. *Close to Home.* Washington, DC: World Bank.

Feliciano, Zadia. 2001. "The Skill and Economic Performance of Mexican Immigrants from 1910 to 1990." *Explorations in Economic History* 38: 386–409.

Fernandez-Huertas, Jesus. 2006. "New Evidence on Emigration Selection." Unpublished paper, Columbia University, New York.

Freund, Caroline, and Nicola Spatafora. 2007. "Informality and Remittances." Unpublished paper, World Bank, Washington, DC.

Gathmann, Christina. 2004. "The Effects of Enforcement on Illegal Markets: Evidence from Migrant Smuggling on the Southwestern Border." Discussion Paper 1004, Institute for the Study of Labor (IZA), Bonn, Germany.

Gould, David M. 1994. "Immigration Links to the Home Country: Empirical Implications for U.S. Bilateral Trade Flows." *Review of Economics and Statistics* 76: 302–16.

Grogger, Jeffrey, and Gordon H. Hanson. 2007. "Income Maximization and the Sorting of Emigrants across Destinations." Unpublished paper, University of California, San Diego.

Hamilton, Bob, and John Whalley. 1984. "Efficiency and Distributional Implications of Global Restrictions on Labor Mobility." *Journal of Development Economics* 14 (1): 61–75.

Hanson, Gordon H. 2006. "Illegal Migration from Mexico to the United States." *Journal of Economic Literature* 44: 869–924.

———. 2007. "International Migration and the Developing World." Unpublished paper, University of California, San Diego.

Hanson, Gordon H., Kenneth Scheve, and Matthew J. Slaughter. 2007. "Local Public Finance and Individual Preferences over Globalization Strategies." *Economics and Politics* 19: 1–33.

———. 2005. "A Dual Policy Paradox: Why Have Trade and Immigration Policies Always Differed in Labor-Scarce Economies." Working Paper 11866, National Bureau of Economic Research, Cambridge, MA.

Hatton, Timothy J., and Jeffrey G. Williamson. 2004. "Refugees, Asylum Seekers and Policy in Europe." Working Paper 10680, National Bureau of Economic Research, Cambridge, MA.

Head, Keith, John Ries, and Deborah Swenson. 1998. "Immigration and Trade Creation: Econometric Evidence from Canada." *Canadian Journal of Economics* 31 (1): 47–62.

Ibarraran, Pablo, and Darren Lubotsky. 2007. "The Socioeconomic Status of Mexican Migrant Families: New Evidence from the 2000 Mexican Census." In *Mexican Immigration to the United States,* ed. George J. Borjas. Chicago: University of Chicago; Cambridge, MA: National Bureau of Economic Research.

Kim, Jinyoung, 1998. "Economic Analysis of Foreign Education and Students Abroad." *Journal of Development Economics* 56 (2): 337–65.

Lucas, Robert E. B. 1988. "On the Mechanics of Economic Development." *Journal of Monetary Economics* 22 (3): 3–42.

Massey, Douglas S., and Kristin E. Espinosa. 1997. "What's Driving Mexico-U.S. Migration? A Theoretical, Empirical, and Policy Analysis." *American Journal of Sociology* 102 (4): 939–99.

Massey, Douglas S., L. Goldring, and Jorge Durand. 1994. "Continuities in Transnational Migration: An Analysis of Nineteen Mexican Communities." *American Journal of Sociology* 99 (6): 1492–533.

Mayda, Anna Maria. 2005. "International Migration: A Panel Data Analysis of Economic and Non-economic Determinants." Discussion Paper 1590, Institute for the Study of Labor, Bonn, Germany.

McHale, John. 2007. "Taxation and Skilled Indian Migration to the United States: Revisiting the Bhagwati Tax." Unpublished paper, Queen's University, Kingston, ON.

McKenzie, David, and Hillel Rapoport. 2006. "Self-Selection Patterns in Mexico-U.S. Migration: The Role of Migration Networks." Unpublished paper, World Bank, Washington, DC, and Bar-Ilan University, Ramat-Gan, Israel.

———. 2007. "Network Effects and the Dynamics of Migration and Inequality: Theory and Evidence from Mexico." *Journal of Development Economics* 84 (1): 1–24.

McKenzie, David, John Gibson, and Steven Stillman. 2006. "How Important Is Selection? Experimental versus Non-experimental Measures of the Income Gains from Migration." Unpublished paper, World Bank, Washington, DC.

Mishra, Prachi. 2007. "Emigration and Wages in Source Countries: Evidence from Mexico." *Journal of Development Economics* 82 (1): 180–99.

Miyagiwa, Kaz. 1991. "Scale Economies in Education and the Brain Drain Problem." *International Economic Review* 32 (3): 743–59.

Mountford, Andrew. 1997. "Can a Brain Drain Be Good for Growth in the Source Economy?" *Journal of Development Economics* 53 (2): 287–303.

OECD (Organisation for Economic Co-operation and Development). 2006. *International Migration Outlook.* Paris: OECD.

Olinto, Pedro. 2007. "Do Conditional Cash Transfer Programs Crowd Out Private Transfers?" In *Close to Home,* ed. Pablo Fajnzylber and Humberto Lopez. Washington, DC: World Bank.

Orrenius, Pia M., and Madeline Zavodny. 2005. "Self-Selection among Undocumented Immigrants from Mexico." *Journal of Development Economics* 78 (1): 215–40.

Ottaviano, Gianmarco I. P., and Giovanni Peri. 2006. "Rethinking the Effects of Immigration on Wages." Working Paper 12497, National Bureau of Economic Research, Cambridge, MA.

Ozden, Caglar, and Maurice Schiff, eds. 2006. *International Migration, Remittances, and the Brain Drain.* Washington, DC: World Bank; New York: Palgrave McMillan.

Pritchett, Lant. 2006. *Let Their People Come: Breaking the Gridlock on Global Labor Mobility.* Washington, DC: Center for Global Development.

Ramos, Fernando. 1992. "Out-Migration and Return Migration of Puerto Ricans." In *Immigration and the Work Force,* ed. George Borjas and Richard Freeman. Chicago: University of Chicago Press; Cambridge, MA: National Bureau of Economic Research.

Rapoport, Hillel. 2002. "Migration, Credit Constraints, and Self-Employment: A Simple Model of Occupational Choice, Inequality, and Growth." *Economics Bulletin* 15 (7): 1–5.

Ratha, Dilip, and William Shaw. 2007. "South-South Migration and Remittances." Unpublished paper, World Bank, Washington, DC.

Rauch, James E. 1999. "Networks versus Markets in International Trade." *Journal of International Economics* 48 (1): 7–35.

Rauch, James E., and Vitor Trindade. 2002. "Ethnic Chinese Networks in International Trade." *Review of Economics and Statistics* 84 (February): 116–30.

Rosenzweig, Mark. 2006. "Global Wage Differences and International Student Flows." In *Brookings Trade Forum: 2006,* ed. Susan M. Collins and Carol Graham. Washington, DC: Brookings.

———. 2007. "Education and Migration: A Global Perspective." Unpublished paper, Yale University, New Haven, CT.

Rosenzweig, Mark, and Oded Stark. 1989. "Consumption Smoothing, Migration, and Marriage: Evidence from Rural India." *Journal of Political Economy* 97 (4): 905–26.

Roy, A. D. 1951. "Some Thoughts on the Distribution of Earnings." *Oxford Economic Papers* 3 (June): 135–46.

Saxenian, AnnaLee. 2002. *Local and Global Networks of Immigrant Professionals in Silicon Valley.* San Francisco: Public Policy Institute of California.

Spilimbergo, Antonio. 2006. "Foreign Students and Democracy." Unpublished paper, International Monetary Fund, Washington, DC.

Stark, Oded, and You Qiang Wang. 2002. "Inducing Human Capital Formation: Migration as a Substitute for Subsidies." *Journal of Public Economics* 86 (1): 29–46.

Stark, Oded, Christian Helmenstein, and Alexia Prskawetz. 1997. "A Brain Gain with a Brain Drain." *Economics Letters* 55: 227–34.

Teruel, Graciela, and B. Davis. 2000. "Final Report: An Evaluation of the Impact of PROGRESA Cash Payments on Private Inter-Household Transfers." International Food Policy Research Institute, Washington, DC.

United Nations. 2005. "Trends in Total Migrant Stock: 2005 Revision." Department of Economic and Social Affairs, United Nations, New York.

Wellisch, Dietmar, and Uwe Walz. 1998. "Why Do Rich Countries Prefer Free Trade over Free Immigration? The Role of the Modern Welfare States." *European Economic Review* 42: 1595–612.

Wong, Kar-yiu, and Chong Kee Yip. 1999. "Education, Economic Growth, and Brain Drain." *Journal of Economic Dynamics and Control* 23: 699–726.

Woodruff, Christopher, and Rene Zenteno. 2007. "Migration Networks and Microenterprises in Mexico." *Journal of Development Economics* 82 (2): 509–28.

Yang, Dean. 2006. "Why Do Migrants Return to Poor Countries? Evidence from Philippine Migrants' Responses to Exchange Rate Shocks." *Review of Economics and Statistics* 88 (4): 715–35.

———. 2008. "International Migration, Remittances, and Household Investment: Evidence from Philippine Migrants' Exchange Rate Shocks." *Economic Journal* 118 (528): 591–630.

# CHAPTER 11

# The Cliff at the Border

*Lant Pritchett*

I begin with John Maynard Keynes's famous description of the world (well, London—well, upper-middle-class London) at the apex of the "first global-ization," just before that world's tragic end in the carnage of World War I. I divide his passage from *The Economic Consequences of the Peace* (1919) into four sections:

> What an extraordinary episode in the economic progress of man that age was which came to an end in August 1914! The greater part of the population, it is true, worked hard and lived at a low standard of comfort, yet were, to all appearances, reasonably contented with this lot. But escape was possible, for any man of capacity or character at all exceeding the average, into the mid-dle and upper classes, for whom life offered, at a low cost and with the least trouble, conveniences, comforts, and amenities beyond the compass of the richest and most powerful monarchs of other ages. The inhabitant of London could order by telephone, sipping his morning tea in bed, the various products of the whole earth, in such quantity as he might see fit, and reasonably expect their early delivery upon his doorstep.

This chapter is based, very loosely, on comments at a workshop sponsored by the Commission on Growth and Development. The author would like to thank Michael Clemens for comments on a preliminary version.

What better description could there be of the benefits to the sovereign consumer of the liberalization of goods (note he is already aware of the role of income inequality in this liberalization—these goods are available to the "middle and upper classes"). This description is even truer today, because technical advances have put even more "conveniences, comforts, and amenities"—such as air travel, cell phones, medical care, air conditioning—on offer, and globalization of the trade in goods has augmented this plenitude, leading to goods of amazing variety (such as foods from every corner of the earth), availability (such as fruits year-round), and low cost. The material lifestyle of the middle class of rich countries today far exceeds that of the nobility of centuries ago. Keynes continues:

> He could at the same moment and by the same means adventure his wealth in the natural resources and new enterprises of any quarter of the world, and share, without exertion or even trouble, in their prospective fruits and advantages; or he could decide to couple the security of his fortunes with the good faith of the townspeople of any substantial municipality in any continent that fancy or information might recommend.

Again, here is a wonderful description of the glories of the liberalization of capital—interestingly both equity and debt, and with more extensive bond markets than even exist today (the "townspeople" of the relatively few "substantial" municipalities are able to issue bonds internationally or, so much more prosaically, invite people to "couple" their fortunes with their "good faith"). But again today, one can, with the click of a button, "adventure [one's] wealth" into index funds of Indian stocks or Brazilian bonds. As for travel:

> He could secure forthwith, if he wished it, cheap and comfortable means of transit to any country or climate without passport or other formality, could dispatch his servant to the neighboring office of a bank for such supply of the precious metals as might seem convenient, and could then proceed abroad to foreign quarters, without knowledge of their religion, language, or customs, bearing coined wealth upon his person, and would consider himself greatly aggrieved and much surprised at the least interference.

Often overlooked in favor of the much more widely cited passages about Londoners enjoying the "products of the earth," this is an excellent description of the mobility of people. Notice that the travel is "without passport or other formality." Note also the sensitivity (or lack thereof?) to the interpersonal distribution of income and to whom these benefits of globalization are available tucked into just how one gets foreign exchange for travel: one "dispatches" one's servant, of course.

This liberality of the first globalization has not been re-created today, in two senses. Even for the elite of the world there is no longer travel without formality—even as a traveler from the most powerful nation on earth and with sufficient funds, I can attest to the need for constant "formalities" to travel. But, more important, at least within certain areas in the first globalization there had been free mobility for all people. Up until roughly 1914 there were open borders for the movement of labor from Europe to not just the Americas, Australia, and New Zealand but also to Latin America. The citizens of Great Britain could move to British colonies and could engage in more complex flows (e.g., some voluntary, some restricted, some forced) elsewhere within the British Empire as well (e.g., the movement of Indians to Africa and the Caribbean). This general free movement of unskilled labor has not been at all restored.

These three passages from Keynes illustrate the first point I wish to make. The world of the first great globalization came to an end, or at least the beginning of its end, in August 1914. The end of this first globalization was followed by some quite nasty bits of history, with two extremely bloody "world" wars, the rise of Leninism/Stalinism in Russia—with its brutality and famines and staggering loss of life orchestrated by the state—and the rise of fascism in Europe—with the attempted genocide of Jews and, again, a staggering loss of life orchestrated by the state.

Keynes himself, conscious of the world having lost the first peace, was instrumental in attempting to win the second peace after World War II by establishing institutions to re-create the globalization that had created the previous "extraordinary episode in the economic progress of man" and to avoid calamities. In this, the world has been fantastically successful in re-creating two of the three liberalities. But in the 30 years between 1914 and 1944 (the Bretton Woods conference) apparently all appetite disappeared for the third element of the first great globalization. There was no attempt to re-create the globalization of labor markets, no creation of institutions to encourage and manage that process, no equivalent of the World Trade Organization (WTO) or International Monetary Fund (IMF) for the movement of people.[1] This failure, combined with the movement for decolonization after World War II, has led us all into the grand experiment I call the world of the POSEBLL, a Proliferation of Sovereigns combined with Everything But Labor Liberalization. This acronym is sufficiently ugly that I must alert the reader about why I use it—to pose a question with a terrible pun at the end: is more than the POSEBLL possible?

The first point I wish to make is that the world of the POSEBLL has led, as expected, to equalization of the prices of goods and equalization of the prices of capital. But, perhaps unexpectedly, it has also led to very uneven progress in the newly proliferated sovereigns, and this, combined with the binding quantitative restrictions on the movement of labor, has also led to massive gaps in the wages of equivalent labor around the world and sustained divergence in the per capita incomes across nation-states.

Keynes goes on to make a much deeper point about attitudes, which leads to the second point I wish to make:

But, most important of all, he regarded this state of affairs as normal, certain, and permanent, except in the direction of further improvement, and any deviation from it as aberrant, scandalous, and avoidable. The projects and politics

---

1  In fact, an International Organization for Migration was set up (and still exists), but the objective of that group was to facilitate the return of refugees rather than to assume the broader policy agendas of the institutions intended at Bretton Woods (only after more than 50 years did the WTO acquire independent organizational status).

of militarism and imperialism, of racial and cultural rivalries, of monopolies, restrictions, and exclusion, which were to play the serpent to this paradise, were little more than the amusements of his daily newspaper, and appeared to exercise almost no influence at all on the ordinary course of social and economic life, the internationalization of which was nearly complete in practice.

What is interesting about this passage (and the end of the one that preceded it) is that "internationalization" was regarded as a perfectly normal course of events, and one would have been "aggrieved" and "surprised" at any attempts to deviate from this obvious and natural pattern of free movement (at least the free movement of Londoners with the wherewithal to have servants). Moreover, Keynes argued, people regarded this situation as "certain" and "permanent." The logic of internationalization was such obvious common sense that it was impossible to conceive of a move to a fundamentally different arrangement. But this world did end dramatically, and for a very long time, as what was so certain about the world became first contested and then obviously false.

Because I have begun with quotes from Keynes, let me now turn to his great predecessor Karl Marx, who wrote in *The Eighteenth Brumaire of Louis Bonaparte:*

> Hegel remarks somewhere that all great world-historic facts and personages appear, so to speak, twice. He forgot to add: the first time as tragedy, the second time as farce. . . . Men make their own history, but they do not make it as they please; they do not make it under self-selected circumstances, but under circumstances existing already, given and transmitted from the past. The tradition of all dead generations weighs like a nightmare on the brains of the living.

The second "globalization," the world of the POSEBLL, is repeating the "great world-historic facts" of the first great globalization, but this time, following the tragedy of its demise, as farce. The real puzzle is why people continue to assert that they live in an age of globalization when they so obviously do *not* live in a world of globalization. They live in an age of *nationalization,* a nationalization that is deep, radical, and unprecedented in the long history of mankind.[2] After all, their *first* encounter in *every* country they visit is with the people who enforce the regulations about the movement of people *intended* to keep the world from being flat—and it is obviously successful (which I will document at length with new empirical results about wage gaps).

The second section of this chapter addresses the conundrum that in this supposedly "globalized" world people think about "equity" in completely *nationalized* ways. This *nationalization* of the lived reality is so deep and so complete that lists of issues of "equity" and "justice" in a globalized world will include the following: (1) the differentials between Guatemalan men

---

2  I return to this point, especially in the second section. What is unique is not that the world is divided into a large number of sovereign states, but that this process of "globalizing" empires followed by fracturing into independent states has been repeated a number of times. What is new this time around is the association of the relatively new concept of the *nation* with the age-old concept of the *state*, which is what I refer to as "nationalization"—the combination of statehood and an ideology of the "nation" into "nation-states."

and Guatemalan women raised as an example of gender inequity; (2) the treatment of indigenous Guatemalans versus other Guatemalans raised as an example of ethnic inequity; (3) the issue of the gap between the landed and landless raised as an example of persistent economic inequity; (4) the reduction in trade barriers causing an increase in inequality across people of different skills raised as an example of the inequities induced by "globalization"; (5) the issue of education gaps between rich and poor within Guatemala presented as examples of perpetuation of poverty/inequality across generations; and (6) the issue of value chains in coffee sold by Guatemalan farmers adduced as inequities in globalization. One can get very far into lists of "equity" and "justice" problems around which people are willing to mobilize before the gap in wages induced by U.S. restrictions on the movement of Guatemalans ever comes up. Thomas Friedman can write that the world is flat in the same way, and for the same reasons Thomas Jefferson could write that "all men are created equal" while owning slaves—the nationalizing "tradition of dead generations" weighing on our (collective) brains.

In discussions of "globalization and equity" I am a triply impolite guest. First, I dispute the premise that, from the point of view of developing countries, "globalization" is a primary phenomenon of this time. Second, I argue that all of the issues discussed in the context of "globalization and equity" around "everything but labor liberalization" are trivial compared with the one that is not discussed—cross-border flows of labor. Third, I argue that economists lack a coherent way of talking about equity that does not depend on an arbitrary advancement of "nationality" to a first-rank justification of acceptable differences in well-being, which is an incoherent way of talking about globalization.

## The Proliferation of Sovereigns

I was born in Idaho, a state in the upper Northwest primarily famous for its potatoes and, at least for a while, for its crazy white supremacists and survivalists. Suppose that in 2009 Idaho withdrew from the (formerly) "United" States and became a sovereign country, with its own flag, military, money, laws, courts, passport—all the trappings of a sovereign state. At independence, suppose Idaho also simultaneously announced a 25 percent tariff on all goods entering Idaho from any foreign country, including the remaining 49 states. Now suppose time goes on and 10 years later, in 2019, Idaho "liberalizes" its trade by reducing its tariff to 10 percent. One could easily find the impact of this policy shift of some interest. But any academic who suggested that the "integration" of Idaho into the U.S. economy was the primary question of interest because of this modest liberalization of cross-border flows would be laughed out of the room. Obviously, the key question of interest would be the *disintegration* of Idaho from the rest of the United States, not the subsequent liberalization.

A central feature of the post–World War II period is the incredible proliferation of sovereign states; the number of nation-states has risen from about 50 to about 200. As illustrated in figure 11.1, this proliferation happened in roughly three waves: (1) one group immediately after World War II (including, importantly, Indonesia and India and Pakistan); (2) a group of primarily African countries gaining independence around the early 1960s (with another group of the once Portuguese colonies gaining independence in 1974 and 1975); and (3) the proliferation from the disintegration of the Soviet Union and some of its satellites (e.g., Czechoslovakia and Yugoslavia). So, although all of the major industrial countries have been sovereign states for 100 years or more, most poorer countries (the obvious regional exception is Latin America) were in some kind of colonial or quasi-colonial relationship that limited sovereignty over policies until relatively recently.

Many of these countries, on acquiring sovereignty over economic policy did pursue a rather aggressive form of the use of trade barriers for many reasons. Those reasons included revenue needs from tariff collections and export taxes in the absence of other revenue instruments, reaction to the enforced liberality under colonialism, and the wish to assert autonomy, as well as a general ideology of state-led industrialization. Since the emergence of the debt crisis, signaled by Mexico's August 1982 announcement that it would not be able to service its debt, there has been a cumulative, gradual, but by now nearly complete shift toward dismantling the more egregious barriers and a general liberalization of trade.

However, very few countries have gone beyond liberalization of the cross-border trade in goods (which has included regional customs unions and "free trade" areas) and the relaxation of control on some types of capital flows to engage in any really significant "deep integration" (e.g., common currencies, free movement of labor, or harmonization of regulation). In fact, about the only significant experience with "deep integration" has been that of the European Union and, to a much lesser extent, the North American Free Trade Agreement (NAFTA).

Which is more important in the experience of, say, Kenya or Jamaica or Indonesia, the nationalization implicit in sovereignty or the globalization implicit in the cross-border liberalization of the flows of goods (and perhaps capital)?

A set of recent studies examined the extent to which trade between Canadian provinces exceeded that of trade between a Canadian province and a U.S. state. The pioneering paper by McCallum (1995) reported that annual trade between British Columbia and Ontario was $1.4 billion and trade with Texas was only $155 million, but could be predicted at $2.1 billion if Texas were treated as a province of Canada and thus there was zero border effect (see figure 11.2). It is striking that one of the most liberalized borders in the world still appears to be a huge deterrent to trade. This suggests that the mere fact of the borders created—along with the creation of different currencies, different courts, and so forth—by the

Figure 11.1 New States Added Each Year, by Region, 1943–94

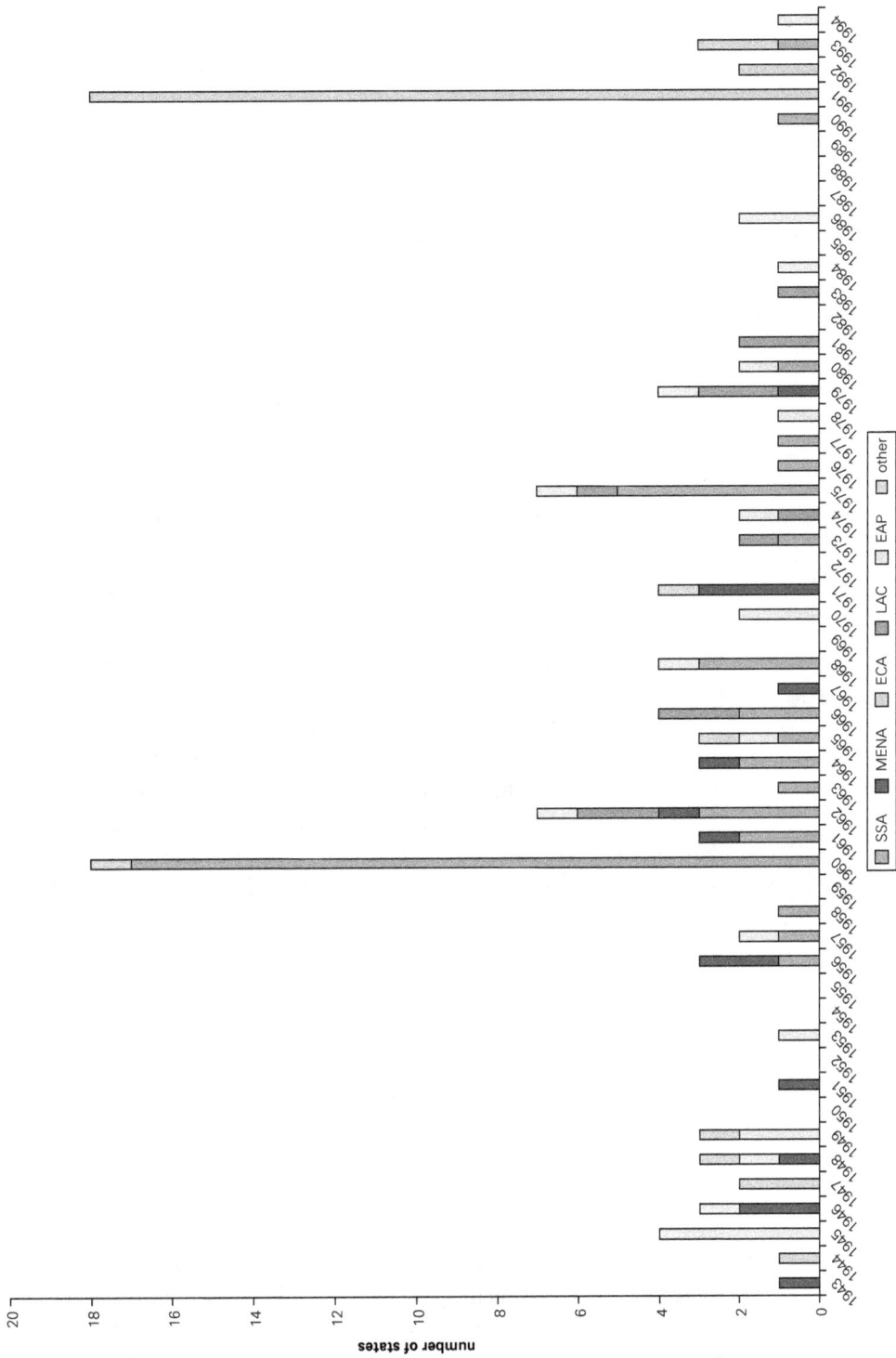

*Source:* Braun, Hausmann, and Pritchett 2004.
*Note:* SSA = Sub-Saharan Africa; ECA = Europe and Central Asia; EAP = East Asia and Pacific; MENA = Middle East and North Africa; LAC = Latin America and Caribbean.

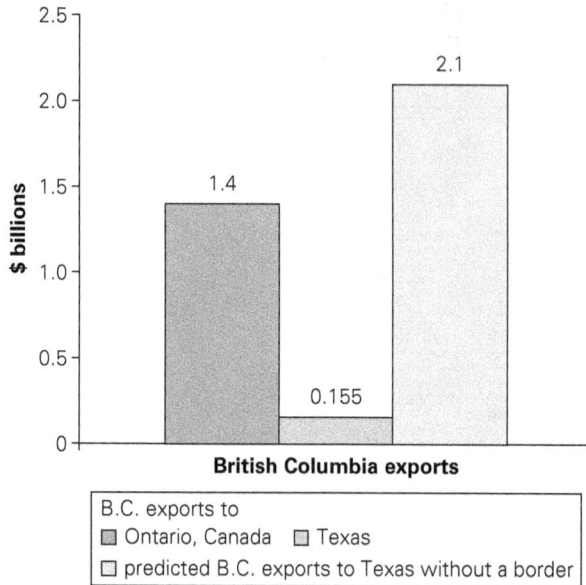

Figure 11.2 Differences in Trade Flows between British Columbia and Ontario and Texas

Source: McCallum 1995.

proliferation of sovereigns may have been only mildly mitigated by the liberalizations to date.

Although there are unquestionably more cross-border flows of goods in most countries and of capital in some, the question is whether this increase implies that the world is in any relevant sense "globalized" or that "globalization" is a useful lens through which to examine recent times. I argue that, at the very least, this implication is not obvious, especially for the poorer countries that acquired sovereignty and thus acquired a set of institutions (e.g., distinct currencies, domestic regulations, independent courts) that, no matter how "liberal" explicit trade policy is, create substantial obstacles to trade.

## From the Top of the Cliff for Labor You Cannot See Other Globalization Issues

That there are gaps in real wages, adjusted for purchasing power, across countries is obvious. These need not be caused by restrictions on the movement of labor, nor should they lead to pressures for labor movement if the differences stem from the intrinsic productivity of the worker. After all, some basketball players make millions of dollars, and yet this in and of itself is not evidence that there are "barriers" to my employment as a professional basketball player other than the fact that, being both short and slow, I would have low productivity in that occupation. But clearly some restrictions are intended to restrict the mobility of persons across nation-state borders—for example, every airplane arriving in the United States is met by (armed) officials whose job it is to prevent the entry of unauthorized persons. The question is, how much more would people from other countries make if they did not face these restrictions and people in the United States could pay them a wage that reflected their productivity in the United States? Or, more prosaically, how high is the cliff that blocks labor at U.S. borders?

A study that my colleagues Michael Clemens and Claudio Montenegro and I recently completed answers this question precisely (Clemens, Montenegro, and Pritchett 2009). We took advantage of two sources of data. The first was a collection of data sets from around the world that recorded wages of individuals and some relevant characteristics (e.g., their years of schooling, age, sex). Using this data, we could adjust the wages that individuals make in their home country for observable characteristics related to their productivity. The second source of data was the U.S. Census. It collects information on wages and the characteristics of individuals such as years of schooling and age. Most important, it also collects information on a person's country of birth and when he or she arrived in the United States.

Let me use Peru to illustrate how these two sources of data can be used. I can compare the predicted real consumption (purchasing power parity [PPP]-adjusted) wages of a Peruvian-born, Peruvian-educated 35-year-old male who has nine years of schooling, lives in an urban area, and works in Peru, with those of the observable equivalent person—a Peruvian-born, Peruvian-educated 35-year-old male who has nine years of schooling (he arrived after age 25, so his education was Peruvian), lives in an urban area, and works in the United States. Figure 11.3 illustrates that this comparison involves estimating a wage profile for Peruvians working in Peru, the relationship between wages and characteristics (illustrated for just one characteristic, X, but in reality it is a multidimensional surface) in Peru, and a wage profile for late-arriving Peruvians in the United States. Then one can "drill down" through those wage surfaces at any given point on the wage profile to estimate the wage gap between observably identical individuals in the United States and Peru. The figure is drawn with squiggly lines to emphasize that the empirical procedure imposes almost no assumptions on the shapes and forms of the two profiles (e.g., we do not impose that the wage returns to schooling are the same in the two countries nor the usual Mincer functional form in either).

The data allowed us to estimate the wage ratios of observably equivalent workers in the United States and 42 developing countries (see table 11.1 for the results). The apparently same worker from these countries makes *five times* as much in the United States as in his home country—that is, on average an annual wage income that is $15,000 (PPP) higher.

Of course, correcting the wages for a few simple observable characteristics may not fully adjust for equal productivity so that it is clear that the gains in table 11.1 would be the gains to a worker moving across the border. Perhaps comparing the wages of Peruvians here to Peruvians there, even correcting for their education, overstates the wage gains from

Figure 11.3 Wage Profiles to Estimate the Wage Gap

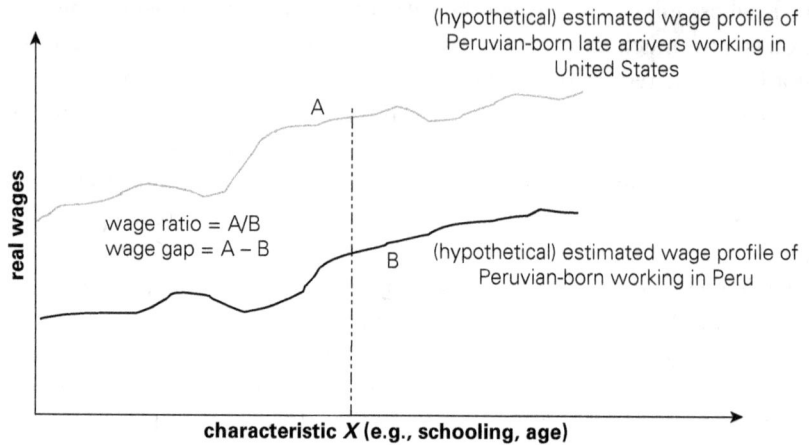

Source: Clemens, Montenegro, and Pritchett 2009.

Table 11.1 Wages of Observably Equivalent Workers across U.S. Border for 42 Countries, Comparing Low-Skill, 35-Year-Old Males

| Country | Annualized wage difference ($) | Ratio | Comparing wages of workers with college degrees at home to workers with primary schooling working in United States |
|---|---|---|---|
| Yemen | 21,772 | 15.45 | 11.43 |
| Nigeria | 17,155 | 14.85 | 7.79 |
| Egypt | 18,660 | 11.92 | 11.93 |
| Haiti | 15,738 | 10.31 | 4.19 |
| Cambodia | 20,737 | 7.45 | 6.4 |
| Sierra Leone | 15,977 | 7.43 | 3.7 |
| Ghana | 17,164 | 7.12 | 4.22 |
| Indonesia | 17,478 | 6.72 | 3.17 |
| Pakistan | 18,019 | 6.57 | 2.95 |
| Venezuela, R.B. de | 17,471 | 6.57 | 3.69 |
| Cameroon | 17,807 | 6.53 | 7.38 |
| Vietnam | 16,753 | 6.49 | 3.92 |
| India | 19,340 | 6.25 | 2.96 |
| Jordan | 16,439 | 5.65 | 3.98 |
| Ecuador | 14,300 | 5.16 | 3.26 |
| Bolivia | 15,455 | 5.03 | 3.34 |
| Sri Lanka | 14,666 | 4.95 | 1.26 |
| Nepal | 11,524 | 4.85 | 4.37 |
| Bangladesh | 14,891 | 4.60 | 2.19 |

(continued)

Table 11.1 (continued)

| Country | Annualized wage difference ($) | Ratio | Comparing wages of workers with college degrees at home to workers with primary schooling working in United States |
|---|---|---|---|
| Uganda | 15,318 | 4.38 | 2.3 |
| Ethiopia | 14,772 | 4.35 | 2.4 |
| Guyana | 16,888 | 3.87 | 1.39 |
| Philippines | 13,615 | 3.82 | 1.42 |
| Peru | 15,149 | 3.79 | 1.6 |
| Brazil | 17,423 | 3.76 | 1.66 |
| Jamaica | 15,421 | 3.63 | 1.55 |
| Chile | 16,057 | 3.53 | 1.6 |
| Nicaragua | 13,412 | 3.52 | 1.42 |
| Panama | 14,368 | 3.36 | 1.54 |
| Uruguay | 20,962 | 3.10 | 1.9 |
| Guatemala | 12,295 | 2.94 | 1.73 |
| Colombia | 12,330 | 2.88 | 1.65 |
| Paraguay | 17,674 | 2.78 | 1.1 |
| South Africa | 20,311 | 2.75 | 0.65 |
| Turkey | 12,877 | 2.68 | 1.46 |
| Argentina | 13,700 | 2.54 | 1.37 |
| Mexico | 10,679 | 2.53 | 1.31 |
| Belize | 14,959 | 2.43 | 1.16 |
| Thailand | 9,859 | 2.17 | 1.04 |
| Costa Rica | 9,982 | 2.07 | 1.24 |
| Morocco | 8,970 | 2.00 | 0.62 |
| Dominican Rep. | 8,912 | 1.99 | 1.3 |
| Mean | 15,411 | 5.11 | 2.99 |
| Median | 15,438 | 4.11 | 1.82 |

*Source:* Clemens, Montenegro, and Pritchett 2009.
*Note:* "Low-skill" means nine years of schooling.

migration, because those who moved would have been more productive had they remained at home than those who remained at home—that is, perhaps people who move have more "pluck" or drive or ambition or some other personal characteristic that makes them more productive in either place. In this case, "positive selection" of migrants would lead to an *over*statement of the wage gain from just comparing observably equivalent individuals. In my study with Clemens and Montenegro (2009) we devote considerable attention to this issue and deploy several new sources of evidence about the range of the magnitude of the adjustment for positive selection we should typically expect (while anticipating it would vary across countries). Overall, we find there is some evidence of positive selection. Indeed, if one wanted to be conservative about the adjustment one could divide the ratios of the wages of "observably identical" workers by a factor of about 1.2 (the range is from 1.0 to 1.4) to determine "equal productivity" workers.

Even after adjusting for the potential positive selection of migrants, this approach still suggests that the gain to a low-skill worker from these 42 countries of moving across the U.S. border is to increase wages by a factor of 4.26, for a gain of about $13,000 (PPP) per year.

Now, it is possible that people are sufficiently wedded to their own place, language, culture, family, and social ties that even this wage gain is not worth the other real and psychological costs of moving. Fortunately, a near "natural experiment" in Puerto Rico addresses this question. Puerto Rico has remained a territory of the United States, where its citizens have the right to live and work. So one can subject Puerto Rico to exactly the same procedure and ask: what is the wage ratio for observably equivalent workers with spatially disintegrated, linguistically and culturally distinct places when there are no obstacles to labor movement? Puerto Rico's wage ratio of equivalent workers is 1.5, which, in view of the very long period during which the movement of labor has been free, might be near a sustained equilibrium—that is, wages would have to be 50 percent higher to induce workers to move to a "foreign" country.

Of course, this ratio is enormously lower than those observed for other Central American and Caribbean countries. Dominican Republic has the lowest observed wage ratio, only 1.99, but most other Central American countries have ratios almost twice as high—Jamaica's is 3.6, and Guyana's is 3.8. The median for Central American and Caribbean countries is 2.94, almost exactly twice the ratio for Puerto Rico. This variation suggests that the observed wage differentials are the result of the border controls, not any lack of interest in taking advantage of the wage gains.

Not surprising, this evidence suggests that for labor movement the border matters, a lot. Even if the estimates of wage differences of observably equivalent workers are discounted by a factor of 1.5 to adjust for selection and the costs of moving, the gains in wages to a low-skill worker are $10,000 (PPP).

Not only is the world not flat, it is not a curb nor a barrier. Rather, the world has a massive cliff at the U.S. border (and, one suspects, most other rich industrial countries have similarly sized cliffs). Lots of other issues are discussed in the context of "globalization and equity," including the movement of capital, the effects of the liberalization of trade, the creation of antipoverty programs in poor countries, and the working conditions of "sweatshop" workers. However, from the top of the cliff of labor restrictions all of these issues are barely visible.

One way of making these comparisons is to ask: how long would a worker have to work at his market wage in the United States (meaning an employer is willing to pay him based on his productivity) in order to equal the benefits from a *lifetime* of other programs or interventions? For example, the provision of microcredit garnered an enormous amount of attention, with one of the pioneers in revivifying microcredit, Muhmmad Yunus, winning a Nobel Peace Prize for his efforts. So how many weeks would a Bangladeshi man have to work in the United States in order to produce a gain equal to a generous estimate of the gain in net present value of a *lifetime* of access to microcredit? A pioneering (if controversial because it is higher than others) estimate by Pitt and Khandker (1998) of the net return on microloans to Bangladeshi women is 18 percent. Taken at face value, this substantial return translates into an increase in annual household income of $65 at purchasing power parity, so that a *lifetime* of continuous access to lending with these returns would return $683 in net present value.[3]

Table 11.1 reveals that an observational equivalent low-skill Bangladeshi male makes $14,891 (PPP) more a year in the United States. To be conservative, one must scale this figure back by 1.5 to account for positive selection and the psychological costs of moving. At that level, he would have to work *four weeks* in the United States to have a gain in income equal to a *lifetime* of microcredit (see table 11.2).[4] Obviously, one would have to add a few weeks to pay transportation costs and some for expenditures while in the United States, but a single seasonal access of three months to a job in the United States could provide savings more than equal to the total *lifetime* financial gain from microcredit.

My colleagues and I have done similar calculations for other (anti-)globalization or antipoverty initiatives intended to address "equity" (Clemens, Montenegro, and Pritchett 2008). For example, antisweatshop activism does appear to have led to wage gains for Indonesian workers, so that a low-skill Indonesian worker would have to work half a year in the United States to equal a lifetime of gains from the antisweatshop movement. Expanding schooling, a policy that spawns social movements, international resolutions, Millennium Development Goal commitments, and the like do produce wage gains. To produce the equivalent of the gross *lifetime* gains from an additional year of school (not even netting out the opportunity cost), a Bolivian worker would have to work in the United States for 11 weeks.

One could multiply these examples, which all hinge on the same basic simple but inexorable arithmetic: most gains from in situ antipoverty interventions are measured in *percents* of local income, while the gains from

---

3   Pitt and Khandker (1998) estimate the return to males at 11 percent, but I use the higher figure for females to be conservative. Average annual female borrowing is Tk 3,415, or $361 at PPP using the average PPP conversation factor from the World Bank (2007) over the relevant period (1986–92) of 9.47. The resulting increase in household income is thus Tk 615 or $65 at PPP. Average life expectancy in Bangladesh during 1986–92 was 55 years, and average borrower age in the sample is 23. A 33-year stream of $65 payments (including one at time 0) discounted at 10 percent has a net present value of $683. At 5 percent the value is $1,091, and at 15 percent it is $493.

4   I am aware of all the problematic aspects of gender implied by income accruing to a man versus a woman, but the regressions were used for men, because labor force participation is so much more complex an econometric issue for women.

Table 11.2 Comparison of Annual Wage Gains from International Movement of Marginal Workers with Present-Value Lifetime Wage Gains to Marginal Workers from Different in Situ Antipoverty Interventions

| Intervention | Country | Present-value lifetime wage increment due to intervention ($, PPP) | Annual wage increment due to working in United States ($, PPP) | Weeks of U.S. work equivalent to *lifetime* NPV of intervention |
|---|---|---|---|---|
| Microcredit | Bangladesh | 700 | ~10,000 | 4 |
| Antisweatshop Activism | Indonesia | 2,700 | ~12,000 | 30 |
| Additional year of schooling (at zero cost) | Bolivia | 2,250 | ~11,000 | 11 |
| Deworming | Kenya | 71 | ~11,500 | 0.3 |

*Source:* Clemens, Montenegro, and Pritchett 2008.
*Note:* NPV = net present value.

labor mobility to the United States are measured in *factor multiples*. Thus the annual gains from labor mobility are typically *two orders of magnitude* larger than even the most optimistic estimates of "development" actions.

This is not, of course, to pose these as alternatives; one could easily both expand microcredit and reduce the barriers to labor mobility. The point is that, at the margin, the gains to poor people from relaxing the existing barriers to labor mobility are enormous relative to everything else on the development table. Therefore, doing one out of concern for the "equity" of globalization and not advocate the other makes almost no sense.[5]

This same logic also applies to the potential gains from further liberalization of the already quite liberalized markets for goods or capital.

Caselli and Feyrer (2007) find that the marginal product of capital (MPK) across countries is "essentially equalized." In fact, by their estimates, which correct the "naïve" estimates of MPK for differences in "natural capital" and in the price of output, the return to capital is *lower* in poor countries than in rich countries (8.4 percent versus 6.9 percent, from their table 2). If this research is to be believed, the gains from facilitating capital flows to poor countries are very modest indeed. Because the MPK is so nearly equalized, their estimate of the welfare gains from *complete* equalization of the MPK across countries is only one-tenth of 1 percent of the world's gross domestic product (GDP)—roughly $65 billion. Even if one went beyond liberalization and subsidized the flows of capital to poor countries, the net gain, the difference between the financing cost and MPK, is limited by the low MPK.

Although borders may create substantial barriers to trade, the gains from *liberalization*, the reduction in trade barriers, are by now quite modest. The World Bank (2005, 128) estimates that elimination of *all* remaining policy barriers to trade worldwide would produce welfare gains to the developing countries of roughly $109 billion in annual income by 2015.

---

5  These calculations are even more dramatic if one factors in costs. Microcredit or a year of schooling, for example, costs real resources, whereas expanding migration, by most estimates, has almost zero welfare cost (and, in many instances, substantially positive gains) for the receiving country. Thus it is, at least potentially, a "win-win."

In contrast to these modest gains from further liberalization of goods or capital markets, estimates of the gains from the fanciful counterfactual of a complete liberalization of labor mobility are that the world GDP would roughly double.[6] At current levels of GDP, this implies gains of $65 *trillion*, roughly *three* orders of magnitude larger than the world gains from MPK equalization or than the developing country gains from all remaining trade liberalization. Another possibility is that rather than even entertaining the borderline facetious estimate of "open borders," one can calculate the gains from a modest relaxation of the constraints on labor flows. Walmsley and Winters (2005, table 4, col. V) use a general equilibrium model to estimate that allowing an additional movement of people equal to 3 percent of the existing labor force of the member countries of the Organisation for Economic Co-operation and Development (OECD) would raise the welfare of those moving by $170 billion.[7] Again, the logic is familiar; because welfare gains grow with the square of the deviation and the existing price distortions of goods are measured in percents and labor price distortions are measured in factor multiples, the gains from labor mobility just swamp everything else on the agenda. Figure 11.4 shows these gains from complete labor, goods, or capital liberality on the same scale, and, as one might suspect, it is impossible to see the gains to further flattening from the spectacularly high cliff of $65 trillion.

The world has run an interesting and unique historical experiment since World War II of dividing itself into smaller and smaller geographic bits, endowing those bits with sovereignty over economic policies, and then promoting modest amounts of cross-border liberality in some transactions (certainly goods, certainly foreign exchange, less so capital), but almost uniformly countries have blocked the movement of labor.[8] Different simple theories of economic growth and international trade made different predictions on how that experiment would turn out, some predicting convergence in per capita incomes across countries, some predicting equalization of factor prices. The experiment with the POSEBLL has now run for about 60 years and the outcome is clear: incomes have not converged (certainly not in absolute terms, certainly not in country-weighted relative terms) and factor prices have not converged. It is not known what real "globalization" might have produced, but the POSEBLL has created a world

---

6   Hamilton and Whalley (1984) estimate a rough doubling of world output per person. Klein and Ventura (2004) use a calibrated general equilibrium model with capital mobility and estimate gains of between 94 percent and 172 percent.

7   The simulations by Walmsley and Winters (2005) are based on rough assumptions about how much of the existing wage differences are attributable to productivity differences that would move with the worker (which they assume is only half), whereas my estimates per worker are based on data. They find a welfare gain to movers of roughly $20,000 per mover, which is close to my estimate for India of $19,900 (PPP), although their estimates are not exclusively of low-skill workers.

8   What is unique is that most, if not all, countries have blocked the influx of labor. Although the movement of labor across "state" borders has always been complex, states in earlier times were at least as concerned about losing labor, and thus they adopted all kinds of arrangements, from serfdom to slavery to peasantry, that bound people to the land to prevent losses of labor (especially in rural areas). They were much less concerned about cross-state mobility.

Figure 11.4 View of the Flatland of Goods and Capital from the Cliff against Labor Mobility

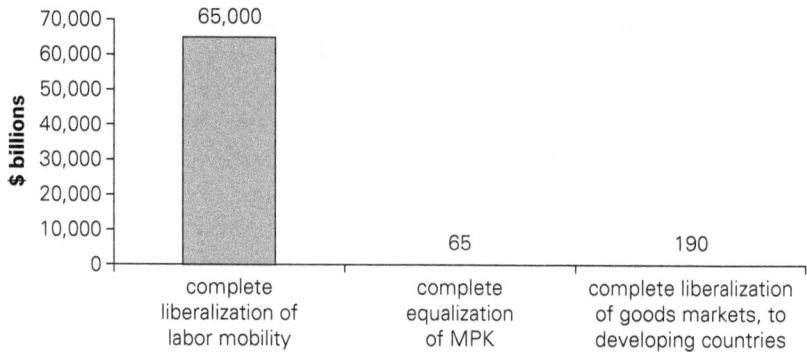

Sources: Hamilton and Whalley (1984) and Klein and Ventura (2004) for labor mobility, Caselli and Freyer (2007) for capital, World Bank (2005) for goods.

in which there are massive differences in the earnings of equal intrinsic productivity workers across countries, differences that are sustained by enforcing restrictions on the movement of poor people.

## The "Nation-State-ization" of Equity

One issue that is rarely raised in discussions of "globalization and equity" is what the concepts of "equity" or "fairness" or "justice" mean in a global or even cross-national context. Although I am not well suited or trained to raise these issues, if not me, then who?

One of the hubs, if not temples, of globalization is the Singapore Changi International Airport. Nearly every experienced international traveler has passed through this marvel of modernity and efficiency, a testament to non-Western wealth and prosperity, and a hive of globalization as businesspeople from every corner of the globe pass by. A few years ago I was headed toward my next flight when I encountered a string of Bangladeshi men, all hand-cuffed and chained together. They were being escorted through the airport, presumably to be flown back to Bangladesh. Their apparent "crime" was an attempt to sell their labor services to willing buyers in Singapore. None of us streaming past paid the slightest attention to this perfectly natural, perfectly ordinary course of events.

One fascinating aspect of the huge divergence in earnings across national borders is that coercion is needed to enforce those restrictions. This coercion, at least in the OECD countries, is carried out by agents under the near-perfect control of democratic nation-states. The support for these restrictions is overwhelming. In nearly all public opinion surveys in OECD countries recently (even before the economic troubles in 2008), a major-ity of people believe that, even with the existing restrictions, there is still "too much" migration. These restrictions raise almost no objections on the grounds of "justice" or "equity," apparently because of what I call the "nation-state-ization" of justice claims.

I would argue that a desire for equality often stems from an even deeper principle of equity that "likes should be treated like likes." Even a very small child will object— "That's not fair!"—if any favor is distributed unevenly if that uneven distribution appears to be arbitrary. However, what constitutes "like" for purposes of justice claims is, as they say, socially constructed, because what differences count in making people "unlike" is entirely a social convention.

For example, there is little that is more obvious about the world than that the biological sexes differ. Nearly every individual is immediately and easily recognized by all others as belonging to one or the other of the biological sexes. Yet in most modern societies these obvious differences between the sexes have been redefined as irrelevant to justice claims as the socially constructed notions have been deconstructed and reconstructed. "Because you are a girl" is no longer considered a socially appropriate rationale for differential treatment.

By contrast, people who are exactly identical in every conceivable and observable respect can be treated in ways that cause their well-being to differ by orders of magnitude—for example, one is denied access to a more productive job—with no apparent violation of justice if those otherwise identical individuals happen to be citizens of different countries. Two brothers, both born to, say, Peruvian parents, one born in the United States and one not, have completely different lifetime claims on rights because this seemingly arbitrary condition of place of birth makes them completely "unlike" for nationalized theories of justice.

Just as one illustration, I can use the multicountry wage data to ask how apparent discrimination against women in wages in the labor market—just simple wage differences between otherwise observably equivalent men and women—compares with the wage gap between observably identical men (including same country of birth). Not surprising, the estimates are consistent with the existence of substantial labor market discrimination against women in nearly every country of the world. In the United States, the estimate is a wage ratio (men to women) of 1.3. Estimating the "male premium" for each of the countries gives a median of 1.4 (shown by the median country, Madagascar, in figure 11.5). The worst observed "male premium" is, again not very surprising, in Pakistan, at 3.1—that is, males make three times more than observably equivalent females. Of course, these very simple numbers are meant to be illustrative and are not corrected for labor market selection, nor do they reflect the many potential dimensions of sex discrimination beyond the labor market (e.g., violence against women, including domestic abuse, which is widespread in many countries; forced marriages; or bias in health care and property ownership). But the simple point is that my very conservative estimate of the wage gap of equal productivity workers willing to move (taking observed wage ratios for observably identical workers and dividing by 1.5) exceeds the *median* male premium (1.4) in nearly every instance (only two countries are less than this amount), and

Figure 11.5 Comparing Wage Gaps across Borders to Wage Gaps within Spatially Integrated Labor Markets

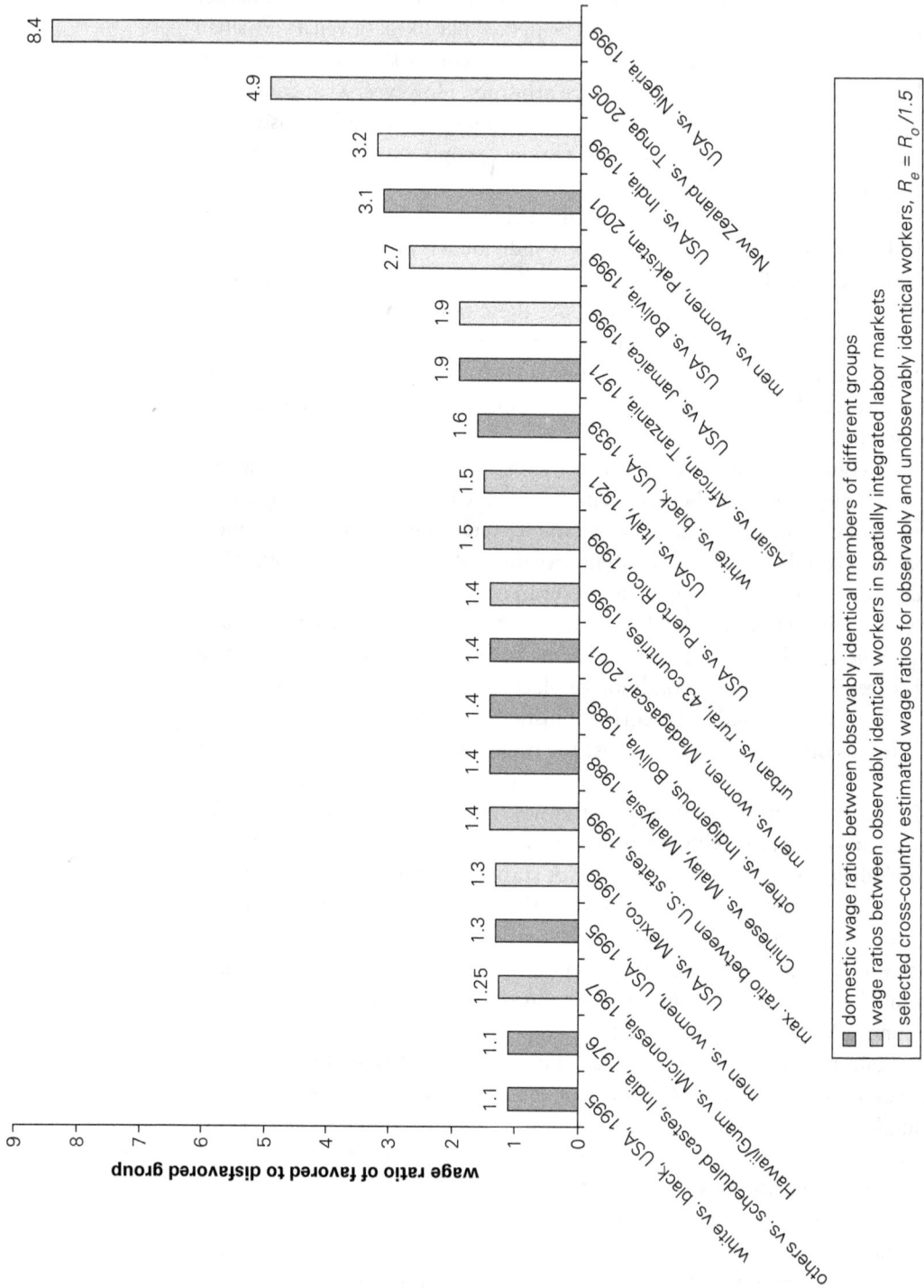

Source: Clemens, Montenegro, and Pritchett 2008, figure 4.

Note: The estimates for wage gaps across borders are from table 11.1, scaled back by 1.5.

in 17 countries the "place premium" for access to the U.S. labor market for low-skill workers is greater than the *worst* estimated sex-based wage discrimination observed in any country.[9]

Similar comparisons can be made with other forms of labor market discrimination. One study (Sundstrom 2007) estimated the degree of wage discrimination against African Americans in 1939—a time in America when discrimination was egregious, blatant, and pervasive. The estimated wage ratio was 1.6—that is, whites made 60 percent more than equivalent African Americans. This was a clear offense to any sense of justice, and many people fought long and courageously to address that injustice. Current estimates suggest much lower degrees of outright wage discrimination, but even the outrageous discrimination of 1.6 is exceeded again by all but two countries (Mexico's estimate is 1.61). Estimates of labor market discrimination against disfavored ethnicities around the world (e.g., versus indigenous groups in Bolivia, versus scheduled castes in India) often reveal persistent and large wage gaps, but they never reach the levels of the discrimination at the U.S. border.

The question is, how does the massive differential treatment of people who are alike in every respect except for their affiliation with a particular nation-state, an essentially arbitrary condition of birth, square with any theory of justice? This is not to ask why there are not in fact open (or more liberal) policies on labor mobility (or, even deeper, the acquisition of citizenship), which is a historical and political question. Rather, why is it now accepted that this differential treatment of "like" individuals is not a violation of the fundamental principle of equity of treating likes like likes? Alternatively, what is the construction of a notion of "difference" in a theory of justice so that nearly all other conditions of birth (e.g., sex, race, and nonbiologically grounded, socially transmitted ascriptive identities such as ethnicity and religion) are absolutely ethically and morally unacceptable as criteria of difference, particularly for action by the state, but a person's location of birth (or parentage) is an acceptable basis for legally grounded and coercively enforced discrimination by states?

I will be the first to admit that I am a puzzled amateur rather than a professional philosopher. To me, the three primary theories of justice when applied to this issue either imply open borders or, in an effort to avoid this obvious conclusion, devolve into a mass of confusion or irrelevance.

One version of a popular class of theories of justice (contractarian) is that articulated by John Rawls in his classic *The Theory of Justice* (1970). His basic argument has two parts: first, a set of social arrangements should be considered just if individuals, behind a "veil of ignorance" and thus with no knowledge of the position they would subsequently occupy in that social arrangement, agreed to those social arrangements; and, second, he makes arguments about what social conditions would in fact be agreed to in those circumstances. The seemingly obvious implication of that setup is

---

9  These numbers are derived from a modestly different technique and functional form than those in table 11.1 and thus are not completely comparable.

that open access to participation in any given set of social arrangements (conditional on fulfilling whatever obligations those arrangements entail) is a fundamental condition of justice, and thus open borders are one corollary of that. Imagine, taking Rawls perhaps a bit more literally than he would prefer, that humans actually existed in some sense as entities capable of reasoning before birth, say, raw "intelligences." In the prebirth conference of intelligences, would I ever agree that you would be born in Denmark or France or the United States and I would be born in Mali or Nepal or Bolivia, and that just you could arrange for coercion to prevent me from working in the territory controlled by your social arrangement, even for a willing employer? It is hard to see why I would. Philosophers such as Joseph Carens (1987) argue that Rawls's approach does imply open borders.

Rawls's initial means of avoiding this consequence of his approach (a consequence which may be seen as a defect, as some might regard any theory of justice that demands open borders as flawed because it implies that the modern nation-state is unjust) was simply to stipulate that the nation-state was a primary and primordial entity and claim that his theory applied only to social arrangements up to the nation-state and no larger. Later he suggested that there were two different theories, one for domestic arrangements and the other between "peoples." Either approach is a radical reduction in the scope of his theory. It means that to have any general *human* or *universal* theory of justice there must be one theory, Rawls's say, for relationships within a nation-state (a potentially arbitrarily formed category), another theory, which cannot be Rawlsian but is otherwise specified, to answer questions about the "just" relationships between individuals across nation-states (including who is admitted), and perhaps a third theory for the behavior of nation-states as actors. For example, are there any conditions for determining new members of a nation-state that are unjust? Could, say, a nation-state deny a person admission as a citizen under precisely the same criteria (e.g., gender, religion) for which discrimination against a national is unjust? This seems like a mass of confusion to avoid a simple, plausible, universal, "veil of ignorance" contractarian theory and its obvious consequence.

The philosopher Robert Nozick proposed a comprehensive alternative view of justice as "process fairness"—that people own the fruits of their labor and are entitled to make voluntary transactions and that any outcome of such a process is fair, no matter how unequal. This theory leads quickly to the conclusion that it would be unjust to bar voluntary transactions across individuals on the basis on some justice-arbitrary condition such as place of birth. The only alternative is to again introduce the nation-state as an unanalyzed primordial with an ability to regulate or ban transactions between citizens of nation-states that it would be unjust to bar for citizens of the same nation-state.

A third alternative class of theories of justice is more "communitarian" and builds notions of justice up from sustained free dialogue among the participants of a community. These theories, while having attractions, seem especially problematic because the conditions under which individuals can join communities and the ability of communities to regulate membership seem particularly intractable. If justice is only community-based, is there then any injustice to a "community" denying new members based on, say, their race? If so, then some other theory of justice must transcend the community, a broader community notion of justice. The problem with this sequence is that there is no reason why this process of envisioning broader communities would just happen to stop at the (imagined) "community" called the "nation-state," which could then deny any and all others membership without any justice claim. In other words, the prior practice of white neighborhoods writing restrictive convenants that prevented the sale of homes to nonwhite individuals within a nation-state cannot be justified—no matter how radically different the nonwhite individuals' "culture" or "values" and their positive or negative contribution to the "community"—within a just nation-state. Yet somehow there is an "imagined community" (Anderson 1983) that people feel can justly do exactly that to others with absolutely no justice claim involved. There are some, perhaps many, things that all human beings have in common, which would seem to imply some universal set of justice obligations and a common notion of "equity" such that, although "communities" may have distinct notions of justice, there are at least some cross-community constraints on the range of acceptable cross-community actions consistent with fairness, equity, or justice.

The alternative to these views is the widespread view, of which Michel Foucault is the most popular wellspring, that, very crudely put, discourse is structured by power and that discussions that pretend to be "rational" discourse on all topics, including justice, are the cloaked attempt of power to control discourse to construct a social reality conducive to its aims. The alternative to this discourse is "deconstruction," the unmasking of the relations of power behind discourse so that alternate realities can emerge. However, this postmodern "deconstruction" is unlike most previous deconstructions in that it has given up any illusions of displacing the "false" with the "truth"—there is no solid, much less transcendent (in the sense of "God" or "Reason" or "History") basis for "truth" or "justice"; it is just discourse and convention all the way down. Thus postmodern analysis is not an alternative theory of justice, but rather a positive theory of justice claims.

Taking Foucault seriously, then, one should look for power not in controversy but in silences. After all, controversy reveals fissures in power, and signifies a topic beyond the real concern of power, an erosion of power, or conflicting powers in which neither party is able to subjugate the other. In issues around which there is overwhelming power, there is no legitimate controversy, only silence, because discourse beyond the specified boundaries is not "controversy" but "craziness." This seems like a good description of the current status of justice discussions about the cross-border movement of people. The claim that "closed borders are unjust" is not controversial; it is just plain crazy.

This lack of a widely acceptable notion of cross nation-state border equity leads the discussion of the movement of people into twists and knots. Let me illustrate with three conundrums.

First, Kuwait has a massive population of non-Kuwaitis, most of whom are explicitly temporary workers and most of whom are not on a path to achieving any long-term claims on Kuwaiti citizenship. Kuwaitis and the government of Kuwait seem perfectly comfortable with co-residence with an unequal citizenship status. One can articulate a view, based on Nozick's view, that this is a just arrangement: "We make an offer of the conditions under which people may be granted access to the Kuwaiti labor market (including limits on rights, not being able to bring families, and less than due process for expulsion), and if people accept that offer, then by revealed preference they are better off. So by process fairness the resulting outcome is just (or at least no less just than the situation before we made the offer and that initial injustice is not our problem)." Many people are uncomfortable with this view; they argue that it will lead to a "race to the bottom" or a "coarsening" of a sense of justice such that *within* national inequality will grow or Kuwait will be unable to sustain social programs. For example, Milton Friedman himself proclaimed that the welfare state and open migration are incompatible. As a general proposition this is obviously refuted by Kuwait (and other Gulf states and Singapore) all of which, for their citizens, have an amazing cradle-to-grave set of social welfare programs, often even beyond those of most European states. What Milton Friedman meant was that social welfare states and open migration are incompatible *if* migrants acquire immediate and full claims on these benefits. The conundrum is that the Kuwaitis' lack of a sense that co-residence creates justice claims leads them to accept a far higher number of workers than they would if each acquired citizenship (which, of course, implies a claim on the revenues from oil). The lack of a coherent theory of cross-border equity means there is no coherent view on whether allowing temporary workers is more or less just than banning them altogether.

A second conundrum is that the conventional wisdom is that a theory of universal human rights does involve allowing certain kinds of petitions—such as "refugee" or "asylum"—but a nation-state has no justice obligation whatsoever with regard to "economically" motivated migration. Suppose that an asylum petitioner could prove that his odds of dying if he were forced to return to his country were one in five within five years. This is a fantastically high fatality rate—for comparison, the fatality rate of the U.S. Army in World War II was 2.8 percent, the British Army 5.2 percent. If a one-in-five fatality risk was demonstrated in asylum hearings, the asylum seeker's petition would be granted. In the poorest countries of the world, the under-5 mortality rate is about 200 per thousand—one in five. So returning a Malian or Somali or Liberian woman who desires to remain on mere "economic" grounds creates this incredibly high mortality risk for all of her future children. Why isn't every southern Sudanese or Somali or Malawian or Nepalese a candidate for asylum, not from political prosecution but from the very real dangers of poverty?

A third ethical conundrum is Americans' ambivalence about the justice of their current situation. Many if not most Americans do not want open borders, but they feel little or no ethical compunction about violating the current immigration laws by employing undocumented workers. The most recent, spectacularly illustrative example was the arrest in December 2008 in the Boston area of the top local official of the Customs and Border Patrol for not just hiring an illegal worker, but actively aiding this person in evading the law.[10] This deep ambivalence, I would argue, stems from the conflict between the vague sense that it is just to enforce borders and the similarly vague sense that it is not unethical to give another person work.

All in all, I find myself confused and out of touch in discussions about "globalization" and "equity," as I do believe in God but do not believe in Sudan, whereas everyone around me seems to have the opposite view. As Benedict Anderson so cogently pointed out in *Imagined Communities* (1983) nationalism is the last acceptable credo, and the "imagined communities" of nationalism have swept the floor with not just kith and clan but God and Class (with a big "C"). The puzzle is not that people believe in *states*; these are an obvious juridical category. The puzzle is that people believe in *nations* and thus *nationality* as a *social* category in which discrimination is possible without any justice claims. Yet the *social* realities of the "Congo" or "Indonesia" or even "India" are that they are "communities" or "nations" that, like Yugoslavia or Sudan, exist only in the most fevered of imaginations. As for me, I'll take Pascal's wager and stick a while longer to the old-fashioned notion that all men and women are brothers and sisters and that a theory of justice should be universal, not contingent on place of birth or physical proximity or "nationality."

## Conclusion

My addition to, or perhaps subtraction from, a discussion about "globalization and equity" is to triply deny the premise.

First, for most poor countries "globalization" is a much less primary phenomenon than sovereignty, and even the most aggressively liberalizing countries have yet to overcome the disintegration consequences of sovereignty.

Second, the range of "equity" issues usually discussed in this context are all dwarfed, by *order of magnitude,* by the wage gaps across equally productive workers created by the enforcement of U.S. (and other rich countries') borders. Given that the typical low-skill worker could triple his or her wages by moving to the United States (or other rich countries), discussing the inequity of cotton subsidies or "fair trade" or inadequate foreign aid or the efficacy of antipoverty interventions leaves one wondering, why this and not that?

Third, I cannot see any coherent way in which to discuss "equity" (or fairness or justice) in the context of globalization that does not seem to boil down to an unsupported claim about the primacy of nation-states as a legitimate ethical category. To me, this seems more like a "tradition of all dead generations [that] weighs like a nightmare on the brains of

---

10 Ironically, as I arrived in Boston in February 2009 a photo of this official still greeted me as I cleared customs.

the living," a nightmare from which, I suspect and hope, the world may one day awake.

## References

Anderson, Benedict. 1983. *Imagined Communities: Reflections on the Origins and Spread of Nationalism.* Verso: London.

Braun, M., R. Hausmann, and L. Pritchett. 2004. "Disintegration and the Proliferation of Sovereigns: Are There Lessons for Integration?" In *Integrating the Americas: FTAA and Beyond*, ed. A. Estevadeordal, D. Rodrik, A.M. Taylor, and A. Velasco. Cambridge, MA: Harvard University Press.

Carens, Joseph. 1987. "Aliens and Citizens: The Case for Open Borders." *Review of Politics* 49 (2): 251–72.

Caselli, F., and J. Feyrer. 2007. "The Marginal Product of Capital." *Quarterly Journal of Economics* 122 (2): 535–65.

Clemens, Michael A., Claudio E. Montenegro, and Lant Pritchett. 2008. "The Place Premium: Wage Differences for Identical Workers across the U.S. Border." World Bank Policy Research Working Paper 4671, World Bank, Washington, DC.

———. 2009. "The Place Premium: Wage Differences for Identical Workers across the US Border." Faculty Research Working Papers Series, John F. Kennedy School of Government, Harvard University, Cambridge, MA.

Hamilton, B., and J. Whalley. 1984. "Efficiency and Distributional Implications of Global Restrictions on Labour Mobility: Calculations and Policy Implications." *Journal of Development Economics.* 14 (1–2): 61–75.

Keynes, John Maynard. 1919. *The Economic Consequences of the Peace.* Macmillan: London.

Klein, P., and G. Ventura. 2004. "Do Migration Restrictions Matter?" Unpublished manuscript.

Marx, Karl. 1937. *The Eighteenth Brumaire of Louis Bonaparte.* Moscow: Progress Publishers.

McCallum, J. 1995. "National Borders Matter: US-Canada Regional Trade Patterns." *American Economic Review* 85 (3): 615–23.

Pitt, M., and S. Khandker. 1998. "The Impact of Group-Based Credit Programs on Poor Households in Bangladesh: Does the Gender of Participants Matter?" *Journal of Political Economy* 106 (5): 958–96.

Rawls, J. 1970. *The Theory of Justice.* Cambridge, MA: Harvard University Press.

Sundstrom, W. 2007. "The Geography of Wage Discrimination in the Pre–Civil Rights South." *Journal of Economic History* 67 (2): 410–44.

Walmsley, T., and A. Winters. 2005. "Relaxing the Restrictions on the Temporary Movement of Natural Persons: A Simulation Exercise." *Journal of Economic Integration* 20 (4): 628–726.

World Bank. 2005. *Global Economic Prospects 2005: Trade, Regionalism, and Development.* Washington, DC: World Bank.

———. 2007. *World Development Indicators 2007.* Washington, DC: World Bank.

# Index

Arneson, Richard, 132
Ashraf, Nava, 113*n*
Asia. *See also specific regions and countries*
  MDG achievement in, 37
  middle class in, 181
Asian Development Bank, 75, 76
asylum and refugee status, 284
Atkinson, Anthony, 131*n*
Australia, immigration to, 233,
    234, 235*t*, 255
Aydemir, Abdurrahman, 248

B
Bandiera, Oriana, 114*n*
Banerjee, Abhijit V., 5, 62, 71, 78, 84,
    87*n*, 90, 94, 105, 175, 176
Bangladesh
  credit
    gender differences and, 112, 118
    microcredit in vs. migrant earnings in
      U.S., 275–76, 276*t*
  growth correlated with inequality, 62
  MDG progress, 20
  worker earnings based on educational
    level, 219–20, 220*f*
Baqir, Reza, 53
Barro, Robert J., 91, 217, 233
Basta, S., 90
BDH (Bono de Desarrollo Humano;
    Ecuador), 117, 117*n*
Becker, Gary, 82
Beine, Michael, 239, 245
Berger, Marguerite, 112
Bergson-Samuelson welfare function, 51
Besley, Timothy, 81, 160
between-group component of
    inequality, 52
Bhagwati, J., 191
Bhorat, Haroon, 47
Bils, Mark, 215, 217
Binswanger, Hans P., 81, 87, 89
Birdsall, Nancy, 7–8, 13, 43*n*,
    61–62, 157
BLEND scenario, 51*n*, 55
Bolaky, B., 197
Bolivia

educational increase and income vs.
    Bolivian migrant worker's income
    in U.S., 275, 276*t*
  infant mortality rate, 163–64
  middle class, 172
Bono de Desarrollo Humano
    (BDH; Ecuador), 117, 117*n*
border enforcement and migration, 247,
    254, 278–79
Borjas, George J., 240, 241, 243, 248
Bourguignon, François, 3, 4, 6, 7, 11,
    17, 27, 54, 131*n*, 200
brain drain, 207, 223–24,
    230–31, 237–40,
    238–40*f*, 249, 255
Brazil
  farm size, 86, 87*t*
  infant mortality rate, 163
  marital rights, 118
  middle class, 173, 175, 178
Burgess, Robin, 81
Burkina Faso
  cash transfer programs and children's
    human capital, 118
  land rights and gender inequality, 110
Buvinic, Mayra, 112

C
Caballero, Ricardo, 74
Cambodia, poverty rate in, 5, 21, 27
Canada
  immigration to, 234, 235*t*, 255
    education level of
      immigrants, 245, 245*t*
    trade and, 253
    inter-province trade vs. Canadian
      province-U.S. trade,
      268–69, 270*f*
Carens, Joseph, 282
Carrington, William J., 232
Caselli, Francesco, 77, 276
cash transfer programs
  in developing countries, 7, 182–83
  evaluation of effectiveness of, 65, 117
  in Mexico, 60, 117
  targeting of, 160

Deininger, Klaus, 56, 81, 91
De Mel, Suresh, 85, 93, 94, 113
Demographic and Health Survey (DHS), 7,
    20, 154, 175
Dercon, Stefan, 17
Desai, Mihir, 249
Detragiache, Enrica, 232
developing countries
    brain drain from. *See* brain drain
    credit access in, 111
    emigration from, trends in,
        230–31, 254
    financial crises and, 192–93
    food and agricultural aid to,
        198–99, 199*f*
    land regulation in, 81–82
    middle class in, 7, 157–87.
        *See also* middle class in
        developing countries
    sustained periods of growth
        in, 158
    U.S. wages vs., 271, 272–73*t*, 285
deworming program, 90
DHS. *See* Demographic and Health Survey
Diagne, Aliou, 112
disadvantaged vs. highly advantaged,
    differences in school enrollment,
    145, 145*f*
discount rate and sacrifices of today's
    generation for future
    generation, 57
Docquier, Frédéric, 233, 239, 245
Dollar, David, 59, 190
Dominican Republic
    employment status of middle class,
        176–77, 178*t*
    immigration from
        to OECD countries, 229–30
        remittances, 251
        wage ratio, 274
Doss, Cheryl R., 115
Duflo, Esther, 62, 78, 81, 84, 86, 90, 94,
    105, 118, 175, 176
Dupas, Pascaline, 113
Dutch disease, 248, 253
Dworkin, Ronald, 132

E

East Asia. *See also specific countries*
    education in, 176
    elimination of occupational segregation
        in, 107
    growth rates in, 62
    remittances in, 250
Easterly, William, 53, 62, 199*n*, 200
Eastern European immigration to OECD
    countries, 233, 234*t*, 236
*The Economic Consequences of the Peace*
    (Keynes), 263
economic development and inequality. *See*
    growth and inequality
Ecuador
    cash transfer program and food
        spending, 117, 117*n*
    immigration to OECD
        countries from, 230
    middle class, 175
education
    access to, 13
    as "advantage," 133
    equality of opportunity and, 133
    gender inequality
        in academic achievement, 148*t*, 153
        in school enrollments, 4, 21, 25–26*f*,
            134, 136–44, 137–42*f*, 143–44*t*
    highly educated, migration of. *See*
        brain drain
    measurement of quality and quantity
        of, 133
    as middle class characteristic, 166,
        175–76, 176*t*
    mothers' schooling, effect of, 116
    primary emphasized over secondary
        education, 158
    primary school completion rates,
        4, 18*b*, 21
    returns to schooling. *See also* Mincer
        model on return to schooling
        gender differences, 104
        on private investment in, 90
        wage inequality and,
            243, 271
    in Turkey, 7, 131–56. *See also* Turkey

*The Eighteenth Brumaire of Louis Bonaparte* (Marx), 266

El Salvador
  immigration to OECD countries from, 229, 233
  remittances to, 251
Elson, Diane, 106*n*
Employment Guarantee Scheme of Maharshtra (India), 60
environmental sustainability, 18*b*
equality-enhancing policies and growth, 60–63
equality of opportunity, 6, 11, 53–55, 132–33
  education and, 133. *See also* Turkey
  Roemerian circumstances and, 133, 146, 154
equity between nations, 3, 8–12
equity within nations, 2, 3–8
Estache, Antonio, 17
ethical goal of reducing inequity, 2
Ethiopia
  food aid to, 198
  land rights and gender inequality, 109
  poverty rate, 21
  trade liberalization and, 192, 194
Europe/European Union. *See also* OECD countries; *specific countries*
  immigrants to
    education level of immigrants, 245, 245*t*
    effect of, 230–31
    trade liberalization, 268
ex ante (opportunity) equity issues, 2, 12–13
Explaining African Economic Growth Performance Project, 24*n*
ex post (outcomes) equity issues, 2, 12–13
external shocks
  negative shocks
    effect on gender equality, 104
    effect on the poor and middle class, 181
  positive shocks, short-term effect of, 159

**F**

Fafchamps, Marcel, 81*n*
family's investment in children, 82–83, 107, 107*n*
Feder, Gershon, 81
Feliciano, Zadia, 241
Fernandez-Huertas, Jesus, 241
Ferreira, Francisco H. G., 7, 54, 131, 147, 153
Feyrer, J., 276
Field, Erica, 89*n*
Fields, Gary, 51*n*, 55, 56
Filme, Deon, 135
financial crises, 192–93, 196
Fletschner, Diana, 112
Forbes, Kristin J., 91
foreign investment and poverty reduction, 192, 193
Foster, Andrew D., 86
Foucault, Michel, 283
fragile states and MDG achievements, 3–4, 4*n*, 21, 21*f*, 23, 37
France, immigration to, 234, 235*t*
Frankenberg, Elizabeth, 195
Freeman, Richard B., 206, 213
Freund, C. L., 197, 251
Friedman, Milton, 53, 284
Friedman, Thomas, 267

**G**

garment industry in India, 94–96, 95*f*
Gathmann, Christina, 246, 247
GDP. *See* gross domestic product
Gelbach, Jonah, 160, 182*n*
gender inequality, 6, 103–29
  access to economic resources and opportunities and, 121
  agricultural technology and, 105, 113–16
  credit market and, 105, 111–13, 118
  documenting gender disparities, 47, 120
  economic development/growth and, 47–49, 104*n*, 105*n*, 118–20
  efficiency gains, 121
  future research agenda, 6, 120–21

India (continued)
    credit market, 75–76, 76t, 84
    Employment Guarantee Scheme of
        Maharshtra, 60
    garment industry, 94–96, 95f
    Green Revolution, 86
    growth correlated with inequality, 62
    immigration from
        brain drain, 249, 250n
        educational progress related to, 250
        high tech industries and, 250
        to OECD countries, 233
    incremental capital output ratio
        (ICOR), 85
    insurance of villagers, 79–80
    land ownership, regulation of, 81
    MDG progress, 11, 20
    middle vs. rich class, 171, 172, 172n,
        175, 179t, 180
    poverty statistics, 44, 46
    school attainment levels, 163n
    SENSEX (index of Indian stock
        market), 94
    trade liberalization and, 191, 192,
        193–94, 196–97, 200
    wealth distribution, 72, 73, 94
    worker earnings based on educational
        level, 217–19, 218f
Indonesia
    assets owned by household types, 167,
        168t, 177–78
    currency crisis (1997), 192, 196
    iron supplementation experiment, 90
    MDG progress, 20
    middle class, 170, 170f, 171f, 175
    poverty statistics, 163
    worker conditions and wages vs.
        Indonesian migrant's wages
        in U.S., 276t
    worker earnings based on educational
        level, 217–19, 218f
industry, underinvestment in, 83–85, 83f
inequality
    between-group component of, 52
    challenges of understanding, 2, 51–55
    gender. See gender inequality

    of opportunity. See equality of
        opportunity
    policy implications of, 12–14
    poverty reduction vs. growth vs., 5,
        41–70. See also growth
        and inequality
    scope of, 1, 12
    wages. See wage inequality
infant mortality rates, 163
information and flow of ideas, 253–54
inheritance and land rights, 109, 109n
insurance, poor's lack of, 78–81,
    87, 87n, 88
International Comparison of Prices
    project, 20
International Conference on
    "Financing for
    Development" (Monterrey,
    Mexico, 2002), 19
International Crop Research Institute
    in the Semi-Arid Tropics
    (ICRISAT), 79, 87, 88f
International Labor Organization, 213
International Monetary Fund (IMF), 85
International Organization for
    Migration, 265n
investment efficiency, 5, 71–101
    "ability bias," 84
    business start-up, 72–73
    credit market, 5, 74–77
    distribution of wealth and, 74, 91–96
        aggregate investment, 91–93
        quality of investment, 94–96
    family's investment in children, 82–83,
        107, 107n
    inequality and diminishing
        returns, 93–94
    insurance market, 78–81, 80t, 87, 87n
    land market, 81–82
    mitigating factors, 77–78
    reinforcing factors, 78–83
    scale of investment, 93–94
    underinvestment, 83–91
        evidence from agriculture, 85–89,
        86f, 87t
        evidence from human capital, 89–91

evidence from industry and trade, 83–85, 83*f*

gender differences, 104

iron supplements, 90

Lubotsky, Darren, 241
Lund, Susan, 81*n*
Lustig, Nora, 62–63
Luxembourg, immigration to, 234, 235*t*

## M

macroeconomic policy
  decline in inequality in Latin America
    and, 27
  in developing countries, 180
  gender inequality and, 119
Malawi, credit and gender inequality
    in, 112
Malaysia and farm size, 86–87, 87*t*
malnutrition. *See* undernutrition
Marfouk, Abdeslam, 233
marginal product of capital (MPK),
    equalization of, 276–77
marital rights, 118
Marshall, Alfred, 82
Marx, Karl, 266
maternal health, 18*b*, 20
Matoussi, Mohamed Salah, 89
Maxwell, Simon, 17
Mayda, Anna Maria, 237
McCallum, J., 268
McCulloch, Neil, 190, 190*n*
McHale, John, 249
McKay, Andrew, 190, 190*n*
McKenzie, David, 84, 85, 93, 94, 113, 241,
    244, 246, 247
McKinsey Global Institute, 171
McMillan, Margaret, 8–9, 189, 198
MDGs. *See* Millennium Development Goals
Mekonnen, Hailu, 115
Mesnard, Alice, 93
Mexico
  currency crisis (1995) and poverty,
    192, 196
  debt crisis (August 1982), 268
  foreign investment in, 192
  immigration from
    illegal immigrants, 235, 247, 285
    migration networks and, 246–47
    to OECD countries, 230, 233,
      234*t*, 236

relationship to wealth, 244
remittances, 252
return migrants, 252
to United States, 241
wage elasticity and, 248, 255
inequality despite growth and poverty
    reduction, 43, 43*n*, 50
middle class, 173, 178, 180
Oportunidades-Progresa (cash transfer
    scheme), 60, 117
poverty rates, 192–93
trade liberalization and, 192, 193,
    194, 197
underinvestment in industry, 83, 83*f*, 93
worker earnings based on educational
    level, 217–19, 218*f*
microcredit, 111, 118, 275
microeconomic policy
  in developing countries, 182–83
  gender inequality and, 118
microenterprises and credit access, gender
    differences in, 113, 113*n*
MICS (Multiple Indicator Cluster Survey,
    UNICEF), 20
middle class in developing countries,
    7, 13, 157–87
  assets owned by, 167, 168*t*, 177–78
  cash transfer programs, 7, 160, 182–83
  characteristics of, 175–80
  consumption and income distribution
    correlated with, 165–66, 166*f*,
    180, 181*f*
  defined, 161–69
  education as characteristic of, 166,
    175–76, 176*t*
  employment status of, 176–77, 178*t*
  exit out of poverty to vs. exit out of
    wealth to, 161*n*
  household size of, 176, 177*t*
  implications for growth and economic
    development, 13, 180–83
  income-based identity of (Gini
    coefficients), 167–69, 168*t*
  macroeconomic policy, 180
  measurement, selection of, 165–67
  microeconomic policy, 182–83

Pritchett, Lant, 11–12, 135, 160, 163,
  163n, 182n, 263, 271, 273
process fairness and justice, 282, 284
Program for International Student
  Assessment (PISA), 133, 135–36,
  147–50, 148–49t, 151f
Proliferation of Sovereigns combined with
  Everything But Labor Liberalization
  (POSEBLL), 11, 265, 277
proliferation of sovereigns
  since World War II, 267–70, 269f
pro-poor growth, 157–58, 161
PRSP (Poverty Reduction Strategy
  Paper), 32
public services, value of, 46–47
Puerto Rico, immigration to U.S.
  from, 241, 274
purchasing power parity, 213

## Q

quotas in migration, 257

## R

Rajan, S. Irudaya, 115
Raju, Dhushyanth, 5–6, 103
Rangel, Marcos, 118
Rapoport, Hillel, 239, 241, 245, 246, 247
Rasul, Imran, 114n
Rauch, James E., 253
Ravallion, Martin, 93, 162, 181, 190
Rawls, John, 11, 132, 281–82
refugees, 284
Reis, John, 253, 254
remittances, 232, 250–53, 251t, 255
Reports on Informal Credit Markets in
  India: Summary (Dasgupta), 75
Republic of Korea. See Korea, Republic of
research agenda, 8–9, 189–203
  agricultural effects from OECD trade and
    aid, 198–99, 199f
  complementarities between globalization
    and other policies, 9, 192, 197–98
  currency crises, effect on poor,
    192–93, 196
  failure of financial integration to help
    poor, 195–96

gender inequality. See gender inequality
  integration of poorest countries, 194
  lessons on links between globalization
    and poverty, 191–94
  measuring effect of globalization on
    poverty, 193–94
  measuring poverty, 194–95
  positive effects of globalization,
    193, 196–97
  poverty reduction not shown by
    aggregate cross-country data,
    199–200, 200f
  unresolved issues, 194–200
resource mobilization at national and
  international levels and
  MDGs, 32–33
return migration, 252
return to specific interventions, 65. See also
  education
Ricardo, David, 131
the rich. See wealth
risk and insurance markets, 78–81
risk and vulnerability
  literature, 49
Robinson, Jonathan, 86, 113
Rodrik, Dani, 60n, 61
Roemer, John E., 54, 132–33, 146, 154
Rosenzweig, Mark R., 9–10, 86, 87, 88–89,
  205, 224, 243n, 244, 244n
Rosero, Jose, 117
rotating savings and credit associations
  (ROSCAs), 112, 113
Roy, A. D., 240
Rubalcava, L., 117
rural vs. urban differences in school
  enrollment, 138, 139f, 143t, 144
Russian middle class, 173, 178, 182

## S

Saito, Katrine A., 115
Sandström, S., 27
Sangraula, Prem, 162
Sawada, Y., 112
Schady, Norbert, 117
schooling. See education
Scrimshaw, N., 90

www.ingramcontent.com/pod-product-compliance
Lightning Source LLC
Chambersburg PA
CBHW080412270326
41929CB00018B/2997